FROM TWO LANES
TO THE FAST LANE:

Stories of Change in America
from Temecula and Murrieta

By Carl Love

From Two Lanes to the Fast Lane: Stories of Change in America from Temecula and Murrieta

ISBN-13: 978-1493619795
Printed in the United States of America
Book design by Robbie Adkins, www.adkinsconsult.com
Cover Photos by Carl Kravats, www.carlkravats.com

This book is dedicated to my family, both two legged and four legged.

FOREWORD

Nobody knows Southwest Riverside County better than Carl Love. He knows the community because he and his family are so much a part of it. Carl is a dad's dad, a sucker for homeless dogs, a teacher who loves his students enough to dream, nurture and protect their dreams. And he's a veteran columnist with a sharp eye for the basic goodness and self-destructive foibles of the large cast of characters that has entered and exited The Carl Love Theater for a quarter century. Read this collection, and you will understand and embrace an American community that happens to be located in "Southwest," but whose values and challenges and tough choices will resonate with readers in American communities everywhere.

Dan Bernstein, metro columnist, The Press-Enterprise

ENDORSEMENTS

As a resident of Riverside County for 33 years, I have always enjoyed reading Carl Love's columns. I equate Carl with his unique writing talents as Norman Rockwell was recognized as an important American artist. Both have a knack for bringing us back into recent history and rekindling the emotions that those precious moments in history created. Carl has witnessed the transformation of our once small and close knit communities into much larger ones, yet still retaining our small town charm. His fanciful detailed stories of life grace these gaps in time. This compilation of his writings over 25 years will invoke emotions of love, empathy, anger, and rage, with the many events he chronicles in our brief history in Riverside County. Thanks for the memories Carl.

Jeff Stone
Temecula Mayor and Councilman 1992 - 2004
Riverside County Supervisor, 3rd District,
2005 to present.

Carl, you have captured so much of the history of our region in your homespun column. I enjoy each nostalgic view you portray of people who have shaped our valleys.

To imagine you compiling all of them into a chronological review is wonderful! Thank you for your dedication to community.

Joan F. Sparkman, community activist

True to his name, Carl Love writes with real love-- love for his family and his community. His heart shines through these columns."

Gayle Brandeis, author of the Bellwether Prize-
winning novel The Book of Dead Birds.

For more than 20 years, Press-Enterprise columnist Carl Love's quiet eloquence chronicled Southwest Riverside County. A survivor of the suburban trenches, he saw how pickups that once hauled hay got traded for SUVs with leather seats and drop-down TVs. He witnessed the growing pains as families struggled to build neighborhoods where once there were only farmlands. He saw it, lived it and wrote about it. Here's a book that week by week captures history, telling Southwest County stories with grace and clarity.

Gordon Johnson, writer/poet

PROLOGUE

It started with open space.

That's the first thing I noticed some 30 years ago passing through Southwest Riverside County. It was basically the middle of nowhere between Los Angeles and San Diego.

My girlfriend Joanne – soon to be my wife – and I would get off the freeway and cruise through the Lake Village and Starlight Ridge subdivisions in what was then called Rancho California.

I got serious about moving here when The Press-Enterprise newspaper sent me to cover a balloon and wine festival in the late-1980s. What struck me was how everybody who lived here seemed happy. What is this, paradise?

The summer of 1988, when we bought our house, was a blur of driving here every weekend to look at model homes on newly paved streets. If 1967 was the summer of love in San Francisco, 1988 was the summer of model frenzy for thousands attracted by affordable prices and country living, all chasing the same dream.

On the last day of 1988, we moved into a small tract house in Murrieta. We celebrated New Year's Eve with dinner at a local winery though my wife Joanne couldn't drink because she was five months pregnant with our first child. Then we came back to our first night in our brand new home. There was a problem with our furnace so we didn't have heat or gas. We couldn't cook. Cable TV hadn't arrived in part of Murrieta so we couldn't watch the tube. We slept on the floor.

It wasn't much to live in. But it sure was wonderful.

Temecula, Murrieta, Wildomar, Menifee and Lake Elsinore were primed for growth.

Temecula didn't have many traffic lights, the Target on Rancho California Road was under construction, Ynez Road was two lanes, and there were hardly any tract houses along Margarita Road or south of Highway 79 South.

In Murrieta there were few if any businesses east of Interstate 15, California Oaks Road wasn't finished, there wasn't a traffic light in town and I didn't know where Old Town was. It seems some people still don't today – but that's another story.

As for Wildomar, I didn't even know it existed. Menifee was ranches and a smattering of tract houses. The Menifee with a lake, golf course and college was mostly developer plans.

Lake Elsinore was the only incorporated city at the time but that wasn't saying much. Heck, The Storm minor league baseball team was out of our league at the time.

Southwest Riverside County was about 50,000 people at the time, give or take a few sheep. Today it is easily 400,000.

So it's changed a little.

I started working at The Press-Enterprise's Temecula office in the spring of 1989. The idea was to make a big push in the area because we all knew this runaway train called growth was fast approaching. In September, the editors in Riverside wanted someone to write a local column. I was lucky the late Mark Petix wasn't interested because he was an amazing writer. Pat Murkland and I tried out and they hired us, me writing twice a week and her once.

Which brings us to this book.

It marks almost a quarter century of this newspaper column and to be honest, I can't believe I just wrote those words. Most newspaper columnists don't even make it a couple years, let alone nearly 25. And yet here I am.

Like everything, this column and I have constantly evolved. I'm different, I started at 31; today I'm 55. When I started I was a full time journalist for The Press-Enterprise, today I'm a fulltime teacher for the Murrieta Valley Unified School District, fifth grade right now. I've written the column as a freelancer for about 16 years.

My columns used to have more humor, my critics would even say sophomoric. Now that I'm nearing my senior years – according to the AARP I'm already there – my writing has perhaps matured, become more serious. Aging does that.

The early writing was that of a small town newspaper with lots of gossip, as if everybody knew everybody.

It's no secret that newspapers had more clout back then, before the Internet age of texting, tweeting, blogging, Instagram-ing, etc. Before the first football game between Temecula Valley and Murrieta Valley high schools, I predicted the Temecula boys would crush their rivals. Later I learned those words inspired the Murrieta players to go harder. They still lost, but the game was closer than expected. I'm glad I did my part.

I was often recognized in stores, and to be honest, I cringed. If it were up to me, I'd be an unknown newspaper columnist photographed with a bag over my head. Today people rarely recognize me. It's for the best.

My favorite topic to write about is my family. And it's not just for vanity. No single topic has inspired more reader feedback in an area that was founded on the developers' premise that if you build affordable housing in a place with smog free skies in Southern California, families will come in droves. So many of you could relate when I wrote about the many adventures of my daughter Julia or my son David because you too were experiencing the same highs and lows with your own kids.

Speaking of the pits, if I had a dollar for every time I wanted to stop writing this column – and had used it to buy Apple stock back then -- I'd be a rich man today. I'm not looking for your sympathy, but coming up with something new to write every week – for many years it was two or three times a week – can be daunting.

Although I long ago lost count of how many columns I've written, it's closing in on 2,000. That's a lot of ideas. And a lot of interesting people to feature -- my favorite kind of journalism.

Somehow, someway this column has endured. The cool thing is that it's a dream come true, given that I decided in college that writing a column was my career goal.

Another dream has been to write a book. And now I have.

This book looks back at our stories and presents them as a keepsake for all of us who lived through these times and as a window of time for others who can see how it was.

Table of Contents

CHAPTER 1

1989 - A new city and a ruined view

It was a big year in Temecula, one in which voters approved city-hood by a whopping 87.6 percent. Locals also OK'd the name of Temecula for the city to the delight of the folks who were annoyed at the thought of another city named Rancho, in this case Rancho California. Temecula is much more distinctive. The City Council celebrated with free champagne at its first meeting. Why not?

My first columns focused on the growth slamming into the area, including the Murrieta newcomers alarmed at the condition of schools in the fastest growing district in the entire state, and an acronym-laced rant against the Temecula traffic.

There was the annual Great Temecula Tractor Race, which high-lighted the great divide between the old-timers who frequented the event and the newcomers who preferred the balloon and wine festival. It's a tale of two communities and what they represent.

I also caught up with the longtime Warm Springs Knolls residents who live across the canyon from the newly built Alta Murrieta neighborhood, full of folks like me. Let's just say they weren't happy to see their view spoiled by all the newcomers.

Finally, there was a growth management symposium that high-lighted the projected development of Southwest Riverside County. At stake was the question of whether we would just turn into another nondescript San Fernando Valley. A quarter century later, I'll let you be the judge.

Murrieta newcomers alarmed by schools
Publication Date: Sept. 27, 1989

Cameron Wilson dreamed of escaping what he considers the urban nightmare of Orange County six months ago when he moved to a tract house in Murrieta.

He recently decided to put his house on the market because of the crowding in Murrieta's schools. He wants to go back to the established schools of Orange County even if it means the end of a dream.

"The schools are terrible," Wilson complained while waiting to pick up his child from Alta Murrieta School. "We love the house but we can't stand the schools."

A lot of Murrieta parents lured to the town by the country living touted by the housing developers are gnashing their teeth over the unadvertised crowded schools.

Alta Murrieta is a stark example of the obstacles facing the fastest growing district in the state. Alta Murrieta opened this year with several portable classrooms and no buildings. There is no grass, a few trees that look more like twigs and a lot of dirt. Hardly the stuff of dreams.

Now the school is two schools. Alta Murrieta and Rail Ranch School students are sharing classrooms until Rail Ranch is finished. Alta Murrieta students go from 7 a.m. to noon and Rail Ranch pupils attend from noon until 5 p.m.

The double sessions at three of the district schools are disrupting home lives, work schedules and sleep patterns throughout the town.

Murrieta mother Nancy Leavitt said she was bombarded with phone calls from desperate commuters when she advertised for kids to baby-sit.

Her neighbor, Jane Wilson, said her husband doesn't get to spend as much time with their three children. He gets home right before the children's new bedtime that was necessitated by the double sessions.

Another result is Murrieta's first daily traffic jam at noon at Alta Murrieta Drive and Whitewood Roads. People triple park waiting to pick up their kids, while Rail Ranch parents dart in and out dropping off their kids. Big trucks with building supplies for even more houses pass by ominously.

Mike Jennings, a captain with the Murrieta Fire Department, stood across the street waiting to pick up his kids. He wondered what would happen if an emergency vehicle had to get through the mess, and questioned why four-way stop signs hadn't been installed at the intersection. "I'm really worried about the kids' safety."

Jennings, a resident of Murrieta most of his life, said he and his wife have trouble juggling their work schedules and the early school hours. "Without two parents working how else can you afford these houses?"

Jean Roberts, who moved from Phoenix about a month ago, said she can't understand why the district can't build the schools faster with the fees developers have paid for new school construction.

Alta Murrieta Principal Buck DeWeese is advising frustrated parents to be patient while the district works through its growing pains. "The parents have been very understanding and very patient."

DeWeese said the district plans construction of buildings for Alta Murrieta soon and hopes to have grass planted next spring. "That is a concern of mine," he said of the lack of places to play. "There's nowhere to have a strong P.E. program."

DeWeese said the school is providing baby-sitting for students until 6 p.m.; and he and his staff are working hard to solve the hazards of the noon rush hour. "Boy, I am open to suggestions on that one."

School administrators certainly get an "A" for trying to ease the crowding. They've taken the dramatic step of sending a letter to developers and real estate agents explaining their growth woes. Under the state's real estate disclosure law the letter must be provided to all prospective buyers.

They have asked Riverside County officials many times for relief from the tract housing onslaught. Their requests are either ignored or rebuffed by county officials who contend it's not their problem.

While the bureaucrats quibble the student stampede continues with no slowing in sight. In the next 10 years Murrieta enrollment is expected to go from about 2,300 students to more than 24,000. By then Murrieta will need 24 new elementary schools and one or two high schools.

Like Buck DeWeese says: Be patient Murrieta parents. Or like Cameron Wilson says: Move on.

%?&#@!& TRAFFIC! drives him crazy

Warning: The following concerns a subject that usually elicits four-letter outbursts from Temecula Valley motorists.

Reader discretion is advised.

Publication Date: Sept. 30, 1989

Let's talk today about traffic. Of course, in the Temecula Valley when we talk traffic we don't mean just plain ol' traffic. We mean the !&*$#©% TRAFFIC!

The worst thing about the $&%#$©& TRAFFIC! in the Temecula Valley is it's only going to get worse.

HAHAHAHAHAHAHAHAHAHAHAHA!

Pardon me. The #(&:%$# TRAFFIC! is no laughing matter to Temecula Valley residents. Indeed it's almost taken on mythic proportions as neighbors and office cohorts relay their latest horror stories.

Being an empirical evidence kind of guy, I did an experiment to determine how awful the $&%$#(© TRAFFIC! really is. Three times I started south on Jefferson Avenue from Winchester Road, turned left at Rancho California Road, left on Ynez Road, left on Winchester and back to Jefferson, a route of about 4.3 miles.

A 5 p.m. week-day trip when the business parks are emptying took 23 minutes while noon on a Saturday when the commuters are back in town took 19 minutes. Sunday at 6 a.m. was done in a mere eight minutes, without one X-rated gesture. Piece of cake.

Now let's identify the groups that could do something about the %&(%$&<§> TRAFFIC!:

YUPPIES or young, urban professionals. Migrants from Los Angeles, Orange and San Diego counties, they came to the Temecula Valley so they could brag to their YUPPIE buddies back at the beach that they live five minutes from a wine country. Of course the Temecula Valley YUPPIES can't afford to go there because they're mortgaged to the max. No problem, say the YUPPIES, who care only about appearances. The Temecula Valley YUPPIES still commute daily to their jobs back on the coast, thus creating !&%$#(& TRAFFIC! wherever they go.

CUPPIES or cute, urban preppies. Direct descendants of the YUPPIES, the CUPPIES are another reason the YUPPIES moved here. Lured by the developers' promises of vast green fields and the lack of #&*(%$# TRAFFIC!, the YUPPIES thought the Temecula

Valley would be the perfect place to raise their CUPPIES. Little did they know.

CURDS, or construction, urban, rude drivers. Definitely a major player in the @&%$#@(TRAFFIC!, they build the houses that drive the area's economy and keep property values on the rise — something the YUPPIES love to talk about. But the CURDS' turtle-like trucks slow the $&%$#©*& TRAFFIC! to a snail's pace, while the houses they build attract more people and more #&(%$©) TRAFFIC! Also, the YUPPIES live in constant fear that one day the CURDS' heavy equipment will squish their CUPPIES. A lot of YUPPIES consider the CURDS CRUD.

KURDS, an Iranian ethnic group. Last seen marching in waves in the Iran-Iraq war of the early '80s, the KURDS are out of work because peace has broken out in their homeland. They need a cause.

Finally, some possible solutions to the $&*($%© TRAFFIC!:

The YUPPIES could have PUPPIES instead of CUPPIES. This would definitely cut down on the number of teen-age CUPPIES on the road. Problem is it would attract a media mob (considering it's a man-bites-dog kind of story) and generate more &%(%#©! TRAFFIC!

The KURDS could invade the Temecula Valley. The CURDS would surely drop their shovels and jackhammers to do battle with the KURDS (remember how upset the CURDS and everybody else got when the Iranians grabbed the hostages back in 79). This in turn would stop the construction boom dead in its tracks. Problem is a CURD-KURD war might get a little bloody.

The YUPPIES, CUPPIES and CURDS could move, leaving the Temecula Valley to the PUPPIES and the INDIANS. Problem is the mass exodus would devastate property values, meaning the departing YUPPIES couldn't brag to the YUPPIES back at the beach about how much money they made living here.

Riverside County could require the CURDS' bosses, the developers, to put in sufficient roads to handle the %&($%©$ TRAFFIC! the houses are generating. Problem is this might impinge on the developers' Constitutional right to make millions of $$$$$$$$, regardless of the consequences.

Call me crazy, but I think one of those might work.

Tractor race the farmers' Indy 500
Publication Date: October 7, 1989

The promoters tout it as The Great Temecula Tractor Race, but to insiders it's The Poor Man's Wine Festival.

The Great Divide between Rancho California and Temecula is never more obvious than during the tractor race this weekend and the balloon and wine fest in May. Don't you dare say to tractor race fans that their festival is in "the Rancho California area." Not unless you're prepared to duck. Them's fightin' words to the Temecula folk who think their tractor hoedown is the epitome of a good ol' time.

Take Buck Kemmis. Now there's a name destined to be a tractor race chairman, which he is. You wouldn't make a Buck a wine festival chairman. Maurice maybe.

Consider the drink of choice at the two events. A tractor race press release said during the first event in 1977 "pit stops were mandatory for the purpose of taking on a cold beer." Word has it there were a lot of pit stops. A wine taster would prefer to savor a successful balloon launch with a good glass of chardonnay, but not too often, lest one get silly.

How 'bout the hay bales that serve as seats for the stage show at the tractor race? Any self-respecting YUPPIE worth his BMW wouldn't be caught dead sitting on hay, unless it was lined with leather.

Tractors racing through the mud? Pleeeeeezzze would say the whine crowd. "What a proletariat thing to do. Think of the mud that would get all over our white trousers. Why can't those people, those HICKS, just be happy with beer and belching. Tractor racing? How utterly ghastly."

Consider the old horse stalls that have been made into concession booths at the tractor race. The noses of the wine-tasting YUPPIES would shoot straight up in the air over the thought of that scene. And it would be from pretensions, not the scent of the stalls' former occupants.

Mud surfing also probably wouldn't be a big hit with the YUPPIES. "You mean they really surf in mud?" they'd ask. "Where's the water? There's a lake right next to the freeway in Rancho California. Surely those nice people at Bedford Properties wouldn't mind if you used their water to surf."

Stop progress! They want off
Publication Date: Nov. 25, 1989

Danny Sheppard blames me for the current state of his view.

"I came out here to retire and you screwed it up," he said with a laugh the other day.

Sheppard and other Warm Springs Knolls homeowners in Murrieta Hot Springs once had uncluttered views of rolling hills. Bobcats, rabbits, coyotes, deer and other wildlife roamed the canyon below their homes. Peace and quiet ruled.

Then a lot of people like me showed up.

Now the rolling hills look as if they might buckle from the tract houses sitting on top of them. Most of the wildlife fled in search of habitat that's not been graded by developers. The peace and quiet that was first smothered by the rumbling of heavy equipment now is lost in the day-to-day living of the thousands of newcomers in Alta Murrieta and Rancho Acacias.

The only thing still the way it was is the rugged canyon. It serves as a moat of sorts, protecting the mobile homes from the invading horde of tile roofs and swimming pools.

Society calls these developments progress, Warm Springs Knolls folks think it's . . . well, they're too polite to cuss. Suffice it to say they're not too pleased.

Retired salesman Joe Zingarelli used to love having his morning coffee on his back porch, watching the wildlife in the canyon below. These days he has his morning coffee somewhere else.

"What is there to see now?" he asked, pointing to the thousands of houses across the canyon. "A lot of people hanging their clothes out, just like in Mexico."

Retired Navy man Larry Haber lived in New York, Chicago and Los Angeles before coming to Warm Springs Knolls 17 years ago to escape those crowded cities. "I can't run anymore," he said. "If I could I'd get the hell out of this mad mess."

Warm Springs Knolls residents can't figure out why everybody across the canyon is in such a hurry. Houses go up seemingly overnight. The newcomers treat the country roads like speedways. Everybody's pushy in the stores.

What's the rush? they ask.

Life's a tad slower on their side of the canyon. They'll talk your ear off if you give 'em a chance. Cars seem to tiptoe through the winding streets. Some building lots are actually vacant.

The elderly residents at Warm Springs Knolls also wonder what the youngsters across the canyon are getting themselves into. Monthly mortgages that run into the thousands of dollars, and hours and hours on the freeways back to San Diego, Orange and Los Angeles counties to jobs that pay enough to cover the bills. Then they complain about stress and wonder why they don't have time for their families.

It all seems crazy, the old-timers say.

Warm Springs Knolls residents moved to Murrieta to escape the big city; now it's sitting across the canyon, staring them in the face. They were here first, some more than 20 years ago, but who cares now?

They're victims of the free market system they went to war to protect from Hitler's Germany and imperialist Japan. What's happened to the rolling hills across the canyon is capitalism, pure and simple.

Most Warm Springs Knolls residents sadly shrug their shoulders. It's a great country, people can do with their property as they please. That's what the good ol' USA was founded on.

One of the many ironies in these developments is that the country living and clear skies that attracted Warm Springs Knolls residents to their park now is used by the developers to entice newcomers to the housing tracts across the canyon. Now experts talk of Murrieta's population being 100,000 by the turn of the century, meaning the country living is going to be somewhere else.

With property in the Temecula Valley appreciating at dizzying rates, I and a lot of newcomers talk about making a bunch of money on our new houses in the next few years and moving to a small town in Oregon or Colorado to pay cash for our dream homes.

Warm Springs Knolls residents thought they'd done just that by coming to sleepy Murrieta many years ago. Now their dream's been buried by an avalanche of progress. And there's not a thing they can do about it.

Hey, guinea pigs! Get involved
Publication Date: Dec. 16, 1989

I'd never thought of myself as a guinea pig until a symposium this week on growth management for Riverside County.

Most panelists at the University of California, Riverside, agreed America's love affair with the car and big housing lots is driving suburbanization further and further into the hinterlands. This generates a lot of environmental bickering, long commutes and social headaches.

Sound familiar?

The Temecula Valley must be a vast laboratory for the mad growth-scientists. They're surely salivating over what our construction boom, job-housing disparities, huge open spaces and tiny pockets of congestion portend for the next decade. We residents scurrying around here amount to experimental guinea pigs — but only in the scientists' minds. No need to get a complex.

The big questions are will the Temecula Valley be another smoggy, congested San Fernando Valley in the 1990s? Or will it be a Utopia, where people live, work and play in a manageable, pristine environment?

The large number of Temecula Valley business, tourist and school leaders at the growth symposium this week in Riverside indicates they have considerable interest in the answers.

Four of them — Murrieta School Board President Austin Linsley, Temecula Valley Chamber of Commerce executive Perry Peters, Temecula Town Association representative Bill Harker and Callaway Vineyard's spokesman John Moramarco Sr. — agree more communication and planning is needed if the Temecula Valley is to sidestep the urban sprawl creeping over Southern California.

They contend it's not too late for the valley to decide its fate but there's no time to dillydally. Another 35,000 homes are planned to be plopped in Temecula and Murrieta in the next decade. That means another 100,000 people will join the estimated 60,000 who call the area home today. Today's population will almost triple.

Everybody here already feels the effects of the growth. Look at the clogged Interstate 15 overpasses on Rancho California Road or Winchester Road. Ask the Murrieta parents feel cheated by developers who didn't advertise the community's terribly crowded schools.

Or check with the Temecula kids who can't find parks among the houses.

Yet everybody here has benefited from the growth. Thousands of jobs have been generated by the construction boom. We have better shopping and more things to do. Property values are going through the roof.

As Peters points out, most communities are starving for such an economic diet. "We have it (development) handed to us on a silver platter. It would almost be sacrilegious to throw it away."

How we handle that platter is another matter. Do we build when the schools can't house the kids? Do we build when the roads can't handle the traffic? Do we build on the fragile Santa Rosa Plateau when so much vacant land sits in the valley below?

Hard questions with no easy answers. And don't forget, this is a free market where people can basically do with their property as they please.

Peters talks of "positive solutions," citing school bond measures passed by voters in Murrieta and Temecula last month. "Stopping the building of houses isn't a positive approach."

Then consider the Murrieta Valley Unified School District, which figures it must spend $1.1 billion to keep up with growth outlined in a plan approved by County Supervisors last month. But the district and the state are financially strapped, and developers complain they can't afford such a tab. That leaves growth control or the residents to pay for more bonds.

Yet, as County Supervisor Kay Ceniceros observes, the residents (the guinea pigs) are basically silent in this great growth debate.

While the growth gurus, the builders, the conservationists and the community leaders do the talking the guinea pigs scurry around making ends meet, too busy to get involved. Unfortunately, as Ceniceros notes, it's difficult to build a consensus on solutions without the guinea pigs' involvement.

Meanwhile, another San Fernando Valley is forming.

CHAPTER 2

1990 - MurriEATa's turn

It was Murrieta's turn to approve cityhood this year. The first City Council included two firefighters Jerry Allen and Joe Peery, and a CHP guy, Gary Smith. Yes, Murrieta's focus on public safety can be traced back to its origins.

Another big news item in Murrieta was a community rite of passage: the opening of a McDonald's on Los Alamos Road. It was the first business of any kind to open amid the zillions of homes popping up between the 15 and 215.

Finally, ground was broken on Murrieta Valley High School, the community's first. The school to be's students threw the first shovel of dirt. Perfect.

In Temecula, folks were talking about the Towering Inferno, Temecula's most prominent building, and its gaudy design. They also were yapping about their squabbling City Council and a potential recall. It never came to pass.

On the home front I wrote about my daughter Julia's first birthday. I remember agonizing about it the whole time I composed it, wanting to make it absolutely perfect. I've since come to realize that, like many aspects of child-raising, it doesn't have to be so.

I also wrote about the trials and tribulations of putting in a yard. Oh the agony of owning a new home.

Murrieta moves up as Big Macs move in
Publication Date: Feb. 17, 1990

Welcome to McMurrieta.

Little ol' Murrieta joined the corporate fray at noon Tuesday with the opening of — what else — a McDonald's on Los Alamos Road, just west of Interstate 215.

Obviously, what's good enough for Moscow is good enough for Murrieta. Or vice versa.

The town's abuzz with excitement, even if the international media aren't on hand to record it. McDonald's has become a tourist trap with locals dropping by to sample the cuisine and just plain gawk at the place. Ronald McDonald might be elected mayor if he were so inclined.

As Murrieta Fire Chief Marvin Curran said, "You are not a city unless you have a ZIP code. If you don't have a ZIP code you don't exist. McDonald's kind of goes with a ZIP code."

Call it a community rite of passage.

Curran and Assistant Fire Chief Joe Whisenand have already dined at McDonald's three times. Why would two esteemed community leaders partake of burgers and fries over and over again?

Because they can.

Apparently a lot of people feel the same. "Business has been very good," said McDonald's owner Alex Mestas. "We were just packed all day and night the first day."

It's the first business of any sort to open amid the zillions of houses dotting the hills surrounding Interstates 215 and 15. And there's a lot more to come:

In the Plaza Las Brisas being built behind McDonald's, a preschool, a gas station, a bank, and yogurt, bagel, spaghetti, sandwich, video and beauty supply stores are planned.

Down the 215 at Murrieta Hot Springs Road is the massive Murrieta Town Center, a 500,000-square-foot center with the first phase set to open this spring. Planned are a market, a drug store, a theater, a toy store, a home improvement store and several restaurants.

Yes, change is coming to sleepy Murrieta at warp speed. A few years ago the rolling hills offered views of wide-open farm land as far as the eye could see. Now the same view is crammed with tract houses and shopping centers-to-be.

Some day when Murrieta's 100,000 residents (or more) look back and remember where the boom started, McDonald's will be one of the first places they'll look.

The restaurant itself has a taste of very early Murrieta. Hanging on McDonald's walls are five water color paintings from Fresno artist Pat Hunter, based on photographs from E. Hale Curran, Marvin's mother. Included are an old train depot and the Fountain House Hotel, where the Currans lived.

McDonald's decor is highlighted by very trendy pastel colors. "We wanted a family atmosphere where it wouldn't be perceived as a hang-out," said owner Mestas, who has five children and lives in Murrieta.

The restaurant was a big hit with Kyle Mitchell, 2, and Ian Robertson, 5, who were munching on McDonald's finest and slurping down sodas. The best part of the meal package was the toy cars they got. Naturally the toys had McDonald's logos — Ronald doesn't miss a trick.

Their parents, Susan Mitchell and Kathleen Robertson, said they were disappointed there wasn't a McDonald's Playland, especially considering the lack of parks in Murrieta's new subdivisions.

Mestas said he hopes to have a Playland at the restaurant within a year, but first he has to get permits for it. "The bureaucratic red tape is incredible."

The restaurant is already a popular morning hangout for neighbors Efraim Moreno and Lloyd Hurley. Moreno makes a 40-minute walk for breakfast while Hurley drops by for coffee on the way to work.

Moreno, who's lived in Murrieta almost five years, said when he moved here he had to drive to Corona to get a burger at night. Now he lives in McMurrieta and can go down the street for a Big Mac.

Talk about increasing your property values.

Tis the season to wrestle the yard
Publication Date: March 14, 1990

Your neighbor across the street, Mr. Do-It-Himself, is making you look real bad. He ripped out the puny front sidewalk the builder gave everybody and put in a curved monolith with a ton of bricks. Then he laid out a carpet of sod that puts lawns in Kentucky to shame. His grass is ringed with a rainbow of flowers and a miniature waterfall flown in from Hawaii. Sunset Magazine is coming by next week for a photo shoot.

Meanwhile, you and your dirt have been figuratively dusted. The recent rains dumped large quantities of your front slope into the street. Your weeds resemble five-gallon shrubs. Code Enforcement Quarterly is bugging you for a picture spread. Do-It-Himself across the street plants you a dirty look every time you step outside. You'd like to rototill his face.

What to do with your front and back yards — that's the topic eating away at you, the new homeowner.

Do you do the environmentally conscious thing and install native vegetation in your yard? Do you put in a vast lawn, ignoring water bills and water conservation? Do you go the couch potato route and make the whole thing concrete and rocks?

Or do you do the easiest, the most affordable and the most embarrassing thing of all — nothing.

Now multiply your plight by thousands. The new houses in Wildomar, Menifee, Murrieta and Temecula need lots of grass, trees, shrubs, flowers, fertilizer, ground cover, sprinkler systems, rocks and other landscape paraphernalia.

A nursery person's dream. A chance for them to make a lot of lettuce, not just grow it.

"We've just been booming," said Thorn Johnson, general manager of the Murrieta Oaks Nursery. His comrades at the Plant Club in Murrieta and the California Garden Center in Temecula echo his joy.

So while you endure marathon commutes to run yourself ragged in the stressful corporate world, the plant people who work outside with blooming flowers and fragrant trees are making pretty good money at it. Maybe we are becoming a more enlightened society.

"They're fun," said Plant Club manager Dawn Vanderlaan of her green co-workers. "Plants don't talk back. I like to watch them through their season."

The nursery folks said lawns are still popular with homeowners, even though grass drinks a lot of water in this arid climate. "They're (homeowners) after the appearance,' said Brad Quick, assistant manager of the California Garden Center.

Also a big hit with homeowner sapiens are mature trees and shrubs, even though they are considerably more expensive than their younger brethren. Apparently instant gratification applies to the yard.

Homeowners are divided between the do-it-himselfers and the hire-somebody-else-to-do-the-dirty-work crowd. The biggest problem for the aspiring do-it-himselfers is their arch enemy, Dr. Sprinkler System. Case in point is the Love household.

After these innocents moved to their new home 15 months ago, Mr. Love watched a few of his do-it-himself neighbors work the land like their ancestors. There was even a do-it-herselfer toiling.

Emboldened with such sights, Mr. Love talked a big game of rolling up his sleeves and getting out there with the REAL MEN and WOMEN to rototill his front yard, install sprinklers and plant seed like his forefathers. GRRRRRRR!!

Mr. Love green thumbed through the do-it-himself manual, marveling at the very pretty pictures of successful lawns. Then he turned to the not-so-pretty Dr. Sprinkler System diagrams, complete with the evil anti-siphon device, the diabolical pressure regulator and the terrifying elbow connecting tubing.

Hmmm, thought Mr. Love, this looks complicated. Way beyond my limited screw-in-a-light-bulb capabilities.

He called a neighbor, a professional do-it-himselfer/landscape contractor type. Three days later, minus a couple thousand green bills, he had a front yard armed with Dr. Sprinkler System.

Mr. Love lived happily ever after. Even if his back yard looks like a vacant lot.

A parent rejoices over the first year
Publication Date: May 2, 1990

Our baby turned one year the other day, which in parent years equates to about nine.

Parents not only age like a dog, they often feel like one. Even stranger, most can't seem to get enough of this abuse. Yet there is logic behind this, though it can only be fully comprehended by those who've been called "dada" or "mama."

Babies have a power over their parents than can't be measured by science or mathematics. But it's there, as real as the diapers. The birth of our child, Julia, is the most powerful experience of my life. I can't imagine a happier moment.

This father-daughter bond was immediate, as soon as Julia came out of her mother's womb. She was crying when a nurse handed her to me for the first time. She started cooing the moment I spoke to her. She's had me wrapped around her tiniest pinky since then.

The same time I was closer to my wife than I've ever been. Joanne weathered the storm of child delivery like a champ. A father can never experience the agony of labor but he can sure love somebody for enduring it.

I remember riding down a hospital elevator the day we came home. An elderly woman looked at Julia and asked if she was our first. When we nodded she smiled and said we were in for the best time of our lives.

She was right.

Nothing compares to the changes of the first year of a first child. Julia has more than doubled in weight and added about 10 inches in height. She can crawl and feed herself. She can stand by herself for a few moments and she says three words, "mama," "dada" and "no." The last word is key. Our daughter has developed her own will and it's only going to get worse. She throws her food when she's had enough. She crawls where she's not supposed to. She screams when she doesn't want to do something.

It's part of the separation from us. Soon she'll be walking. Then she'll be playing outside. Then she won't miss us while we're gone. Then she'll be gone to school. Then she'll be gone for good.

A parent changes too. Free time takes on a new significance because a parent so rarely has any. Change the diaper. Clean up the mess she's made. Feed her. Pull her away from something. Give her a bath. Read to her. Try to get her to sleep. Pick her up because she just wants to be held.

My childless friends often ask me what it's like being a parent. Well, it's a lot of work, a lot of lost sleep, a lot of frustration, a lot of worrying. It's almost like you're no longer an adult, like you have to answer to somebody new — your child.

Being a parent also is a way to relive your childhood. Babies get the greatest pleasure from the simplest things. They love to splash the bath water, smash food in their face, crawl around in the grass and roll on the floor. A parent can't help but laugh with them.

Most importantly, being a parent gives you a purpose. You're not just earning a paycheck so you can eat a nice meal out or take a great vacation. You're providing for somebody.

Yes, I tell my childless friends, being a parent makes you feel better about yourself.

Children make a parent think about the future.

So many who've moved to the Temecula Valley did so for their children. They want to live in a place where the air is clean, the fields are vast, the schools are small and the streets are safe.

But a lot is happening to the valley in a very short time. Indeed, the place is changing almost as fast as our children. The smog is creeping in on both ends of the valley. The fields are filling up with tract homes. The local schools are having trouble keeping pace with the growth. Two people are murdered in a house just a couple blocks away.

It makes a parent afraid.

Dry farming flooded by tract houses
Publication Date: May 26, 1990

A mile stretch on Los Alamos Road is home to Murrieta's past and future.

At Interstate 215 and Los Alamos is the Murrieta to be. A McDonald's and Mobil gas station have opened and a strip shopping center is going up. Apartments surround the west side of the intersection and more shopping ventures are planned for the east side. Thousands of acres of jammed tract houses spread from the intersection like roots from a massive tree.

Continue east on Los Alamos around the bend and enter the Murrieta that was. The road drops to two lanes and the vegetation turns from manicured to native. The houses thin to one every few acres and the animals are farm, not domestic.

Marvin Zepede is in the middle of this time change. His land at Ruth Ellen Way and Los Alamos used to be dry farmed. Now it's slated for houses, apartments and a school.

Zepede is the most recent example of the dry-farming-gone-subdivision trend. His plans were approved by Riverside County supervisors last month despite complaints from a few of his rural neighbors that the area doesn't need another harvest of roof tops.

Zepede, a retired hardware distributor, said he respects what his neighbors are doing. He too isn't happy about the growth that has hit Murrieta like a tornado. But stopping it is like trying to stop the weather — it can't be done.

Dry farmers learn about weather the hard way. In the years that it rained they made a decent living off the land. In the years that it didn't they agonized.

Zepede stopped leasing his land for dry farming in the early '80s when the water and the money dried up. The last year's crop didn't even cover the grain, let alone the labor.

He wasn't the only one. John McElroy, the leader of Murrieta's cityhood effort, used to dry farm about 5,000 acres, including Murrieta Hot Springs, Alta Murrieta and California Oaks. Now that land and other acres that were once dry farmed are littered with suburbia.

It was always too expensive to import water to Murrieta. Then the price of fuel and farm equipment soared, the bureaucrats restricted the pesticides and the demand for more housing drove land prices sky-high. Dry farming didn't have a chance against those forces.

"It was either quit or go broke," McElroy said.

Not to mention the people who trampled on your hard work. The motorcyclists, the campers and the vagrants used the land as if they owned it. "Every day it was a fight," McElroy said. "It was just like a battleground. It wasn't pleasurable."

Still, it was a good life for McElroy from 1969 to 1976. He and his son, Gary, worked the land sun up to sun down. They grew oat hay, wheat and barley. The oats would grow as tall as your head.

"It was hard work but I tell you I never enjoyed something as much in my life," McElroy said. "I was my own boss and we were creating something and not taking anything from anybody."

The Murrieta then also was a nice place to live. Peace and quiet thrived and folks weren't in such a hurry. "People aren't nice on the road anymore," McElroy said. "It used to be everybody waved and everybody knew each other."

Like his friend Zepede, McElroy is trying to take advantage of the changing economic climate on Los Alamos Road. In March he had his 61.9 acres at the corner of Monroe Avenue and Los Alamos changed from rural residential to commercial.

Zepede said he wants to do something with his property while he still can. He's had a lot near San Luis Obispo for about 10 years. It has an ocean view and Zepede has long planned to build a house there. But the government there won't let him. "All you can do is look at it."

He's afraid his neighbors, both rural and tract, could do the same thing in Murrieta if he waits. "It irritates me," he said. "If they don't want me to do it, then buy it."

Just what's in a name? Ask the ancestors
October 20, 1990

Temecula, Murrieta, Wildomar and Menifee are rather oddly named.

For many years this wasn't a problem because there weren't many newcomers and the kangaroo rats didn't care.

But now that we're booming and the rats are fleeing, more and more out-of-towners are moving in and having fits with the name of their new hometowns:

"How do you spell that?"

"Isn't Murrieta in Georgia"

"Where the hell is Temecula?"

How'd you come up with Wildomar?"

"Menifee? Do men pay fees to live there?"

"Isn't that part of Rancho California?"

The last question is fightin' words to diehard community activists. Many out-of-towners (including yours truly before I moved here and reformed) lump Southwest Riverside County into Rancho California. Real community names are usually seen as "quaint," but nothing newcomers would want to spell, explain or claim as an address. "Why not make it Rancho Anything?" they ask.

Consequently, many new arrivals don't know the significance behind the strange names of their communities. Well, boys and girls, gather 'round for a little history lesson, compliments of our local experts:

Temecula is an Indian word meaning "land where the sun shines through the mist." The name is taken from the Temecula Indians who settled here about a thousand years ago, according to Bill Harker of the Temecula Town Association.

The original Indian name was "Temeku," but the Spanish settlers preferred to give their communities a sex, so they added a feminine "la." Apparently, Temeku wasn't studly enough to warrant the masculine "Temekulo." If only they'd known that their local descendants would one day worship the male commercial god "Mervyn" and his grand opening ritual.

The English-speaking folks arrived and changed "Temekula" to the Anglo-Saxon spelling they liked, "Temecula." Fortunately for local residents, the Russians never made it to Temecula to add their touch, "Temeculadostoevski." That would have been a crime and a punishment.

Murrieta dates back to Don Juan Murrieta, who wandered into the area in the 1870s, said local resident Arleen Garrison in her book about the town's history, "My Children's Home."

Don Juan drove sheep from Merced to this area. The town was named after him "because the early settlers held him in high esteem and appreciated his honesty, generosity and kindness," Garrison writes. Too bad he's not running for office today.

Unfortunately for local gigolos, the settlers didn't opt for Don Juan California. And despite the modern-day inhabitants' penchant for settling important political matters with a potluck dinner, the town's name is not spelled Murrieata.

The name Wildomar was brought about by the three folks who settled the town in the 1880s, Donald Graham, William Collier and Margaret Collier. Local historian Dave Brown said Margaret decided to name the place after the first syllables of their first names, Wil-do-mar.

Attorneys today are upset that Wildomar wasn't settled by Lyle and Bill and modified over the years by tort-minded invaders to "Liable." Developers would prefer that Hy and Turner had moved to Wildomar first and passed down "High Return," while doctors wish Xavier and Ray had arrived to illuminate their descendants with "Xray."

Menifee came from a young Kentuckian named S. Menifee Wilson. He found a gold quartz mine in the 1880s about eight miles south of Perris and others soon rushed to the area in hopes of striking riches. Alas, most came up empty.

Today, dreamers of a different sort rush in by the thousands to the four ancient communities of Southwest Riverside County. Let's hope they don't forget their ancestors in their haste. Otherwise, they may lose their historical riches.

Those cakes that Murrieta forgot & why
Nov. 10, 1990

Welcome to the city of Murrieata.

Cityhood was three years in the oven and election night local eaters let loose with a party. Oddly, considering the town's, uh city's, culinary rep, a potluck wasn't planned. But about 30 dishes that wandered in off the streets were greeted with open mouths. Call them Murrieta's homeless cuisine. If America is the great melting pot, Murrieata is the great crock pot.

Odder still, the city birthday cakes were ignored. Said head chef Dottie Renon: "Everybody got so busy and so anxious watching the results and drinking that they didn't bother eating the cakes."

The forlorn cakes, compliments of candidate Rob Scott and councilman-elect Gary Smith, will be turned over to the Murrieta Garden Club for a seniors' luncheon. 'Till then they're under lock 'n' key in Renon's freezer.

Enough of the seconds, Murrieatans. On to the votes, the party and the memories of one brief shining moment that made you forget to eat a couple cakes:

First item on the agenda (better get used to agendas, Murrietans) is congrats to the council members-elect Jerry Allen, Joe Peery, Fred Weishaupl, Gary Smith and Dave Haas.

The council should be ready for any emergency with local fire-fighters Peery and Allen and CHP Officer Smith. They swear they won't break the open-meeting law and discuss council biz at crash scenes. But beware if you see contractor Haas directing traffic and civil engineer Weishaupl lighting flares at a Murrieta emergency.

Regards to the hard-working losers. So much for being the only woman on the ballot, right Hattie Hedrick? So much for putting up a lot of campaign signs, right Doug Irvine, Jack Taylor, Brian Padberg and Jerry Gorman?

Now that the campaign's signed off, remember Padberg being ripped by his rivals for having illegal signs? Well, Padberg's illegal sign on Los Alamos Road had plenty of friends stuck to it election day — smaller placards from Bill Knight, Ron LoPresto, Smith and Taylor.

Longest faces at the election bash belonged to Padberg's supporters. At one point they gathered for a group photo and it didn't look easy to crack the obligatory smile. "It's one of those things," Padberg said of his election owee.

The kingmaker of Murrieta award goes to old-timer Jack Johnson. Kingmaker took out newspaper ads anointing eight of the 19 candidates for election. Four were elected and the other four finished sixth, seventh, tenth and eleventh. Not too bad, kingmaker. His big whiff was Peery. Kingmaker said two Murrieta fire officials was one too many. His subjects thought otherwise.

Kingmaker institution is the Murrieta Fire Department, considering Allen and Peery ran one-two. Makes you wonder what would have happened if Mischief the fire dog had gathered enough paw prints to get on the ballot. Fire Chief Marv Curran said he had no regrets about not running. Apparently fires provide enough heat for Marv.

The would-be kingmaker award goes to John Haskell. The Murrieta Springs Mall honcho was at the party pressing flesh. The new council's first gut check should come with Haskell's request to kick back half of the mall's sales taxes to his project. The city is entitled to all of it but Haskell says he needs half to build. Stay tuned.

Peace pipe award goes to Temecula Councilman Sal Munoz, who called to wish Murrieta winners good luck. Munoz offered to discuss common issues and help with the transition to a city. He didn't offer to donate any of Temecula's ample traffic. Greedy, Sal, greedy.

Speaking of Temecula, the mayor there is Ron Parks. Murrieta's honorary mayor is Rita Park. That explains where all the parks are.

Finally, Murrietans, is it just me or does everybody feel better driving around our home knowing we're now a city? Thank you John McElroy and your many, many hard-working cityhood helpers.

CHAPTER 3

1991 - "Time" for a movie and a dream

It was a year of bizarre. There was Temecula City Councilman Karel Lindemans and the Royal Flush, his solution to the drought. So why would a city leader be talking about toilets? It was one of those you-had-to-be-there things.

There was the campaign to ban a movie, "Boyz N the Hood," from Temecula theaters, due to of fears of gang violence. After one local theater cancelled plans to show the film, another stepped in and showed it anyway. Take that Thought Police!

Folks also were mad about the Temecula City Council's retreat to Laguna Beach; the group's third such commune since they took office. Thank goodness today's councils don't take their shows on the road so much.

There was our 15 minutes of fame, when Temecula and Murrieta were highlighted in a special issue of Time magazine: "California The Endangered Dream." Our growth wasn't just making local headlines.

I profiled Murrieta City Councilman-elect Dave Haas and his odd hats, including one with multiple rattlesnakes. Local politicians were more colorful back when the area was quainter.

I also came up with a creative list of ways to save water; a piece I then shipped to the writers of Johnny Carson's Tonight Show in the hopes of landing a job. The head writer actually responded with a personal letter talking about my talents, but also saying the only way to make it in the Big Show was to come into LA and he couldn't make any promises. I passed and to be honest, no regrets.

Bribes, diapers, beer offer ways to save water
Publication Date: March 6, 1991

Got those drought tolerant blues, I do, I do. Saves what I can and I can't saves no more. Now they're talking 'bout more of them dang water cutbacks. What's I gonna do, Doc Precip?

You've come to the right place, water worrier. We'll fix you right up with this home remedy brew. Take at least two of these and call us first thing in the morning, if you make it that far:

– Don't take showers. If the folks at the office whine about B.O., tell the boss to give you a longer lunch hour. The company might even give you a paid sabbatical if you go several months without taking a shower. Make the drought work for you, not against you.

– Drink your swimming pool water. Besides quenching your thirst, you won't have to worry about algae forming on your internal organs.

– Wash your car with beer. The drawback is you might get pulled over by the cops for operating an influenced vehicle. You could wash the car with coffee, but then you risk getting nailed for driving a speeding vehicle.

– Soak your lawn with a highly toxic grass killer. This will save enormous amounts of pain and suffering for you and your beloved grass because it's going to die anyway.

– Soak yourself with a highly toxic grass killer. This will probably get you admitted to a hospital, where you can waste their water with reckless abandon. Plus you won't have to see your grass suffer its slow death.

– Wear diapers. Your friends — if you still have any after you do this — might think you're a little strange, but remind them that it saves water. They'll understand. At least we hope for your sake.

– Abstain from meat and invest heavily in soybean futures. Farmers use tons of water for the grass that cows eat. If we didn't eat beef we wouldn't need the cattle and the grass wouldn't need the water. Makes a lot of sense to us. Which is why it will never happen.

– Abstain from sex. Hey, it couldn't hurt.

– Bribe your water meter reader. These are the guys who control your destiny. Get to them and you get to the drought. But be careful. Heard of a guy in the last drought who went too far and got a meter reader to turn in a negative reading. Homeowner claimed he was pumping water back to the district from a mountain spring in the back yard of his Murrieta tract home. Now he and the meter reader are doing hard time, changing filters at the district's sewer treatment plant.

– Use public restrooms whenever possible. Sure it's inconvenient, tacky and at times embarrassing. ("No, I don't want to buy anything; I just want to use your bathroom as soon as possible.") But remember our motto, "I'm using their water, not mine."

– Flip out. Turn on every source of water in your house full blast, then run down the street laughing and screaming "why do they let farmers grow rice in California?" Eventually you'll be arrested and sent in for a complete psychological overhaul. Eventually you'll lose your job, your home, your family and your life as you know it.

But you'll never have to worry about saving water again.

Politicians take 3rd retreat at public expense
Publication Date: March 9, 1991

So what's on tap this weekend? Pull a few weeds in the back yard. Take the kids to the park. Rent a video. Aw what the heck, get wild and order out for pizza.

Your Temecula City Council has a little nicer weekend lined up. Two nights and three days at the Surf and Sand Hotel in Laguna Beach. Sounds great. But here's the best part: It's FREE! Guess who's picking up the tab, pepperoni breath.

Yup the council members are drowning themselves in the public trough this weekend to the tune of about $14,000. It's another one of those touchy-feely team-building sessions, the council's third commune since they took office. Sample topic for discussion: "Like wow man, check out the vibes of this proposed ordinance."

Seems the city isn't getting the great advice from its new PR firm: Trump, Helmsley & Canseco. But our lavish leaders can make amends with their follow-up retreat, which we all know they're going to tell us they need 'cause this one was just soooo successful.

Came across an internal memo from a rival PR agency, Mother Teresa & Associates. It reviews the locales the might consider for its next gathering with the goal of a more ascetic image:

– Saddam's bunker: The experts think it will be available real soon. Council members would dine on Iraqi troop rations and review Saddam's plans for a topic they are very familiar with – how to handle a sudden invasion of outsiders. The bunker is built to withstand a nuclear blast, which would shield council members from public flak.

– Siberia. Best time to go would be the middle of winter. Council members could pitch tents on the frozen tundra or stay at the The Rack Hilton. Problem is most visitors never make it out of there alive. Oh well.

– Slumber party at Karel Lindemans' house, sleeping bags optional. Let off some steam in Lindemans' Jacuzzi. Take a cue from the amiable City Council in Murrieta and have a potluck. Beware, Ron Parks, if San Munoz makes you drink a particular glass of spiked punch. Finish off with a game of Twister.

More retreat fallout:

Munoz was the lone council member to vote against the commune, contending it was (get this) too expensive. Munoz went anyway, saying he wanted to get his "two cents" in on talks about the future of the city. Considering his extravagant colleagues, Munoz might want to weigh in with more than a few pennies. Perhaps a fully loaded Brink's truck, Sal.

From the bulging why-your-mom-should-have-raised-you-to-be-a-consultant file comes Sentient Systems, which is charging the city $11,235, plus expenses, for the three-day love fest.

An anonymous caller left this message at City Hall: "Hope the council chokes on their steak and lobster." Sounds like yet another happy constituent.

Haas keeps an image under his black hat
Publication Date: March 27, 1991

There was a time when Dave Haas hated hates. Sure, and Tommy Lasorda doesn't like pasta.

But it's true about Haas. He never wore a hat while growing up in the Midwest. Then about 15 years ago his nose and ears started to get sore from the sun. It was wrestle skin cancer, get out of the building business or wear a hat.

Welcome to an image.

Haas is to hats what Jimmy Carter as to peanuts. You can no more separate Haas from his hats than you can part Ronald Reagan from his jelly beans.

Obviously, Haas isn't in that political league. He is a Murrieta city councilman-elect, not the leader of the free world. But Carter and Reagan didn't have three snarling rattlesnakes perched on their heads when they met with vising heads of state. If you own such a contraption, you don't have to be president to be noticed. You just wear it.

Take one of Haas' favorite hats, a black Western number. It includes a nasty looking eastern diamond back rattlesnake, badger fur, an Arkansas toothpick, rabbit jawbones, pheasant feathers and suede ties with some poor little bunny's vertebra.

You're gonna mess with somebody wearing that? Heck no. Otherwise your dead head might be dangling from his next hat.

"I decided if I'm going to wear hats, I'm going to wear interesting ones," Haas says. "Regular hats just don't cut it with me."

Obviously. Haas has seven rattlesnake hats, each equipped with a full range of animal body parts. Other hats feature a cobra head, and alligator and badger paws. Add it all up and Haas' head is a swiveling zoo, taxidermist's full employment act and animal-lover's nightmare.

The hats are out of Texas, from an outfit called "Charlie 1 Horse." The company's previous foul-mouthed motto is etched in a few of Haas' hats: "If it ain't Charlie 1 Horse, it ain't …."

Haas' wife Shirley picks up the hats for birthdays and Christmases at about $400 a crack. "It adds a little something individual to his personality," she says.

No kidding. Haas has taken to the hats like Madonna takes to lingerie. "Now it's a part of me," Haas says. "I feel naked if I leave my house without one on."

And no matter what Reagan and Carter might think, they are a political asset. Nineteen candidates ran in last fall's Murrieta council campaign and standing out was almost tantamount to getting elected. The dude with the weird hats stood out.

Haas played to his brim-image with a contest to design a new hat for him. A flier advertised him as a "man of many hats," including hard, cowboy, golf, chef and top. Entries stored in the Haas scrapbook include Mickey Mouse from Tyna Petrich, Oktoberfest from William Leppsaar, a sombrero from Jane Coscarelli, ear muffins from Arlean Garrison, a fire helmet from Marvin Curran, a Sherlock Holmes investigator version from Stephen Boyer and a Murrieta cityhood party hat from Carol Kravagna.

The winner came from Dick Gibbo, a local architect, who designed a western hat featuring a rattlesnake, Murrieta cityhood button, top hat, hard hat, fork and spatula. Gibbo's prize was a gift certificate from the Orange County store where Haas gets his hats. Gibbo opted for a cowboy hat with a bullet hole, figuring it had to be safer.

"I'm afraid of fangs too," he says. "I know the bullet's not coming back."

Haas like the rattlers 'cause of their reputation. "It's a tough critter. Don't mess with me. Take your shots, but don't mess with me."

Not even Haas can fool with his hats. As he was getting out of the car once he pricked his finger on a snake fang. The finger swelled for about three days and was sore for a week.

Aw, what's a little pain to a guy with dead animals on his head.

The "Boyz" gets a bad rap, but still shows
Publication Date: July 17, 1991

Thank you, James Edwards Sr., for having the courage to show "Boyz N the Hood" in Temecula.

Thanks you for standing up to the pressure from local churches, civic groups and Temecula Mayor Ron Parks. All wanted the movie about life in a black ghetto in L.A. banned in Temecula because of possible gang violence.

Pressure from the same groups got to Gary Richardson, general manager of SoCal Cinemas, which owns Temeku Cinema in the Palm Plaza. He canceled the movie from Temeku last week, deciding it was in the best interests of the city to do so. Edwards, owner of Tower Center Cinemas 10 on Ynez Road, stepped in and picked the film the same day Richardson dropped it.

I saw "Boyz" on Sunday afternoon in Temecula. It's a very human story about the very real violence in south-central Los Angeles. It made me realize that the body counts on the local news every night are more than numbers; they're friends and lovers, brothers and sisters, sons and daughters. And it's not happening in a faraway land, it's happening about 80 miles away.

A lot of people moved here from Los Angeles because they wanted a better place to raise their children. They're so determined that they're willing to spend three and four hours a day on freeways driving back to Los Angeles for work.

These intentions are admirable. Everybody wants their children to be safe; not everybody is willing to make the sacrifices that go with it. These people are.

But we can't build moats around the 'hoods where we live. Sure, we can hire more police officers. We can ban gang colors in our schools. We can tell our kids to stay away from trouble. We can install fancy security systems in our houses and we can even stash guns in our bedrooms. But I think we go too far when we try to keep movies out of our theaters.

Supporters of the ban centered their campaign on violence. Before the movie was even released, they were arguing that "Boyz" wasn't fit for their kids. "Boyz" has two violent scenes, not much when compared to the carnage I've heard about in Arnold Schwarzenegger's "Terminator 2: Judgment Day." I haven't heard of anybody trying to save Temecula from the Terminator.

Backers of the ban argued that gang members from throughout Riverside County would be invading Temecula to see the movie. Last weekend, besides Temecula, the film opened in the county cities of Corona, Moreno Valley, Palm Springs, Rubidoux and Riverside. The theater I was in Sunday afternoon wasn't packed with gang members. On opening night on Friday, two people were arrested outside the theater for fighting. The Temecula Police Department is patrolling the area and no other problems have been reported since then.

Bottom line, I think the opportunity to see a powerful illustration of what it's like to grow up black and poor in modern-day America is worth putting up with a fight in a parking lot.

Temecula city officials got about 70 calls last week asking that "Boyz" be blacked out in the city. Mayor Parks no doubt heard from many of these ban supporters, then said he too didn't want the movie in Temecula.

"I don't back censorship in any way, shape or form," he said. "I just don't want any unnecessary trouble in our community. I am sure that if somebody really wants to see this, they can see it in other towns around here."

Sorry, Mr. Mayor, I think banning a movie is censorship. I don't want to have to go to another town to see "Boyz N the Hood." I want to be able to see it in my town.

Surprise: Abortion is a big issue
Publication Date: October 30, 1991

I am holding my breath while I write this because today the topic is abortion.

Crusade For Life Inc. raised this volatile issue with the Temecula and Murrieta school board candidates via a six-question survey in mid-September. It asked candidates for "yes" and "no" responses on questions about abortion, parental consent, school-based clinics and sex education. At the time, Crusade For Life's local chairman, Edward Day, was a Temecula candidate. He has since pulled out of the race.

Included with the survey was an anti-abortion brochure with color pictures of aborted fetuses, including one labeled "human garbage." It certainly gets the point across.

In response to the survey, Murrieta candidate Gil Rasmussen in a letter to the editor said he thought abortion was "a peripheral issue" that didn't need to be addressed by the candidates. "Reasonable men and women will have to resist the lure of single-issue politics if they want to build a positive school community for their children," he wrote.

Day fired back in another letter to the editor, urging candidates to respond to the questionnaire ASAP. "Any sincere answer will gain you more respect and credibility than 'ducking the issues' by non-response," he wrote. "That approach only shows an unfortunate contempt for the public's right to know!"

Finally, enough candidates responded for Day's group to put out "voter information guides" based on the results. Day isn't letting reporters see the guides because, "It would be best to distribute them directly rather than put it in the paper." It seems the same logic didn't apply when he wrote the letter to the editor pressuring the candidates to respond.

Crusade For Life has passed out about 1,200 guides to churches, businesses, private schools, community groups and acquaintances in the past couple of weeks, and may get out as many as 2,000 by election day on Tuesday. In small communities like ours, these guides could be powerful stuff.

Rasmussen is a former evangelical minister who is "getting more pro-choice as I get older." He says he resents the "insincerity" of the Crusade For Life questions. "They're portraying themselves as representatives of the unborn, but in truth their desire is politics, politics on the cheap."

Another Murrieta candidate, Shauna Briggs, is a mother of four who says, "I do not believe in abortion as a means of birth control." She says she agonized about the survey for weeks because of the volatility of the topic and the graphic nature of the anti-abortion brochure. Finally, she decided to send her own written statement, but not answer the questions.

"As a candidate it was scary because no matter what you say, somebody's not going to like it," she said. "I had to do what I felt was right. Your integrity is based on how you believe in things. There are a lot of parents who would be very concerned about these types of issues. We cannot take away parents' rights as parents."

From the for-what-it's-worth file:

Four of Temecula's nine candidates answered the abortion questions: Barbara Tooker, Linda Cloughen, J. Eric Brown and David Eurich. Eight of Murrieta's 21 candidates responded: Paul Cartas, Scott Morris, Keith Penny, Edward Benthale, Judy Rosen, Patty Julian, Alan Gordon and Ellwyn Hughes.

Rasmussen calls the anti-abortion brochure "revulsive" and "pornographic." Day says mailing it with the questionnaire "may have been a tactical mistake in terms of the approach, but I make no apology for it. It wasn't a moral mistake. Those little kids who were killed by abortion were not killed by Crusade For Life."

Rasmussen and Briggs say they were not questioned by any pro-choice groups. Day says he personally questioned the City Council candidates for Temecula and Murrieta and made recommendations in those races. He says Crusade For Life will ask future local candidates about abortion.

You are hereby advised, candidates-to-be.

Time to cram some bleating in; bad dream
Publication Date: November 16, 1991

Temecula is on the map.

But Murrieta is the centerfold.

That's part of the play of our two fair cities in this week's special issue of Time magazine: "California The Endangered Dream."

Temecula is identified on Time's version of a California map, right above a drawing of some grapes. Either the Temecula Valley Wine

Country is gaining prominence or the Temecula City Council's sour grapes are getting national exposure.

Murrieta appears in what Time calls its "gatefold photographs," which feature a shot of two bicycle riders in the Santa Cruz Mountains on one side and the California Oaks housing tract on the other side. The Cal Oaks spread covers almost four pages; far and away the biggest photo in the mag. Alas, the caption identifies Cal Oaks thusly: "A new housing tract sprawls across hills 60 miles southeast of Los Angeles. . ."

Centerfold Mayor Jerry Allen says he's heard worse. "At least they don't say the uhhhhhhmmmmmmm Valley area." (For those of you not sensitive to Murrieta's ego, Allen is referring to that neighboring city mentioned on the map.)

The centerfold depicts thousands of rooftops marching into the hills. It justifies America's worst stereotype about the crammed SoCal subdivision. Jeff Minkler, president of Kulberg Ltd., master developer of Cal Oaks, agrees the centerfold is hardly flattering. "I guess negative publicity is better than no publicity at all."

Temecula also is identified as a classic example of suburban sprawl gone berserk. Temecula is called "a sudden-growth city" where lights go on at 4 a.m. "By 5 one can stand on the hill above the Winchester Collection tract, and, to the sound of sheep bleating in the darkness, look down on the streams of headlights coming down the feeder roads to the Route 15 Freeway, two hours to San Diego."

America's image of us: Murrieta: The city that crams. Temecula: The city that bleats.

Other Timely matters:

Time is not timely. The centerfold was shot about a year ago, according to estimates from Minkler and Pam Egan, saleswoman for the Siena homes that are prominently displayed.

"It took the guy a long time to write the article," Minkler says.

Time's timing couldn't have been worse for Siena. The photo has a billboard advertising Siena homes from the $ 120,000s. Egan says Siena lowered its prices to the $110,000s this week.

Since when is Temecula two hours from San Diego? Since Time began (writing about us).

Wednesday night's broadcast of the Temecula council meeting on Inland Valley Cablevision was a riot. Seriously. Station techs goofed and broadcast the voices of British actors and a laugh track while our esteemed council was shown in action.

I'm told at one point Mayor Ron Parks was on the screen saying in a British accent: "This isn't a massage parlor."

Let's hope Time's editors weren't watching.

Now our own Endangered Dream. We moved here to escape the smog, congestion and gangs that afflict urban California. We wanted to make our valley something special.

Now the smog is creeping in from the north. Our traffic is already legendary. And last week a kid was wounded when three punks in a BMW fired three shots outside the Yellow Brick Road arcade at the Temecula Town Center.

"If they shoot at us, we'll get our own guns and shoot back. We'll go hurt them."

That's Temecula Valley High School student Jason Halbert talking, not some L.A. gang member. They're here folks, as real as the concrete-tile roof on your dream home.

Councilman Karel Lindemans wants the city to open a rec center A.S.A.P. KRTM-FM deejays John Hunneman and Tony Marino want a 9 p.m. curfew for youths and a $500 fine for parents whose kids bust the curfew. Arcade manager Greg Heer wants the cops to take control of loiterers. Police Chief Rick Sayre wants the arcade workers to make citizen arrests. Ruth Chesher wants to form a teen council.

We better do something soon, dreamers, if we really want to be something special.

CHAPTER 4

1992 - Death and life

This was the year of the gut-wrenching Border Patrol crash at Temecula Valley High School. Locals who lived here know I need not say more. Fortunately, I was off work at the time and so didn't write much about it. I'll explain why later.

There was lots of good news this year for a couple institutions that could use it: Murrieta schools and Temecula's library.

The state finally stepped in and committed to building real campuses for Avaxat, Alta Murrieta and E. Hale Curran elementary schools, replacing portables with permanent buildings. Things were so bad in cash strapped Murrieta that legendary baseball player Barry Bonds, also a local at the time, held a fund-raiser for the high school at his home of Bear Creek.

Two years after construction started, the new Temecula library finally opened, replacing a facility that at that time served Temecula and Murrieta and was smaller than most of the tract homes being built in the area. It was a time of great rejoicing for a community that loves to read.

More good news arrived when the Murrieta Police Department finally got started. While other Southwest Riverside County cities relied on the sheriff's department to provide such services, independent Murrietans said they would do it themselves. And so they have, 21 years and counting.

More bad news came when Temecula ended its legendary traffic guard program, the one where paid people stood on freeway overpasses guiding motorists, providing the best traffic flow since the days of no stop lights in Temecula so long ago.

On the domestic front my second child, David, arrived that year, which meant I was off three weeks to help. The Border Patrol crash occurred then, which was fine by me, given that my reporter colleagues said it was the saddest thing they've ever written about. Much better to celebrate life.

Finally, with the help – such as it was – of my 2-year-old daughter Julia, I baked a birthday cake for my wife Joanne and lived to talk about it.

And what else is this in Murrieta? They played a high school football game for the first time. Wow, something to do in town.

Chasing the pot of gold for schools
Publication Date: February 12, 1992

Even Mother Nature knows baseball players are rich.

A rainbow was spotted Monday morning on my way out to a golf tourney sponsored by Murrieta's most famous resident, baseball man Barry Bonds. The rainbow seemed to end at the Bear Creek Country Club, host of the Murrieta Valley High School fund-raiser. No doubt there was a pot of gold at the end of it. Or at least the baseball equivalent – a multimillion dollar contract.

Baseball players make a lot of money. No, make that an obscene amount of money, with all due respect to Murrieta anit-porn crusader Trudy Thomas. Bobby Bonilla, one of the ballplayers at the tourney, just signed a $29 million, five-year contract. His pal Bonds is expected to get an even bigger contract next year.

By comparison, Murrieta voters last year twice voted down a $46 million bond measure that would have built five badly needed permanent schools. Two strikes was an out for the school district that won't try bonding with voters again anytime soon.

Outrageous salaries for baseball school and a dollar drought for schools, we do indeed live in strange times, right Murrieta School Board prez Austin Linsley?

No comment, says Linsley, who played in the tourney. "The important thing is that people like Barry Bonds, who have resources, mobilize those resources for the community that they live in, which is what Barry … did," Linsley says.

To his credit, Bonds, the father of two children who may one day attend local schools, is aware of the Murrieta money problems. He wants to make next year's fund-raiser even bigger and says we'll be "shocked" at what can be done for local schools.

His fellow Murrietans hope he's as good at raising money as he is at hitting a baseball.

Baking a big surprise and other treats
Publication Date: March 18, 1992

Since when is baking a case a test of one's manhood.

Since John, the husband of your wife's friend, baked one.

You and your 2-year-old daughter are forced into this test of skill when you wife demands a homemade cake for her birthday. Nothing store-bought this time if you really love me, she warns,

Oh-oh.

You start by forgetting. Ninety minutes before she's due back for her cake, you remember the edict. Ninety minutes may be an eternity for Betty Crocker, but for you who have never made a cake, it's panic.

Ten minutes later you've dismantled the kitchen and you still haven't found baking's most basic tool, the mixer.

"I know where it is," says your daughter.

Hallelujah, you exclaim.

"It's lost," she says.

Just in time you remember your vow to never throttle your own offspring.

You finally find the mixer, right where it's supposed to be. You toss eggs, water and batter into a bowl and turn the mixer on high. Now the cake is splattered all over the kitchen.

"You're making a big mess," says your daughter.

You salvage what you can of the cake and put it back in the bowl. This time you put the mixer on super slow and make a brown sludge that looks toxic. You consider dialing 9-1-1, but before you can, your 2-year-old smashes the egg that you forgot to put away.

"Sorry, daddy."

This is the least of your worries because now the size of your baking pan does not match what is recommended on the back of the cake box. You've come too far to turn back now, into the oven she goes.

You debate whether to evacuate or clean up, then decide the real man toughs it out. Thirty miraculous minutes later, the kitchen is clean and the battle-scarred cake is cooling. And thank goodness for frosting, which covers the skid marks and leaves your cake looking like a Bon Appetit centerfold.

Just in time for your wife, who is surprised that you remembered. "It looks beautiful," she says.

Take that, John.

This town's door is open and closed
Publication Date: April 4, 1992

The aptly named Don Juan Murrieta was the first Murrieta newcomer in 1870. The place was practically inundated when the Buchanans and the Doolittles arrived in 1884, the Thompsons in 1887 and the Sykes in 1888.

Modern Murrieta measures its growth by the tens of thousands, not individual families. In the last five years Murrieta has grown from about 3,300 to more than 25,000. It is a Don Juan of modern-day suburbia, romancing big-city escapees with its country. (How corny is that comparison? Don Juan is probably turning over in his grave.)

Anyway, this onslaught has created a fair amount of tension. The old-timers feel their turf is being invaded by rude city slickers; the newcomers blame the fuddy-duddies for not planning better.

In recent months this resentment has spread from the whispering-behind-the-back in coffee klatches to open warfare in the public domain, primarily because of plans for a pool hall and a pirate-theme park in Murrieta.

Groups of mostly newcomers have organized to oppose each project, contending they fled the big cities to get away from such things. Old-timers scoff at the complaints, saying if they'd acted on their objections to growth; the newcomers would still be stuck in their metropolises.

It's a bitter feud, proving once again that Murrieta's politics are anything but dull. A Planning Commission meeting on the pool hall got so nasty that the police were sent to the next session. The local letters-to-the-editor have been as vicious as a celebrity divorce battle.

"I kind of feel the people have the doorknob tied to their butt when they come here and close the door behind them," says Councilman Dave Haas. "These people that come in here and want to complain about everything that goes on should have thought about that before they moved here."

Theme park opponents like Steve Montelli say the council is more interested in pleasing developers than residents. "I guess there is always another election," he warns his leaders in a letter-to-the-editor. "Nothing like a short political career, eh fellas?"

Adds Anne Greenstone in another anti-park letter: "This project is a gaudy, garish, obnoxious cheap shot that will undoubtedly draw gangs, trouble and more trouble. Worst of all, it will label Murrieta as 'that place with the stupid-looking phony boat.'"

The high seas were never so rough on the real pirates. Perry Peters, one of the Haunted Galleon park's owners, says he's shocked by the opposition, especially because so many newcomers complain there isn't family entertainment here.

"The real bottom line is they don't want any growth in this area, period," Peters says of the critics. "While I sympathize with them, that's not gonna happen, whether we build there or not."

The old-timers compare the whining newcomers to NIMBYs, or Not In My Back Yard. To NIMBYs, anything is fine, as long as it's not next to them. To carry this caricature to its extreme, nothing would ever be built because nobody wants anything next door.

"It's a small mind that wants to shut everybody out," Haas says. "They're (NIMBYs) usually the first to complain about their rights, yet they want to prevent everybody else from having their rights."

Newcomers like Michael Hoffee (theme park opponent) and Christine Brunskill (pool hall foe) say they too favor growth; they just want it better managed. Each says it's silly to locate these places next to them.

Brunskill talks about the newcomers who flee the gangs, the smog and the congestion of Los Angeles, Orange and San Diego counties for the safe, clean and easy life of Murrieta. They want to keep it that way as long as possible.

"Everyone moving here genuinely cares about what's going on because it's brand new for all of us," Brunskill says. "For the old-timers, they're kind of laughing at us in a way. If I were them, I'd feel very sad for how things have changed."

This library is worthy of a great epic
Publication Date: May 6, 1992

Once upon a time in a very near kingdom, the people were most unhappy with their library.

It was smaller than many of the affordable tract cottages that the people found when they fled from the big, bad cities. These people knew that their master-planned kingdom, especially their children, deserved a better library.

So they got off their duffs and raised money, 500,000 gold coins to be exact. The federal and county kings chipped in, and work on the new library began in an age when many others were closing. Temecula was the little kingdom that could.

Alas, the happy ending wasn't to be because the work stopped a year later. The county kings, uh supervisors, decreed the contractor in default. (What's that word doing in a fairy tale?) A "KEEP OUT OR MONSTERS WILL EAT YOU UP" sign was posted, a barbed wire fence was put up and nothing happened for months. It was a sad time, indeed, in the kingdom.

A white knight — another builder, actually — finally came to the rescue and the new library was finished two years after it began. What a beautiful castle this was! Shiny purple, yellow and brown colors on the outside. The gorgeous children's mural inside. A clever story room, a grand ; entryway, thousands of new books, a computerized catalog — oh, it would take an encyclopedia to list all the ways the new was better than the old.

The people rejoiced on a bright Sunday afternoon with music, song, stories, paintings, food, drink and speeches from the evil politicians who hogged the spotlight.

The people in this kingdom lived happily ever after until the summer when they had to cross the freeway while Rancho California Road was under construction.

Going to work and leaving the womb
Publication Date: June 24, 1992

"Hi-ho, hi-ho, it's off to work we go."

So sang my 3-year-old daughter as we walked to the car Monday morning. It was fitting for my transition from the world of make-believe to the all too real world of newspapers.

I'm now a nuclear family man in this age of reduced nukes and Murphy Brown. David Max Love joined us at 11:06 a.m. May 28, giving me a wife, a daughter, a son and two enormous college bills.

I'm ahead of myself by about 5,000,000,000,000 diapers. First the basics – there's nothing more wonderful than watching the birth of your child. (Note the emphasis on watching as opposed to giving.) I was in tears, terror, goose bumps, chills, smiles and shock all at once. If this sounds like babble, well, it's one of those things that words can't describe.

The birth itself went as well as those things can go. My wife had an epidural, a pain medication that is to childbirth what the cold drink is to thirst. Last time my wife got the drugs too late, couldn't push, was in agony the whole time, and the doctor had to bring out everything but a tow truck to pull out the kid. This time my wife was merely uncomfortable, shoved out David in six minutes, and was talking afterward about having 10 more babies. Then the drugs wore off.

We were kicked out of the hospital 24 hours after the birth because that's all the insurance company will cover. Can't say I blame them, considering the bill for a perfectly healthy baby with absolutely no complications is $5,000 and counting. Perhaps the politicians will fix our health care system by the time David's great grandchildren are great grandparents. Perhaps.

David hit the scales at 8 pounds, 12 ounces. He's already put on three pounds, outgrown an outfit and changed diaper sizes. At this rate he should be in the NFL by the time he's potty trained, especially if his pushy dad has any say in it.

Why David? Because it's safe. Gotta be careful with the last name of Love. We ruled out Summer, First and Puppy, no matter how persistent the jokesters at the office were. Naming a kid after me would have saddled him with a lifetime of fast-food puns. Finally, so many boy names reminded mom and dad of the many male jerks they've run into. (Take note feminists, we didn't have this problem with girl names.) This convoluted process of elimination left us with Waldo, Orville and David.

David is a mellow fellow and obviously has his dad's wonderful personality. He's already smiling — you would too if all you had to do was eat, sleep and poop. He also naps a lot during the day, so much so that we call him Baby Sominex. His tireless sister is the NoDoz Kid.

This duo has made the last three weeks a blur of sleepless nights, laundry, dirty diapers, tantrums, more laundry, jealousy, demands, arguments, spills, vomiting, more laundry and no free time. I've never been happier.

A wise friend once warned that the workload from the second child increases exponentially to the point of exhaustion. Another wise friend advised that a second offspring creates a family and a sense of childlike bliss in mom and dad.

They were both right. And no, I'm not so tired that I'm in some weird state of nirvana. A family is security, providing, protecting, teaching and, most of all, loving. In a corny kind of way, a family is like a womb that shields us from the rest of this stressful world.

But I'm no Dan Quayle when it comes to families. Not everybody has what it takes to get excited when your daughter flushes the toilet and waves bye-bye to her poo-poo. Or cuddle up with your two children and read the same book six times in a row. Or hold your sleeping newborn in your arms and dream about his life. Or put on a costume and be a handsome prince to your daughter's Snow White. Or change your son's diaper and wonder why he pees on you in the middle of it. Or look at your incredible wife when you're both collapsed in bed at the end of another 22-hour-day and realize, you've made two really special little people.

Calling all units: The P.D. is here
Publication Date: August 5, 1992

This is not a good week to go on a crime spree in Murrieta.

Murrieta Blue is on the streets giving the bad guys the blues. Corny, you say, but remember, you can never curry too much favor with the cops. And all of a sudden there are a lot of cops to keep an eye on in Murrieta.

It's the new Murrieta P.D., the origins of which can best be explained by the community's unofficial bureaucratic motto: "We don't trust that dang county, we're gonna do it ourselves!"

The independent cusses in Murrieta went off and opened their own p.d. last weekend, a rarity in these tight budget times in California. Before that, they began their own fire department and their own city government. Next they're gonna start their own foreign policy.

There is police presence and then there is Murrieta presence. The cops took over from the county sheriff Friday night at 10:01 p.m. and made their first arrest at 10:05. At that rate they should have every Murrieta criminal arrested, prosecuted and behind bars by this afternoon.

Not that we're expecting a lot from our new police department. Police Chief Larry Dean reports that Murrietans last weekend did a lot of double takes at the large number of cops on local streets.

I can relate. Last Saturday night while I prepared to do my customary roll-at-a-stop-sign-on-Whitewood-because-there's-never-a-cop-in-Murrieta, I saw a strange white car coming up the street. Then the universally recognized flashing red lights went off and some other surprised motorist was nailed. I made a completely legal stop, went about my law abiding way and realized Murrieta will never be the same.

Of course, some things never change. From the outside the Murrieta police station could be easily confused with a trailer you see at a housing project before the models are done. The purple canopy, the new landscaping, the workers still putting on the finishing touches — it's the perfect p.d. for model-home infested Murrieta.

Now Dean and his 34-member staff are hoping to build a model police department. The chance to start a force is a police chief's dream, which explains why Dean was selected from more than 100 applicants last February. Ditto for working in a new department — just ask the more than 500 people who applied for the Murrieta P.D. jobs.

It sounds like Murrieta has an all-star squad. And in the interest of praising a cop whenever possible because you never know when you'll need a break, I hereby proclaim Murrieta the Dream Team of police departments. The bad guys might as well turn themselves in now 'cause they ain't got a chance. And you're dreamin' if you think that's gonna happen.

The change of the guard with lights
Publication Date: August 29, 1992

It wasn't that bad. Honest.

We've long dreaded the day Temecula's waving traffic guards waved goodbye. And about 1:30 p.m. Thursday they did when the signals on the Rancho California Road-Interstate 15 overpass were turned on.

Surprise, it wasn't instant gridlock. Yours truly crossed the freeway at 2 p.m. and 5 p.m. Thursday and each trip took another minute or two because signals had replaced guards.

Sure, you could argue that those minutes add up if you cross the freeway a couple of times a day every day for the rest of your life. Not to mention what your children, grandchildren and great grandchildren might pile up.

But that amount of time is offset by what the signals save when the guards weren't there and the stop signs took over, like weekends, middle of the day and nights.

Add it all up, subtract the difference, divide by the four-letter words used on the Winchester Road overpass at rush hour, multiply by the $250,000 the city spent on the guards and you're as confused as I am. Let's just call the signals vs. guards debate on Rancho Cal a draw.

So why is Winchester so much worse? The difference is all those extra lanes they've put on Rancho Cal. You don't have to be a mathematician to figure that more lanes moves more traffic. That's why people will continue to use Rancho Cal even though our beloved guards are gone.

Not everybody thinks guards and signals are the same.

Bill Kouvelis, the guards supervisor since they began, watched the Rancho Cal signals debut on Thursday night and wasn't much impressed. He says an accident backed up traffic plenty, a situation his crew would have handled much more efficiently. A cop also had to direct traffic at one point because the signals malfunctioned.

"You can't replace the human element," Kouvelis says.

Here's some traffic guard trivia you can impress (or bore) your friends with:

Traffic guards had a one-week trial run from Jan. 29 to Feb. 2, 1990. The $4,300 tab was picked up by local developer David Lowry. Keep that in mind the next time someone says developers don't ever do anything positive. That someone then will ask you who got us in the mess in the first place.

The guards became a permanent fixture on June 14, 1990. They served 803 days through sizzle, cold, rain, hail, sleet, snow, (Well, they would have if it ever had.) There was never a major accident attributed to their directions, a fact the city's insurance carrier appreciates.

Kouvelis says the city isn't planning anything to remember the guards by.

I've said it before, I'll say it again; for the past 803 days the traffic guards were as much a part of Temecula as Old Town, the wine country and affordable housing.

This thankful motorist suggests a waving guards monument on the Rancho Cal overpass. And in the spirit of the "They Passed This Way" monument in Old Town, our traffic guard memorial could read "We Passed This Way Thanks To Them."

A first for everything this night
Publication Date: September 16, 1992

There were a lot of hoarse people in Murrieta last weekend.

The Murrieta Valley High School opened its season Friday with a 29-0 victory over visiting Temescal Canyon.

So what's the big deal? They always play high school football this time of year.

Not in Murrieta. It was the first ever varsity football game in the city. On the Murrieta small-town new barometer, this was the equivalent of Elvis hosting "The Tonight Show" live.

Goosebumps were the emotion of the evening, beginning with the thundering ovations that Murrieta's starters received as they were introduced before the game. Could a 17-year-old know that life doesn't get any better?

The game started at 7:37 and Johnny Bush scored the historic first Murrieta touchdown just 15 minutes later. As the score indicates, everything went right for Murrieta and the excited faithful screamed for every highlight. On this magical night — it even looked to be a full moon — it seemed the home team could have whipped a major college team.

By the way, Murrieta plays at Notre Dame this weekend. Is Murrieta ready for them already?

It was a night of firsts and first downs in Murrieta . . .

Anybody who is a Murrieta somebody was at the game. The Who's Who that I saw or heard was there included Mayor Jerry Allen, school boss Tate Parker, school board members Austin Linsley, Al Christenson, Shauna Briggs, Judy Rosen, and Margi Wray; and City Councilman Fred Weishaupl.

Plus I saw five of my neighbors at the game. Who says there's nothing to do in Murrieta on a Friday night?

The first arrests in Murrieta football history were two Inglewood teenagers after a ruckus on the Temescal side in the third quarter. Eight officers and six cars arrived in a major show of force from the new Murrieta Police Department.

Strangest ad in the game's program was a half-pager from Astro Burgers in West Hollywood, a community most Murrieta parents would not want their kids in on a Friday night.

The crew working the sideline chains included Murrieta Police Chief Larry Dean and his lieutenant, Rick McIntire. After the game Murrieta police directed traffic to the freeway and the parking lot was empty in less than half an hour. Now there's a full-service p.d.

The youngest Murrieta twins/fans were probably Benjamin and Andrew Walters. Their mom, Mary, is a teacher at the high school. The 5-month-old boys watched from a twin stroller parked on the Murrieta side of the field. Their proud papa, Karl, says they were so excited about the game that they couldn't sleep the night before.

The biggest Murrieta booster was Shelby Brzezinski, a.k.a. Ned Nighthawk. The Murrieta mascot was jazzed about the community's spirit. "This will be something everybody will remember, hopefully." Ned says he hopes the game will establish a tradition that Murrieta can be proud of. "We're tired of being snubbed by Temecula."

Guess who Murrieta plays for the first time on Oct. 9?

This is, after all, high school. Tony Carroll, John Viramontes, Derek Robertson and James Sackett are hanging out, scoping the girls, watching the game, talking trash, scoping the girls, making plans, ripping each other, scoping the girls. . .

In the second quarter they eagerly tell a passing student that they're being interviewed by "the newspaper." "They're all losers," the kid yells. "Stupid sophomore," Viramontes fires back.

The students say the football game is already the place to be; it puts McDonald's to shame. But they probably won't go to the dance after the game because — like a lot of things in their world — it's stupid. And girls, the reason they're not talking to you is because they're still deciding who they want. It goes without saying that you want them.

We cross paths again in the third quarter and they still haven't talked to any girls. What did some girls think of the Don Juan wanna-bes? We'll never know because "the newspaper" — harking back to his own high school days — couldn't work up the courage to ask them.

CHAPTER 5

1993 - Mudville and a political bathroom

Here comes Wal-Mart and there goes the mall!

Wait a minute, history didn't happen that way. Yet in 1993 it sure looked that way as Temecula officials considered placing the mega retailer on part of what is basically now site of The Promenade mall. Saner heads prevailed and Wal-Mart was shown the door, though folks in Murrieta still rue the day because they might have welcomed a mall in the ill-fated Golden Triangle instead. Oh well.

Another big story was the January rain that flooded Southwest Riverside County. Besides the memorable stuff in Old Town Temecula, there was a not-so-memorable moment involving an Ortega park district meeting in a bathroom. Trust me; I don't make this stuff up. At one time Ortega provided parks to the Wildomar area.

In Murrieta they decided to temporarily hire their own traffic guards to ease the rapidly growing gridlock there. Given how Murrietans always turn up their noses at Temecula's traffic, it was a matter of swallowing some pride. Better than sitting in traffic.

In Temecula schools there was controversy over a book and the one year anniversary of the God-awful Border Patrol crash was recognized.

What's really going on in there?
Publication Date: January 9, 1993

The week's rains brought the usual results. Old Murrieta was a mess, roads were flooded with flooded signs, Murrieta Creek boiled but didn't burst and drivers did stupid things.

Then there was Wednesday night's Ortega park board meeting. No, the session wasn't canceled by the downpour. It just had to be moved somewhere else - the bathroom.

Blame Mother Nature and a grumpy audience for the bizarre nature break. The board met like it always does in a small, one-room building. When it came time to go to a closed session, the board did what it always does and asked the crowd of about 20 to step outside.

No way, said the masses. It's a monsoon out there.

Somebody (I'm not sure who because events were moving fast. You know how it is when you gotta go.) suggested the board meet in the bathroom.

Life truly being stranger than fiction, the board agreed to do it. Board prez Ray Grage assured us the meeting would last "just a couple minutes" `cause the district's attorney, Joe Aklufi, was involved and his legal meter was running.

Take note, wherever you are Thomas Jefferson, democracy adjourned to the men's room at 7:34 p.m. with Aklufi, Administrator Alain Grenier, Grage and fellow board members Charley Johnson, Pat Desjardins, Don Hickman and Elizabeth Lindsey in attendance.

Of course it stopped raining as soon as the closed session started. And of course nobody in the audience interfered with history and told our elected officials. This was something to tell the grandkids - we were there when government really did go down the toilet.

Oh, the pun possibilities were endless. The heads of Ortega meet in the head. Considering they were discussing personnel, would they can somebody while in the can? Some say the district needs more park facilities, but obviously it has some "facilities."

The audience had lots of yuks. "Let's hope they didn't take in the sports section," somebody cackled. "Who's sitting on the urinal?" another guy wondered. "Government really smells this time!" and, "Let's hope the ladies keep their eyes closed!" were also heard.

For once it was acceptable behavior to have your mind in the gutter at a public meeting.

Dick Ashmead had his mind somewhere else when he accidentally opened the men's room to take care of his business. Imagine his surprise when he realized the politicians were taking care of theirs.

Weren't they supposed to be in the ladies room? a "flush" Ashmead asked as he headed there himself. Yet another first for a public meeting - nobody tried to stop a guy from using the ladies room.

The men's room was finally vacant at 8:45 p.m., 71 minutes after it was first occupied. It's a good thing the board was in a hurry. On this weird night, government gridlock and constipation were one.

There was no joy in Mudville
Publication Date: January 20, 1993

Wow.

I think we better do something about Murrieta Creek. It's already too late.

In case you live under a rock or in new Murrieta or new Temecula, the rest of Southwest Riverside County spent the weekend in the bathtub. But it was hardly relaxing. Or cleansing.

Murrieta Creek finally did what everybody was afraid it would. Old Murrieta just did what it always does when it rains. Only worse than ever before.

People were flooded, stranded, evacuated, financially ruined, and, most tragically, drowned.

All this made for THE BIG STORY, which explains why five LA TV station news vans, two media helicopters and dozens of newspaper types were rolling around in our mud. And that's just what I saw.

Andy Warhol was right. This weekend was our 15 minutes of fame. I hope you enjoyed it.

Everywhere people were saying, ``I was just interviewed by Channel (fill in the blank)."Talking to little ol' me ain't quite the same.

My big moment came Monday morn when I was on Channel 5 twice. First, I was in the background while Pujol Street resident Shannon Nickol was interviewed.

I moved front and center on the TV screen a couple minutes later while some National Guard guy was yapping. Fortunately, from a job security perspective, I was furiously taking notes in both instances. Good thing the bosses don't see me off camera.

My wife got calls from friends saying guess who's on TV right now. The only problem is we don't have TV 'cause we turned off our cable this month. Who says I don't have timing?

A couple neighbor kids called me a big star yesterday morn while I was out changing my wife's flat tire. They also asked why I don't have a rain coat. And what was with the goofy hat? I thought one of them said nerd but I'm not sure. Not that I care what they think anyway, now that I'm a big star. So why do I still have to change a tire?

After my air time, I was with one of my newspaper-reporter-geek brethren when one of the perfectly-manicured-man-that-guy-must-get-a-lot-of-babes TV reporters walked by. Of course we snickered.

Not everybody was excited about the media horde that gathered like vultures to see if Old Town would be inundated again. Said Old Town merchant Bruce Becker: ``There will be a lot of disappointed people if it doesn't."

Fortunately (honest), it didn't.

The city is spending more than $500,000 to pitch Temecula as a place with "everything under the sun." Now the nation knows Temecula as the place with "everything under water." Or if you prefer; "everything under the mud."

A year later and it still really hurts
Publication Date: June 2, 1993

I've given a lot of thought to writing something about today's first anniversary of the Border Patrol crash. But what can you say that either (A) hasn't already been written, or (B) won't get you vilified by one side or the other of this extremely emotional issue?

By my unofficial count, there have been 103 articles in the P-E in the past year on the Border Patrol crash. There were 40 in the first week and 60 in the first month. Media blitz, indeed.

It's unfortunately the biggest story to ever hit here, Temecula's equivalent of the Kennedy assassination. I'm sure most folks around here remember where they were when they heard the numbing news that a Chevrolet Suburban, loaded with 12 Mexican citizens and trying to evade Border Patrol agents, plowed into a car and two pedestrians at Temecula Valley High School.

The worst accident in city history left six people dead and a controversy that may never die.

(Even this morning's memorial service is a point of dispute. Residents have been calling City Hall asking who's going to pay for the police protection needed to put it on at Margarita and Rancho Vista roads, the site of the crash. The city will pay the tab, inquiring taxpayers.)

I was starting a three-week vacation a year ago when I heard the news on the radio at a Temecula gas station. It takes a pretty big story for Temecula to make KNX, so the reporter in me wanted to race out and cover it. The human being in me said I don't have to because I'm on vacation. Thank goodness.

My son David was born five days before the crash, and I wanted to talk to people about life, not death. For the next three weeks I totally tuned out the crash story by not looking at the newspaper and changing the channel when it came on the news or the radio.

I still feel that way, so it was with great difficulty that I looked at the past year's blizzard of stories. No matter how much has been written, I still can't find anything to smile about.

I want to cry when reminded of Gloria Murrilo, who arrived at the crash as a reporter and left as a victim. She learned at the scene that her two oldest children, Gloria and Jose, died in the wreck. Wow.

I feel the same when I think of Linda Davis, who lost her husband, John, and her son, Todd; or Michael and Stephanie Emilio, who lost their daughter, Monisa.

And I get just as upset when I imagine the parents of Eniceforo Vargas Gomez, the 21-year-old undocumented worker who died five days later from injuries he suffered while riding in the Suburban.

I know listing Gomez with the other five is a source of anger for many in Temecula. One just has to see the two nearby memorials, which include five rose bushes and five trees, to realize how he has been forgotten. But the bottom line is that nobody's child deserved to die that terrible day.

On this one-year anniversary of that tragedy, I'm going to think of death, just like many of you will. But as a parent who just celebrated the one-year anniversary of his son's inspiring birth, I'm also going to think of life.

Living in a place that's on the move
Publication Date: July 21, 1993

Let me ruin your day with some talk about repos and moving.

We've all become familiar with repos in these troubled times, especially my neighborhood. My house sits on a corner and on one street there are three repos among its 12 houses. A neighbor told me last weekend it's about to get much worse - two now-empty houses are going to be repoed.

When and if his information comes true, that would make five repos on the street, including all four houses on one side. In baseball they call this a grand slam, in a neighborhood we call it depressing.

Two of the houses have brown lawns; two others had yards of weeds for the longest time. The good news in the case of the latter two is that the bank came in when they were repoed and fixed them up. Now they just sit empty because it's not easy to sell houses these days.

One reason we moved to Murrieta was because we wanted peace and quiet. Now we have too much because half the houses on the street are empty. I just shrug my shoulders when my 4-year-old daughter complains there aren't enough kids to play with. How can you explain a repo to a child?

I'd thought about getting into the particulars of how each house became a repo, but decided why embarrass the folks involved. They've got enough problems without being singled out by their nosey neighbor who writes for a newspaper.

I'd also thought about trying to make light of the situation, like launching a contest to locate the local street with the most repos and the most-empty houses. The grand prize could have been something silly; the only problem is that there's nothing funny about it. So all I can do is offer my condolences if your street's repos or empty houses are worse than mine.

Our neighborhood is not alone when it comes to repos. The latest figures in Riverside County show the repos are up 71 percent over last year. A breakdown for communities isn't available, but locally we certainly have more than our share if the "bank repo sale" signs and the boom-gone-bust construction industry are indications.

While we're getting depressed about repos, my wife and I have noticed another discouraging trend in the 4 1/2 years we've been here: So many people are coming and going. It's like nothing we have ever experienced before.

Local reporters focus on arrivals because they can be quantified with numbers: new homes, new businesses, new schools, etc. It's a lot harder to identify departures because they're harder to identify. Nobody counts when you leave here, only when you arrive.

Still, it seems that people are moving out of here almost as fast as they are moving in here. For instance, some good friends from the neighborhood left for Colorado two weeks ago. That makes eight families who've departed after we got to know them.

Then there are the passing acquaintances who left before we got to know them. And don't forget all the people who talk of moving. My wife is almost afraid to make friends because then they'll go.

You comics out there would say it's "us" that our friends are fleeing, but I think it's more disturbing than that. (At least I hope.) My hunch is our environs have become a refuge of last resort for people fleeing SoCal's problems.

Here's how I figure: The majority of people who move here are running from something on the coast, be it high housing prices, crime, bad schools, congestion, etc.

They get here and it's not Utopia (What is?) But because they don't have any established ties to the community to hold them, they're more likely to move on. Some go back to the coast because they're tired of the commute. Others, like the eight families we knew, leave California because they've had it with the place.

But no matter why they come or go, the effect is that in this most mobile of societies, we live in one of its most mobile places. It's a distinction I could live without.

Signing off & signing up a new career
Publication Date: September 25, 1993

Mornings just aren't the same around here.

John Hunneman - the loud, opinionated, informative and witty mouth that many of you were addicted to for the past two years - signed off forever Tuesday morn on his KRTM show, 88.9 FM on your local radio dial.

It was vintage Hunneman in that he said and did exactly what was on his mind. A lot of folks dream about quitting their job, Hunneman did it.

He broke the news to his audience at about 8:10 a.m. He signed off for good at about 9:50 a.m., advising that KRTM will go on, it'll just have to go on without him.

Hunneman made live remotes a way of life around here. Whether it was those obvious plugs for sponsors or major news events such as last winter's floods, Hunneman always seemed to be broadcasting on location.

"You'll just have to have your fires without me," is how he put what major news events will be without him.

Mum's the word on why he's quitting. All Hunneman will say is it's personal and that it has nothing to do with his muckraking in local politics. "Nobody put any pressure on me to leave, nobody called the station to say get rid of me. It was totally my decision."

Hunneman did it his way, which meant no long, drawn-out farewells, like his sports heroes. He talked it over with his wife a few times, then let her know it was all systems go a mere five minutes before he announced it on the air. The phone's been ringing nonstop at his Murrieta home ever since.

"There's nothing wrong with me," he assures his devotees. "It's just time to do something else."

Is there an election in his future? "That's within the realm of possibility," he says. He's thinking state Assembly because the local incumbent, Republican Ray Haynes, is hoping to move up the political food chain to state Senate.

He's registered Democrat, which means he'll never be elected around here. He says he'd run as an independent considering he's a middle-of-the-road guy anyway. He's already got a campaign slogan: "Vote for John, he needs the money." At least he's being honest about why he's running.

He also mentioned writing for a newspaper. In other words, he's after my job. Well, he can have it because I've had it. I quit. The Press-Enterprise will go on, it'll just have to go on without . . .

Just kidding, boss.

Anyway, back to the end of our story. Hunneman's kid is named D.J. So does that mean he's gonna alter the lad's name to Super-cool Guy (otherwise known as a newspaper writer) or Super-dummy (politician, obviously)?

"No, he's going to go by `unemployed' now," Hunneman says.

We're going to miss that wit in the morning.

Hunneman is also the reigning Temecula Valley Chamber of Commerce Citizen of the Year. He notes that the big business of the year, Doubletree Suites, and the small business of the year, Jazzercise, are both gone. Now he's unemployed.

"Not to say anything bad about the honor, but people might want to consider this before accepting," Hunneman says.

Riding and writing for a good time
Publication Date: October 20, 1993

A cowboy I'm not, not even a suburban one.

So what's a city type like yours truly doing on top of a horse trying to prod a reluctant cow into moving over this here line?

Having a good time, that's what.

Some guy named Rocky Hill - sounds more like a boxer than a cowboy - roped me into this escapade last Friday night.

Looking for a little free publicity for this weekend's team penning event in the Temecula Pro Rodeo at the Temecula Showgrounds, Hill suggested I come write about my ride on a horse named "Buck."

OK, I made the name up. This being a 35-year-old-couch potato who hasn't been on a horse since his free pony ride days, the idea of climbing on any horse not in a full-body cast is extremely terrifying.

But my false machismo got the best of me, like it usually does. So I ventured out for my ride into history, my date with destiny, my . . . talk about a load of horse manure.

Before I get to any of the glory, I've got to find the place. Hill's directions would have gotten Daniel Boone lost. After 10 minutes of stumbling around old Murrieta, I discover the Murrieta Arena quite by accident: I almost crash into some horse trailers. This must be the place, said my trained reporter eye.

"Where's Rocky Hill?" I ask the friendly woman at the gate.

"Is that a street or a town?" she wonders.

More investigative reporting leads me to one of the two Rockies in attendance tonight. Fortunately, it's the right Rocky, who takes me to my partner for tonight's ride, Abbey.

Rocky's wife, Debbie, tells me some trivia about Abbey: She was thrown and her back was broken by another white horse with the same name. Hahaha, what a funny coincidence, I mutter to myself, as I climb aboard my white Abbey.

Then Abbey moved.

What happened to the full-body cast that was promised, I'm wondering, as Abbey follows Rocky and his horse into an arena where a crowd of about 75 is gathered like famished Romans waiting for the slaughter of helpless Christians.

Now Rocky is giving me these complicated rules about do's and don'ts of team sorting of cattle. Like I'm going to remember. Team Survival is all I care about.

Now we're riding into the middle of the arena and they're announcing my name on a loudspeaker. Whatever happened to learning to ride a horse in the privacy of your own barn.

Now I can't find my stirrup. Granted, I don't know a lot about horses, but even I know you need stirrups, especially when your mount is in the middle of a 0-to-60-in-six-seconds gallop.

AHHH! AHHHH!! AHHHHH!!!

I basically choke Abbey to death while pulling the reins, but she stops and only needs a little horse CPR. Rocky has found my stirrup that fell off, perhaps from all the pressure calm-and-collected me was applying. Oh well.

Rocky, his daughter Erin, and I finally get to team sorting. We finish last, basically because I use about 89 of the allotted 90 seconds getting one cow across the finish line. That left one second for Erin and Rocky to round up the other nine cows. Some help they were.

Now we're lounging on the sidelines and I'm doing interviews on horseback, of all things.

Tag Gaines, the guy who helps maintain the arena, rides up for a chat on his horse, Quiet Kahlua. We share a laugh about the wonderful names that ships and horses get, then the city person in me asks a really dumb question, like how's a guy make ends meet on maintaining a little place like this.

"It's a labor of love," Gaines says of his free time.

This is a family sport, that's what people get out of it. Murrieta west of the freeway is still a horse town, Gaines says, despite the stampede of tract houses and strip centers everywhere else.

"If you note the zoning, it shows equestrian in the different areas," he says of city zoning maps. "It's there for a reason."

I spend about an hour on Abbey, quite a feat. Not so much for me, but for the horse. She was as gentle as could be.

I gave Abbey a good night kiss (I hope my wife will understand) and thanked Rocky and Debbie for a good time. Then I rode off into the night in a car, aware that I'd stumbled onto something really special.

A bridge to controversy in schools
Publication Date: November 10, 1993

Walt Swickla and Leslea Pedersen both consider themselves Christians.

Yet when it comes to the politics of last week's Temecula school board election, neither thinks the other acted like a Christian.

School board member Swickla is furious that Pedersen and her husband, Chris, put out a flier in the campaign's last week that he thinks likened a vote of his to the support of profanity.

Pedersen is angry that Swickla wants to keep a book in the classroom that she and other parents find offensive.

The dispute encompasses issues like censorship, last-minute political smears, parents' rights, the growing influence of religious activists in schools and the troubled state of public education. It's basically political nitroglycerine.

But even though the campaign's over, this stuff needs to be talked about because it says a lot about what's happening in Temecula today.

We'll start with the spark that ignited this. The book, "Bridge To Terabithia," is a wonderful piece of work about a boy and a girl and Terabithia, their secret kingdom in the woods. Swickla says he had a tear in his eye when he finished it. A sentimental fool like me was almost bawling when I completed it yesterday. A children's book that makes two grown men cry needs to be experienced by children.

Or does it? The book doesn't waste any time getting to the Pedersens' issue. On the second page is this sentence: "He figured if he had worked at it - and Lord, had he worked - he could be the fastest runner in the fifth grade when school opened up."

Or how about this thought on page 9: "She (the boy's mother) never canned except when it was scalding anyhow, and all the boiling turned the kitchen into some kind of hellhole."

On Page 12, the boy's father asks, "What are they teaching in that damn school?" Page 15 has, "Not like stubby school crayons you had to press down on till somebody bitched about your breaking them."

Perhaps the author of the book, Katherine Paterson, answers the profanity question herself on Page 63 when the story talks of cheap racing cars that kept breaking down "until his father was cursing them with impatience."

Note that Paterson doesn't tell us what the father said.

After the book was used in their Rancho Elementary School fifth-grader's class, the Pedersens and other parents asked the Temecula school board last year to remove it. The board voted 4-1 to keep the book, with David Eurich dissenting.

This prompted the Pedersens to spend $368 to produce 20,000 fliers that were distributed on the street and in The Bargain Bulletin a few days before the election. It was headlined, "What Is Your Child Learning In School." The words "reading" and "writing" were crossed out on the flier, leaving their answer, "PROFANITY," in bold red letters.

It quoted board member Rosie Vanderhaak: "My daughter had difficulty in College because she was not exposed to 'such language' earlier. When asked then why not 4th grade. She did not answer."

The flier quoted Swickla: "Children must learn about the Real World . . . we cannot shelter them. Somebody has to know there are cultures out that talk that way. I could understand it if my boy got up in the night and stubbed his toe and swore, just not all the time."

Vanderhaak, the leading vote-getter in last week's election, declined to comment on the flier. Swickla, who finished eighth among nine candidates, is irate because he thinks the flier takes everything out of context and makes him look like he's advocating atheism.

Ironically, neither Swickla nor Pedersen is happy with what this episode means for the future.

Swickla, who has lived in Temecula 17 years and served on the school board 10 years, has never seen such a vicious campaign here. He attributes it to the growth and figures it'll only get worse as the town continues to change.

Pedersen, a homemaker, and her husband, a self-employed business appraiser, moved here four years ago from the San Gabriel Valley. She's so disappointed in Temecula schools that she's thinking of home-schooling her four children.

I'll settle this the best way I know how: Go read "Bridge To Terabithia" and decide for yourself.

CHAPTER 6

1994 - Zero tolerance for zany Zev

Two words sum up this wild year, Zev Buffman.

The developer showed up in Old Temecula pitching a massive entertainment project that drove the community crazy.

There were other politics, as always. Up and coming Jeff Stone, then of the Temecula City Council, hosted a night of the stars for Temecula with two U. S Senators showing up at his house. Not to be outdone, Sonny Bono appeared at another local event. And the beat goes on.

There was perhaps my favorite local scandal of all, the Temecula beauty queen who relinquished her crown, in part because it was revealed she had appeared in Playboy. Oh the controversy in a community that was then so prim and proper. Today, with a massive casino in our midst, there might be less of a fuss.

The disparity between education in Temecula and Murrieta became apparent when Temecula opened another middle school of permanent buildings while Murrieta's middle schools remained as mostly portables. Thank goodness we've remedied that problem.

In Murrieta, homeowners continued a massive protest against a proposed housing project while yours truly wondered if maybe they were damaging their cause by carrying on for so long.

Domestically, my daughter Julia started kindergarten. Oh the grief. It's all relative, given that 12 years later she went to college on the other side of the country.

Then there was the hue and cry that resulted when I suggested that staying at home and watching the kids wasn't so hard after all. Those are fighting words with moms.

And I'll never forget the piece that generated more reader protests than anything I've ever written, the one describing my wild days in high school and how silly I thought it was to possibly expel local school kids busted for drugs. I wrote a follow-up about all the reader responses, including one who called the Murrieta PD to see if I could be arrested for all the alcohol and drug laws I'd broken some 20 years prior.

Fortunately for me – not for her -- the statute of limitations has run out. I hope.

Being foolish and being tolerant
Publication Date: February 12, 1994

Remember how irresponsible you were at 17?
If you were like me, you thought you had this life thing wired. But I didn't, and I bet you didn't either.

This comes to mind because of the Murrieta and Temecula school districts' anti-drug rules. Under them, students are recommended for expulsion for any offense involving drugs or alcohol.

It's a good thing I didn't go to school here. It makes me wonder about sending my kids to school here.

I had a big drinking problem in high school, along with my friends - the student body president, the star cross country runner and the straight "A" student.

We used to get drunk three or four nights a week in our senior year. One memorable time we were arrested by the cops for underage drinking. Imagine how pleased our parents were to pick us up from the police station.

School didn't interfere with our drinking. We'd buy "Mad Dog" liquor every Friday at lunch to drink and drive with. Then we'd chew gum and go back to school blitzed out of our freaking minds.

We'd even drink in class. A lot of my partying buddies were on the high school newspaper staff and a photographer used to smuggle bottles into the dark room. No wonder it was our favorite class.

I could write a book on my drinking in high school. The time I stumbled down five rows of bleachers at a school basketball game, the time I drank a case of beer in four hours at our senior-class graduation party, the time I drank a six-pack in a half hour, threw up, then had one more six-pack, the time I, well, you get the point: I was really stupid.

I could write another book on my drug use in college. The time I was thrown out of a dorm, or, the grand finale to my school career, the time six of us were sued for millions of dollars for trashing a Northridge home that was a real "Animal House."

Most school districts counsel or suspend first-time drug and alcohol offenders, a system that might have helped my friends and me. Temecula and Murrieta can expel their students, a decision that might have destroyed us.

My point is that a lot of kids today are just as foolish as we were 18 years ago. I doubt our two school boards of well-meaning adults are going to change that fact of life by throwing out students. Maybe in a Utopia, but not in America today.

I remember how steamed my dad was the night he fetched me from the police station. I also remember how "cool" I was the next day in school. My drinking didn't make any sense to my parents; it made perfect sense to my fellow teen-agers.

And in case you get the idea that I grew up in South-Central L.A. or some other tough burg, I graduated from high school in Bettendorf, Iowa, a small town remarkably like Temecula and Murrieta in character.

Yup, the Bettendorf school district is known as one of the best in Iowa, a state with arguably the best public education in America. The community of Bettendorf back then didn't put up with alcohol and drugs any more than Temecula and Murrieta do today. But Bettendorf didn't expel first-time offenders from its schools.

I know the backers of the anti-drug rules say they're the best way to keep drugs and booze out of our schools. I also know a lot of

Temecula and Murrieta students are doing the same things I did in high school. Those two situations can't co-exist without destroying lives and generating lawsuits.

I solved my problems by growing up. I have about a beer a week now, I haven't smoked pot in years, and I don't ever plan to drive drunk again. My wife even teases me about how straight I am.

But my comeuppance awaits.

My 4-year-old daughter and 1-year-old son are going to be teenagers before I know it. They'll probably try alcohol and drugs, and I know I'll try to convince them not to. I pray that I'm more successful than my parents, but I'm not kicking them out of the house if I'm not.

I hope this ultra-tough drug policy works in our schools, but it'll defy human nature if it does.

Wondering if my buddies made it
Publication Date: February 16, 1994

This being a free column and a free country, let's hear from people about what's right with the Temecula and Murrieta school districts' tough anti-drug rules.

Heaven knows I have since Saturday when I wrote that a first-time drug offender shouldn't be expelled like they can be in our local school districts.

I supported my case with my own high school days, which were consumed by drinking and drugs. I might not be writing this column today if I'd been kicked out of school 18 years ago.

Right, says Tom Kasper of Murrieta, you might be a Pulitzer Prize winner today if somebody had shaken you out of your stupor in high school.

He and others cite Tommy Moe, who won the Olympic downhill on Sunday, eight years after he was kicked off a ski team for smoking pot. His dad got strict with Moe and turned his life around. Now our school districts are getting strict with our loaded kids and turning their lives around.

Or so goes the callers' argument.

I thank Kasper, Pam Barret, Barbara Carnesecca and Marianne Monfils for understanding where I'm coming from and telling me where they come from. As for the other calls I didn't return before I wrote this yesterday, I'll get back to you. A call from one reader is considered a great response in newspapers, so the 11 calls I've gotten so far is an avalanche.

I knew I would hit a nerve in our conservative cities with my column, but I didn't think a woman would ask Murrieta police Lt. Rick McIntire if I could be arrested for the alcohol and drug laws I broke some 20 years ago. McIntire says the statute of limitations has run out, but he's looking into legal precedents. I think he was kidding.

Thanks to the callers, I now know the rationale for the "zero-tolerance" approach like I know the back of my hand. It's all about accountability: Get caught with a beer or a joint in school and get ready for extreme punishment, including possible expulsion.

It's that basic. If you take the risk, be ready for the consequences. The earlier youngsters learn that lesson, the better off they'll be in life, the backers of zero tolerance contend. In an age where so few people accept the consequences for their actions, that's a powerful argument.

My approach - the same one used by most school districts - is to suspend or counsel first-time drug offenders. But callers say schools are being over-run by drugs and alcohol because of this "lenient approach."

I certainly don't quibble with their goal. Like a lot of us, many of the zero-tolerance backers have moved from LA area schools that are plagued with drugs and guns. They have brought an admirable zeal to their quest to protect our community from these scourges. After all, we all live in fear that a few years from now Southwest Riverside County will be just another part of the drugged-violent-congested-polluted Southern California urban blob.

The emotion behind zero tolerance is best expressed by Barret, a mother of five who last week presented the Murrieta school board with a letter signed by about 1,000 people backing the tough rules.

She says her family has a terrible history of alcoholism, including her brother who drinks and drives with his 1-year-old son in the car.

"He was never stopped in high school, never in college," she says, fighting back tears. "He never got the message. He doesn't even see the danger involved in driving around with my nephew. I don't want my kids to be a part of that."

The most profound caller was Kasper, who started our conversation with how mad he was about the influence I'll have on kids who read my story. I can hear the party animals telling their parents now: "See, he did it and look where he is today. It's OK."

It's obviously not OK, but I'm not big on preaching. Just take my word for it, animals.

Kasper, a 1966 high school graduate, also got me thinking when he talked about his high school reunion and how everybody's doing today. The kids like me who partied their way through school regret what they did, the ones who stayed straight are happier.

It reminded me of my own high school reunion and how my three drinking buddies turned out: The straight-A student came to the reunion and was now a city planner; the cross country runner and the student body president didn't make it to the event. Nobody at the reunion even had a clue as to what happened to my two old pals. I hope to God they're OK.

Keeping pace with Zev and his dream
Publication Date: March 19, 1994

Get ready Temecula, because Zev Buffman is for real.

So says yours truly after spending a power-lunch hour with him.

Heretofore Zev has been a blur of headlines to me. Ain't he the guy that claims he's gonna turn Old Town into the country-western capital of the west?

Yeah, right. And I'm Dolly Parton.

Then the city last week lays out $125,000 for Zev's vision. Whoa there, pardner. The city of Temecula is loaded, but they're not rich enough to blow that kind of dough on a whim. The guy must have something there.

Which brings us to the lunch hour in Old Town on Thursday in a typically busy day in Zev's life. He's just been in a big meeting at City Hall, so the first thing he's going to do is relax.

"Now that I'm out of the city building, there goes the tie," Zev says as he takes it off.

I like Zev and we haven't even shaken hands.

Zev's winded from the night before because he caught the last flight from West Palm Beach to Orange County, then drove to a Temecula hotel in an hour. "I drive very fast," Zev says. No kidding.

Zev does everything fast, even if he's 60 years old. He wants to open his extravaganza in Old Town by - I hope you're sitting down - Memorial Day, 1996.

"I have a reputation for building things on time," Zev reminds us.

A couple years ago Zev sees a piece of land near San Bernardino. A mere 14 months later, the $15 million Blockbuster Pavilion - yup, another Zev dream - opens to rave reviews. Now that's moving.

This is all happening because Zev needs gas one day last April while on his busy way from San Berdoo to San Diego. He gets off at Rancho California Road for the gas, and then cruises through Old Town, where he hears gunfire and sees cops.

But instead of trouble, Zev finds an opportunity. It is one of those fake shootouts and Zev is entertained. He sees the antique shops, the old buildings, the beauty, and, most importantly, the character.

This is real, Zev thinks, not some contrived fun that so many entertainment places today are based on. All this gets Zev to dreaming: Southern California has a ton of country-western music fans, Temecula has so much to offer, the I-15 is a major freeway and nobody has taken advantage of this combination.

By now you know that the difference between Zev and most of us is he acts on his dreams. He calls then-City Manager Dave Dixon ASAP, meets with him as soon as he can, finishes his . . .

Ooops, a woman is now interrupting Zev's story, asking if she can sit at the end of our table because she can't find an empty one in the busy restaurant we're in.

Go right ahead, says Zev.

I'm thinking, can you imagine most entertainment moguls, let alone people, agreeing to share a table with a stranger? I'm impressed, Zev, I'm impressed. Even if the woman never does sit with us.

Now, let's get back to Zev's Temecula dream: An opera house, a large showboat in Murrieta Creek, an 1890s-style tent theater, six virtual-reality theaters, two cabaret theaters, saloons, TV and recording studios, and a radio station.

Nobody says Zev thinks small.

Actually he's just revving up. Zev plans to comb the country for the top young talent and bring them here to perform every night for a year. Sort of a country-western college. Zev wants the big name stars here too, and they'll be welcome to stay at the La Cresta spread he's buying.

"This is Temecula, the music capital of the West," Zev says, as if it's really going to happen.

Oh-oh. In a recent letter-to-the-editor, Stacey Tescler of Murrieta compares Zev's dream with Branson, Mo., another small town turned music capital. He says Branson gets 5.5 million visitors a year, the town is gridlocked and the hills are lined with motels and restaurants.

"It's a great place to visit but you wouldn't want to live there," Tescler argues.

Zev hates the comparison and here's why: Branson wasn't thought out, Temecula will be. Zev says he knows how to work with the bureaucrats and the music industry big shots to make sure this is a great place to visit and live.

Let's hope so, Zev, let's hope so.

At last! Something to do here
Publication Date: April 20, 1994

Thank you, Lake Elsinore.

You take a lot of guff from the rest of the valley. Wildomar treats you like the plague; Murrieta and Temecula blame you for the growing gang problem.

But you were the only one willing to take on minor league baseball, a fact not lost on this or the other tens of thousands of excited folks who have "stormed" the gates since your glorious stadium and awful team debuted.

Much has been made of the ball diamond's $18 million cost, more than double the original estimate of $8.2 million. It's a hefty price tag for a modest community like you, one that even the extravagant city of Temecula passed on last year.

Your courage in this matter is much appreciated. It's given the rest of us in this deadly dull valley something to do without taking on any of the risks of such a high-finance venture. My kind of odds.

Not that you don't stand to benefit. You hope this endeavor will give you a new image, something to replace the smelly lake, the dead fish, the tough prostitutes and the rough gangs so many of us unfortunately associate with you.

You've already hit a home run on the sales pitch. There's nothing like the green grass of a beautiful ballpark to cover over a community's black eyes. I certainly have a new impression of you after Friday night's grand opening.

Baseball is a fountain of youth for a guy like me. Going to a ball game always brings back my glory days on the diamond, the times I would run down line drives in the gap and hit towering drives into the bleachers. Too bad none of it ever happened.

I am here in an official capacity as a working member of the press. This allows me to tag along on an interview in the locker room with Joe Magrane, a certified multi-millionaire big leaguer - Aren't they all? - who was down for something called a "rehabilitation assignment." This kid in me never passes up an opportunity to talk to a real big leaguer.

Magrane mechanically answers the queries about his physical condition and pitch selection, but he gets animated when asked about the park and the commotion the Lake Elsinore Storm is creating.

"It really is a beautiful stadium," Magrane says. "It's big league in every way."

The ultimate compliment, Lake Elsinore.

Back up at the action, I come across two guys who had a lot to do with what's happening here, Temecula Mayor Ron Roberts and Temecula Councilman Ron Parks. I say this because by all accounts Temecula was the Storm's top choice when it was looking to move from Palm Springs last year. When Temecula didn't step up to the plate, Lake Elsinore did.

Any regrets, guys, from the perspective of a packed house on a beautiful night in a wonderful setting?

No, says Roberts.

Yes, says Parks.

Regardless, says Parks, we're supporting it like it's ours. He points to the outfield wall which is lined with Temecula advertisers and to the countless Temeculans he's seen tonight.

"It draws the whole valley together," Parks says.

For that we can thank an unlikely source, Lake Elsinore.

Parting is such sweet sorrow
Publication Date: May 21, 1994

Got together with some friends the other day. We argued, laughed and solved the world's problems, just like I often do with people I like.

Then we went our own ways, knowing we'll never see each other again.

Why? Because I met these people in jury duty, one of those situations in life where circumstances force you to get to know your neighbor because there's nothing else to do.

Talking to strangers is a novel concept in these terrified times. It was so odd that it seemed as if we were acting out a play, though it was definitely off-Broadway. Downtown Riverside to be precise.

Our production opens in a corner of a big room with hundreds of people waiting out their jury duty fate. I sit against the wall scanning a magazine. Next to me is some guy about my age reading his book. Against another wall are two young women who seem to know each other. A couple middle-aged men sit at a table in front of me, one reading, the other marking papers.

The first conversation I notice are the two guys at the table talking about their shared profession, teaching. This grabs the interest of the two women who wonder if the public schools are as bad as everyone says they are.

Look at these and see for yourself, says the teacher who is grading papers.

These are awful, the women decide a couple minutes later.

The four of them launch into a tirade about today's youth while the rest of us not-so discreetly eavesdrop. We learn the women are college students, the men are fourth- and seventh-grade teachers.

"I think the public school system is a farce," throws in a big man sitting at another table, adding he should know because he's a school bus driver.

It's the parents' fault, says a teacher, who relays an anecdote about this, his first year on the job: He tried to talk to the mother of a problem student, but she couldn't be bothered to help her kid because she was too busy with her own life.

I crash the conversation with my favorite pet peeve: The evils of TV. That woman would have more time if she unplugged the tube, I pronounce all knowingly.

Here! Here! says the guy next to me, piping up for the first time.

Now we're all jabbering about everything. One of the students is amazed that the junior high teacher has more than 140 youngsters and that he only meets with their parents once a year.

"I would call them every week," one coed insists. The rest of us laugh, knowing there's nothing quite like the idealism of a college student.

The guy next to me is a budget supervisor for the LA Sheriff's Department and he tells us of the time he spends in court on deputy child support cases. One officer he testified on is 33 and has six children from five different women. Now there's a pillar of society, not to mention the father.

We go on this way for more than an hour, acting like we'd known each other for years, not a few minutes. We settle into roles like good friends usually do. The coeds display their innocence and we even tease them about it. Meanwhile the old bus driver just thinks everything is screwed up.

The first-year teacher tells us he educates his kids at home. We rip him and he laughs; then notes teachers do more home schooling than any other profession. They must know something we don't.

Our fun is rudely interrupted by a court official on the intercom who starts reading off names of prospective jurors who need to go elsewhere. He does about 50 and there's almost a sense of relief that none of us are called and we can get back to our party.

The loud speaker is back on a few minutes later and this time one of us is nailed, the bus driver. We all say bye, see you around, etc. The next batch claims a teacher and the sheriff's budget supervisor. Those of us left break for lunch a couple minutes later. The first-year teacher talks of getting something to eat but everybody else has to go.

On the way out I run into the sheriff's budget supervisor, the guy I like the most, and yap about how maybe we should have gone into teaching like we wanted to. We step outside the courthouse and I want to say something about getting together. But this is the '90s, and, with work and family, I barely have time for the friends I have, let alone a new one. So we part, knowing we'll never see each other again because that's how things are today.

Living out a life in the past
Publication Date: May 25, 1994

It's hard to say which is more fascinating, Leverne Parker or her house.

Parker is 80 years of proof that you don't have to slow down when you get older. She makes her stocking dolls, does her watercolor pictures, arranges family get-togethers and still keeps up with her enormous house.

Temecula Hotel, one of the oldest buildings around, is Parker's home. It's 24 rooms and 5,250 square feet of history that Parker has restored to look like the 1890s, not today's '90s.

The hotel is smack in the middle of Old Town, on the south side of Main Street up against the east bank of Temecula Creek. It's hard to spot because Parker had to remove the Hotel Temecula sign two years ago after her insurance company said the marker made the building look like a business, not a home. Too bad.

Parker doesn't open up her home to the general public, so yesterday's tour was quite an honor for yours truly. The two-story hotel was built in 1891 by the Welty family and served as an inn for travelers and a boardinghouse for quarry men, Chinese railroad workers and cowboys. The history of your tract house pales by comparison.

The hotel was sold to the LeClare family in 1925. They lived downstairs and rented the upstairs rooms to local characters like Ivan Hewett, Temecula's postman back then.

Parker and her husband, Horace, bought the hotel and surrounding two acres in 1960. Then came five years of renovation, from rewiring to replastering to reroofing to basically re-everything. A do-it-yourselfer's paradise.

The Parkers knew what they were doing because the hotel looks like a museum. It's loaded with assorted memorabilia from bygone days, including an ancient wood stove, portable commode and phone switchboard. The antiques are so dominant that the modern conveniences - the TV and the refrigerator - look out of place.

Each of the rooms has its own history. One bedroom is Bessie Barnett's, named after a woman who grew up in an abode house that today is at the center of Adobe Plaza on Jefferson Avenue in Temecula. The renovated adobe is a sore spot with Parker because, she says, it doesn't look authentic.

Where's the ivy, the old shingles, the hammock?

"That's the way it should look," says the woman who knows a thing or two about making something look historic.

To what lengths will Parker go? The cranberry colored lamps that hang from the ceiling of the upstairs hallway give a certain red-light district feel. A sign on the wall suggests, "Ladies Will Do Their Soliciting Discreetly."

It seems every artifact has a tale. Horace Parker needed help moving an old square grand piano, so he went to a nearby saloon to offer a pitcher of beer to prospective assistants. Four pitchers of beer later the piano was where it belonged in the dining room.

The sign above an old barber's chair tells another story. "Shoe and haircut, 2 bits. Teeth pulled while you wait. Choice of Anesthetic." The grim choices hang on the wall - a bottle of liquor or a club.

Another room is dedicated to Horace, who died in 1977. It has the books he wrote about the history of area events and places. Hardly surprising that he liked to write about history.

A huge collection of Leverne's handmade dolls resides in the ladies' sitting room. The figures include baseball manager Tommy Lasorda, Freddy the Flasher, E.T. and other portly characters. Parker has wonderful stories about the lives they lead. "I'm in my second childhood," she says. "I like my dolls."

Larger homemade life-sized dolls also have names, including "Agnes Mae Castleberry," who lives in the parlor; "Carly Cruthers," who lives in the outhouse; and his wife, "Clarebelle," who lives in a shed. She's sneaking a nip on Carly's bottle of whiskey, so don't tell him.

Parker's art studio is out back. It's decorated with her beautiful water color portraits, most of which are based on historical area photos. The same pictures now hang in Tony Roma's restaurant on Jefferson. My favorite painting is of St. Catherine's Church on Dec. 13, 1967, the day four inches of snow fell in Temecula.

I've run out of room to tell the hundreds, maybe even thousands, of other stories that have gathered on Parker's property. It's quite a life she has there. No wonder she says, "I love it. It's my pride and joy."

The start of school & the end of an era
Publication Date: July 20, 1994

An enormous part of me died recently - my first child started kindergarten.

It's a moment I've dreaded almost from the day Julia was born five years ago, because I've always wanted her to remain a baby. Kindergarten represents the real world trying to take her from me. It's enough to make a dad feel old.

Despite the emotional buildup, our actual separation was anti-climactic. My wife Joanne had the honors of staying with Julia in her first hour of school because somebody had to be with our 2-year-old David.

We were all in the classroom with the other parents and new students, but David was having way too much fun destroying school supplies. I reluctantly kissed my daughter, told her I loved her and whisked away my screaming son before he was banned from the public school system for life.

David and I walked to a park while I wondered: That was it? My baby's gone and I didn't even get a chance to get sentimental and embarrass her. Life sure isn't like the movies.

The end of the first day was more like what I'd envisioned. I got to pick up Julia because my wife has a temporary teaching job and I'm home watching the kids. So David and I were there when the new kindergartners got out of school for the first time.

My daughter was in the back of the pack of kids and she looked so forlorn because she couldn't find us. Her little mind probably figured her family had abandoned her.

Then Julia saw her goofy dad waving at her. She bolted past the teacher and crashed into me, giving me the biggest hug I've ever had from her. It was enough to bring tears to her old man's eyes. Good thing I was wearing shades.

More tugging at the heart a couple minutes later when Julia told me she was scared a few times and wondered where mommy and daddy were. But she toughed it out anyway. Life can be that way, even in kindergarten.

But, oh, how she loves it now. And why not, considering all they do is listen to stories about friendly bears, make darling crafts, eat tasty snacks and romp around on the playground with their new friends. I'd settle for just one of those treats at work.

Still, like most of us, she doesn't realize how good she has it. Every day I ask what she did in school and all I get is a shrug of the shoulders and an "I can't remember." She'll remember in 30 years when she's stressed out about work, her paycheck's spent before she cashes it and her kids frequently don't appreciate what they have. Not that I'm plotting revenge, of course.

Kindergarten has been hardest on our son, who keeps wondering why his best friend isn't around as much. "Need sister," he'll say several times in the course of a morning. When we finally pick her up, David climbs out of his stroller and gives her as big a hug as his little frame can muster. Then sister pushes him, he shoves back, and it's as if they never left each other.

Mom and dad are adjusting too. Our first back-to-school night is coming up (alas, I've got to work), we've got to start collecting cans for the first big field trip and we're trying to juggle our schedules so we can volunteer in the classroom. All of a sudden I'm really interested in public education issues. Watch out, local school boards.

This brings us to her first teacher. How many times can I say in this newspaper space that she's the most wonderful, talented, intelligent and caring teacher I've ever met, without appearing to curry favor for my daughter.

We'll see.

The end result of all this is that my little girl is growing up no matter how much I kick and scream. Indeed, for the first time she's asking me to only put the good stuff about her in the paper, like when she gave things to her friends because it was the right thing to do. I'd better heed her advice, too, because she'll be reading it before I know it.

"Don't put bad things about me in the paper," she warns me repeatedly. "I'm not a baby anymore."

Working to earn money & raise kids
Publication Date: July 30, 1994

We all know it's not nice to fool Mother Nature.

It's also not nice to fool around with moms.

Before you and my wife get the wrong idea, I don't mean it in the adultery way. I mean it in terms of the do-moms-who-stay-at-home-to-raise-the-kids-have-it-easy? argument.

I stumbled into this quagmire - health care is nothing compared to the intensity of the battle of the sexes - earlier this week by advocating the delights of staying home over the stresses of working a full-time job.

I based this on a month I spent as Mr. Mom with the kids while my wife had a temp teaching job. I told my bread-winning-dad colleagues that stay-at-home moms have a pretty good gig going.

Talk about crashing into a raw nerve.

First off, say the moms (including my steamed wife), they have a full-time job too. The difference is that theirs is 24 hours a day. None of this eight hours a day stuff. That's for weaklings like dads.

I also mentioned how luxurious the stay-at-home mom lifestyle is. Drop one child off at school and take the other to the park. The angel romps around while the parent reads the paper or contemplates how wonderful life is.

The feared street gang, "mad moms in Menifee," set the record straight on that scenario in a drive-by letter aimed at yours truly.

Bottom line, the mad moms fume, "there would not be one mom complaining about being stuck at home raising kids" if all they did was what I just described.

But what about turning "dirty stinking socks right side in" so they get clean? ask mad moms. Or "cleaning toilet bowls that you men can't manage to aim straight at."

If you find that disgusting, mad moms are just warming up.

"What about grocery shopping, dreaming up what to cook to please everyone, dishes, trash, mopping floors . . . changing the bedding . . . scrubbing the scum from the tub and shower stall, vacuum, dust, windows, oven, refrigerator, budgeting bills, lawn and the cars.

"Yes Carl, if the ONLY thing we had to do was sit at the park and pick our nose while the kid played, yes Carl it would be the `great' lifestyle. Get a CLUE."

Hey, I did laundry, cleaned toilets, fixed meals, vacuumed, scrubbed the shower and got the oven so clean that my wife even noticed. Per your other allegations, mad moms, I won't dignify them with a response in this family newspaper.

Sincerely, mad dad.

I got lots of other feedback on this topic, at the office, on the street and at the home. (Boy, did I ever get it there.)

But the one that made the most sense - and not just because she halfway agrees with me - comes from Julie McGuire, a good mom in Murrieta.

Of course, McGuire had to start the conversation by saying I must be crazy for thinking that staying at home is a tranquil life. Obviously, I never had to barricade myself in the kitchen just to get a few moments of peace and quiet from the kids like she's had to. (Would that work with a boss?)

However, says the mom of two, "it's the most rewarding job you can have and I don't want to miss any of their significant moments. But it's also the hardest."

McGuire figures she has the best of both worlds because she gets out of the house to work two days a week. Then again, her husband Tim is usually on the road two weeks a month, so it's non-stop action without backup from dad in those times.

"Every time he leaves I just want to die," she says. "He leaves with a smile on his face."

Tim's gonna get his though because Julie is planning a weekend getaway for the first time and she's insisting he watch the kids solo, i.e. without help from grandmother.

McGuire says stay-at-home moms get a bad rap. It's not just lounging around watching Oprah and doing the lunch thing with other moms. Just like working full-time isn't just standing around the water cooler talking sports.

In closing out this furious debate, McGuire agrees with me on this point: When we're all old and gray and we look back at what in the heck we did with this thing called life, we're probably not gonna think much of grinding out paychecks.

No, we're probably gonna look back and realize the most significant thing we did with our lives was raise our children right. Sure, there were the toxic diapers and getting up four times in the night, but there were also the dances of joy and rocking our babies to sleep. The stay-at-home moms will have more of those wonderful memories than the bread-winning dads.

A beauty of a scandal in Temecula
Publication Date: August 3, 1994

When last we got together, we discussed stay-at-home moms and the wholesome children they raise.

It's time to shift gears a bit in the area of the fairer sex and discuss the Miss Temecula pageant, allegations of lying and . . . PLAYBOY!!!!!!!!!

Yes, a delicious scandal has rocked our family environs, though details are frustratingly few. (Obviously the people running the pageant didn't go to the O.J. Simpson School of Scandal Publicity. Too bad, 'cause we're just dying to know what's reeeeeeeeally going on.)

The end result of the situation is that Tracy Richer resigns from Miss Temecula, a mere 10 days into her reign. Chamber types say it's for personal reasons and that's about it. The chamber was looking into an allegation that Richer lied about a college degree on her pageant application, but she quit before the inquiry was done.

Then there's the matter of the picture of Richer in the May edition of the above-mentioned scholarly publication. (I know I speak for my fellow men when I say that the articles are what attract me to Playboy.)

Richer wears only a sheet in the photo, but from what I've heard of Playboy standards that's tame. (I wouldn't know, of course, being that I've never seen anything but the stories.)

Alas, by our community standards, where the discovery of newsstands with X-rated advertising was cause for angst, the idea of Miss Temecula appearing in the world's most noted distributor of pictures of naked women must have been cause for alarm with some folks.

Richer pooh-poohs the photo, saying she would never bare all because she wants to be a Superior Court judge someday and doesn't want any nude shots hurting her prospects. Still, if you've seen the photo, you know she isn't exactly promoting judicial reform.

The text accompanying the photo - see, I do read what's in Playboy - is . . . well, I'll let you be the "judge," just like Richer wants to be.

It's titled "Where the Sheet Meets." The caption says, "Model and actress Tracy Richer appeared on film with Danny Glover in `Angels in the Outfield' and in `American Me' with Edward James Olmos. Also featured in the 1994 Miss Playtime Reno calendar, Tracy is picture perfect."

Now Richer can add a brief stint as Miss Temecula to her credits. And if Richer ever makes Playboy again, think of the publicity our little town will get. And while we're on the topic, anybody for a Miss Playtime Temecula calendar?

Think before you damage your cause
Publication Date: September 14, 1994

Their plight was one all homeowners could relate to.

They thought their property values and their lifestyle were threatened by a developer's plans. But instead of sitting around and just whining with their neighbors, they did something. They organized into a political force, turned out in record numbers at Murrieta City Council meetings and picketed housing tracts in other cities. It was an inspiring example of civic involvement.

But they keep losing. And now it may be time to move on while they're still ahead, at least in the political world.

I never thought I, the crusading homeowner, would say this, but I'm actually starting to sympathize with the de, de, de, de, developer. There, I said it.

I'm starting to think Kaufman and Broad is in the right in its much-chronicled dispute with homeowners in the neighborhood near Shivela Middle School in California Oaks.

To make a long story as short as possible, Kaufman and Broad wants to build 189 homes ranging in size from 1,241 to 1,907 square feet. That's your basic housing tract, especially in these recessed times when smaller houses sell the best.

The problem is that the area is surrounded by much larger homes, some more than 3,000 square feet. These were built back in the boom times when big houses were the rage. Kaufman and Broad's would be the runts in this neighborhood.

They're also perfectly legal runts. The developer has the right to build smaller houses because Riverside County made it so back in the 1980s when the entire neighborhood was dirt and weeds, not just Kaufman and Broad's acreage.

Murrieta city staff looked at it and said yeah, it's legal. The council tap-danced around the issue for two months - withholding Kaufman and Broad's building permits, hosting a meeting between developer and residents, wincing when the company sued the city - before finally conceding the obvious last week and allowing construction to roll.

But the homeowners won't give up. Leader Steve Amante vows to do anything possible to keep the smaller houses from selling. His group, Murrieta Citizens For Quality Growth, plans to keep picketing and meeting with Kaufman and Broad to convince the company to build houses that would be more compatible with the neighborhood.

Amante also objects to the impression that his group looks down on owners of smaller homes. The sentiment was illustrated last week by the owner of a large house who said Kaufman and Broad is building "outhouses" across the street. And we all know what vile stuff they collect.

Funny, I never thought of my home-sweet-home as a disgusting outhouse. But at 1,560 square feet, my home is just about the average size of what Kaufman and Broad is putting up.

I'm not alone either. Murrietan Helena Paniccia, who lives in a tract of smaller homes, snarled at the outhouse description in a letter to the editor. "Small, yes, but clean, neat, well-landscaped and a nice quiet place to bring up children and above all be safe," she wrote.

Murrieta Mayor Jack van Haaster adds that he's received several calls amid this controversy from smaller house owners who are offended by the idea that they're bad people because they either don't want or can't afford a larger home.

Amante says the outhouse comparison is "an unfortunate comment" and is not the opinion of his organization . Hey, Amante lived in a 1,200 square foot house himself and says home size has nothing to do with the character of the person living there.

Contrary to the calls the mayor's getting, Amante says his group isn't a bunch of rich snobs just out to protect their investment. He says their focus is good planning and whether it makes sense to put homes right next to others twice as big.

I wish you well, Amante and company. But Kaufman and Broad didn't get to be a big developer without some staying power.

But regardless of what happens, Van Haaster has the best advice of all: Stay involved in the community. The town that doesn't have concerned folks like you is the one that's really going down the toilet.

And the beat goes on with Sonny
Publication Date: October 8, 1994

It should come as no surprise that this politician has stage presence. He arrives at the campaign debate about 20 minutes late and there is a murmur in the crowd of almost 100 as soon as he walks in.

"There he is," a few say excitedly.

Just after he sits down at the candidates' table, an elderly gentleman pops up from the front row and gleefully takes a picture of the famous candidate.

His two rivals look on impassively, though they're probably burning up inside. If only they had the same impact on the voters.

By now it should be obvious that Democrat Steve Clute and American Independent Party nominee Donald Cochran are not competing against any ordinary politician in this race for the 44th Congressional District seat. No, they're up against a man who once slept with Cher. Balancing the federal budget pales by comparison.

Yes, the one and only Sonny Bono is in our political midst this election season.

Grace Van Nalts and Alice Garrison typify this sudden interest in the political process during Thursday afternoon's debate at the Kay Ceniceros Senior Center in Sun City.

They're your basic sweet, little, old ladies who are proud to say they're here solely to see "Sonny." Politics, smolitics, as far as they're concerned. But their equally spry colleague, Harriet Sellers, swears she's come just to pick up an absentee ballot.

A likely story, especially when you hear her talk about the time on a cruise when she wore a long black wig so she would look like you-know-who and lip-synched "I Got You Babe" with some old guy.

"I ended up punching him," she says with a hoot.

The challenge is to take a candidate seriously on the issues when he made millions crooning "The Beat Goes On" while in bell-bottoms. Then again, look at some of our recent presidential timber. Sonny looks almost Lincolnesque by comparison.

Sonny looks the same, by the way. Although he's 59, his hair is dark and he's got the same mustache he wore back in the '60s. His wide smile is still there, though he doesn't flash it as often now that the subjects are federal mandates, not a shtick with Cher. And the voice is still nasal, proving any little boy can dream to be president and sing on a best-selling album.

The oft-repeated chorus in Sonny's current hit is that government is growing out of control. "Pretty soon bureaucracy will take over everything," he warns ominously. His anti-government tune strikes a chord with the seniors who applaud his remarks more than anybody else's.

Sonny can still provide the theatrics too. At one point he gets into a tiff with a moderator while trying to respond to a Clute zinger when he's supposed to stick to the question asked. "You just heard a professional politician at his finest," Sonny fires at Clute.

Garrison, Van Nalts and Sellers - the three little, old ladies sitting behind me - are eating this stuff up. Go get 'em, Sonny.

The theatrics are spreading. Cochran refers to Clute as a socialist, to which the Democrat stands up as if he's going to ask his rival to step outside and settle this man-to-man. Clute then proclaims he's a former Navy pilot who doesn't have to take such flak. "That is a bunch of hooey," he barks. Go get 'em, Steve.

The scene borders on anarchy when a Ming Roberson roars up to the front of the room and blasts the organizers of the debate for not asking her questions. "You are manipulating all these retired people," she fumes before a couple elderly gents gently escort her away.

After the debate about a dozen seniors run up to Sonny and he stands and poses for few more pictures. I stop and chat with Sonny for a couple minutes, but I can't bring myself to ask the critical question - Do people take you seriously?

Maybe his performance provided some clues. He seemed to give a couple of weird answers, but I was willing to give him the benefit of the doubt because maybe he misunderstood the question and hit the wrong recording button in his brain. Cochran, the sharpest of the three candidates, had a similar stumble.

Then I heard his talk with Robinson after she chased him down in the parking lot to ask him his position on planned parenthood.

"You were talking about the CLAS test?" Sonny wonders.

Sonny should fit right in Washington.

An affordable night with the stars
Publication Date: October 14, 1994

It was, by all accounts, the most political firepower Temecula has ever witnessed.

For starters, we had not one but two U.S. senators in our midst Sunday eve, Phil Gramm and John McCain. But they were merely a warmup act for the main event - U.S. senate candidate Mike Huffington.

California's latest political phenomenon drops by the palace of Temecula's own rising political star, Councilman Jeff Stone, for a barbecue. As might be expected at such a Republican gathering, the Democrats are on the grill.

The prez is the main course, with a generous serving of Hillary bashing on the side. Blah, blah, blah.

No, the most interesting part of this night is the people watching. It's as good as it gets in Temecula.

Call me star struck, but I'm fascinated by celebrities. And whether it's all his money he's spending on this race, whether it's that he's more Texan than Californian, or whether it's that his wife Arianna is maybe even more interesting than he is, Huffington is definitely hot.

So it's with real awe that I watch him work the crowd like only a polished politician can. Have you ever noticed how long a politician spends shaking someone's hand while they talk to the person? If you or I did that we'd be thought weird, but for a politician, well, it's normal.

Gramm, the Texan who's running for prez in '96, and McCain, the Arizonan who launched a political career after doing time as a POW in Vietnam - you cynics will say he's doing time in Washington now - share this same magic with we the people.

Temecula's most connected Republican, John Affolter, introduces me to celebrity - as opposed to mere citizen - McCain. "It's a pleasure," he says warmly. "How are you? It's great to see you." I feel like I'm his best friend.

He moves on to the guy next to me. "It's a pleasure. How are you? It's great to see you."

The exact same words he tells me, his best friend, he's now telling a total stranger. I love politicians.

McCain gives the best line of the night by comparing the nice introduction he gets from Affolter to one he got in Arizona the day before: "Here's the latest dope from Washington."

If you know Ray Borel, you know he despises politicians as much as anybody. Ray's a farmer from French Valley and he looks like he'd rather be shoveling manure than sitting at one of these things. Ray will also tell you there's not any difference. But he's gotta play the political game because he wants to do all this building in French Valley and rubbing elbows with politicians is how you get that kind of stuff done.

So guess who's applauding as much as anyone while the three famous politicos speak? None other than the sly farmer himself.

Still, as much as political celebs enthrall, methinks Huffington shovels a little manure himself when he says his campaign really got going with a visit to Temecula last year. Wanta bet he says that wherever he goes?

There are more than 200 people here, so there's some good local people watching to do too. Temeculan Diane Bainbridge says she is surprised to see how many folks she knows in the crowd. "Now you know who thinks like you."

Locals include planning consultant Larry Markham, Old Town boosters Bill and Evelyn Harker, former Temecula city manager

Dave Dixon, winemaker John Moramarco, City Clerk June Greek and even my dentist, Russell Soon. This means I watch what I say about socialized medicine the next time I'm getting drilled.

Temecula Republican honcho Mary Petersen credits Jeff and Bev Stone for the good turnout. She says a local fund-raiser for Gramm a few years back was $250 a plate. Rubbing elbows with all this political clout tonight only cost $35, a bargain as such things go. Just call the Stones the Wal-Mart of discount political fund-raisers.

So what of our own rising political star, Mr. Stone? He says he's interested in Congress and if Mark Takano beats Republican Ken Calvert, he might go after him. Otherwise he's thinking Ron Packard's seat when the veteran congressman hangs up his politics. Oh don't you just love political star watching?

Boys and girls and everything in between
Publication Date: November 2, 1994

We've got a little identity crisis going on at the house and we're not sure what to do about it.

It involves our 2-year-old son, or at least we think it does. Then again, it could be our daughter.

This much we know for sure: It concerns David. After all, at least he hasn't changed his name. Yet.

David likes to wear dresses. He likes to wear girls shoes. He likes to wear headbands in his curly blond locks. Basically, he wants to be just like his big sister, who's all of 5. It's so bad that sometimes he wants to change dresses every five minutes just like, well, I better watch it before everybody in the family is mad at me.

The 97 percent of me that is the enlightened male of the '90s has gone along with this for about a month now. We put on his boy clothes - the pants and shirts - and then, after only the kind of tantrum that a two-year-old can muster, we throw on a dress over it. The headband and/or heels often complete this "snappy" ensemble. Brother, it's a good thing they don't keep a "Top 10 worst dressed list" for 2-year-olds. Or should that be sister?

Fortunately, my wife Joanne and I were able to keep this behavior in the closet, so to speak. We only let him do it in the house and always made him take off the dress when we went out. I'm not gonna let some little kid manipulate me. Grrrrrrr!!!!

Alas, two weeks ago we are running late to a child's birthday party and David is throwing a fit about you-know-what, so we give in. Sure enough, some woman I've never met before comes up to me at the party and says, "Your little girl is just adorable."

When I tell her she's a he, the woman gushes about how enlightened I am about his behavior.

"It is just a phase after all," she assures me. "He'll be out of it before you know it."

That's easy for her to say. Suppose she, I mean he, doesn't snap out of it. Suppose David tries out for the cheerleading squad instead of the football team in high school. Suppose he wants to be homecoming king and queen. Suppose he is, well, the possibilities are limitless. Especially in these "enlightened" times.

But this is nothing compared to seeing the colonel last Saturday. Now the colonel is my dad, a retired 25-year Army vet who is about as macho as they get, bless his heart.

We take David out with his dress because once again we are late. Even worse, he is wearing the dress inside-out and off one shoulder, like he is some kind of mixed-up sexpot. He'll be flashing cleavage before we know it.

The colonel blew when he saw this production. It's the maddest I've seen him since he had to fetch me from a police station 20 years ago. He told me that no grandson of his is going to be, well, you know.

Come on dad, he's 2. It's just a phase.

But the colonel gets me thinking. Maybe we need to get tough. Like my dad says, I'm the boss.

Be a man, not a sissy.

So on Sunday my wife and I vow to not put a dress on David. Of course the whining goes on. And on. And on. For days, or at least an hour. "You're a girl, not a boy," my flustered wife shouts at one point. Great, that'll set him straight. Next we'll get him a subscription to Playgirl.

You parents of little kids know how it ends. But before I give in, David and I have this talk about the birds and the bees and the differences between boys and girls. All the while I'm thinking: I thought he'd at least be out of diapers before we had to do this.

So we console ourselves with the fact that he likes to hit his sister and even be mean to her. He loves to throw things and play with cars. He's into "Power Rangers" and runs around the house shouting, "yaa, yaa," when the show's on.

And for Halloween he said he wanted to be a boy. Oh boy.

Remember, it's just a phase. That or we have to get David's big sister to start dressing like a boy.

Weather isn't only hot stuff around here
Publication Date: December 7, 1994

The curvy model looked at him longingly, passion coursing through every part of her voluptuous being.

"Kiss me," she told the newspaper columnist she knew best for his studly reputation. "Oh, kiss me."

"If I must, but only if you insist," he said.

"Oh, yes. Oh, my. OH, BABY!!!!!!!!!!!"

Oh, hi there. I'm just doing a little romance writing. Guess who gets the girl?

Romance writing comes natural to us Murrietans. How else to explain why we have a trio - a trilogy if you prefer - of acclaimed romance authors in our passionate midst - Val Whisenand, Linda Randall Wisdom and Mary Anne Wilson.

Wisdom's book, "Sometimes A Lady," was even set in Murrieta. It's about a police detective assigned to protect a sexy lady veterinarian from a killer. Of course, this could be considered redundant because everyone and everything in Murrieta is sexy. Here's an excerpt for you readers who are unfortunately stuck in Temecula, Wildomar and Menifee:

When the tip of his tongue dipped into the hollow of her throat, Elsie doubted she could remember her own name. "Dean, please." She wasn't sure if she was pleading with him to stop or continue. She was too busy concentrating on not melting to the floor. Slowly she lifted her arms. Her hands didn't need any direction as they tunneled through his thick dark hair, her fingers tangling among the silky strands that curled with a life of their own. His kiss came next, sending flashes of fire through her veins and leaving her short of breath.

This type of thing breaks out in public places throughout Murrieta. It happened to me just the other night while I was checking out at Lucky's. And the stuff that used to go on in the Murrieta Von's! Now you know why it was so painful to see the store close. The coupons weren't the only things that were multiplied, if you know what I mean.

Not even the three authors can explain how a small town could produce so much steamy writing.

It's the water, jokes Whisenand, who notes that both she and Wilson didn't start writing until they moved here. Then again, it could be the steamy water at the nearby Murrieta Hot Springs.

Wisdom, who was writing before she moved here in 1990, thinks the small town has something to do with it. They have more characters and you tend to see them over and over again. She finds some while on errands to the Murrieta post office, in case you're dying to be fodder for a book.

A few years back, Wilson found inspiration for a book about babies born to drug-addicted mothers in a cowboy standing outside the Stater Brothers market neighboring Temecula and trying to console a screaming child. She has no idea who the guy was, but thanks for the material, whoever you were.

How good is the romance around here? Whisenand has churned out 15 books, Wilson 20 and Wisdom is about to start her 50th. Talk about the throes of passion.

For those of you who can find the time to read - we Murrietans are too busy being sexually fulfilled to bother - the trio's books can be found in supermarkets and drug stores everywhere, even sedate Temecula:

Whisenand's recent titles include "Daddy's Back" and "A Father Betrayed." Wisdom just dished out "Double Jeopardy," and, as her contribution to the Harlequin American Romance's STUD Series, "He's A Rebel." Wilson's "False Family" is just out and "The Bride Wore Blue Jeans" will be released this February.

Finally, Murrieta history buffs know the real reason why the town is home to three romance writers and, no doubt, many other wannabes. (An ex-neighbor, in fact, was working on one that was quite good, but then she moved. Now she'll never be published.)

Yes, even the founder of Murrieta must have been a romantic guy. Why else would he have been named Don Juan Murrieta?

CHAPTER 7

1995 - Dogs move in, politicians move out

Coming, going, and what in the hell were they thinking?

It was a year when Temecula's first mayor, Ron Parks, said so long to his City Council colleagues. He was one of the early proponents of the growth that defined the community. One of his frequent council critics, Sal Munoz, also departed, leaving a trail of questions you could write a book about. Maybe someday.

The Pechanga casino opened that year. Just like that, it was hard to whine that there was nothing to do around here.

As for going, there was Calvary Chapel and its purchase of the famous Murrieta Hot Springs resort. Given that the property included a bar, you can see it was an interesting meeting of spirits. The bar is now long gone and we know which side prevailed, at least in this world, if not the afterlife.

My weekly column about Lake Elsinore debuted that year as well, adding to the two I was already writing about Temecula and Murrieta. The more the merrier, right?

And who can forget the proposed name for a fund raiser in Temecula. It was called a slave auction, which for some reason created a ruckus. Go figure. If you ever want to say attitudes toward minorities in Southwest Riverside County have changed in the past quarter century, one need look no further.

Of course, the same year African American Chuck Washington was elected to the Murrieta City Council. So it was a year of one step forward, one step back, in terms of cultural awareness.

Finally, there was the arrival of two of our dogs. Smiley, and six weeks later, Midnight. Please don't get me started on why we got two dogs in such a short time. I still bark about that.

So daddy, why are you going insane?
Publication Date: February 15, 1995

The questions from children, they'll drive you nuts.

"What does nuts mean?" my daughter might ask. "I thought you ate them."

See what I mean? You parents know what I'm babbling about. Kids look to us for guidance for we are their teachers. So our children ask us questions when they come across the things they don't understand in life. And ask. And ask. And keep asking until you the parent wants to just strangle them to death. Anything to stop the questions.

Take the nice young lad in my daughter's kindergarten class, the one who innocently asks, "Why is your name Mister Love?"

Well, my first name is really Carl.

"Why do you go by mister then?"

Because mister is a sign of respect and your teacher wants you to respect adults, so you kids call me mister.

"What does respect mean?"

It means you look up to me, that you look to me for guidance.

"What does guidance mean?"

By now you've figured out this is a slippery slope I'm navigating and there is nowhere to go but down. Every answer, no matter how definitive it may appear, always prompts another question. Always. Only a question - what else - from another kid extricated me from the interrogation described above. And don't you dare ask me what extricated means.

Being the father of a 5-year-old girl and a 2-year-old boy, my life is full of questions. (Not to mention the ones that the onset of middle age presents.)

Last weekend my daughter was asking, "Why did Tonya Harding hit Nancy Kerrigan?"

Because she wanted a gold medal.

"What's a gold medal?"

I somehow maneuvered my way around that line of questioning, only to be hit with, "Why didn't Nancy Kerrigan hit Tonya Harding?"

These are the toughest of all, the ones oozing morality, sexuality and legalities, because you don't want to set your child on the wrong course. So you tippy-toe around queries like, Have you ever done drugs? Why do you drink beer if it's bad for you? Why do you want to kill your boss? Where do babies come from?

Nothing is more delicate with kids than sex. (Funny, the same holds true for adults.) In our house, my wife Joanne has always told my daughter Julia that a girl can't get fertilizer for her seed until she marries a boy.

So my daughter announces the other day that she doesn't want to get married, but she still wants to get the fertilizer. (Ohhhh boy.) My wife thinks fast on her feet and says she could go to a fertilizer bank. My daughter asks her mom if she could drive her there. Yup, I'm gonna be a grandfather before I know it.

A parent these days needs to be an expert in a lot of fields. In conferring with my adult colleagues, recent questions range from "How do planes stay in the air?" to "Why do dogs have fleas?" to "How do earthquakes happen?" to "How does Santa Claus get down the chimney?"

Look at the vast expertise involved here. Everything from aviation to veterinarian to seismology to fairy tales. No wonder kids are advised to finish school before they start a family.

Then there are the silly questions, the ones like, "What if your name was Mike instead of Carl?" Or "Why did God make mosquitoes?" (While we're at it, why did God make politicians?) Then there's my personal fave, "When you're keeping an eye on me, what do you do with the other eye?"

But nothing bothers a parent more than the question that's asked multiple times. You know, the one that's asked over and over and over, like a broken record. Ad infinitum. (Don't ask me what it means, look it up yourself!)

The other day we went to grandmother's house, about a 45-minute drive. Five minutes into the trip my daughter asked, "How long before we got to grandma's?"

Alas, this was only the beginning. In the course of our pleasant outing she must have asked the same question a thousand times if she asked twice. (What, you think I exaggerate? Parents know I don't.)

Spliced in between these repeated inquiries were other oldies but goodies: "How long to my birthday? When are we getting a dog? What will I get for Christmas? What will I get for Easter?"

It'll drive you batty.

"I didn't know bats drive. Don't they fly?"

Great 'slave' debate
Publication Date: March 18, 1995

Here's a news flash: Temecula is changing.

But it can also be news when Temecula isn't changing.

Take this afternoon's fund-raising auction hosted by the Firebirds Ladies Auxiliary. It raises money for the Temecula Valley Volunteer Fire Co., an endeavor everybody supports.

What got people steamed about this seemingly wonderful event was the name of it: "Slave Auction."

Numerous local black residents objected to the term, but organizer Niecee Thorne said they didn't understand what the auction was about. She said in terms of the fund-raiser, the word slave was intended as an "attractive name."

That hardly placated critics, who were thinking of picketing today's fund-raiser. This intriguing small-town debate - Is it racism? Are the blacks being too sensitive? - got the attention of two Los Angeles television stations, with, no doubt, more to come if the story had progressed.

Fortunately for the fund-raiser and the city's image, the word slave was dropped by Kurt Verhoef, the president of the volunteer fire company and a man who obviously knows how to put out a fire.

A lot of locals seemed surprised by the controversy, noting that "slave auctions" were used off and on for the past 15 years with hardly a peep of protest. Now all of a sudden it's a major news event.

What's changed, obviously, is Temecula. The small town is growing up into a more cosmopolitan place. A place that hardly had any blacks now has a lot more, with surely more on the way. The desire to escape the grime of metropolitan living isn't confined to white people.

Many of the community leaders involved in the event are people who've been around here since it was a small town. They presumably had no qualms with the word "slave" then or now.

And no doubt a lot of locals - maybe even some of those same community leaders - are now muttering privately: "What's the big deal?" Indeed, a few folks who I would consider "enlightened" about race issues have said the same thing to me.

Does that attitude make them racists?

I certainly can't answer that question. To me the issue of whether someone is a racist can only be answered by that person. Only they know their true feelings about the skin color of their fellow man.

Am I a racist?

I like to think I'm not. At the same time, I certainly empathize with the growing opposition to affirmative action and racial quotas. I can't tell you how many times I've seen opportunities open up for minorities and wondered, "Would that person get that chance if they were a white male like me?"

But then I think of what happened to me when I was on a junior varsity basketball team in 1973 at an American high school in Germany. I was one of only two whites on the 12-man squad. Everyone else was black, along with the coach, the assistant coach and the trainer.

I had several nicknames among my teammates, including "Goldilocks," "Blondie" and "Rabbit." You may have noticed that these relate back to the color of my skin. These were usually said good-naturedly, but they were said nonetheless. I wasn't known as "Carl" or "Love," I was known by the color of my skin. Just like black people are every day of their lives.

Now I always thought of myself as a good basketball player, especially for a 5-foot-10 guy who can't jump. I certainly thought I was good enough to play regularly on that team and maybe even start. But I basically sat on the bench.

Was I discriminated against by the black coaches? I thought so. In fact I was so frustrated that I quit in the middle of the season and joined another team. I ended up being most valuable player of the squad, which had several black players and was coached by a white man.

Looking back on that chapter in my life, the thing I'll always remember is what it felt like to perhaps be a victim of racism. It's something I'll never forget. I was lucky because I could walk away from it. Others are not so lucky.

So the next time we as a community are confronted with a question of race, I hope we look back on the controversy over the "slave auction" and remember what it meant to black people. Only then will we have changed.

Diamonds from the rough
Publication Date: April 8, 1995

Just when you're about ready to give up on humanity ever doing a decent thing again - this only seems to happen every other day - along comes something to restore your faith.

Today's restoration project comes compliments of the Murrieta Valley Pony Baseball people. In the annals of good deeds, this ranks with about anything I've come across.

These folks built six baseball fields. Not one, not two, six. They did it all with donated materials and their own bare hands. A lot of those hands are calloused now and a lot of wallets are lighter too, but when you realize some 700 kids have a place to play ball that is probably worth $500,000 - well, like Murrieta Mayor Jack van Haaster himself said - it's a miracle.

It all started in November with Ron Lane and Pat McGehee, the guys who got the tractors and started grading 13 acres that were wall-to-wall tumbleweeds. If you need more proof, look at the raw land that surrounds the six fields today. The green ball diamonds stand out like emeralds.

Getting it done required lots of faith. Beyond the obvious obstacles of such an enormous task, the good guys had to overcome some bad guys who ripped off about $2,500 worth of construction supplies in January. Like we said, just when you're about ready to give up. . . .

But those fields were going to be ready for opening day no matter what. You get the sense that a stray meteor could have slammed into the area and this resilient crowd still would have met its deadline.

"We learned one thing in all of this," says volunteer John Duncan. "Things are never as bad as they seem when you can look at a pile of rust and end up with a field of dreams."

You knew we had to get to the movie allusion eventually. And no cinematic detail is unreachable for these real-life dreamers, right down to the corn field that they're planning in their Murrieta field of dreams. Just like the flick.

The pile of rust, by the way, was donated by some fence guy. It's believed to date back to World War II. The volunteers cleaned it up and today it stands as backstops for the fields. The stuff Charlie Van Deusen, the fields' director of construction, pulled off.

It's remarkable how things came together. The good guys would be sitting in a pizza joint late at night wondering how they were going to get electrical conduits, some folks at the next table would overhear, and the next morning the materials would be on the field free of charge. Time after time things like that happened.

By the way, notice we're not listing any businesses. The good guys would like to name the companies that helped, but, being the conscientious types, they're afraid to leave someone out. The good Samaritan businesses surely didn't do it for the name recognition anyway.

And let's not forget the moms who kept their households intact while the volunteer dads were working on the fields all hours of the night. Then there are the people who manned the phones, asking anybody and everybody to donate. They certainly got their share of nos, but they obviously got enough yeses.

All the effort paid off this week when the games started. From 5-year-olds struggling to hit in T-ball to 14-year-olds hammering distant home runs, it was a sight to behold. History buffs will note that the park's first-ever round tripper was delivered by Jake Davis.

The construction was still going on this week in preparation for the grand-opening festivities today. Several of the dugouts were getting roofs, bleachers were being finished and trees were being planted. Four months of hard work and it ain't over till it's over, to quote a baseball philosopher.

Maybe technical writer Mike Adriance, the coat-and-tie guy who learned to pour concrete and hammer in fence posts, explains best what it all means: "There are pieces of all of us in these fields. It really feels like it belongs to us."

E. Hale Curran fills 95 years with memories
Publication Date: April 12, 1995

History. That's what comes to mind when you observe E. Hale Curran.

She's celebrating her 95th birthday, so she's witnessed a little bit of it in her time. When it comes to Murrieta, she's seen just about everything in this century. That's a lot, especially with all the growth of the past decade.

So it's with awe that a 36-year-old like myself looked at Curran during her birthday party. This is, after all, a woman with an elementary school named after her, stuff usually reserved for political legends like Lincoln and Washington. Curran is a Murrieta legend.

As wonderful as it is having a school in the California Oaks subdivision named after you, it has one drawback: People are always calling your home thinking you're the school, not the person.

"Some can be very nice about it and some can be very mad because I'm not," she says with a laugh.

There's a lot of laughter in Curran's life. For example, she thinks it's great to be 95.

"You ought to try it sometime," she says.

OK, how have you managed to live so long?

"I was careful how I chose my ancestors," she says with a hoot.

One of her longtime friends, Arlean Garrison, says it's her wit that keeps Curran going. "Without a sense of humor today you're dead."

Maybe the laughter explains why Murrieta has so many old-timers. The town has a remarkable collection of longtime families, from the Currans to the Thompsons to the Dunhams to the Sotellos to the Rails to the Buchanans.

Like the witty Curran, they must all be cards. They're not something you want to build a house out of, but a community sure seems to work fine.

Garrison wrote a history of Murrieta in 1963 and called it, "My Children's Home," in honor of all the people with well-established roots.

"A lot of these families have four generations here," she says.

Three are familiar to the thousands of Murrieta youngsters who have moved here in the recent past. Rail is an elementary school and Thompson a middle school, in addition to Curran.

These schools were well-represented at Hale Curran's party. Raymond Thompson, Murrieta's first fire chief, was there, along with Floyd Rail, a retired firefighter. The party was at the home of Hale's son, Marv, another retired fire chief. Yes, the party was in good hands if a fire broke out.

By now you may have figured out that there were plenty of elderly people in the party's guest book of more than a hundred. I'm still a whippersnapper to this crowd. What fun.

There were a few other kids there, too, including my 5-year-old daughter, Julia. Like me, she was in awe of Curran, though for another reason.

"Boy, does she have a lot of friends," Julia said.

That she does, but I'm more impressed with the years Curran has logged in her life. It seems the older I get the more I'm amazed by older people. They've experienced so much in their time.

I'm reminded of this by a mother who took her young son up to meet Curran. The boy was obviously not too interested - hey, I was the same way when I was 7 - until his mother said something that makes him take notice: Curran was alive when there were no cars. She also lived when there were no planes, no TV and no computers.

The lad looks surprised, like how could a person manage without such necessities. (And imagine what we'll invent by the time he's 95.)

Gadgets aside, it seems Curran appreciates the basics the most. She lives by herself on the same land she's resided on since 1906. She still keeps up her garden, she enjoys her numerous friends and she obviously loves a good laugh.

But the thing she mentions most while we talk is that she's blessed with a wonderful memory. "If the memory dries up and blows away, then you have nothing."

Fortunately for us, Curran still has something wonderful to share.

Old Munoz, new Munoz, no Munoz
Publication Date: May 24, 1995

At a big bash to celebrate Temecula's birth as a city more than five years ago, Glenn Richardson talked excitedly about the political future of one J. Sal Munoz.

He's young, he's articulate, he's smart, he's a hard worker, he's a natural, Richardson the political expert was telling me. This guy's really going places.

But Munoz never went farther than the City Council seat he resigned last night. You could write a book about why.

It would be an interesting tale. He is the city's most famous politician, having made enough headlines to last a political lifetime, not a mere 5 1/2 years on a small-town city council.

Whether it was accusing his enemies of dirty tricks, taking a guy to court for dumping a cake on his back, going to work for one of the biggest builders in town or losing a local radio talk show because of his attacks on fellow council members, Munoz sure knew how to make news.

It's tempting to say Munoz is leaving because he prided himself on being the people's friend in a town that prided itself on being a friend to business. In doing so, it was only a matter of time until his enemies would exact their revenge.

But if it was merely a matter of too much political heat, Munoz would have given up long ago, not now.

No, in quitting Munoz perhaps is admitting what has been apparent for some time: The man ran afoul of himself.

This people's champion was politically neutered a year ago when he went to work for Kemper Real Estate, one of the city's largest developers. Munoz rationalized it by saying he would be looking out for the city's best interests from inside Kemper's den.

But arch-enemies, like former councilwoman Pat Birdsall, called it for what it was: hypocrisy. It would be easier to accept if Munoz had simply said he was doing it for the money, which he was.

The move effectively muzzled Munoz on key development issues, including the critical question of what builders are going to pay for in building new schools. The old Munoz would have led the charge to make the builders pay the full cost; the new Munoz had to excuse himself from the discussion because he had a conflict. What a shame.

Then there was March's election on Zev Buffman's proposed western entertainment attraction, only the most important decision ever faced by Temecula.

The critics said the project puts the city at financial risk and predicted it would be death to Temecula's small-town atmosphere. Both arguments were vintage Munoz concerns.

The new Munoz agonized about the issue - Buffman critic Phil Hoxsey says the councilman had tears in his eyes when he met with the project's opposition - but in the end, the people's once fearless leader sided with the Temecula establishment and supported the Buffman project. Considering it only won by 46 votes, it's obvious Munoz was the difference.

Imagine trying to rest at night with that political demon dancing in your head.

The Temeculan who knows him best, Giovanna Munoz, agrees the political life changed her husband. Giovanna was there in the beginning, going door-to-door in 1989 when he miraculously won an election in a city he'd moved to just six months before. But today the couple are separated.

Giovanna says the Sal of then wouldn't like the Sal of now. "I think Sal is tired. A lot of people see he's made compromises. He's not the person he was before."

So maybe it's best he step down. One of the many things I've always admired about Munoz is his courage. To walk away from something he obviously loves but just as obviously destroys him takes real courage. If we can't have the real Munoz, it's best we have none at all.

Thanks for the memories and the community service, Sal. We'll miss you.

Nicer spa may appear, likely without beer
Publication Date: June 7, 1995

Is Calvary Church going to be good or bad for our beloved Murrieta Hot Springs?

It's a question a lot of us have grappled with since the church announced it's buying the place. I've been going to the resort since I moved here seven years ago and am quite attached to the tranquility I always find there. The possibility that anybody might mess with it is disturbing.

My mind's more at ease after spending a few hours there last weekend watching the new owners in action. One thing nobody can argue with, Calvary will be great for the place's appearance.

More than 500 church volunteers gave it a badly needed make-over. They were even scraping weeds from the roads; that's how meticulous they were. Not to sound sacrilegious, but hallelujah!

"They've trimmed more trees in two days than have been trimmed in two years," spa director Marcia Bennett says. "It's wonderful. For anybody who loves this property, it's a joy."

Bennett also is instructive because of the uncertainty she was experiencing a month ago when news of the sale hit the streets.

Back then, rumor had it that the church might close the spa, seal up the hot springs and ban the public from the entire 46-acre property.

It's much better today, Bennett says. The church people are quite considerate of what she and her spa customers want. She can see a good relationship coming of this shotgun marriage between church and spa. After all, Calvary plans to turn the resort into a retreat, a place for people to heal. Ever since Fritz Guenther opened the resort in 1902, this land has always meant that. Now it will just be a different style of healing.

John Jackson, one of the Calvary people coordinating this massive volunteer cleanup, made me feel even better. He said the church wants to restore the rundown buildings to their "original glory." Yes, he reassured me, the public will be able to come to the restaurant, stroll the grounds and use the spa.

Leaving Jackson's office, I headed to the front lines of Calvary's restoration - the volunteers. The hum of weed whackers and tree trimmers was everywhere. Kids, moms, dads and seniors were all working for free on a muggy afternoon. Most had come from at least an hour's drive away. These people were truly inspired.

Clara Welles, a 43-year-old church member from Santa Ana, took a break from raking a hillside to tell me about coming to the resort as a kid. Now she can't wait to come back after her church has fixed up the property. "I plan to be out here a lot."

One of the oddest sights was 17-year-old Samantha Peterson, who was lying out in a bikini by a pool while 20 feet away a bulldozer tore up concrete. She too was working earlier, but now she was taking a breather.

She and everybody with the church appeared remarkably happy. A cynic might say they were too cheery. You're not supposed to be that happy, at least not in this life.

We close with the one downer of the day, the crowd at Shakespeare's British Pub & Grill. The place is obviously on borrowed time with its new landlord, but a yellow flier defiantly proclaimed Shakespeare's religion - LONGEST HAPPY HOUR IN TOWN!!! It's the kind of happiness you just can't find in a church.

Inside the bar, Bob Seideman and Jerry Lurwick were lamenting the loss of their Shakespeare's, a sorrow I share. It's the best place around to sit and have a beer, a real community asset.

While we talked, some joker stuck a sign on the front door, reading "Please Keep Out - Private Property." Just what every successful business needs.

Many in the bar complain the Calvary people want to close Shakespeare's down as soon as possible.

Lurwick put us in a better mood, telling us a yarn about how Jimmy Hoffa was supposedly at the resort three days before he disappeared. Who knows, maybe he's buried here, he suggested a little too matter-of-factly.

And maybe the Calvary people will dig up him up today, I cackled. The followers of Calvary and Shakespeare's might even agree such a find would be a miracle.

I left Murrieta Hot Springs in a better mood than when I arrived. I won't be able to get a beer there, but it'll look a lot better and I'll still be able to visit. I'm happy.

Dangers of doing the right thing
Publication Date: June 21, 1995

Richard Melgar Jr. did something a lot of people won't do anymore. He cared enough to try and set some troublemakers straight. And it may have cost him his life.

According to the cops, Melgar was beaten and later died Saturday night in old Murrieta. It happened after his son's Little League game, of all things. Relatives of the suspects differ with the police version, contending Melgar wasn't beaten. The suspects were arrested on suspicion of involuntary manslaughter.

It all started when Melgar left the game and saw a black pickup that had been speeding earlier that evening, disrupting the game.

After telling his older son, Michael, to pull over, the former Gardena police officer advised the people in the truck that they should be more careful because of the Little League game.

But when they taunted him, Melgar made the mistake of getting out of his car. He was pounded with rocks and branches until he collapsed in the street, police say. A nurse, Stephanie Brouse, ran from the ball field to try and save him, but it was too late for Melgar, a 48-year-old man with a bad heart. He died in the ambulance.

And if that isn't bad enough, it's believed one of the suspects took a tree trunk and bashed it through the back window of Melgar's car, where two children cowered inside. Fortunately, Melgar's son,

11-year-old Drew, shielded his granddaughter, 2-year-old Payton Melgar, from the flying glass, and she only suffered a small cut near her eye.

Of course, the little girl woke up Sunday morning with nightmares of her grandfather lying in the street bleeding. She and Melgar's other loved ones may never recover from the mental scars left by this incident.

There are so many chilling things about this story that it's hard to even think about it without getting disgusted.

But there are lessons to be learned, including what this means for the idyllic state of Murrieta. An armed robbery a few weeks ago was thought to be the first such crime in town in almost a year. How quaint, until last weekend when even a Little League game wasn't safe. It makes you wonder what's in store for Murrieta's future.

The thing that gives me the most angst, though, is what this says for speaking up about the wrongs that all of us come across. After seeing this, it's easy to see why so many people just turn their heads. If an ex-cop can't get involved, who can?

It makes me think of the last time I did something, about six years ago at a late-night party in the neighborhood. (The neighbors have since moved, so I think I can safely tell this story.)

Anyway, our first child was just a couple months old and sleep was at a premium in our house. I was really steamed when music from the big bash down the street woke me from sleep I desperately needed.

If it were today I'd call the cops. But this was back in the days before Temecula and Murrieta became cities, when it seemed there was one sheriff's deputy patrolling both towns. Loud music was hardly a priority call.

So I took matters into my own hands and stormed over to the party. Angry words were exchanged and I left in a huff, the music as loud as ever.

But I must have earned some sympathy points because a few minutes later the music was turned down. Then the party host came over, rang the doorbell, and asked me if I was happy now. Yeah, and thanks for waking my kid with the doorbell.

The next day I shared the story with other neighbors and they told me how lucky I was, considering they thought the kids who lived there might be gang members. That's why they didn't do anything about the noisy party. But, hey, thanks for doing what needed to be done.

There were other times when I'd played cop and lived to tell about it. But not anymore. As frustrating as it is to watch some of the things that go on in this world, it's too dangerous to get involved anymore. Sure, it's a sad commentary on the times, and it's certainly not the "right" thing to do. But right and wrong just don't mean what they used to. Just ask the family of Richard Melgar Jr.

They all speak the language of fishing
Publication Date: August 2, 1995

Fishing was definitely the international language at a public fishing spot on Lake Elsinore one recent morning.

Six languages, but only a little English, are used by the 10 anglers in the area in the 1500 block of West Lakeshore Drive.

It makes for a tough assignment for a reporter who only speaks English and very little Spanish. Fortunately, the peace and quiet found here doesn't need to be translated. Especially at 7 a.m. on a Friday when there isn't a cloud in the sky and the lake shimmers like a jewel. They call it chamber of commerce weather.

The most interesting-looking people are three elderly men who have surely caught a fish or two in their day. They sit by themselves with their trusty poles, like characters out of a Hemingway novel.

I ask if anybody speaks English and one of them rattles off, "Armenian, Romanian, Greek, Russian." Seems everything but English. Oh well.

I ask the family sitting nearby if any of them can understand me.

"Are you the inspector?" the wife asks. Her husband shows me the fishing license dangling from his neck, just in case.

They are Gevork and Marion Semirdjian. Their three teen-agers with them are John, Samuel and Karine.

They come once a week from Glendale, which seems like a long way to go for the five fish they usually catch. They had to leave home at 4:30 a.m. to be here by 6 a.m.

They're originally from Armenia, just like the three old men. "But we don't know them," Marion says.

She goes over to her fellow countrymen and asks if she can translate for me, but they say no. Some things just aren't meant to be.

On the other side of the Semirdjians is a Hispanic man with a T-shirt that reads, "YOUR NEXT IBM COMPUTER SHOULD BE A MACINTOSH." Surely he speaks English.

He shakes his head no, then takes me to a van where his son-in-law, Atilio Lopez, is trying to catch up on his sleep. Fortunately, Lopez is an easygoing fellow who doesn't mind being disturbed.

His father-in-law, Paulino Gonzales, comes to fish twice a week from Corona. This is Lopez's first trip and he had to get up at 4 a.m. to make it down here by 5:30 a.m. The three old guys were already here by then. A park sign says the "designated fishing area" hours are from 6 a.m. to 10 p.m. That means the old men are here before the place even opens. They're dedicated.

"Fishing is better when you get up early," Lopez says. "This is so beautiful. It's so relaxing."

So much so that after we're done talking, Lopez closes the door, covers the window with a shirt and goes back to sleep.

Perhaps it seems odd that a guy would get up early in the morning to drive 30 miles to go back to sleep. Then again, it's fishing.

I've never been much of a fisherman myself. Not enough action, I guess. It took a buddy who loves to fish to set me straight: People who fish are trying to get away from action. They're looking to catch some relaxation; if they happen to catch some fish, too, well, that's just fine.

Across Lakeshore is a convenience market with a sign in the window advertising fishing licenses and bait. The manager, Abdou Jaloul, says he gets lots of fishing-related business, especially on weekends when the public fishing hole across the street will be packed with anglers from Los Angeles. A hundred people will be there at times.

Jaloul is a fisherman himself, but he doesn't have time, even if there's a place so close. "I work long hours," he says.

Back at the fishing hole another fisherman, Carlos Morales, pulls up. He doesn't speak much English - by now I've come to expect it - but at least I understand him enough to learn he comes twice a week from Riverside. He says the fishing here is good, and to prove the point, he hauls out a fish five minutes after starting.

Morales scoops some of Lake Elsinore into his cooler and tosses the fish in there. The Semirdjian family keeps their catch in a cage buried in the lake. The three old men toss their fish on to the beach, where they flop for a few minutes before dying. Everybody has his own style.

Back in the van, Lopez moves his shirt to keep pace with the sun that's rising in the sky. Think of all the action he's missing.

Gambling is just down the street
Publication Date: August 9, 1995

My neighbor Joe Cantone gambles about once a year in Nevada. But now the Murrieta retiree also can drive just 10 minutes and play. And considering he only lost $4 when he did, it seems Joe has found some awfully cheap entertainment.

As we leave after our first visit to the new Pechanga Indian Reservation casino just outside Temecula, Joe says he might come down a time or two a week. "I gotta have a place to hang out."

We can gamble in our own hometown. It's a dream come true and a nightmare waiting to happen, all in one.

The casino, at the corner of Pala and Wolf Valley roads, is about a quarter of a mile from the nearest subdivision. Is there another town in America where houses and "the house" are so close?

The tribe opened the casino last month with little publicity. Usually a gambling establishment debuts with as much fanfare as can be afforded. Not the Pechangas and their stealth casino. But hey, it's their business.

About 200 people have found the place by the time Joe and I arrive Sunday afternoon. The Pechangas eventually plan a permanent casino that would abut the back yards of several homes.

But for now, gamblers are relegated to a couple trailers, one for cards, one for machines. Nothing fancy, but like a real gambler cares.

Inside one trailer, the 200 slots are humming, clanging, rocking, well, I'm not quite sure what verb best describes the racket made by gaming machines. Music to the Pechangas' ears, that much is certain.

Standing there and taking it all in, I'm struck by how much the place feels like Vegas. It's exhilarating and terrifying for a compulsive gambler like me. The last thing someone like me needs is a blackjack table down the street 24 hours a day, seven days a week, 52 weeks a year.

To boil down a long story, I had a little problem with blackjack almost a decade ago. Card counting, being asked to leave casinos, the works. My best buddy and I were obsessed with the game until

I had a mental meltdown one Saturday night at the Stardust in Las Vegas. I've hardly played since then.

Joe and I head over to the card room and the blackjack tables. I'm overjoyed at what we find because I'll probably never play here. Unless I'm the banker, i.e., the casino.

That's not a misprint. Unlike Vegas, in this version of blackjack, each player pays the Pechangas 50 cents a hand to play. Blackjack is hard to win at anyway, but when you're spotting money every hand, it's really tough.

The banker can be anybody except the Pechangas. (That's how the tribe gets around state law that basically bans blackjack otherwise.) The banker handles the bets, win and lose. But considering most people lose - why do you think they keep building bigger and bigger casinos in Vegas - bankers usually wins.

Joe's no dummy, so he gets the dope on how to be a banker. Sure beats working.

Now we're back over in the slot room, paying close attention to some nickel poker machines that pay escalating jackpots for a royal flush. Every time somebody plays and doesn't get such a hand, the grand prize goes up two cents. Neon lights update the jackpots of each of the machines, the highest being $2,218.71 when we start watching.

A middle-aged guy sitting at that machine says he's been there for more than three hours. He plays 40 nickels a hand and it's hard to keep up with him because he goes so fast. He does some hands in five seconds.

He started with $30 and he's still about even. Like most gamblers, he's waiting for the big payday, which is at $2,219.69 as I move on.

Joe grabs a slot machine, while I walk around for a few minutes, agonizing over whether to play. I give in to a poker machine, play two hands and lose a buck.

It's all the money a suburban family man feels like losing for now. A few minutes later I find a dollar on the floor. Getting even was never so easy.

On our way out to reality, I notice that our friend the nickel poker player has moved on from the poker machine with the "progressive jackpot." It stands at $2,222.81 as we leave.

Joe and I decide it's basically a good thing, this casino. It's probably not something you want for a neighbor, but for the rest of us it's something to do 24 hours a day, seven days a week . . .

6 BR, 9 BA, gym, pool, pizza oven
Publication Date: September 16, 1995

So how nice is Barry Bonds' house?

Hmmm, where do I start? His 1,700-square-foot master bedroom is bigger than my entire house. His 30 stereo speakers are 28 more than you-know-who's. And with a Jacuzzi in the guest bathroom, well, you've caught the drift by now.

Realtor Doug Irvine Jr. says Bonds' is the nicest house in Southwest Riverside County. By my modest tract home standards, it's the nicest house in the entire galaxy.

Bonds is listing the Bear Creek home for sale at $3.2 million. Irvine says the superstar for the San Francisco Giants baseball team is relocating to the Bay Area, ending his four-year reign as Murrieta's most famous resident.

As you might expect from a ballplayer who puts up incredible numbers on the field, his house is loaded with equally impressive figures. Like 10,500 square feet of living space, a 2,000-square-foot garage, 300 indoor recessed lights, 24-karat gold trim in the guest's bathroom, a dozen phone lines, nine bathrooms, two washers and two dryers.

But the best thing about this house is its class. It's not just some gigantic slab of stucco with endless rooms that all start to look the same. After all, Bonds' house has only six bedrooms. Some tract homes have that many.

It's the little touches - OK, the millionaire's touches; that make this more than just another big box. It's the kind of house I would have built if I had the chance. Dream on, Love.

There is a room with a 37-foot-high ceiling and a bank of skylights. Amazingly, the room sits empty. Bonds wanted to put a piano in it but never got around to it. He's also got a $3,000 pizza oven he's never used. Rich people.

Computerized control panels in every room resemble the "intelligent house" we're all supposed to live in some day. Using those panels, Bonds controls TVs, stereos, videos, lights, drapes and even bathtubs. (He can push a button in his car and run bath water.) The only gadget missing is a cone of silence.

Bear Creek is a gated community, but Bonds has electronic gates outside his home as well. No surprise there, considering his celebrity status. For good measure, each gate is marked with a "B" for his two initials.

Bonds didn't exactly pick up his letters down at Home Base. His builder and good buddy, Mike Taylor, says they're replicas of Bonds' own signature, cut by laser from solid brass and weighing almost 75 pounds.

Bonds could operate a pretty fair sports memorabilia shop from his home. His trophy case is stocked with three Most Valuable Player awards, five Gold Gloves and five Silver Slugger bats. It was all I could do not to drool at this display.

Bonds has framed autographed jerseys from 27 athletes hanging throughout the place. They range from Joe Montana to Charles Barkley to Willie Mays to Wayne Gretzky to Jerry Rice to Delino DeShields. (Delino DeShields?)

"I love these," says giddy sports buff Irvine. "Just give me these for the commission."

By the way, you may recall Irvine from running Primadonna's restaurant and trying to bring minor league baseball to Temecula.

Of course the workout amenities are incredible in the Bonds' home. The exercise room has a dozen workout machines, the pool is lagoon style and big enough to do laps in, and there are Jacuzzis everywhere. The only commoner's touch is the basketball hoop in the driveway that looks suspiciously below regulation height. Even puny me could maybe jam on that thing. Tsk, tsk, Barry.

The look of money goes on and on. The black granite counter tops are from Sly Stallone's place, the wrought iron handrails are from Cher's house, the pool has a waterfall, spa, slide and fire ring, the electric panel would power up an industrial building, the wet bar is the size of my kid's room, the. . . .

But just when you think it's too much, that you could feed a family for a year with what was spent on an oven that's never been used, that capitalism has truly run amok when a baseball player owns the best pad in the valley, that, that . . . God, I want to live here.

Smiley comes equipped with instant love
Publication Date: October 4, 1995

I'm a firm believer that kids teach us as much as we teach them. Take the matter of a dog.

Our 6-year-old girl, Julia, pestered us to get one for a couple years. But all I could see was more work and another mouth to feed, and this one wasn't even a tax write-off.

Alas, my wife Joanne and I realized she wasn't going to stop until we gave in - after all, kids are as tenacious as pit bulls. So, 10 days ago, Smiley joined our happy clan. Today, thanks to a mere animal, we are even happier. Our kid was right again.

The joy was instantaneous. We took Smiley on a walk and I had warm, fuzzy feelings all over. It wasn't quite as great as seeing two kids join the world, but then Smiley doesn't cry as much, either.

Actually, Smiley doesn't cry at all. She also doesn't whine, demand, pout or display any other negative emotion. All she basically does is smile and wag her tail. No wonder she and her fellow dogs are considered man's best pals.

Yup, the boss can be steamed, the family ornery, the bill collectors unrelenting, and all Smiley ever wants is her tummy scratched.

It is easy to get real attached to such a sweet animal. I slept with her on the living room floor the first night in our house because I was worried that she might freak out over her new surroundings. She had four walks the first day she was with us; her previous owners hadn't given her that many in the past year.

Our two kids, David and Julia, did their part by following Smiley around everywhere. In tandem, they brushed her, scratched her and fed her. It was like watching a queen and her court.

Three-year-old David likes to walk up to Smiley and throw himself on her like she's a bean bag chair. Or he'll yank on different body parts, checking for anything that isn't attached. Smiley never snaps or growls during the ordeal; she just lumbers off into another room.

Being the youngest human of the household, David is used to being blamed for the most mischief. Now he's got somebody else to take out three years of frustration on. The other day I heard him bark at Smiley, "You're messing up the game. Go to your room."

Of course, Julia jumped to the dog's defense. She is Smiley's No. 1 advocate, always lobbying on the animal's behalf for walks and treats. She is keeping a running total of how many times Smiley kisses her. It was 64 times by Tuesday morning. Note that she's not keeping track of the kisses anybody else gives her.

Yet, as much as I cherish Smiley, she has her downsides. The living room, her favorite room and mine, now reeks of dog. Now it's just her favorite room.

Then there's the matter of the dog going to the bathroom. Considering the amazing things they do with technology these days, you'd think they could invent something that isn't as disgusting as the pooper-scooper.

At least we didn't have to teach Smiley about where to take care of business. She's probably about 5, so she's way beyond the giddy puppy years. She's a mix, looks to be part golden retriever and part Labrador. She is a good-sized dog with brown hair, and the best description of her came from a fellow dog owner who said she looked like a "Rusty." She's no "Fifi," that's for sure.

She came to us equipped with the name Smiley, but her past is unfortunately nothing to smile about. The people who gave us the dog said Smiley's previous owners had probably beaten her, which helps explain her meek personality. Others suggested at the dog pound that they thought her puppies were taken from her right after birth and killed. If Smiley was human, she'd be in therapy and/or popping Prozac.

Fortunately, the people we got Smiley from took good care of her. But she didn't bark enough for their tastes and they just didn't want a dog anymore. We were happy to welcome her into our family.

Sometimes I think she's getting a little spoiled - she seems to almost expect a walk whenever the front door is opened - but then I think of what she's been through. She lost her puppies, for God's sake.

Smiley can have her tummy scratched anytime.

The Don't 'Show' Me City
Publication Date: October 7, 1995

Here we go again, Temecula.

Another movie has been seized from our midst because of community protests. Four years ago it was the riveting "Boyz N the Hood." This week it was the awful "Showgirls."

Last time, Temeku Cinema chickened out because of community concerns that "Boyz" might spawn gang violence. Town Center Cinemas 10 rode to the rescue and showed the movie.

This time, a small group of protesters objected to "Showgirls" because they considered it pornographic. Thanks to their efforts, you'll have to go to Lake Elsinore, Hemet, San Jacinto, Moreno Valley, Corona, Riverside or other apparently less-wholesome communities to see "Showgirls."

Brandy Makosky and Chris Rush, who were in the theater with about 15 others for the last day of "Showgirls" in Temecula, think this is wrong.

Makosky, an 18-year-old who just enlisted in the Army, and Rush, a 20-year-old maintenance worker, wonder what the big deal is. Hey, it's a movie with lots of nudity, sex scenes and bad language. What flick this side of Disney doesn't have the same elements these days?

Makosky has the most interesting take on the movie: "This is what the '90s is about."

A group of people in Temecula seems to think it is its duty to protect the rest of us from what it considers the evils of today's society.

First it was "Boyz," a movie about life in a black ghetto in L.A. Now it's "Showgirls," an NC-17 rated production about a woman's raunchy climb to fame. What's next?

Ed Elder is the most prominent member of the group objecting to "Showgirls." The retired Marine is active in political affairs, from promoting conservative Temecula school board candidates to backing black conservative presidential candidate Alan Keyes to organizing movie protests.

You might even be surprised to learn I like Elder. He's got a sense of humor, he loves to debate issues and he doesn't hold a grudge.

Elder is also effective. After Temecula's "Showgirls" flap hit the papers, somebody called from Corona asking how that town too could rid itself of the movie. Elder had a simple recipe: Call up a few friends, make a couple of signs, let the newspapers know, and presto - No more movie.

Though Temecula has had thousands turn out for anti-abortion demonstrations, only about a dozen people made the "Showgirls" demonstration.

Elder says "Showgirls" is like dumping a little poison into our community well. He says kids snuck into the movie, though no one under 17 was supposed to be admitted. (For what it's worth, Rush and Marosky were both carded when they bought tickets.)

I wouldn't argue that Temecula's community well is pretty pure, but why only single out "Boyz N the Hood" and "Showgirls?"

Stallone's new R-rated movie, "Assasins," opened at Temeku on Friday. Think there might be a little violence in that movie?

Elder says he hadn't thought of taking on that cause. "Too busy of a docket. That's a good idea, Carl. Maybe I'll do that next."

But what about the gambling at the casino on Pala Road? Or the beer drinking that will go on at the tractor race this weekend? Think gambling and drinking promote family values? Where are the protesters?

Where do we stop? Or start?

Whether they realize it or not, Elder and his helpers are having a chilling effect on Temecula. Of six people I talked to in the theater where "Showgirls" was playing, only two eagerly gave their names. Like one guy said, you think I want the people in this town to read where I'm at?

There's a sense among more than a few people in Temecula that if they just try hard enough, they can keep out the ideas that they don't want.

And they're succeeding. While I yawned my way through "Showgirls," I realized that the lifestyle depicted on the screen is about as different from Temecula as you can get. The great thing was that I didn't have to go outside of town to see this contrast. Now I'll have to.

A welcome addition to the family?

Publication Date: November 15, 1995

No. Never. Over my dead body. Not in a million ice ages.

How many ways can you say no? That's what I was trying to calculate 11 days ago when my wife Joanne walked out of a pet store with a puppy.

She had one of our children on each side of her to help plead her case that this was a necessary addition to our family, a household that already included one of man's best friends.

Kids and a puppy. Who could say no?

I could. Nope. Nothing doing. Unh unh. Negatory.

We were having what is commonly known as "a scene." We were in a Murrieta shopping center on a Saturday afternoon, performing before scores of witnesses. Nothing like a spectacle.

Stalling for time, I said let's get a puppy from a pound. How can anybody in good conscience get a dog and not save a life in the process, I barked.

Nothing doing. Joanne wasn't letting go of that dog until it was hers. She even had a name for the guy, Midnight. It was a black lab, and I had to concede it was a perfect fit.

She wanted me to hold the animal, knowing it takes a cold person to say no to a puppy after cuddling it. But I didn't relent until she handed the dog to me while she reached for the charge card. Of course the dog took care of business on me. Then on the way to the car, a group of little kids accosted me as if I was carrying Barney.

So we have a puppy. I still can't say that I'm ecstatic, but if I have to have one, why couldn't it have happened sooner?

You should see the way women flock whenever I show our latest bundle of joy. It makes me wonder why I didn't get one when I was doing the singles scene.

My fellow men, insensitive louts that they are, just laugh when I tell them about Midnight. "You wimp!" "We know who's wearing the pants in your family!" "Replaced the carpet yet?" Yuck, yuck, yuck, yuck.

At least Joanne is getting hers. She told me a couple mornings ago she had a nightmare about taking care of Midnight's poo-poo and pee-pee. I'm too good of a person to say, "Told you so." Sure was tempting though.

Our kids naturally love Midnight and not just because they don't have to clean up after him.

Julia, our 6-year-old, treats him as if he is her first born, holding him delicately in her lap and kissing him, at least until he tries to bite off her nose.

David, our 3-year-old, is a little rougher on Midnight. The dog often takes off when David comes into the room, for fear of which body part he'll yank on next. But as the pups of the family, Midnight and David share a bond. The scenes of David riding on his tricycle and Midnight chasing him, his little tail a blur, are pretty special.

Our other dog, Smiley, is coming around slowly to her new canine colleague. She used to just lumber out of the room when Midnight came crashing into her, always nipping at her playfully. But now the old girl is starting to joust with him and at times now it's the puppy who needs the rest, not Smiley.

His elder also is teaching Midnight to dig, a development of dire consequences for our beleaguered back yard. Another problem is that, like most dogs, Smiley and Midnight love to be scratched. A growing percentage of my day is devoted to such duties, along with feeding, bathing and walking.

To think I've got 15 years of this ahead of me. Plus black labs get as big as horses. It reminds me of when I was in high school and our neighbors had a black lab. He was named Moose for a reason.

But for now Midnight is a little guy who is as vulnerable as any newborn. The first night at our house he was yelping up a storm in the night, so I tossed some newspapers on the floor, laid him beside me and held him. He just needed to be reassured about these strange new surroundings. He slept soundly until morning, just like a baby.

But I still don't want him. At least I don't think so.

A step in the right direction
Publication Date: November 18, 1995

Chuck Washington is a lot of things. Family man. Airline pilot. School volunteer. Chamber of Commerce citizen of the year. Murrieta city councilman-elect.

Washington also is the first black person in recent memory - if not ever - to be elected to public office in Murrieta or Temecula.

It's hard to gauge how much this says about the state of local race relations because I'll bet more people in Murrieta know Colin Powell is black than know Washington is.

Still, it says something that a black man can be elected in a town that is mostly white, especially in the volatile world after the O.J. verdict, where anything to do with race seems to have some larger meaning.

It's definitely a positive sign, at least if you are concerned about improving race relations around here. Obviously, not everybody here is, judging by some recent events at Temecula Valley High School.

A couple weeks ago - during the homecoming pep rally of all things - some white boys allegedly used some racial slurs against a performing group mostly made up of black girls.

More than 35 black parents and community members picketed the high school Monday and observed students during lunch. The parents said they were afraid the white kids posed a threat to their youngsters. School officials are working feverishly to cool things off.

Amid these disturbing developments comes the news of Washington's election to the Murrieta council last week. If you're concerned about racism around here like I am, it's good news.

I'd never even talked to Washington until I called him to inquire about his election and the topic of racism. I felt awkward bringing it up, but Washington put me right at ease and didn't seem to mind talking about it. That alone says plenty about the man.

Washington says we have a real dichotomy in this country: Racism is alive and well, but people are more likely to judge an individual by his merit, not his color. Our new councilman seems to be an example of the latter.

Washington says he knows his race may have been an issue with some voters, but it was never raised to him. He says his core support came from families, including many who knew him before the campaign even began. Race has never been a factor for them.

Washington says he's heard of incidents of local racism and he himself may have been a victim at some point. But he says his personality is such that he doesn't dwell on such matters. He'd rather focus on the local people who've been so supportive of him.

The new councilman says he hopes he can be an example for all of us. For blacks, he's trying to demonstrate that you can take control of your life and be a success. Yes, he's black and, yes, he could spend his whole life looking for someone to blame; he just prefers to focus on other things.

As for the rest of us, Washington hopes he can help combat the stereotypes. As he so aptly puts, he's an example of a black man who isn't being thrown up against the side of a police car.

But in talking to Washington, there is no question he's out to make Murrieta a better place to live in every way, not just racially. He's already heard of concerns from kids about the Police Department and the local curfew, so he's talked to the cops about the situation.

It's certain he'll be working a lot with youths. He met this week with a student ethnic advisory council at Murrieta Valley High School and reports that they don't feel there are many racial tensions on their campus. With Washington involved there is a better chance it'll stay that way.

I got off the phone with the new councilman feeling a lot better about racism in our community.

Obviously, it isn't going to magically disappear because we've elected one black person. But it's a step in the right direction. And with racial tensions the way they are these days, it's a big step.

Chuck Washington isn't just the man of the year, he's the man of the hour.

CHAPTER 8

1996 - A mom who never quit

It was a frustrating year for a lot of people.

For the fourth time Murrieta voters rejected a school bond measure and the town was left with still too many schools of mostly portables.

The same year, Murrietans had to sit and watch while the city of Temecula ponied up money for extra services that everybody in the two cities use. Because of its weak finances, the city of Murrieta stood idly by. Some people in Murrieta even moved to Temecula at the time while others, including yours truly, thought about it. I even wrote a piece about why Murrieta was still good enough for me. Considering Murrieta is now more than 100,000, it seems plenty agree.

Folks in Temecula were left dumbstruck by Karel Lindemans, who delivered a speech at a black tie event that had a lot of people seeing red. That Lindemans sure had a mouth. Meanwhile, people sat and waited for Zev Buffman to do something about his massive project in Old Town Temecula. And to this day they are still waiting.

Lenny Pechner made quite a ruckus by daring to rent out adult movies from his video store. Never mind that it was perfectly legal, both then and now. Only in Temecula.

As for me, I wrote my favorite column of all time, a tribute to my mom who died in September of that year. She defied all the odds by surviving for years with ovarian cancer, which was basically a death sentence at the time. She never quit, a virtue she passed down to me.

Bizarre new world
Publication Date: January 13, 1996

There are laws and there is logic. Then there are CC&Rs.

Helen Miller knows all about that. She is the 77-year-old violin teacher who lives in The Colony retirement community but who has run afoul of the area's CC&Rs, or covenants, conditions and restrictions as the legal guys refer to 'em.

The Colony board silenced her violin lessons recently, citing the all-mighty CC&Rs.

In a legalistic nutshell, the board objects to the traffic - all 11 cars a week of it - that Miller created by giving lessons in her home.

Oh, and a sibling of a child who was taking a lesson was seen playing in Miller's front yard at least once. This is thought to be a violation of those CC&Rs because the child was there due to the violin lessons Miller is dealing from her home.

A kid playing in a yard - heavens to Betsy. Next thing you know L.A. street gangs will be rampaging through the Murrieta development.

Miller's plight went public this week when about 40 of her supporters stood outside The Colony's gates in California Oaks to protest the board ruling.

It appears it's all for naught though, because the board doesn't look like it's going to change its mind. Doing that could mean tampering with the CC&Rs. A blizzard is more likely to hit The Colony before that happens.

This case opens the proverbial Pandora's Box of interesting questions, but for today we'll confine ourselves to this core issue: What's the world coming to when a sweet old lady can't teach violin out of her house?

The answer, according to board member Jay Dawson, is that The Colony is another world.

It's a world where you can't have family members stay with you more than three months a year. It's a world where you can't put aluminum foil in your window. It's a world where you can't interfere with your neighbor's "quiet enjoyment."

All this - and more - is from - you got it - the CC&Rs.

Dawson qualifies as an expert in the field as a semi-retired manager of homeowners' associations. He says The Colony's CC&Rs aren't anything out of the ordinary. A frightening prospect indeed.

It comes down to this, as far as Dawson is concerned: If you move into The Colony, you don't just play by the rules; you play by the CC&Rs. If you don't want to, you move on, which is what Miller is doing by putting her house up for sale.

Miller certainly isn't going without a fight. Miller says she was told when she bought the house four years ago that the violin lessons would be OK. But she did not get it in writing.

Now before you go off thinking that Dawson has a cold heart, he actually thinks this whole thing is "a darn shame." (The guy's so mild that he can't even bring himself to swear.)

He thinks Miller is the nicest lady. The board members even spent hours with an attorney trying to find some way to help her without gutting their sacred CC&R provision on "commercial activity."

But amending the requirement would have required numerous OKs, including two-thirds approval from The Colony's homeowners. That is highly unlikely, Dawson contends. Indeed, he's been bombarded with phone calls from homeowners who support his stand. Not a one has called to beef.

So Miller leaves; the CC&Rs stay. The poor lady never really had a chance.

We close with a look at the world created by The Colony's CC&Rs. If you're into an antiseptic environment, The Colony is your kind of place. Everything here is uniform and neat in appearance, from the windows to the front yards. No slum neighbors in this place.

It's kind of sterile, but living in a gated community has its advantages. They no doubt walk the streets of The Colony at night without fear. Peace and quiet also prevail. So do the CC&Rs.

So many of us move to this area to escape the hazards of the outside world. Here in The Colony, the seniors are taking it one step further and creating their own world. It sounds appealing, until you realize what exactly is being created.

Blue jokes make some cheeks red
Publication Date: April 6, 1996

Considering Temecula's latest mayor is the one-and-only Karel Lindemans, it's no surprise that the most recent mayor's ball was a one-of-a-kind affair.

It wasn't just the mayor's ball, it was "The Mayor's Black Tie Bluejean Ball." He made a dramatic entrance by pulling up in a horse-drawn carriage. His dreamy first dance with wife Lydia was like something out of a fairy tale.

Then there was the matter of the mayor's monologue, which was more X-rated than children's story.

It was vintage Lindemans, meaning it was like somebody tossing an electrical appliance into your bath water. Shock city.

There were the prostitutes, the sex toys, the Lorenna Bobbett-Giovanna Munoz comparison - the usual stuff mayors talk about at official functions.

A few people walked out of the room at the Temecula Creek Inn on Sunday night, apparently unable to stomach any more of the "fun." More than a few eyes were rolled during the show.

In defense of the mayor's sense of humor, a lot of it apparently really was funny. To wit:

o Councilman Ron Roberts was visiting somebody in a hospital on a recent trip to Japan. The guy told Roberts something in Japanese, repeated it and then died. Roberts ran to the nurse and told her his last words. She translated, "Sir, you're standing on my air hose."

o Councilman Jeff Stone is always shuttling between the dias and the audience during council meetings. Stone has property in Old Town and must abstain during any Zev Buffman business. Lindemans compared Stone to a keno runner in Vegas. Back and forth, back and forth ...

And then there was the stuff that wasn't so funny to some in the audience:

o There are a lot of sex shops in Lindemans' native Holland. Customers who don't pay their tab are tossed in the canals that also are plentiful in Holland. Those who can't swim are thrown the "necessary inflatables to save them."

o Anti-Buffman activist Sam Pratt brings to mind the lone Chinese man who stood up to the tanks in Tiananmen Square. Lindemans says Pratt may well stand fast in front of Buffman's bulldozers when they're ready to roll. "We never heard what happened to the Chinaman, maybe afterward we won't hear what happened to Mr. Pratt."

o Giovanna Munoz - involved in a bitter split with ex-hubby, ex-councilman Sal Munoz - reminds Lindemans of the infamous Lorena Bobbitt. "Mrs. Bobbitt was happy with a little thing and she (Munoz) goes for the whole enchilada."

Lindemans insists his humor was all in good taste and he hasn't heard from anybody who thinks otherwise.

"They all thought it was funny and they enjoyed it," he says. "I was there to make people laugh and that's what I did."

He won't get any argument from Temecula Valley Chamber of Commerce President Joan Sparkman. "I thought he was a scream," she says. "I think he hit most everybody in town."

And because he's the mayor, nobody is hitting back, at least publicly. I've talked to several people who say they were offended by Lindemans' routine, but nobody wants their name in the newspaper.

Those who do want to talk publicly are choosing their words oh-so-carefully.

Councilman Stone says, "He was a little more colorful than I expected him to be."

"I don't think Karel meant any harm to anybody," Stone adds. "I think Karel meant to go out there and have a good time."

Another butt of Lindemans' humor, Councilman Roberts, says he wasn't offended by the jokes. As for the folks who were, Roberts says perhaps they don't know Lindemans as well as he does.

"I've known Karel for a long time," he says. "It's different than people who really do not know Karel. Karel says what he thinks. He doesn't hold back."

Lindemans isn't the first comedian to go too far for some people's tastes and he certainly won't be the last. But he may be the first mayor to do so.

A daughter's maturing mind a path to hope
Publication Date: May 21, 1996

Sometime between diapers and high school diplomas, kids start to mature.

I think my daughter Julia, who just turned 7, is starting that bizarre process.

For one, the other day Julia, the budding adult, asked my wife Joanne if she and I ever have sex. Moments later, Julia, the fading child, wanted to know the names of Santa's reindeer.

There's a transformation taking place inside her little body and it offers all kinds of delights and sleepless nights for her parents.

The one I find most intriguing so far - the sex inquiries are too frightening to think about just yet - is the talk about a career. She's decided she wants to breed horses for a living in Idyllwild, of all places. She is going to have 20 horses and 12 huskies - her imagination has such detail - on her land. And she is going to be a painter on the side.

Julia doesn't want to work in an office or have a boss because it doesn't sound like much fun.

Hmmm, I wonder who she got those concepts from.

Her aspirations mean that our recent night in a cabin in Idyllwild is more than just a mini vacation. It's a fact-finding mission as well.

It's easy to see why she wants to settle in Idyllwild. Nestled in the San Jacinto Mountains above Hemet, it's the kind of small town - about 2,500 people - that Temecula and Murrieta were as recently as the mid '80s.

Squirrels hang out in downtown Idyllwild. Everybody seems to know everybody. We don't see a cop the whole time we are there because they probably don't need them. The wonderful fragrance of pines isn't from some deodorizer. And while Temecula and Murrieta bake in the early summer heat, the temps are in the mid-70s up here.

After we settle into our woodsy cabin next to an awesome playground, right in the middle of downtown, the first words from Julia's mouth are, "Can we live here?"

Chimes in her 3-year-old brother David, "Can we stay here forever?"

Their parents try to explain that we are just here for a night, that we have jobs we have to get back to and bills to pay. The usual garbage adults spew.

Our kids aren't buying it. And you know, why should they?

This explains why their father on an early morning walk hunts down the office of the local newspaper to get a copy and to see if an editor is in. Just curious, mind you. Unfortunately the newspaper office isn't open yet.

Meanwhile, their mother is grabbing every piece of real estate literature she can find. One of our favorite places - two bedrooms and three private decks - is headlined "ARTISTS, WRITERS, LOVERS." Should we live there or what?

I'm dreamin' you say? Well I'm a big believer in the notion your kids teach you as much as you teach them.

Julia's aspirations aren't ruined yet by the aging process. She still thinks dreams, no matter how farfetched they may seem to grown-ups, can come true. And who's to say she can't live in a beautiful place and breed 20 horses for a living. I'm not.

I've often thought we here in Southwest Riverside County have it as good as it gets in Southern California right now. We have the advantages of the climate and the beauty without all the problems of the cities most of us fled.

But Temecula and Murrieta are changing really fast. For better or for worse, for richer or for poorer, Temecula's not going to be the same if Zev Buffman builds his western entertainment center. And Murrieta, which prides itself on not having the "congestion" of Temecula, sure has a lot more than when I moved there eight years ago.

I'm not trying to take sides in the growth debate because there's a lot of good that's come with the development. And to think you can just stop these changes is a true fantasy.

I remain convinced that Temecula and Murrieta are as good as it gets in Southern California, within the confines of having to be close to a job that pays better than what most artists make. But there could be something better out there some day (i.e., Idyllwild) and it took a child to teach me that when you stop dreaming of such possibilities you might as well give up.

Apathy wins; shabby Shivela; no Taj Mahals

Publication Date: June 8, 1996

The message board at Shivela Middle School says it all about this week's Murrieta school bond election:

"Apathy 4, Schools 0."

Murrieta schools took it on the chin again when Measure C crashed and burned. Sure it got 61 percent of the vote, but these measures need two-thirds approval.

Shivela's scoreboard recounts that is the fourth time in four tries that a Murrieta bond measure has failed in the 1990s. In a town of mostly families, theoretically people should be willing to spend more money on their schools. Yet, apathy seems to be pitching a shutout.

Considering the same measure lost by just five votes last November, bond backers were really hopeful they could dig up the extra support this week. Instead they lost by a much wider margin.

Perhaps nobody is more depressed about this bonding experience than the staff and students at Shivela.

The school has been housed in trailers since it opened in 1989. The first permanent building on campus - a fine-looking P.E. building that looms large over the rest of the shabby-looking middle-school - is supposed to open when the next school year starts in July.

But other than that it is portables. And no place is in worse shape than the science classrooms. Each has to get by with warped floors, a sink and no Bunsen burners.

The rooms also aren't big enough to house supplies, so teachers like Cindy Lauvray and Donise Lei haul in materials from somewhere else. Teachers and kids say the obstacles make learning harder.

"Small, crowded," says sixth grader Adam Barret of his science classroom.

"There's not a lot of equipment," adds classmate Karen Nierva.

Hardly sounds like youngsters loaded with school spirit. Rah, rah. Or is it raw, raw, as in the deal these kids are getting classroom wise?

There's some big-time resentment among the Shivela kids I talked to about the environment they have to learn in. They can't figure out why the adults won't do something about it, like approving bond measures.

Notes a frustrated Shelby Tolbert: "They want all the money for themselves and they don't want to share it with us."

Jerry Kellett is one of those adults who opposed the bond measure. He says it's not a matter of being for or against kids - he's all for them - it's a question of spending too much money on building schools.

Kellett cites the $38.5 million high school bond measure that local voters, including him, supported in 1989. Kellett says then the district put in a chandelier in the performing arts center and a plush new pool at the new school.

"They build Taj Mahal schools," he says. "It's not necessary. You can build a nice school for a lot less money."

It's all pretty depressing for a Murrieta parent who has a first grader and a 4-year-old a year away from kindergarten. Will my kids end up in a school as dreary looking as Shivela someday?

It's my town and it's good enough for me
Publication Date: June 28, 1996

Murrieta, Murrieta, Murrieta.

I say this to a town that I care about it deeply, even though it tries my patience constantly.

Murrieta is celebrating its fifth year as a city and in that time my hometown has raised and dashed my hopes more than I care to remember.

Just when I'm about to throw up my hands and say, "That's it, I'm moving to Temecula (or wherever)," Murrieta seems to scurry over to make up, like some whimpering puppy that's just whizzed on the carpet.

How can I move now, I sigh.

Most people zipping through on the I-15 probably can't tell any difference between Temecula and Murrieta. To them, our two cities are just one solid mass of tile roofs marching into the hills.

Those who live under those tile roofs know otherwise. Temecula is efficiency, as in new parks, seemingly on every other corner, a community recreation center that's to die for and permanent schools built when they're supposed to be.

Murrieta goes about its business in a more haphazard fashion.

Just last February the city opened its first park since incorporation. Murrieta is struggling just to rent space in a shopping center for a little community center. And school district voters have turned down so many bond measures that the town's biggest middle school has been in trailers since 1989.

One thing about Murrietans though, they never give up. The town could have easily given in to the grand vision of Temecula in 1988 and allowed itself to be swallowed up in one massive city.

Some plucky Murrietans - sparked by John McElroy, Tex McAlister and George Walker - thought otherwise and launched their own competing city proposal. Somehow they survived, with a remarkable 82.8 percent of the townsfolk supporting the new city. Who says Murrietans can't agree?

Of course, Murrieta had to start up its city at the dawn of the worst recession in California in the past 50 years. The new city's two meal-ticket projects - Murrieta Springs Mall and a fancy six-story hotel to be built by some German guy - never made it off the paper they were drawn up on.

There have been other struggles as well. Murrieta went with its own police force at a time when most new cities do the safe thing and contract with the Riverside County Sheriff's Department.

Sure, the city had lots of problems, but Murrieta is still standing tall with its own P.D.

Even the local fire department - the community's pride and joy before the city was started - was in all kinds of financial trouble when the city took over the place. Nevertheless, Murrietans still have their own firefighters today.

There's a pattern here. Murrietans have to do everything by themselves, even though they sometimes seem to have no idea what they're getting into. It's an independent streak that has both cursed and preserved Murrieta.

Now our city leaders are talking about more than mere survival. The "Madison Avenue Corridor" - Best Buy, Home Depot, etc. - is trumpeted as Murrieta's goldmine. Combine that with the mall, and Murrieta, not Temecula, could be the retail powerhouse of our valley. Fancy that.

For me, the best thing about Murrieta is that it still feels like a small town.

I see Mayor Jack van Haaster dropping off his kids at the same school my daughter goes to. City Manager Steve Harding lives just a few blocks away. School Board member Al Christenson is just around the corner from me. The town's former fire chief, Marv Curran, is nearby as well.

Somehow I don't think people with tract homes in L.A. can say the same thing about their leaders.

Even more telling is that most of my non-celebrity neighbors haven't changed since I moved here in 1988. Considering how mobile the rest of Southern California is, Murrieta must be doing something right.

So is this five-year old city a success? Who cares. It's Murrieta and that's good enough for me.

Illusion versus reality
Publication Date: July 23, 1996

So how's it feel to be living in a suburban laboratory?

Not too long ago, the big national newsmagazines - Time and Newsweek - used Temecula and Murrieta as classic examples of modern suburbia.

Now comes the academic perspective. Sociologist Ray Maietta has weighed in with his dissertation on making - or at least trying to make - friends in this area.

Maietta's just-finished work - "Lost In The Shuffle: In Search of Wayward Friendship" - is making the rounds of the university types and one aspect of our lives really intrigues them.

It's the notion of a master-planned community, where everything we'll need for a happy life can be penciled in on paper.

Maietta says Temecula and Murrieta seem to be among the pioneers of this concept, which accounts for the play in the news magazines.

Temecula and Murrieta are about as master planned as cities can get. Great homes, fine schools, big parks and convenient shopping centers are just some of the goodies promised by our local builders.

Developments are advertised with slogans such as "Everything you want . . . Everything they deserve." Happy people are always photographed in the ads. A couple riding bicycles, a family having a barbecue, kids romping around a park.

As those of us who live here have found out the hard way, a few of the master planner's images haven't materialized yet.

You can put a great looking park on paper in a developer's bro-chure, but what if you live in the City of Murrieta which is having a hard time coming up with the money to build places to play?

The roads on the builder's plans can look like they'll do the job. But when's the last time you saw congestion on the Rancho California Road or Winchester Road bridges over Interstate 15 featured in an advertisement? Unless it was for ridesharing.

Obviously, every town has its problems. Except Temecula and Murrieta, judging by developer ads.

Maietta talked to 96 local people for his study and the majority were disappointed by the reality of Temecula and Murrieta vs. the perception advertised to them.

The long commutes definitely weren't part of the plan, excuse me, "master plan." Nor was how difficult it would be for some of us to make friends in a town where everybody is new and nobody has any free time.

Maietta says it's hard for any town to live up to the image of the "master plan" because some things can't be controlled, such as who your neighbors are. Consequently, a lot of folks may never give Temecula and Murrieta a fair shake because it doesn't immediately fulfill their grand expectations.

I know I used to fall in that boat. My wife and I moved here eight years ago thinking this was going to be perfect. Even a cynic like me was sucked in by the images touted by the builders.

We were both disappointed when reality sank in. I used to plot ways to move to Oregon, my wife even gave serious thought to moving back to the Ohio town she grew up in. During a trip there we went house hunting for a couple days and I plotted a way to get a job there.

Then something happened on the way out of here. We grew to accept Temecula and Murrieta for what they are, not what they are supposed to be.

Murrieta doesn't have enough parks, but there are enough for us in the neighborhood where we live. Temecula's traffic is bad - in some spots. It could be better, but it could be Anaheim too.

We haven't made as many friends as we'd like, but we certainly have enough considering how little free time we have while raising two kids.

We haven't thought about moving for a couple years now and I can't imagine us considering it again anytime soon. I sometimes wonder how we'd feel if we hadn't given Temecula and Murrieta time, if we'd just moved on like some others I used to know. On to the next so-called "master-planned community."

A son remembers his mom
Publication Date: September 28, 1996

This is a special day for my mom. Her memorial service is being held this afternoon at her brother's home in Oceanside.

My mom died in her living room at 6:53 a.m. Sunday. It was dawn, the birds were singing at the time.

Perhaps the best way to describe my mom's life is to start with the profound way it ended.

Her last night was a difficult one as she struggled with her impending death. But by early morning she was finally resting comfortably, her pain mercifully under control thanks to the angels of Elizabeth Hospice.

My dad, my sister and I collapsed in exhaustion, having been up with her all night.

We revived ourselves about an hour later and started to come to terms with her fate.

While my dad knelt by his wife and talked about how it was almost 40 years to the day since he'd met her, my wise sister crawled into her hospital bed and cuddled with her.

The moment was too much for me and I collapsed to the floor with a cry that can best be described as a wail. I've never felt such pain.

My father comforted me, then suggested I too join my mom. I gently hoisted myself over the hospital bed railing and settled in on the other side of her.

Five, maybe 10 minutes later, my mom died. She couldn't leave until her children made safe her passage.

I've shared this story with many people the past few days and I compare it to a religious experience. No, corrected my best friend, it was a religious experience.

I've always thought there would be nothing like witnessing the birth of my two children. I've found something comparable.

My mom fought ovarian cancer for nine years. It was a remarkable feat, considering her first doctor said she had six months when she was first diagnosed.

She was in and out of remission so many times I lost track. Her last cancer doctor said she was the most spirited patient he'd ever seen. My mom the big sports fan would be happy to know I consider her the Michael Jordan of cancer patients.

Even a great talent needs a supporting cast to succeed. My mom's teammate in battle was my dad, at her side every step of the way with care and love that were at times superhuman. I am forever grateful.

My mom was only 64 when she died and many tell me I've been cheated. True, but I'll take quality over quantity every time.

Besides being the best mom a kid ever had - I know that goes without saying - she was a special person.

I had the honor of calling her legion of friends to announce her death and it was so moving to hear their reactions. It's clear her family won't be the only ones who miss her.

My mom was such a giving person. She was a pioneer in the Trauma Intervention Program, or TIP, a group providing comfort to victims. Her last job was as coordinator of Red Cross volunteers for the Camp Pendleton Marines, a position she had to regretfully leave due to her illness.

She also loved politics and served nine years on the Oceanside Manufactured Home Fair Practices Commission.

I could go on and on about my mom, perhaps even write a book. But for now I'll close with my collaborator in this tribute, my sister and fellow writer, Theresa. She wrote a poem to mom shortly before she died:

FOR MY MOTHER

"Sometimes I long for - as though an injured bird lighting
Under the canopy of some great tree, struggling to feed, warmth
    may
Shadow me - some unknowable, precise absence; in order that
    a seed
Awakening within,
Nourishment perhaps, would embrace us both; her tender, opu-
    lent wings
Justly brushing our fine, pure skin; just as you must long for
Another day free of suffering – nevertheless
Nature's great processional proceeds, each of us

Ever closer to the unknown: an almost empty forest,
Light touch of rain, thunder calling loudly
Overhead as you lie silently
Very still, your life a day in May, a dance
Ever more before you, ever more again."

Soccer season brought a sense of community
Publication Date: November 19, 1996

Life won't be nearly so frantic at our house. No more getting the kids out of bed at 7 a.m. on a Saturday, fed, dressed and on their way to a game when they'd rather be sleeping.

No more dashing home from work, skipping dinner and hauling the children to practice when many a time we just wanted to stay home and take it easy.

Best of all, no more fund-raisers.

Soccer season is over and despite the above-mentioned hassles, I'm definitely sad.

This was our first go-round with the youth sports routine and it was a kick. And not just because it was soccer.

There was a real sense of community when the games were played Saturday mornings at Avaxat Elementary. It seemed we'd see half the parents we knew in Murrieta, all of us chasing after our little soccer guys. It was really cool.

I felt the same vibes at the Sports Park in Temecula on a Saturday in September when I wrote something about the local soccer boom. The notion that we still live in small towns is alive and well at kid sports events, no matter the population growth.

As for our local soccer moms, they were even a political force this fall: Elected types were using it as a catch-all term for the baby boomer women racing through the '90s, juggling jobs, kids and hubbies.

Just one thing though: What about the needs of soccer dads? Apparently they don't count to the politicos. Or anybody else it seems. Not that this soccer dad is overly sensitive, of course.

As for the kids of my soccer wife Joanne and I - 7-year-old Julia and 4-year-old David - they learned a lot about the sport and about life in general. Funny what a simple game can teach.

Beyond the dribbling and passing, David was exposed to something called a work ethic. There were times at the start of the season when he didn't want to go practice. But we'd drag him there - one of my favorite lines was to say I didn't want to go to work either but I had to go - and David always had a good time with his new pals, the "teammates."

By the end of the season he was genuinely bummed soccer was over and he can't wait for next year. Now if I could just learn to develop the same enthusiasm for going to work.

Julia's problem was harder to handle. (And it's even harder to write about in a newspaper because she can read.)

Anyway, my daughter had done well at most everything until she tackled soccer. For one of the few times she wasn't excelling at something and it was tough to take. For her and her parents.

We talked about it a lot and tried to get across the point that nobody is good at everything they do. What matters is having a good time, something she was still having.

She persevered, she really tried hard, her coach Mike Rabehl supported her, and by the end of the season she was a better player and person.

The thing that most impressed me about the soccer experience though was the general concept, fun. I remember it was the first thing David's coach - Dave Pettersen - talked about at the start of the first practice on some 184-degree August afternoon: Let's have fun.

They didn't keep score for David's games and I thought it was great. Granted, the competitive parents - me included - knew the real score anyway, but that's our problem.

And last Saturday at closing ceremonies, both of my kids got trophies, as well as all their teammates. It didn't matter how their teams, Iguanas and Wonder Girls, had done.

These personalized trophies had their names. The figure on Julia's trophy even sported a ponytail. Let me tell you, my kids were pumped.

Unfortunately they won't always get trophies as they get older because there will be more emphasis on those stupid wins and losses.

So thanks Iguanas - Richard and Gizzy Aldersley, Aroha Allen, Demar Butler, David Love, Andrew Olivares, Greg Pettersen, Nathan Pollard, Andrew Reyes and Kyle Stiefel - and Wonder Girls - S.R. Grunow, Breann Keating, Julia Love, Ashyln Lozano, Jennifer Northway, Nicole Stump, Alexy Tilkey, Nicole Tosches, Britni Tuthill and Hillary Wragg - for reminding me of what really matters: Fun.

Angel helps team win big game
Publication Date: November 23, 1996

Some wore jeans and sneakers. After it was over, a couple even had suckers in their mouths.

The Murrieta Valley Junior Pee Wee Redhawk football team came out in force Wednesday at the memorial service for Lisa Muzic. The youngsters figured it was the least they could do, considering what they believe she did for them.

Muzic died early last Saturday morning, five hours before her 10-year-old son Tyler and his teammates took the field in Ramona to play the mighty San Dieguito Crimson Tide.

The Palomar Conference Junior Pee Wee championship was on the line and if the Vegas bookies had bothered to post odds, the Tide would have been heavily favored.

But Redhawk coach Tom Wisniewski figured it was his team who had the advantage. They had an extra player on the field that morning, Lisa Muzic.

How else to explain that her son Tyler scored the game's only touchdown on a 25-yard run.

The play was designed to go for three yards. But five defenders miraculously missed tackling Tyler and the lumbering kid somehow outran the fastest Crimson Tide player on the field.

"We had an angel on the field for us Saturday," Wisniewski said. "If you had seen Tyler's run, you would have seen her block for him."

Then there was the play near the end of the game: a wide open Crimson Tide receiver dropped a pass in the end zone and lost the opportunity for a game-tying touchdown. Wisniewski, who had scouted the opposition, said he'd never seen the sure-handed kid muff a pass.

"It's like somebody batted it away," he said, his voice breaking off.

Wisniewski, 45, knows what Ryan is going through. Wisniewski's father died of a sudden heart attack when he was 10, the same day he too played in a kids' football game.

"I've been pretty close to Tyler the last few months," Wisniewski said, his arm wrapped around his own 10-year-old son Thomas shortly before the memorial service began.

Wisniewski dedicated the game to Lisa Muzic before it started. The effect was profound; the coach said he's never seen Tyler or his team play with so much fire.

When the game ended, when the Redhawks had somehow beaten the powerful Tide, Wisniewski ran on the field toward his team.

"I swear to God Tyler floated five feet in the air into my arms," the coach said. "He hit me like a feather. I couldn't hug him enough."

A few moments later Tyler's excited teammates carried him off the field on their shoulders.

"That was O.K.," Tyler said of the memory, flashing one of his big grins that said it was much more than just that.

Tyler was honored that a dozen of his teammates could come to the memorial service. His mother no doubt was touched as well.

Lisa Muzic was 37 when she died. She was diagnosed with breast cancer shortly after Tyler was born. Her only son played his greatest game not knowing his mother was dead.

Her memorial service was held at Callaway Winery, where she worked as hospitality manager until she went on disability. After Muzic's brother Rick tried to come to terms with his little sister's fate in a moving tribute, the young Redhawks talked with me about what they've been through.

Like their coach, Travis Lopez, Matt Schaeffer, Jimmy McGehee and Drew Stevenson are certain Lisa Muzic helped them in their big game. It's as certain as the championship they won that day.

Still, it was just a game. More importantly, they know their friend needs their support off the field. They'll be there to carry him on their shoulders anytime.

And while many of the adults wept with grief during Lisa Muzic's memorial service, young Redhawks such as Travis Lopez tried to find a reason to be joyful as well.

"It's bad that she had to suffer," Travis said. "It's good that she's up in heaven."

Chapter 9

1997 - Disarming cops and the real Clinton Keith

Weird things were popular this year.

There was a proposal to disarm Murrieta police officers. Interesting thought in the land of the Second Amendment and the NRA.

There was a Temecula activist who was criticized for criticizing. When it came to the growth in Temecula, you had to be careful. Funny thing, the same can be true today.

There was an election in Murrieta in which 11.26 percent of the voters in one precinct took part. Yes, apathy was alive and well. In Lake Elsinore, some parks were closed, an annoying habit we have had in Southwest Riverside County historically, especially in Wildomar. Let's hope we can cure ourselves of that affliction once and for all.

Personally, my son David headed off to kindergarten (There is something sad watching your youngest child starting school), my daughter went to her first dance (I'll always be able to say I shared the first one with her) and we laid my wife Joanne's father to rest in a small town in Tennessee that harkened back to the days when Temecula and Murrieta were once so country.

Murrieta's council looks out for future
Publication Date: January 11, 1997

One of the many things people like about living here is that they feel they have a say in the future.

It's not like the big cities where everything was said and done long ago. In those places, it's truly a case of love it or leave it, because you ain't gonna change it.

Temecula, Murrieta, Wildomar, Lake Elsinore and Menifee are places where people can still make a difference.

What transpired at this week's Murrieta City Council meeting was a classic example of what can be accomplished if people take the time to think about what they're doing for the future, not just today.

The subject wasn't one of those hot issues that attract the masses. It was a "final parcel map," an item government bodies rubber stamp in the blink of an eye.

Heck, the issue seems to be so anti-climactic that grading has already started on the project. And what a project. It would include Murrieta's first movie theater, a whopping 17 screens. It would be the largest in all of Riverside County and it's due to open this summer.

But even the movie makers would have a tough time topping the drama that unfolded over this minor bureaucratic matter.

Let's set the scene. The project is planned at California Oaks Road and I-15, a major piece of real estate. All kinds of developing is going up on Cal Oaks, including fast food, gas stations and other stuff. You don't have to be a traffic engineer to see gridlock coming.

And the best way to prevent it is to build loop ramps on and off the freeway at Cal Oaks to move traffic faster than any other means.

One minor detail. The city needs land for the ramps, land now owned by the developer of the movie theater and shopping center. What better time to dicker with the builder to buy that land then when he has a project waiting for city approval.

If the council says nothing and approves it, the developer has less reason to make a deal. It could mean gridlock forevermore at a major Murrieta intersection. All this because the council didn't try to do something.

The ramifications begin to dawn on the council members, particularly Jack van Haaster. Before you know it, they're talking about delaying a vote on the parcel map to see if they can find a way to buy the land they need for those ramps.

Nothing gets the attention of an anxious developer faster than talk of delay. Project rep Robert Grimmick leaps to the podium, contending postponement could result in the end of the entire development.

And nothing gets the attention of a Murrieta City Council faster than that kind of talk. The last thing the cash strapped city needs is to lose a cash cow like the biggest movie theater in the county.

So what's it gonna be councilmen – the gridlock or the bucks?

At this point, not only can you feel the strain the council is under, you can sense the history that will be made by this suddenly momentous decision.

The council decides to see if Grimmick is bluffing and delays the project. The councilmen promise to find a way – as soon as possible of course – to reserve the land they need for the ramps while they try to hustle up the $1 million they need to buy it.

Only time will tell if Grimmick is indeed bluffing about losing the project and if the council can somehow come up with the money.

Van Haaster is optimistic the city will have the happiest of endings – the movies will start on time and the gridlock will be prevented. Let's hope he's right.

More importantly, the drama serves as a powerful reminder of what's up for grabs as development picks up again after a numbing recession.

Fewer than 10 people were in the audience that night. But the outcome will affect whoever passes through that busy intersection forever. Wow.

Our elected officials are making decisions that affect more than those living here now. And like the Murrieta council this week, one can only hope our leaders take the time to consider all the ramifications of all their choices. Before it is all said and done.

Fitting tribute to a fighter
Publication Date: January 28, 1997

We should all be blessed with as much willpower as Mary Phillips. Her resolve is what got the Seniors' Golden Years of Temecula Valley group up and running about six years ago.

And that was the group that was the driving force behind the opening of the city's senior center in Old Town in 1993.

Now it sounds as if it may be the only thing she has left.

Phillips, 84, has been at Sharp HealthCare Murrieta for about 10 days. She's been in a coma about a week.

Stan, her husband of 40 years, says the doctors don't know if she'll come out it. "They aren't giving me much hope."

Some of her friends have been saying for days that Phillips could go anytime.

Indeed, Karel Lindemans, probably her favorite Temecula city councilman, was already talking about Phillips in the past tense last week. He recalls that she made the council aware of the need for the center.

"She would never give up," he says. "She was wonderful and it really was because of her that center is there, with her persistence and begging and pleading. I loved her. She was a great lady."

Lindemans' fondness for Phillips also was demonstrated at the dedication of the senior center. He said they got along so well because each was a C.P.A. He was the more traditional one, certified public accountant, she was the more unusual one, "Constant Pain in the A…"

Another friend of Phillips, Ellie Holliday, describes her determination more diplomatically. "She pushed and shoved in her kind way," she says.

Many still remember the Temecula council meeting where Phillips wept for joy after the plans for a senior center were finally approved.

"She made it easy for you to know when she was happy and when she wasn't," former Temecula councilman Sal Munoz says with an affectionate chuckle.

Phillips had good reason to be emotional about the new senior center. Her husband, Stan, says the couple was foiled in their attempt to build a senior center in Valley Center in San Diego County. She was apparently extra determined when she arrived in Temecula in 1988. Look out.

I only met Phillips once in my life, at her 80th birthday party, also at Sharp. The party was originally planned for the Temecula Community Center, complete with a limousine ride and other treats.

The organizers thought about canceling the big bash because of her health, but the doctors said the celebration must go on. Phillips cried with joy - there she goes again - when about 50 people sang

"Happy Birthday" to her. And though she couldn't talk, she showed her appreciation by squeezing and kissing the hands of the people who greeted her.

It was one of the most moving birthday parties I've ever been too.

In looking back at a newspaper article about the event, I saw Phillips had been hospitalized because of two strokes. "We didn't think she'd be here," her daughter, Chris Peurifoy, said at the time. "She's fooling everybody."

Phillips never has been one to let poor health stop her. Norma Matkovich, the first vice president of the Seniors' Golden Years club, says it was hard to hear Phillips back when the group was first forming.

Phillips, who was the group's first president, would tell Matkovich what she wanted to say. Then the vice president would repeat it so everyone else could hear. "I was just her mouthpiece," Matkovich recalls.

Phillips' health has gotten so poor in recent years that she rarely visited her beloved senior center. Irven Rhodes, current president of the Seniors' Golden Years club, says many of the members don't know her. In time, probably not much time, she'll be mostly forgotten.

One way to prevent this would be to name the senior center after her. Four years ago when local seniors were surveyed about their preference for naming the place, "Mary Phillips Senior Center" finished runner up to "Old Town Temecula Senior Center."

While there is certainly nothing wrong with that choice, it's doubtful anyone wonders why the senior center was named that way. Name it after Mary Phillips and people will always wonder why. Then they'll get to get hear about the awesome willpower behind it. What an inspiration.

Link between what is, what used to be
Publication Date: February 8, 1997

Took a trip back in time this week, back to the way Temecula and Murrieta used to be.

The setting was actually a couple little towns in Tennessee, Celina and Hilham. The occasion was my father-in-law's funeral.

Gene Fiske, 78, was born and raised in Celina, a community of a couple thousand in the Tennessee hill country. It's two hours northeast of Nashville, just below the Kentucky border.

This is a town where the old courthouse is the center. Retired men sit in front of the place whittling on sticks and talking all day.

The pace was a lot like Temecula and Murrieta were not much more than a decade ago. Except our towns didn't have the traffic light. Hard to believe but true.

The Fiske family is legendary in those parts. The patriarch, Moses Fisk, (somebody threw an E on the name later), founded the first girls' school in the South there in 1806. A replica of his house is now a state monument. Celina is named after one of his descendants.

So it's big news when a Fiske passes on. Sort of like a Thompson, a Curran or a Rail dying in old Murrieta, or a Vail or a Roripaugh in Temecula. The Borels of French Valley come to mind as well.

Even though Gene Fiske hadn't lived in Celina since he went away to work on a newspaper in his early 20s, close to 75 folks showed for his memorial service. It seemed everyone there knew him as a kid. My wife Joanne, her brother Steve and I were the youngest people there by several decades.

The old-timers had lots of stories about growing up in a small town. How everybody rode horses because most folks couldn't afford cars. How they had dates at their parents' houses because there was nowhere else to go. And to think kids here have the nerve to complain about nothing to do.

After the memorial service we all piled in our cars for a funeral procession that was led by a sheriff's car. Another deputy - maybe the only other one in town on duty - stood at Celina's major intersection and held up traffic while we passed. It's hard to fathom the same thing happening at Rancho California and Ynez today.

I was driving right behind the hearse and after a few minutes it dawned on me that every car going in the other direction was pulling off the road and stopping until we passed. A moving sign of respect for someone's final journey.

Joanne's father was buried in the Fisk cemetery, about 10 acres off a gravel road in Hilham. This is a community with a gas station, a little market, a mechanic's shop and not much else.

A tent was put up at the grave site to protect us from a driving rain. The minister spoke a few words about the body being just a house and how Gene Fiske's spirit had moved on to another home. Beautiful.

As we prepared to leave I noticed a grove of barren trees on the next property. In the middle of the trees was a lone white horse staring hard at us. It was spooky, considering how much Gene Fiske loved to ride as a boy.

When I got back from Tennessee I shared these and other anecdotes with a trio of local old-timers, Arlean Garrison, Leverne Parker and Thelma Bronson.

They said funerals used to be handled that way when Temecula and Murrieta were hamlets, not the booming bedroom communities of today.

Bronson, whose maiden name is Buck, remembers that her grandfather in the 1920s and '30s had a horse-drawn hearse that was used for the funerals. They'd have processions through town as well, though the cars kept their distance from the horses so as not to spook them. Drivers coming in the other direction would pull off the road and turn off their engines because they made so much racket.

"They can't do it (a procession) very well here anymore because it would cause too many traffic jams," she said.

Garrison, a Murrietan for 57 years, said everybody used to turn out for the funeral of a local resident. It was tradition.

"Now we have funerals in town and we don't even know who the people are," she said. "It's sad."

It can happen in Temecula
Publication Date: April 12, 1997

It's a gorgeous cul-de-sac. The gigantic, two-story tract homes with front balconies look like palaces. The unobstructed views of the mountains wrapping around southeastern Temecula are inspiring. The perfectly green lawns are a slice of paradise. There probably isn't a weed on the entire street.

But there is something terribly wrong. Something so wrong that it's frightening.

Distinctive yellow crime scene tape is stretched across the street. Police officers keep outsiders away. Neighbors huddle in hushed groups on those manicured yards.

And 15-year-old Michael Brian Calkins lies in the garage of one of the two-story homes, killed by a self-inflicted rifle shot to his head late Tuesday afternoon.

His parents, Georgia and Bob Calkins, believe their son was copying the suicide of rock star Kurt Cobain, who killed himself three years ago the same day.

Suicides disturb like nothing else. But especially when it is a teenager taking his life in an immaculate house in suburbia.

It's real, though, as real as the view. It can happen here just like anywhere else. Palace or no palace, people have problems.

Even the professionals trained to handle these matters are numbed.

Temecula Police Chief Pete Labahn says some deputies at the scene had children of their own. "It has a profound effect on us as well. You're left feeling if that person had made it through one more day, just one more hour, he would have had another 60 years."

Tragically, young Calkins' decision is not that unusual. Mitchell Rosen, a local counselor and radio talk show host, calls suicide among kids an epidemic.

Rosen, who designed and implemented the Corona-Norco school district's suicide-prevention program, says kids today don't know how to deal with adversity.

They see their role models, parents, solve marital problems by getting a divorce. Or tackle other difficulties with pills. In the old days parents sucked it up and persevered. Now they want a quick fix, Rosen says.

Consequently, some kids today don't have the fortitude to survive the end of a romance, the poor grades, the teasing or the other difficulties they invariably face. They figure they can't go on, so they end it all.

Such a choice is unfathomable to common-sense people like Lori and Walter Kubacki. The retirees moved from Illinois in 1991 and you get the sense they're still trying to figure out this California place.

The Kubackis know all they want to know about teen suicides though. Ten years ago, a 16-year-old boy hung himself in their suburban Chicago neighborhood. Now a youngster kills himself just down the street in this Southwest Riverside County city.

The Kubackis think today's kids are under too much pressure. Sex. Drugs. Alcohol. Excelling in school. Trying to gear up for a work world that only seems to get more demanding.

"It's time we start thinking more about why these boys are under so much pressure," Lori says.

Then there are the parents, both of whom often have to work to pay for the big mortgage and all the other expenses they've taken on. Throw in the long commutes so many in the Temecula Valley endure and it's a wonder there's time for anything besides the job.

"It's tough to raise kids today," Lori says sympathetically.

It wasn't that way with the Kubackis. Lori stayed home and was there when their three boys got back from school. Whenever they came home with problems, she was there.

"These kids today come home to an empty house," she says.

Then Lori mentions her own 15-year-old granddaughter and it's obvious how much she means to her. "She still seems like a little girl to me. What could possibly be so wrong with their lives to do what they're doing?"

I talk to the Kubackis the morning after young Michael Calkins took his life. As I leave their beautiful neighborhood I notice a small piece of the yellow crime scene tape is still wrapped around their street sign. It looks like a yellow ribbon, like the ones made popular by the corny Tony Orlando song of so many years ago.

It was big when I was 15.

Clinton Keith road was named after whom?
Publication Date: May 6, 1997

Our story begins when Louise Kuzminski of Murrieta asks us to do a write-up on Clinton Keith, the guy with the local road named after him. With a new bridge on Clinton Keith about to open over Murrieta Creek and all the development happening off the road, she figures it's good timing.

I call Keith and we agree to meet at his home in Fontana. Then I ask someone in the newspaper's library to dig up information about him.

Imagine my surprise a few minutes later when the librarian calls back. Keith died in 1995.

Wow, this is some story.

His obituary says Keith worked for Riverside County for 47 years and was county road commissioner and surveyor when he retired in 1971. That's why the road was named after him.

The living Clinton Keith says he made his name by helping to start a treatment program for problem drinkers at Kaiser Steel in Fontana, where he used to work.

Years ago, Keith says, some guy claiming to be a Riverside County supervisor congratulated him at a Fontana parade for having the road named after him.

"It was news to me," Keith says of the surprising honor.

Keith had never heard of any other Clinton Keith, so he figured the road had to be his.

I talk to Kuzminski, our source for the story. She knows Clinton Keith from her nine years of work at the Fontana Federal Credit Union, where he is a member.

Kuzminski first noticed the road in Southwest Riverside County about 1990. She asked him and Keith verified it was named after him. Workers at the credit union like to good-naturedly tease him about the road.

"He's a nice elderly gentleman," Kuzminski says. "I'm sure he's the one it's named after. I don't think he'd make up any stories."

Mark Bernas, assistant county surveyor, confirms the road was named for Clinton Keith, the former county surveyor, on Dec. 28, 1971. It was previously known as Santa Rosa Ranch Road.

"It's interesting, because we've never even heard of that Clinton Keith," Bernas says of the living one.

Needless to say, I feel uncomfortable on my way up to see Keith. Talk about bursting someone's bubble.

Keith shuffles out to meet me. His hair is silver, he talks a little slow and he seems a little hard of hearing. He's 80 but, with a little chuckle, says he feels like 90.

He says he's overcome his own troubles with alcohol and he speaks proudly about the program he helped start in the 1960s at Kaiser with the union and company management.

Until the program began, workers with drinking problems were often dismissed. He says the program offered them treatment. Many jobs were saved as a result. Later, the program was expanded into the community to help drunk drinkers and others with alcohol-related offenses. A recovery home for alcoholics also was opened.

Keith talks movingly about how many people supported the cause. "One person can't take credit for it. There are so many people involved."

He's always figured Clinton Keith Road was named for him because of the program's success. Asked if he thought it was strange that a road in another county more than 50 miles from his home town would be named after him, Keith says, "It didn't make any difference to me."

Mr. Keith and I looked over the other Clinton Keith's obituary. The county added more than 3,000 miles of roads during his tenure. Adna Clinton "Bud" Keith also had a reputation for quietly and quickly taking care of business. It sounds like he too was a class act.

As I get ready to leave, Keith says of the other, "I hope I haven't disturbed his family."

I thank Keith for taking the time to clear up the confusion. "It's no problem," he says, smiling. "Time's one thing I have plenty of."

Heading back to the office, it strikes me that perhaps both Clinton Keiths deserve to have something named after them. Both did good things with their careers for others, something more of us should strive for. It seems a shame the other Clinton Keith doesn't have something to be remembered by.

And yes, I still feel badly for him. Some things are best left alone.

Daddy doesn't get last dance, but he gets 1ˢᵗ
Publication Date: June 3, 1997

It is 7-year-old Lily Rainey's first dance. And she couldn't have a better date.

Her happy daddy, Dick Rainey, says it's an honor to be the one.

More than 500 people are here at Murrieta Valley High School gym Saturday night for the big Father-Daughter Sock Hop put on by the local Girl Scouts. The daddies are doing the big hunk contest, the Macarena, the funky chicken and assorted other activities they wouldn't be caught dead doing anywhere else.

When it comes to their daughters though, anything is possible.

"They're daddy's little girl," says Bob Stuppy, father of two, Samantha and Emily. "There's not a whole lot they can do wrong."

Father-daughter relationships are one of those things words can't really describe. They're just there, as special as can be.

Moms/wives deserve lots of credit, though, too. And not just for biological reasons. This great event is organized by Marisa Stuppy, Kirsten Boyd, Karen Kerr and their families.

And as for you moms and sons out there, Marisa Stuppy cites the dance for them she went to at an elementary school a few years ago. Basically, the boys ended up on the playground while the moms sat around and chitchatted. Boys.

At the father-daughter deal, all the girls are dressed in poodle skirts and blouses while the dads are in white T-shirts and jeans with the bottoms rolled up.

Or at least 99 percent of them are. One clown is there in a Hawaiian shirt. We won't mention any names; let's just say he's the guy with the reporter's notebook.

What can I say? Even my 8-year-old daughter Julia noticed my one-of-a-kind status. "You didn't wear the uniform but you were a good dancer," she tells me after the dance.

Yes, this is one night where daddies can do no wrong. Not even the Big Hunk Contest that hopefully nobody got on videotape. Otherwise there are several hundred local dads hoping their buddies never get a copy.

Let's set the scene. The deejay asks the girls to make two lines while the so-called "hunks" form one big line. Next, the deejay cranks up some song with lyrics like, "you're too sexy," and asks the girls to squeal as loud as possible. Last, the dads are supposed to make like John Travolta in "Saturday Night Fever" and walk the down the middle of this screaming mob.

Rainey gulps just before he starts his strut down the aisle, thinking: "This is for my daughter."

I'll bet 90 percent of the dads there take part in this ritual, an amazing statistic when you consider male behavioral patterns. And now you know why little girls have their daddies wrapped around their finger.

The winners, by the way, receive candy bar titles such as Big Hunk, Mr. Good Bar, Sugar Daddy and Milk Dud. You can tell moms organized that contest.

The participation rate is just as high for other events. You know how it is when you go to most school dances and all the boys are standing around fidgeting, trying to work up the nerve to be rejected.

No problem this night. It's the dads for once who dance the night away, sliding their little girls through their legs, tossing them in the air or hoisting them up on their shoulders.

It's a slow dance though toward the end of the night that is - what else? - too precious for words. Here goes anyway.

Many of the girls barely make it up to their daddies' waists. The fathers have to stoop over to try and touch their daughters' heads.

Many of the couples move awkwardly, probably because people with such height differentials aren't made for slow dancing.

I notice my daughter has her head nestled securely into my Hawaiian shirt and I sense how much this means to her and to me. I think of the future, when she goes out on dates with boys and what that's going to be like for her and me. And what it will be like when I dance with her at her wedding.

I kiss the top of her head and comfort myself that I'll always be the one who took her to her first dance.

Kindergarten blues to part Dad, 'baby'
Publication Date: July 5, 1997

Monday mornings are always rough, but this one coming up is going to be a doozy.

On Monday, my last baby starts kindergarten.

Sure, 5-year-old son David isn't physically a baby anymore. But he is the youngest of our two children, so in some sense he'll always be a baby to his mother Joanne and me.

We're not alone in this sense of loss. Last month at David's final day of preschool, I was struck the number of parents who talked of how sad it was that their youngest kids, their "babies," were growing up. Kindergarten is a demarcation line in the aging process and when your youngest crosses it, a part of you seems to die.

"I try not to think about it," says one of those preschool parents, Marisa Stuppy. "This is a tough time. It really is."

Her youngest, Emily, starts kindergarten Monday too. And her oldest, Robert, begins middle school the same day. It wasn't easy last week at his last day of elementary school.

"We were crying and then we were laughing and then we were crying," she says of the emotional roller coaster.

Fortunately, my oldest child Julia only starts third grade Monday. I can only take so many of these life phases at once.

Laurie Verstegen has found herself following her prospective kindergartner Ivy around more lately, trying to read to her more, trying to play with her more, just trying to be with her more.

"I can barely say it without getting a lump in my throat," she says.

A lot of local parents are going through the same thing. In Temecula there are 1,042 kindergartners starting Monday. In Murrieta it's 740 and in Menifee it's 413. That's a lot of local trauma.

I didn't know what I was getting into when my daughter Julia started school three years ago. Unfortunately, now I know better. David's going to have a lot of other things vying for his attention now that he's in school, including his teacher, more friends and more things to do. Hanging out with dad is going to pale by comparison.

Theresa Ledley says her husband Ben is trying to find the positive side. With their youngest child Michelle venturing off to school, he figures it means they'll have more time for themselves.

Theresa doesn't sound as convinced though. "I feel sad because I love having them around," she says.

David and I have been around each other a lot as well. I've stayed home with him two mornings a week the past three years while his mother worked and his sister was in school. This wasn't always the easiest thing to do because of the demands of a full-time job, but I was fortunate to have a sympathetic boss.

Like Ben Ledley, a big part of me has looked forward to when David went off to school. It would make my life easier.

But now that our mornings together are ending I'm feeling different. We won't be going to the park as much, David and I. We won't be walking to Warm Springs Creek as often to see who can make the biggest splash with a rock. I won't be reading as many books to him because he'll be reading before I know it.

Maybe I'm being selfish though. Marisa Stuppy and Laurie Verstegen talk about how excited their daughters are about going to school. They've watched their brothers and sisters do it for five years and now, finally, it's their turn. Yippee!

David is excited as well. Every morning the past couple weeks we've reviewed how many days it is until kindergarten starts. It's just like the birthday and Christmas countdowns and we know how momentous those occasions are for kids.

David seems to have mixed feelings though. He's been more emotional lately and Joanne and I think maybe it's because of kindergarten. It's a big change for a little guy.

Then there was our final morning together. At one point I mentioned to David that this was it and he started crying. "I don't want this to be out last morning together," he said repeatedly through his tears. I started crying too and told him I felt the same way. We held each other as if we never wanted to let go.

Respecting one devoted to 'the cause'
Publication Date: July 19, 1997

This week's Murrieta City Council meeting was packed with important matters: whether two housing projects should proceed, what to do about a couple possible tax elections and who to appoint to a controversial citizens' committee.

Then there was "the cause."

It's Murrietan Michael Lee's proposal to disarm local police officers. That's not a misprint. Lee really wants Murrieta police officers to work without guns. Wants the same for Temecula as well.

Lee stands at the podium Tuesday night before a packed house and reads a speech he calls, "Peace."

"Peace is what every child is promised," he says. "Peace is the steady flow of wisdom and its tributaries. Peace is a dream."

Wow. Not your typical council meeting banter. The council members themselves look a little perplexed. Zone changes, contract awards, license agreements - those they can handle. But "peace," what do they do with that?

The council members dispatch the issue to their public safety commission, though Lee insists on a vote that night and that police officers presumably be disarmed ASAP.

I'd like to think we've all got a little of Michael Lee inside of us. I know I do. I have any number of causes I'd like to take up, chief among them the elimination of all TV. Think of what a better place the world would be if all that viewing time was put to more productive use.

Maybe your cause is the end of taxes. Or mandatory breast-feeding. Or the arming of everybody.

Whatever your dream, odds are you're not doing much to make it happen. Otherwise our local city council agendas would be overflowing with presentations such as Lee's.

He has been taking on causes for 20 years. He's 39, which means he grew up in the '60s. His dream was to go to UC Berkeley and protest the Vietnam War, but it ended before he could get there. Bummer.

Lee lives with his folks in the house he grew up in in Old Murrieta, makes a living in dry walling and carpentry, and looks like he stepped right out of his beloved '60s.

Lee is proud to call himself a hippy and his long hair is proof of it. His first cause was trying to protect the coastline, an issue he promoted with a surfing magazine he published about four months.

Over the years he's worked on such diverse issues as protecting the Santa Rosa Plateau from development, to legalizing marijuana, to pushing the Peace Corps, to abolishing the death penalty.

Lee got carried away one time. He was sentenced to three years' probation in 1996 for scuffling with the cops and making a threatening phone call about the death penalty to local Assemblyman Bruce Thompson's office.

Usually, he works more within the system. Lee has written more than a hundred letters to big-city mayors across the country regarding disarming local police. He's also made calls to the United Nations to take his cause globally. His main argument is the success of the unarmed police in England.

He's spoken before the Murrieta council a couple times and councilmen Warnie Enochs and Chuck Washington are well versed in his arguments.

Enochs says Lee means well; he's just not sure that what works in England will work in America. "If we took away all the guns from the crooks, then yeah, I'm all for it."

Washington also doesn't think it's very practical to disarm local officers. "On the other hand, I have a great deal of respect for Michael. That's how some of the great ideas started, when everybody else thought it was a nutty idea. We need people like that. That's what creativity is all about."

As natural as it seems for Lee to tackle causes, though, it's not. "I force myself to do this," he says. "I say (to myself), `If you want peace, you better work at it.'"

He's sympathetic to those who say they don't have time to take on their favorite issues. "I think people are too busy. They've got to make the thousand-dollar-a-month payment to the house." It can be a burden.

On my way out of Lee's home he hands me a handful of Peace Corps buttons to pass out. He makes sure I have phone numbers and addresses for Amnesty International and Greenpeace.

Just before I reach my car he calls, "Peace."

Peace.

Debating the dissent of man
Publication Date: August 5, 1997

David Micheal wants to make one thing clear before we start: He's for the mall and he's for growth.

If it sounds like he's worried, he is. He doesn't want fellow Temeculans to get the impression he's opposed to either. Anything but that.

All trepidation aside, Micheal is concerned about how the powers that be treat those who dare question what's happening in Temecula.

"We're a good town and we've got a lot of good people," he says. "The people are deserving of respect. Just because they ask questions and challenge, that's what democracy is supposed to be about."

Specifically, Micheal points to the recent political pummeling of Sam Pratt. He's the guy making such a ruckus asking council members to take another look at the mall's traffic plan before construction starts.

Micheal recently arranged a meeting between Pratt and Councilman Karel Lindemans to settle their differences. Unfortunately the peace-talks failed.

Pratt is now Public Enemy No. 1 among the Temecula elite and Micheal is concerned about the harsh tone of attacks on him.

"Do you want that to happen to you?" Micheal asks. "What's happening to Sam scares people off from getting involved."

Pratt has been savaged in letters to the editor and newspaper commentaries from city officials, including Councilman Jeff Stone. Lindemans expressed a desire to see "the end of Mr. Pratt," then apologized.

Despite their treatment of Pratt, Lindemans and Stone insist the city isn't trying to stifle dissent.

"I don't criticize Sam for bringing up issues he thinks need to be addressed," Stone said. "The problem with Sam is he meets with staff, then he completely disregards what he hears and goes about his own agenda again."

It sounds as if Lindemans is tired of hearing Pratt complain. Others seem to think Temecula is a fantastic place to live, he notes - the council must be doing something right.

Among those rallying to Pratt's defense are former TOTAL group colleagues and Murrieta Councilman Jack van Haaster.

Phil Hoxsey and Kay Cassaro - TOTAL members who led the opposition to Zev Buffman's entertainment center - say Temecula's pro-business forces are showing their true colors, black and blue, with their pounding of Pratt.

"It's almost like living in another country when you live in Temecula," Hoxsey insists. "If anybody gets in their way, they're going to intimidate them."

Adds van Haaster, about Pratt's predicament: "You don't attack somebody for merely exercising their rights within the system. He's not arming himself and trying to overthrow the government."

It's hard to argue with the way the powers that be have handled things so far in Temecula. The local electorate agrees, judging by how incumbent - and establishment-endorsed - Steve Ford annihilated Pratt in last year's council election.

But Pratt has hit on the Temecula elite's Achilles' heel, which is traffic. Maybe the developer has sufficiently addressed the mall's traffic needs, maybe he hasn't. Only time will tell.

But while the movers and shakers can't build the mall fast enough, two things will not change: Traffic is already Temecula's worst problem and the mall is going to produce a lot more.

Traffic is part of a bigger issue: growth. Temecula today is home to 42,000; but population projections for the future, including areas possibly to be annexed, are close to 200,000 people. Meanwile, Murrieta is having a civil war over its plans to expand to just 100,000. In Temecula it's full speed ahead.

Cassaro, Pratt's ally, says the Temecula establishment is portraying anybody who questions the growth as a fanatic. "If you use logic and common sense, rampant uncontrolled growth is not good for anyone. We're going to end up exactly like the places we moved from."

But those who jump in front of the growth train do so at their own risk.

89-year-old is keeping up the good fight
Publication Date: September 30, 1997

Jim McGowan is snoozing at his kitchen table when I arrive at his patio door.

He snaps to attention when I tap on the glass and guides me to the front door. He sits up in his chair, gives me a firm handshake, and wonders why I'd possibly want to write about him.

"Because I hear you're so interesting," I explain, noting that it's unusual for a white man to head up a chapter of the NAACP, which McGowan did until declining health forced him to give it up this year.

Local school board member Sonja Wilson, a charter member of the NAACP chapter, says he was the main organizer of the group in the mid-1970s. "He feels very badly about what happened to the black people in the South. He's very devout and very devoted."

Adds Loraine Watts, the black woman who succeeded McGowan as president of the NAACP: "He's one of a kind because of the obstacles he's overcome. He just keeps going."

His beliefs sure have been tested. The nearly 50-year local resident used to cause a stir by taking black friends to restaurants known to discourage such patrons. More dramatically, his local television repair business was burned down about 40 years ago by what he says were white supremacists.

"That's the risk of offending the ultra-reactionary society," he says.

McGowan has done a lot of offending in his 89 years. He was a Depression-era union organizer and his activities were mentioned in two books.

"Forged in Fury" author Michael Elkins says of McGowan and other farm worker organizers in the Central Valley in the '30s: "They were hounded and jailed by the police, beaten and tarred-and-feathered, and two of them lynched by vigilantes. The law in the valleys was the employers' law and none other."

McGowan gave up his union activities to help care for his wife, Ethel. They came to Lake Elsinore from Los Angeles after World War II because something about the area, perhaps the clean air, made her better.

He hardly modified his politics to suit his new surroundings. At the height of the Cold War he was considered ones of the town's most prominent communists. He was questioned by investigators of the House Committee on Un-American Activities, the group made famous - and infamous, too - for trying to ferret out communists.

"Am I a communist?" he says now, repeating the question. "It's hard to come up with an accurate label for me." (For what it's worth, he's registered to vote with the Peace and Freedom Party.)

What's more certain is his fading health. He relies on a walker to get around. He has a hard time hearing and gets dizzy often and his memory isn't what it used to be. He lives alone in a small hilltop home near downtown because Ethel is confined to a hospital.

"I'm getting ready to die," he says matter-of-factly. "I keep telling people I've already been to my funeral and nobody showed up."

He likes to joke about his age. He says it's his silver hair that makes him hard-of-hearing. When he can't recall something - it happens often now - he says he asks people for their phone numbers so he can call them at 2 in the morning when it comes to him.

McGowan is all business when conversation turns to union and political matters. "Labor is the only thing that creates value and wealth," he contends. "Capital doesn't create anything."

Not surprisingly, he doesn't think much of the incentives his city government has used to lure more commerce to town.

"They say we're running the government like a business," McGowan says, getting more and more animated as he talks politics. "They're not supposed to run a business. They're supposed to take the taxes and turn them into benefits for the citizens. It's the kind of sickness that pervades all levels of government."

McGowan has the passion for his beliefs you don't see much of today. He's not afraid to call 'em as he sees 'em, even if it concerns his mortality.

He gives me another firm handshake as I prepare to go. "When you write the piece, your editor will strike out most of it," he says.

He has the kind of modesty you don't see much of anymore either. Keep up the good fight.

CHAPTER 10

1998 - "Daddy, What is oral sex?"

Transition was the theme this year.

The Ortega park district, arguably the source of more controversy than any other public agency in the quarter century I've lived here, was winding down. Citizen activists and journalists throughout the area bemoaned its loss. Talk about an endless source of fun.

Tract homes moved into French Valley, turning yet another community into a slice of suburbia. And Temecula's first housing tract, Hill 27, turned 30 years old. Check out the area sometime, it shows how development has changed.

Meanwhile, construction on a mall in Temecula continued and Zev Buffman took his big plans to Murrieta. Lucky them.

Trend wise, it was the time of the Bill Clinton-Monica Lewinsky sex scandal and local kids were asking their parents way too many questions way too early about, well, you know what I mean.

Things were looking up in Murrieta and Lake Elsinore with finances rebounding and fewer residents plotting their departures. Like the Bill Clinton campaign once famously said, it's the economy, stupid!

Finally, I left the newspaper business full-time and started teaching third grade at Rail Ranch Elementary School in Murrieta. My column dropped from three a week to one.

Change is good.

Urbanization sprawls down country roads

Publication Date: January 6, 1998

It's the kind of sign seen at a lot of housing tracts around here: "Fresh Air - Great Country Living."

Too often such signs are plopped in the middle of a sea of tract houses, rendering such "country living" advertisements a bit of a stretch in many parts locally.

At the Forecast Homes in French Valley project, the sign is still legit. Though maybe not for long.

Yup, tract homes are being built in French Valley, a community heretofore known for pastoral living, not suburban sprawl.

But that's changing, as evidenced by this first housing tract near state Highway 79 North and Thompson Road, a couple miles north of the airport.

The state of Thompson Road is a perfect illustration of the transition French Valley is about to embark on. The stretch of road in front of the project is paved. The project has French Valley's first residential street lights, curbs, gutters and sidewalks, things city folk take for granted.

But Thompson Road past the project remains what it's always been. Dirt. Now that's country living.

Retiree Howard Cantrell, who will go down in history as the second person to buy a French Valley tract home, likes to take Thompson across the highway. He stays on the dirt road until it hits Los Alamos Road, which he follows to his bank in Murrieta.

It's a gorgeous country drive, even if it's a little rough in places, Cantrell says.

He and his wife Gertrude moved into their home in the middle of November. They have one of 14 houses on Van Eyck Court, the first block of homes built by Forecast.

The single-story houses look extremely out of place, considering the surrounding farmland. Not for long though, considering the developer has plans for 156 houses in the 40-acre project. Plus, Forecast district manager Jim Calvi says the company may buy another 40 acres to extend the project.

Just like that there could be more than 300 homes, close to another thousand people in French Valley.

And more are on the way. Local real estate company owner Ray Borel predicts there will be 4,500 homes built in the next 10 years. Along with that are another 800 acres of commercial and industrial land, including 650 such acres owned by the Borel family.

Yup, the Borels may be country folk - they've been here since 1886 - but they're no bumpkins. The family has a lot of land surrounding French Valley Airport.

Borel says change is coming to French Valley and it's coming fast. "I can feel it from the action we're getting from different clients."

Borel obviously stands to profit from all this development, but he's well aware that a lot of the current French Valley residents aren't as excited about it.

These are the people who bought five-acre parcels in recent years to escape the housing tracts. Now the subdivisions are nipping at their heals again. Expect to see a lot of conflict between these folks and the builders in the future.

Despite the opposition that's sure to arise, it seems inevitable that French Valley will be jammed with tract homes, strip malls and industrial parks before you know it.

And when it is, think back to the suburban pioneers, folks like the Cantrells and Roy and CarolDawn Flippen.

The Flippins talk about what it was like back in the beginning, when they called the utility companies to hook up and heard "What tract homes? Not in French Valley."

The utilities have caught up with the times, but other conveniences haven't. It's still a toll call to Temecula, they still can't get newspaper delivery, it's still six miles to the nearest grocery store, and it's still three miles to get gas.

If all of this development seems a little surreal - can the Golden Arches in French Valley be far behind? - consider what Roy Flippen has to say about what it used to be like driving on Murrieta Hot Springs Road.

He came to Lake Elsinore about 15 years ago and he remembers coming to Murrieta when it was all open country. Now look at it.

It's coming, French Valley, and it's coming fast.

LOCAL VIEW a New Path Changing careers at 39 means focusing on the positive aspects of a new life while overcoming the many nagging reasons to resist change.

Publication Date: January 11, 1998

When I was asked to write about what it's like going through a career change, I was stumped.

I don't think of it that way, even though I'm about to go from covering City Council meetings to teaching third graders.

A few people think I'm nuts to do it. I've got a wife who works part-time, two small kids and a big mortgage. I'm four months from my 40th birthday and I'm supposed to be entrenched on the career track, not jumping off it.

Then there's my job, writing a newspaper column about Southwest Riverside County three times a week. Folks tell me it's a dream job. I get paid to spout off on whatever I want and I get my picture in the newspaper. What more could a guy want from life?

Don't think there haven't been times I haven't asked the same question in the nine months I've worked on a career change. After all, I don't just like to write, I love to write.

Funny thing though, I haven't asked myself that question recently, not even after the trauma of substitute teaching for the first time. More than anything else, that tells me I'm doing the right thing.

Maybe it's because life for me has always been an adventure. I've been in need of a new one for a while and switching careers is the ultimate one.

For one thing, it means learning a whole new way of doing things. Sure it's hard, scary and time-consuming, but it's also really exciting.

Perhaps it was because I was too busy having a good time in high school and college, but I never fully appreciated the joy of acquiring an education. Now that I've been out in the "real world" - whatever that's supposed to mean - for 17 years, I've found I really love to learn.

Then there is the idealistic nature of the field I'm entering, teaching.

My wife Joanne, also a former journalist, has taught English to immigrants for the past six years. She raves about the rewards, which have nothing to do with money and everything to do with helping people.

One reason journalism has always appealed to me - and still does - is the sense that I'm making the world a better place. Whether it's exposing corruption or telling the story of someone in need, there's a feeling I'm contributing something worthwhile.

Counting my high school and college newspaper days, I'm now closing in on 23 years of bylines. As much as I still enjoy journalism, there's a profound sense of, been there, done that.

Now what?

I've thought about being a teacher for a long time. I remember sitting in a UC Riverside teacher orientation about nine years ago. Just after that I got my first column writing job, something I'd always dreamed of. Teaching was put on hold.

About five years ago I went to another teacher orientation at Cal State San Marcos. The job prospects seemed awfully slim at the time and I didn't pursue it any further.

Three things since then changed my mind: Volunteering in a classroom, class-size reduction, and the death of my mom.

Every able-bodied person should volunteer in a classroom. I started by helping out once a week with my daughter Julia's kindergarten class three years ago and saw how great it can be working with kids.

For starters, there are the hugs you get, something bosses don't exactly dispense on a regular basis. The positive feedback is unreal.

Most importantly, there's the sense that you're right there in the trenches, making the world a better place. Granted, it's backbreaking work, but it's all worthwhile because of what you're working toward. Plugging away for a business motivated by profits just can't compare for me.

Ironically, I filled in as a classroom aide for about six months right out of college. Although I enjoyed it, I was doing it to make ends meet. Helping people didn't matter as much to me then. Now that I'm 39, not 22, I value things differently.

With this mindset, class-size reduction in the elementary grades of California was like manna from heaven for me. It's created a huge demand for teachers.

Classes I take two nights a week at Chapman University are packed with real estate agents, business owners, nurses, cops, homemakers, you name it. All people who've thought about teaching over the years because they wanted to do something more meaningful. All of a sudden, look at the opportunities.

My mom's death in September of 1996 from cancer made me really assess what I was doing with my life. Lying on a parent's death bed will do that to a person.

I wondered what it will be like for me. Will I be satisfied with what I did with my life? Did I try everything I wanted to try?

I started studying to be a teacher last spring; still not sure I was doing the right thing.

Now I realize that I have been consumed. I want to help kids learn. I want to educate myself. I want the adventure. None of this would be happening were I still writing for a living.

As for the obstacles presented by a career change, I don't have time. The pay cut, the prospects of starting on the bottom rung of a new career ladder, the responsibility of providing for a family, the fear of trading something I love to do for something I'm still learning how to do . . . .

Yes, there's no shortage of reasons not to change careers.

But because I'm not thinking of it in those terms, I'm not looking back. It's full-speed ahead, the way life should be.

Longest night is when kids sleep over
Publication Date: May 5, 1998

The guests are due at 6 p.m. but this is one time where nobody is fashionably late. By 6:01 p.m. everybody is assembled, the "drinks" are flowing and the "appetizers" are going fast.

It's a kids' slumber party, an annual tradition for my daughter Julia's birthday. Such a bash means the drinks are juice and the appetizers are candy.

Once a year we take one of the most popular kid activities, spending the night, and go berserk. We borrowed the idea from another Murrieta mom who several years ago let 10 girls spend the night, including Julia. It's also the last time the mom hosted a slumber birthday party. She's still in recovery.

Spending the night is one of those rites of passage - kids' first chance to venture out on their own. It's amazingly popular, something the third-graders I teach talk about constantly. Who's sleeping with whom is as much a source of gossip for little kids as it is for adults. Their gossip is just more innocent.

Kid sleepovers present scheduling nightmares for parents. If one of your kids has a friend spending the night and the other doesn't, look out. The left-out sibling is liable to be on the phone endlessly, trying to set up their own rendezvous. Failing that, the odd child out insists on playing with the would-be slumberers, leaving the parents to constantly break up fights. Oh, what fun.

There can be one advantage for parents: If your kids are spending the night elsewhere, you're spending the night alone. It amounts to free baby-sitting.

Thus, on Friday night, the three girls arrive at precisely the appointed hour. Of course, this is nothing compared to three years ago, when we had seven girls over. It's amazing there wasn't an accident in front of our house, so anxious were parents to race off and ditch kids.

This year, it is three minutes before we encounter our first life-threatening situation. Trying to avert fights, we have invited a friend, Nathaniel VandenBerg, to hang out with our 5-year-old son, David, for a few hours.

This seems like a good idea, until Nathaniel lodges his arm in a hollow Lego table leg and can't get it off. His arm is solidly encased in what amounts to a cast from shoulder to wrist. That anxious look on Nathaniel's face tells me he wonders if it is ever coming off. With thoughts racing through my head of trying to comfort his parents as surgeons amputate his arm, I pull hard on the "cast." Fortunately, it comes off. The party is salvaged.

After a pizza dinner, my wife, Joanne, and I toss out two big bags of candy. The six kids practically maul each other. Hoping to quell the disturbance, we serve cake and ice cream, prompting the little darlings to plant candies in the dessert instead of putting them away. A fully involved sugar inferno is now roaring out of control, and it's only 8:15 p.m.

It's going to be a long night.

Take two: It's 3:30 a.m. and I'm awakened by the theme song from "Grease" going full blast on the stereo. This is the 95th time I've heard it in the past eight hours, meaning I'm about to go nuts if I haven't already. In that time span, the kids have had a talent show, watched two videos, eaten a mountain of junk food, sung the "Titanic" theme song too many times and literally danced the night away.

Now it's 5:45 a.m. and our two dogs are barking for a walk. The living room where the four girls are sleeping looks like a war zone, with clothes, blankets, toys and sleeping bags strewn everywhere.

Guess who gets to clean it up?

The girls wake up at 8:45 a.m. and immediately go through a dozen donuts in a matter of seconds. Their sugar tanks full again, they begin to talk most proudly of the night's stellar accomplishment - staying up until 4:50 a.m.

When it is time for pickup, the first parent to arrive is former Murrieta City Manager Steve Harding to pick up daughter Sarah. "What?" he exclaims upon hearing her bedtime.

"But I slept in," she assures him.

David VandenBerg rescues daughter Virginia. The elder VandenBerg wonders if the kids were up until midnight, implying that would be a reasonable bedtime. Maybe at your house.

The last one to go, at 1 p.m., is Danielle Honda. Just before she leaves, David says, "That'd be cool if Danielle spent a month with us."

She and her cohorts just did.

Dreading this question from children

Publication Date: September 22, 1998

"Daddy, what's oral sex?"

My 9-year-old daughter Julia is asking the question. My mistake was turning on a radio talk show as a broadcaster is going off on our president's sexual appetites.

While I scramble for an answer - the birds and the bees I can handle; Lewinsky and Clinton I can't - my 6-year-old son David pipes up with a question about his soccer team.

Grateful for the diversion, I ramble on way too long about the virtues of the sporting life. By the time I'm finished, Julia's forgotten her question.

But the predicament is one local parents dread. To all the experts who advise moms and dads to talk openly and honestly to their kids about the president's affair, we've got one thing to say: "It's easy for you to say."

I can't find any parent who is eager to talk to their kids about the Clinton matter. Most parents I talk to are doing everything they can to divert their children from the news.

Scarlett Duffy of Murrieta doesn't turn on the news now until her kids are safely in bed. She wants visions of sugarplums dancing in their heads, not kinky sex.

Duffy says her children - Jordan, 8, Katie, 6, and Taylor, 5 - are interested in the scandal. But so far they've kept questions to relatively tame matters such as: "Why does the president have a girlfriend if he's married?" Morality is one thing; oral sex is another.

"I'd have fallen off my chair if I'd had to explain that one," Duffy says of my daughter's question.

Here's an example of the lengths parents go to now just to discuss politics. Duffy is talking to her kids at a Murrieta park when I ask if she'd like to be interviewed about the controversy. Sure, she says, but let me get my kids out of here. One of her daughters tries to hang around - have you noticed how some kids' ears perk up when grownups are talking politics now? - and Duffy has to firmly tell her to go play.

What's the world coming to when a child would rather eavesdrop on a political discussion than run around on a playground?

Sharing current events with classmates is another matter that's become delicate. Kate Carr says the teacher of her 8-year-old son Jake asks that parents screen the articles the children are cutting out of newspapers and bringing to school. Otherwise, look out!

But it's not just Clinton's sex life that's inappropriate for kids. Janice Fujii of Temecula - who feels fortunate her 9-year-old daughter Cindy hasn't asked much about the president's mess - says violence is another thing that dominates the news.

"How many mothers kill their children, and it's all over the place," she says. "How do you explain that to your child?"

As troubling as the news can be, one parent can still find humor in it.

Laurie Sims says her fourth-grader Dylan is so busy with school and football that he doesn't have time to watch the news. As for the cartoons he catches in the little free time he has, those shows aren't interrupted with the latest bulletins from Washington, Sims notes with a smile.

Lorraine Martin is the only parent I found who routinely lets her kid watch the news with her. "I'm not a censor mom," she says.

So far, daughter Ashley's questions have been limited to political and moral questions. Nothing yet about the stuff that's prompted newspapers to run advisories warning that articles about sex acts may offend some readers. Who needs pornography when you've got the Starr report?

Like many adults, Ashley, a fifth-grader, is sick of the controversy. Martin reports: "Now, whenever Ashley sees Monica on TV, she says, `Not her again.'"

As further evidence of how disturbing this issue is, the only child I'm comfortable discussing it with is my own. I might come across as a sicko if I started asking anybody else's kid about it.

My daughter Julia says that unlike the adults she is around - hmmmmm, who could that be? - she and her friends don't ever talk about Clinton's mess. "I'm not that interested in it because they keep saying the same thing over and over," she says.

If nothing else comes of my interviews with parents, one local wag gave me a comical response for the next time Julia asks about oral sex: "It's when a man says to a woman, `I love you.'"

Still living good life on Hill 27
Publication Date: October 20, 1998

It's the fall of 1968. The Vietnam War is a living nightmare. Richard Nixon is about to be elected president. The Beatles are still together.

And people are moving into Temecula's first housing tract.

While everything else has changed so dramatically, Hill 27 basically remains what it was three decades ago - a quiet residential neighborhood.

It's named for the first 27 houses built on a hill off Rancho Vista Road just east of Ynez. There are 36 homes now, but nobody's bothered to change the name. Why mess with perfection?

Hill 27 is like no other Temecula housing tract. The trees are so big they produce the closest thing to a forest in Temecula. You can actually hear the green giants sway in the afternoon breeze.

And it is remarkably quiet, considering the place is now surrounded by a thriving city. Traffic is kept to a minimum because there are no through streets. Quite a concept in modern-day Temecula, land of gridlock.

Hill 27 also possesses a certain quaintness not found elsewhere. Old-fashioned wooden mail boxes line the streets, not today's metal contraptions. Houses are spaced far apart, not shoulder to shoulder like they are now. On Camino del Sol, the neighborhood's main drag, three benches offer convenient places for people to sit and visit. That's something the busy go-getters of the modern tracts don't do enough of.

Hill 27 is also stable. Of its original 27 homeowners, six remain. Quite a statement for a transient society. I don't see one for-sale sign while I'm there.

"We love it here," notes one of the old-timers, Steve Struikmans. "That's why we never moved."

Struikmans is a familiar name to many. He heads up Rancho Community Church, a congregation of more than 1,400.

The hill has other movers and shakers. Temecula City Councilman Karel Lindemans has been there since 1983. Vic Saraydarian, a local judge for years and now headed for Blythe, has a place. Jack Liefer, a school board member before local trustee legend Joan Sparkman, has lived on the hill 30 years. Nathaline Liefer's maiden name is Nicolas and her family has been here since the 1880s. Yes, that's where the Temecula elementary school got its name.

There's a sense of community involvement on the hill that has been around since the first home went up. Liefer, Struikmans, Don Jacoby and the Diaz brothers - the latter the guys who built the Hill 27 homes for workers in their aircraft manufacturing plant (also the guys with the local road named after them) - helped organize the first volunteer fire department.

At the time, Temecula had fewer than 300 people. Old Town was simply "town." You had to go Fallbrook for fast-food. Hemet, Sun City and Fallbrook offered the closest supermarkets. Rancho Vista, now a busy street, dead-ended just past the hill.

"Amazing," I blurt out when another hill original, Bill Wolter Sr., relays the last detail.

"It wasn't amazing, it was neat," Wolter corrects.

So you can understand why some hill residents long for the past. The Temecula they knew was a place where you literally knew everybody. Traffic didn't exist, and peace and quiet were everywhere, not just on Hill 27.

Most are careful to say they still like Temecula; it's just different now.

Struikmans best reflects the mixed sentiments. His church was started in 1968 with just seven families. Now look at it. He's glad Temecula is closing in on 50,000 people because "it gives me an opportunity to share Christ with more people."

But he also clearly enjoys telling stories about how wonderful the town was 30 years ago. "I wouldn't trade those years for anything," he says wistfully.

Says Diana Wolter, "Now we have the inconvenience of the traffic, but the convenience of the stores."

So at times it may still take you 15 to 20 minutes to get to a fast-food restaurant, but at least now you're going only a couple miles instead of to Fallbrook.

But one long-time hill resident, Leena Seeman, doesn't mince words about Temecula then and now. "I hate all the changes," says Seeman, who has taught school locally for 26 years. "The traffic is just horrendous."

Seeman moved to the hill in 1972. At that time, she'd look off her back patio and see four rooftops. Now she sees a mass.

Still, Seeman isn't about to move. She loves her job, her home, the local climate. The only place that meets that criteria is Hill 27.

Others aren't moving, either. The Wolters took refuge on the hill from the San Fernando Valley 30 years ago and raised seven kids there. You had to go Lake Elsinore to find a high school because Temecula didn't have one then, let alone two.

Their children are grown now, but six have settled in Southwest Riverside County. Diana Wolter says she can't see going anywhere. "Where else you going to live? I wouldn't move back to the city if you paid me."

"Di, the city has come to us," her husband notes wryly.

In the end, there is no denying it. Liefer, who's lived in Temecula since 1943, figured the area would someday be as big as it is now. He just never imagined he'd live to see it. It seemed so far in the future when a town was just a couple hundred people.

A sign on Rancho Vista identifying Hill 27 also calls it a "country community." It's true, too, even now. Liefer likens the small neighborhood to an island of tranquility. It's definitely surrounded by a sea of humanity.

A temple's tale presents cause to celebrate
Publication Date: December 8, 1998

Today the former Murrieta Hot Springs resort is a Christian conference center. Yet in its heyday as a resort, the development played a role in creating the area's largest Jewish synagogue.

Jewish people such as Celia Stern Silverstone loved its extravagant meals, soothing hot waters and quaint country lifestyle - not to mention the big-name entertainers it drew such as Merv Griffin, Paul Lynde and Kay Ballard.

Silverstone, who lived in the Los Angeles area and started coming to the resort in 1950, couldn't believe it when she saw homes arrive nearby some 30 years ago. "That's for me," she exclaimed.

Jewish people by the hundreds joined her, moving to the mobile home parks sprouting in the hills behind the resort. A quarter century ago the newcomers organized Congregation B'nai Chaim. Their history is being celebrated with a gala dinner Saturday night.

The congregation began modestly enough, meeting in a mobile home park's clubhouse. By the early 1980s worshippers such as Al and Rose Ginsberg realized they needed something more.

"They were the ones who said, `It's time we built a house of our own,'" recalls longtime congregation member Louis Ross.

Seven co-founders, including David Davis, each donated $10,000 to build a temple. Others pitched in by raising money. "We begged, we pleaded," Davis remembers.

In 1985 some 100 people joined in a rare procession to take their congregation's Torah - sacred parchment scrolls - to their new home.

The excitement of that time will be renewed Saturday at the bar mitzvah commemorating the 13th anniversary of the move to the temple at Murrieta Hot Springs Road and Via Princesa. Tickets are $25 and the public is welcome.

Bar mitzvahs traditionally honor Jewish boys turning 13, the age of religious responsibility. Bat mitzvahs are celebrated for girls.

There was a time when bar mitzvahs were few and far between for B'nai Chaim members. As congregation president Fran Rifkin notes, "They literally built the building with no intention of young people coming here."

Then came the late 1980s. Thousands of homes sprouted in Murrieta almost overnight. Residents of all faiths moved into the Murrieta Hot Springs mobile home parks as well.

Meanwhile, the grand resort that first lured the Jews to the area fell into disrepair. A series of ownership changes left the property in the hands of Calvary Chapel, which uses it as a conference center.

Bernie Rocco estimates the mobile home parks were about 95 percent Jewish occupied when he moved in about 15 years ago.

Today, of the thousands of homes there, probably less than 40 percent are inhabited by Jews.

By necessity, B'nai Chaim's congregation has changed. The temple was built without classrooms, so Louis Ross bought two portable buildings that are now a Hebrew school for about 50 children. And only about 115 of the congregation's 250 members live in the Murrieta Hot Springs mobile home parks.

The changing congregation needs look no further than Lake Elsinore to see what can happen to a group that can't attract younger members.

More than 1,000 Jews settled in Lake Elsinore after World War II, accounting for more than a fifth of the city's population. Tragically, 20 years later, the Hebrew Congregation's synagogue at Main and Limited streets was destroyed by arson.

The incident heralded the decline of Lake Elsinore's Jewish community. Most moved away. Others now rest in western Riverside County's only Jewish cemetery. By 1989 Congregation Beth Isaac consisted of 14 elderly people and was disbanded.

Congregation B'nai Chaim's members feel fortunate they've not experienced anti-Semitism. B'nai Chaim's members have taken part in four of the Thanksgiving worship services for several faiths held in Murrieta. Three were held in the temple.

Members of B'nai Chaim, now the area's largest Jewish synagogue, hope their congregation will thrive for another 25 years. Here's hoping they're right, for religious diversity in our valley is a wonderful thing.

CHAPTER 11

1999 - The mall moves in, we move out

The big story is one that continues to impact us forever more (drum roll please): The opening of The Promenade mall in Temecula.

The development marked a tipping point. Locals now could do their shopping here rather than taking their money to Riverside or Escondido. It also meant the community's transformation to suburbia was complete. Housing tracts, strip centers, a mall -- now we're just like so many other Southern California communities.

Also in Temecula, comedian/ City Councilman Karel Lindemans sadly ended his memorable run. Council meetings haven't been the same since. Sam Pratt, driven to fix Temecula's traffic woes, joined the group. Given that the mall and all of its congestion emerged the same year, his timing couldn't have been worse. Or was it better?

It was also the year my family was moving on up, from a one story home to a two-story place. We weren't alone; lots of locals were doing the same as the area's first wave of newcomers from the late 1980s shifted to bigger quarters to accommodate their growing families.

Finally, there was one of my favorite local stories ever, the Temecula saloon that morphed into a church on Sundays. I don't make 'em up.

A real loss for Temecula's art community
Publication Date: January 26, 1999

A local doctor comes up to Randy Holland during an intermission at one of the concerts at the Temecula Art Gallery.

"God, this is a great place you have here," the doctor tells Holland, the gallery's proprietor. "What a wonderful hobby."

"This isn't a hobby," Randy says. "I'm trying to make a living."

Make that "tried to make a living."

On Sunday, Holland will close the place. When it comes to business, bottom line rules. Holland crunched the numbers last week and realized he couldn't put off any more what he'd talked about with friends for months - he couldn't afford the upstairs gallery he's had on Main Street in Old Town since September 1995.

"I sat up here for a while and cried," Holland says of the moment. "Dreamers take this stuff really hard."

He's not the only one.

Murrieta painter Theresa Bell is one of numerous local artists who've profited from finally having a classy place in the area to display their talents. "We're losing THE gallery. I don't know what Plan B is for a local artist."

Barbara McLean, a board member of the Arts Council of the Temecula Valley, says the gallery has been a cultural mecca for visual and performing arts.

She says Holland supported a long list of local art projects. "He didn't put himself first. If he had done what a lot of people did and put himself first, he might still be in business."

Unfortunately, community support for Holland has run hot and cold.

The way local residents stepped forward to help while he battled tonsil cancer 18 months ago is one of the most touching stories I've covered.

People were so concerned about his business that volunteers operated it for two months while he was in the hospital. Almost $8,000 was raised at local fund-raisers to help pay Holland's medical bills.

Although the inoperable cancer didn't kill Holland like he once thought it would, it eventually killed his business.

Sales dropped by 50 percent while volunteers ran the gallery. It certainly wasn't anyone's fault. Holland is forever grateful for what his friends did just to keep the place going.

But the bottom line - there it is again - is that the salesman, the gregarious Holland, wasn't there to pitch the product. A good business person knows that just keeping the doors open isn't enough. Good intentions only go so far.

Holland returned to work on a part-time basis a year ago. I say part-time because he was working 70 to 80 hours a week before he was sick. He could only put in about 40 hours a week on his return.

The next blow came in July when entertainment director Rob Anderson - who worked for free - got a big promotion at his real job, Caltrans, and had to relocate to San Francisco.

With his tireless promotions for the gallery, Anderson made the weekend music program the hit that it was. But when he left, it was left to the weary Holland to run both the art and the music.

He knew the end was near last month when he hosted a concert for Laurence Juber, noted guitarist for Paul McCartney's band "Wings" in the '70s and '80s. Holland sent out more than 2,000 invitations, got plenty of local press in advance of the event and 19 people showed up. A guy can't cover more than $3,000 of monthly business expenses on that support.

What's happening to THE local gallery also says something about what's happening to us as a community and Old Town as a business district.

Holland says he's heard the greatest things from folks about how great it is to finally have a real art gallery in our area. Everybody was always promising to come down and decorate their new homes with original art, but it was mostly just talk.

Holland also has doubts about the future of Old Town, no matter how great the place looks after last summer's $5.3 million facelift. While people love to hang out in the new Old Town now, they're still not buying. And wait until the new mall opens next fall.

There is some good news in all this. Holland can afford to stick around, in part because he gets free rent from the Fallbrook apartments he manages. He's representing many local artists, he can type 120 words a minute and he knows computers. A guy who beat cancer and was a pit boss in Vegas will survive. As for the local art scene, that's another matter.

To grasp cities' road squabble, put it in reverse
Publication Date: February 2, 1999

Today Temecula and Murrieta officials argue about how to pay to improve the roads that connect the two cities.

Ten years ago they debated something more fundamental - whether they should be one city or two.

Imagine how different things would be today if they had settled their differences and agreed to the idea of one city.

There wouldn't be any squabbling about fixing the roads. The mall might be under construction at a more logical location, between Interstates 215 and 15, instead of at Winchester and Ynez roads in Temecula, where traffic could be a nightmare.

By the same token, one town's identity, probably Murrieta's, would be gone. As for a name for one unified city, how about "Murriecula" or "Temietta"? If that's unsettling, how about a developer's moniker, "Rancho California"?

Yes, it was clear history was going to be made when folks from the two communities gathered in Riverside in early 1989 to settle their differences before Riverside County officials.

The Temecula cityhood group, led by local businessman Jimmy Moore, was pitching a united city that would have sprawled from the Pechanga Indian Reservation on the south to Wildomar in the north.

The Murrieta group, led by John McElroy, John Reidy and Tex McAlister, preferred to have its own city. Temeculans could go their own separate way, as far as the Murrietans were concerned.

After passionate arguments from both sides, the county officials cut down the Temecula proposal, basically paving the way for two cities.

Temecula residents said yes to their 26-square-mile city later that year; Murrietans OK'd their 25-square-mile city the following year.

Looking back on those momentous times of 10 years ago, Temecula City Councilman Karel Lindemans can't help but wonder what might have been.

Lindemans, the only current councilman in either city to play a major role in the dispute, says he tried to bring the two feuding sides together.

One of those attempted peace talks ended with combatants from both sides on the verge of exchanging more than words. That pretty much severed any chance of getting together.

Moore, the Temecula leader, lives in Maryland with his wife Peg who served on the first Temecula council. He concedes the Temeculans were naive about the historical tensions some longtime Murrietans had toward their neighbor.

"Had we been a little smarter and maybe tried to include those Murrieta people more in the beginning," things might have turned out differently, Moore says.

McAlister, one of three Murrietans who launched the rival city-hood group, says it's possible the two sides could have found common ground if the Temeculans had been more neighborly about it.

But McAlister and Reidy, who was vice president of the Murrieta incorporation group, are happy with how things turned out.

Murrietans say the two towns simply do things differently, noting how their city has its own police and fire departments while the neighboring community contracts with the county for such services.

Moore still isn't convinced one city wasn't the way to go. "The people of Temecula live better because of the split," he says. "I think the people of Murrieta got the short end."

Financially they have. Temecula is far wealthier due to the car dealers, shopping centers and industrial parks there. Murrieta incorporated with the idea it would get the mall to pay for more public services. Oh well.

George Campos has an interesting perspective on this tale of two cities, considering he was part of the Temecula cityhood group, but now lives in Murrieta.

His choice of home towns isn't by happenstance either. Citing Temecula's traffic, Campos says he couldn't live there now. "If I want to live in my car, I'll go back to Orange County."

Campos, who's been in commercial real estate 18 years, says the two cities have to come up with a joint solution to the congestion. "How the traffic goes, so goes the economy of the whole area."

Lindemans and Murrieta Mayor Chuck Washington talk about working together to solve the traffic problem. One can't help but think it would be easier if the two sides had found common ground 10 years ago.

Saturday's saloon is Sunday's church
Publication Date: May 25, 1999

High on the wall hangs a portrait - a buxom blonde leaning out of a window with the kind of come-hither look that drives most men crazy - representing the epitome of sin.

Standing under this temptation, Derek Thomas sings the praises of something even more intoxicating for him: "Lord, I lift your name on high. Lord, I love to sing your praises. I'm so glad you're in my life."

The odd scene - sin and salvation in the same space - occurs Sunday mornings when God's Country worships at Temecula Stampede in Old Town. The church began meeting in the saloon Easter Sunday.

Saturday nights the Stampede is jumping with music, liquor, dancing and all kinds of devious thoughts. Sunday mornings, almost miraculously, the place is awash in religious songs, Christian banners and morality.

Well, almost. For all their work to transform the place from bar to church, co-pastors Thomas and Steve Richard can't totally cleanse the place.

Ads for Jack Daniel's, Budweiser and Skoal compete with the pastors for the worshippers' attention. Although they're turned off, the neon signs for Corona and Bud Lite beers are still hard to miss. Then there's that portrait of the fetching blonde.

The pastors generally show up about 9 a.m. Sunday mornings to set up for their church service, even as workers from the Stampede continue the clean-up from the night before.

"It's a changing of the guard, that's for sure," Thomas notes.

Clearly, one has to have some irreverence to preach in such a place. Richard and Thomas both can see the humor and irony in their choice of worship.

The surprised response Thomas gets when people hear where he preaches has him thinking of a new message for the church: "`YOU MEET WHERE????' That could be our slogan," he jokes.

Just before the 10:30 a.m. service starts, Richard asks me, "Would you like some lemonade or coffee? The bar's open." I ask - just out of curiosity, of course - if I could have a beer.

"That bar's not open," Bob Hemme notes. This church hasn't applied for a liquor license.

There is some method to the church organizers' madness. If one of the goals of religion is to show people the sins of their ways, what better place to start than in a bar?

Thomas, who's been in Temecula since 1979, has long thought the Stampede would be a wonderful place to worship in. Its huge wooden dance floor has plenty of room for the worshippers' folding chairs. When the morning sun pours through the skylights in the ceiling above the floor, it makes the setting look almost angelic. (Emphasis on almost.) Finally, where you going to find a better sound system than the cavernous Stampede? You just might be able to sing to the heavens.

"We wanted a place where we could meet the people and maybe reach a segment of the town that other churches don't get to," Thomas notes. He found it.

There are parallels between the two extremes, considering that folks attracted to both the bar and the church lifestyles are searching for something. Just not the same thing.

There is even historical precedence for God's Country. Richard says the westward expansion of the 1800s meant that ministers had to move out of the established churches of the East to find new converts. It wasn't unusual for traveling ministers to preach in bars in the tiny Wild West towns that sprang up back then.

These modern-day Wild West pastors are confident they'll find similar success. The church attracted about 50 people Easter Sunday, though there were only 14 people the day I attended.

"We feel we've had a good response already," Richard notes. He knows something about opening a church. In the Seattle area, he began one with six people. He and his wife, Patti, and their family came to Temecula last fall. This is the first ministerial experience for Thomas, a local CPA.

Passers-by such as Linda Wilson can't help but stop for a peek inside a bar with church songs pouring forth. She sees a certain logic to the setting. "It's only a building. God can be anywhere. With all the sinning that goes on Saturday night, maybe they're cleansing it Sunday morning."

I don't know whether to say "Amen" or "I'll drink to that."

Graduate class size reflects march of time
Publication Date: June 15, 1999

The parade started Friday night with 513 graduates finishing up their careers at Murrieta Valley High School. By the end of the month, more than 2,000 diplomas will have been passed out to graduates in the Lake Elsinore, Temecula and Murrieta school districts.

Lilah Knight remembers a time when those three communities produced a graduating class of about 30. It wasn't that long ago either.

She's a proud member of the Elsinore High School Class of '45, a group that included kids from Temecula, Murrieta, Wildomar and Alberhill.

It's hardly news that the growth of the past 15 years has brought a lot of change to our area. We've all seen the stats about the houses, shopping centers and traffic added in that time.

A less publicized figure is the high school graduation numbers. Up until 1985, there was still just one high school, Elsinore, doling out diplomas to the kids of the five communities mentioned previously.

Temecula opened its first high school that year. Three other high schools - Murrieta, Temescal and Chaparral - have opened since then. Two more high schools from Temecula and Murrieta are planned. Within 20 years, the area will have gone from one comprehensive high school to seven.

Knight and the other old-timer graduates I talked to - Leverne Parker of Temecula, Hugh Walker of Lake Elsinore, and Lucy Dunham of Murrieta - talk about how great it was to know kids from all over the valley. It's doubtful today's grads know of many kids outside of their own schools, even towns.

"It was just one big happy family," Knight says of going to high school in the '40s. "It was wonderful. You knew everyone. Now I don't think it's that way."

"It was a gang, we were pals," Walker says of his cronies from Temecula, Murrieta, Elsinore and Wildomar. That was back in the days when gangs weren't such a bad thing.

The old-timers represent a different age. Knight went to school in World War II, a time when the whole country was united, not just the valley. Dunham, Class of '37, finished up while America was emerging from the depths of the Great Depression. Parker (1932) and Walker (1930) witnessed the end of the Roaring Twenties and the start of the aforementioned economic calamity. Imagine being a high school grad entering that job market.

The accommodations were a little different too. Today it seems no high school is complete without its own swimming pool. Grads of yesteryear had their own swimming pool too - Lake Elsinore.

Going to high school at what is now Elsinore Middle School on Graham Avenue, the lake was across the street.

Learning has also changed. Dunham was amazed that her granddaughter was being asked by her middle school teacher to make a graph about the stock market. "They do a lot of different things than we did. We did reading, writing and arithmetic," she says.

Then there is society at large. Back then, people were more settled, not bouncing all over the country like they do today, the old-timers say.

Numbers tell the story. Walker's graduating class in 1930 was about 30. Knight's class was about the same size in 1945. Contrast that with the growth spurt that's gone on here the past 15 years.

Dunham, who played basketball and baseball in high school, says she knew the people from the other towns because she'd see them year after year. Her husband Lawrence, a graduate of Elsinore High in 1930, had lived in Murrieta since he was 5 months old. He died three years ago at 83, still a Murrieta lad.

The kids of yesteryear confined their defiance to harmless pranks. Walker recalls the Halloween night he and three pals moved an outhouse from a church to the Four Corners area of Lake Elsinore.

They were apprehended eventually by Arthur Barber, Elsinore's chief of police at the time. He took them down to his "holding cell," really a human cage behind City Hall. They stayed there a few hours, until they were appropriately chastened. The chief even drove Walker home after his "sentence."

Times are just a little different now.

A two-way love affair
Publication Date: June 29, 1999

With the end of the school year here, a lot of people are asking how my first year of teaching went.

Perhaps the best way to respond is to tell you about one recent morning when it occurs to me that I don't have much time left with my kids. In this case the kids I refer to are my 19 third-graders, not my biological children.

The realization that I'm about to lose my kids makes me sad because I've grown really attached to them. It's something teachers experience. It's hard not to.

Later that same morning, a classroom aide comes by to work with my kids. When she's done, she notes how much she likes my students. The feeling is mutual.

I see the aide again at lunch. She's one of the many people you find in education who have so many positive things to say. She delivers again when she says: "I think you're going to be one of the teachers those kids never forget. I can tell they really like you."

You can't imagine how good that makes me feel.

I pick up my kids after lunch and they read for a few minutes on their own, just like they always do. (I've found kids crave routine.) Meanwhile, I look out a window and start to think about the aide's compliment and how much my kids mean to me.

Just then one of my students comes up to my desk and hands me a drawing. "Here, Mr. Love, I made this for you," she says sweetly.

Now kids make pictures for teachers all the time. It's really no big deal. But this one is different, both because of the subject and the timing.

The girl - the best artist in the class - has drawn a beautiful rainbow. Underneath it she's written, "Thank you for teaching me."

I whisper a thank-you - I can barely talk, I'm so choked up - then turn away to gaze out the window again. I take a minute or two to compose myself, then stick the picture on my bulletin board to forever remind me of that moment.

Fortunately, this isn't an everyday experience as a teacher. Otherwise, I'd be a basket case. But I have to note that in my 17 years as a full-time newspaper reporter there was only one time that I wept over a story. Funny, that one also involved a kid.

It's hard to explain what my first year of teaching has done for me. I certainly don't want to leave the impression it's been all Kodak moments. There have been just as many times I wanted to run out of the classroom door screaming.

Then there are the moments that are priceless. The times you try explaining something to a confused child in a different way and then hear the magic words: "Now I get it." The moments you go up to a crying child and console her. Within seconds she's better because you're someone she trusts. The times a kid mistakes you for a parent, calling you "dad," once even "mom."

Teaching little kids provides the highest of highs and the lowest of lows. Daily, if not hourly. It's way more intense than I imagined. You don't know what tired is until you've spent six hours with a roomful of 8- and 9-year-olds trying to get them to do something they really don't want to do.

And it's only Monday.

Yup, teaching is not for everybody. I've had any number of people look at me almost reverently when I tell them I teach third graders. I try to tell them it's not as hard as it seems, as long as you like being around kids nonstop. That's a big if, of course.

But because I enjoy hanging around kids so much, I haven't regretted my career change once. I came into it hoping to make more of a difference in people's lives. Mission accomplished.

You can't believe how good I feel about the growth some of my kids have made this year. It's a high knowing that I helped them learn to multiply and divide. Or made them better readers, spellers and writers. Most importantly, they're better people.

These are skills they'll have for the rest of their lives. Wow. I know there aren't many jobs that provide the same impact.

The best way to close is with the kids from my first - but not last - memorable class. I had a great time, David Bates, Breanna Bennett, Chad Collingwood, Brittany Redmond, Albert Ruiz, Kevin Hauser, Jordan Koeppen, Jackie Landwehr, Logan Mason, Jesse Perdue, Chris Syers, Casey Vanderpool, Sarah Vega, Tyler Monteleone, Alyssa Way, Mychal Yup, Kalie Schaal, Christian Reynolds and Warren Kennedy.

Awesome mall adds a touch of sameness
Publication Date: November 2, 1999

I hate malls.

Now that I got that off my chest, let's talk about the mall of the moment, The Promenade in Temecula.

In a word: Wow!

"Wow" from someone who's lived in Southwest Riverside County since 1988 and grown accustomed to the small-town building. Now there's a facility with more than 750,000 square feet. Standing outside Robinson's May, the buildings dwarf those towering skinny palm trees.

"Wow" also at the huge number of people strolling around the mall on a weekday afternoon. I know it's new and everybody has to race down to see it, but still, it's hard to believe the number of folks who apparently live within driving distance of the mall. It's the most powerful indicator yet that Southwest Riverside County is growing by leaps and bounds.

"Wow" as in how well the traffic is being handled. I recognize it's only a weekday, but I had no trouble getting in and out of the mall. Ditto for Saturday afternoon when I cruise by. I still have tremendous doubts about future gridlock at the mall, but so far, so good.

Finally, "wow" for what the mall says about Temecula and where it's headed. Last December when I toured the mall construction site, I predicted its opening would mark the end of Temecula as a small town.

That prediction, made in the abstract, I can now say concretely, now that it's a finished product with a lot of shoppers.

Look at Winchester Road from the Interstate 15 to Chaparral High, for instance. It's the first local thoroughfare to resemble something out of bustling Orange County. Just a couple years ago the land was mostly open country. Now this.

And those Robinson's May sales associates -- in mall speak, nobody is a mere worker -- decked out in a spiffy coat and tie straightening a pile of expensive shirts that don't need to be straightened.

Heretofore, Temecula store employees -- OK, "associates" -- didn't wear coats and ties, and they certainly didn't need to busy themselves tinkering with perfection. When you're accustomed to shopping the likes of Kmart, bargains matter more than appearances.

Then there is the scene of the harried moms with strollers, the cackling teens with the spiked hair -- and everybody else for that matter -- nonchalantly passing by the seductive displays of Victoria's Secret.

At one time here, conservatives led by Temecula school board member Ed Elder routinely protested theaters and video stores promoting anything remotely resembling porn. While Victoria's Secret isn't X-rated, the store isn't exactly about chastity. Still, nobody even flinches at the sex display at the mall.

So the new mall represents a creeping sophistication in the valley.

Look, I'm not naive about this stuff. I know as well as anybody that you can't fight progress. You might delay it every now and then, but you can't beat it.

The mall -- and the proposed Zev Buffman entertainment center that lurks nearby in Murrieta -- represents the ultimate in progress. I've heard many local residents say that the mall's opening means there is finally something to do around here. I can't help but wonder though: Is that what I was looking for when I came here, entertainment venues?

More than anything else for me, the mall represents Temecula moving closer to the sameness of other Southern California suburbs. I know, naysayers will say we still have Old Town, we still have the wine country. But they seem so far away when you're standing in a crowded, noisy mall. You could be in Escondido, Moreno Valley, Westminster or Northridge. What's the difference? You're in a friggin' mall! Temecula's lost some of its charm with The Promenade.

Enough whining. On my way out of the mall I see a sign pointing to valet parking, the first time I've seen such a service offered in these parts. There was a time -- well, you get my drift by now. Let's just say I'm struggling to adjust to life in a new town.

Temecula's traffic fighters gain new clout
Publication Date: November 16, 1999

Take heart you who fear Southwest Riverside County is being steamrolled -- not to mention paved over -- by a runaway growth train.

There is hope in your world. Sam Pratt has triumphed.

Temecula's newest councilman, known for battling Temecula's endless traffic and Zev Buffman's endless entertainment venues, is stepping into the wolves' lair, considering how fervently the Temecula panel pursues growth.

It's a new era, proclaims the gang that's stood with Pratt all these years, folks such as George Buhler, Joseph Terrazas, Phil Hoxsey, Leverne Parker, Pat Keller and the like.

They've waged a guerilla insurgency of sorts for nearly a decade, firing off letters to newspapers that wouldn't always print them, being shouted down at public meetings by those who support the growth gusher, filing lawsuits that critics consider frivolous and destructive, and standing on street corners to campaign against the traffic they sense is destroying a quiet lifestyle that lured them here.

Pratt is now part of the power structure they've so despised. It's not often David topples Goliath, even in this Bible Belt of Southern California. They toast their miraculous fortune the other night at Parker's ancient hotel in Old Town.

"Boy, are we relishing this," Buhler says.

The victors jokingly celebrate not just Councilman Pratt, but the possibility of "Senator Pratt."

I remember standing in the same place with the same crowd almost five years ago. I was there to write a story about the new group they were forming to battle Buffman, the Temecula Old Town Advancement League, or T.O.T.A.L.

Foes said they were out to TOTAL Temecula progress, the notion that Old Town was meant to be a country music Mecca. They narrowly lost the first round, a public vote on the Buffman project, but triumphed when the developer was chased off to Murrieta. (Gee thanks, say the Buffman opponents in that town.)

Now the old TOTAL group has pulled off another shocking coup, electing Pratt. Three years ago the hero was trounced by an almost two-to-one margin by Steve Ford in a council race. It seemed the traffic crusader was too extreme to ever win favor in pro-business Temecula.

But there's change in the air in the city and it's not just the increasing smog levels. Judging by the election of Pratt and Mike Naggar, another guy harping about the traffic, it seems to be dawning on more people that sprawling growth -- Shock of shocks! -- has its drawbacks.

The new converts include Pamela Miod, May Lorah and Michelle Anderson. Although they were not major players in the old TOTAL group, they spearheaded Pratt's successful campaign.

The three women are talking about organizing a new watchdog group, perhaps something such as Saving Temecula Our Priority, or S.T.O.P. They want to run more candidates in 2001 when seats held by Stone, Ron Roberts and Jeff Comerchero are up for grabs. Judging by the group's success this year, the incumbents better be careful.

They're promising to make Temeculans more aware of the staggering projections that call for the city's population to swell from nearly 50,000 today to 150,000 or more in the future.

"People need to be aware of all the development that's planned for Temecula," Lorah says. "We want to save Temecula from becoming another Orange County."

They represent a force that's heretofore been uninvolved in Temecula -- and for that matter Lake Elsinore and Murrieta -- politics. They are the recent arrivals, the ones who've been too busy commuting and raising a family to get involved. Let's hope this trend spreads to neighboring cities.

The victory party also attracts Murrieta rabble-rouser Rita Gentry. She pulls me aside to object to my recent contention that her city will never have anything like the traffic problems of Temecula.

Gentry says such thinking breeds complacency. Murrietans need a wakeup call before traffic from their rapidly growing town and nearby French Valley clogs routes such as Murrieta Hot Springs and Los Alamos roads, she advises.

Consider yourself forewarned, Murrietans.

Rescuing a kid can call for team of heroes
Publication Date: November 30, 1999

It's a typical weekday afternoon for Francy Honda: pick up the kids from school, dole out a few snacks and let the children watch a little TV. Meanwhile, Honda goes to the study to finish a letter on the computer.

About 20 minutes later, she hears a commotion at the front door. It's two uniformed Murrieta officers returning her 4-year-old son, Nathaniel.

What happened in between is every parent's worst fear. It's also proof that people still care enough to get involved.

Our story starts with Nathaniel's 7-year-old sister, Tara. Returning with the mail, she closes the front screen door, like she's supposed to. But she forgets to latch it, like she's also supposed to.

While Tara and 13-year-old sister Danielle watch TV, Nathaniel -- who has Weaver syndrome, a rare disorder that's delayed development -- comes around to a front screen door. Bingo! He's out the door.

He cruises down the street, crosses two more streets and motors out to Whitewood Road, one of the busiest streets in town. He's trucking in the bicycle lane, happy as can be, cars whizzing by him at 40 to 50 mph.

Off-duty firefighter Rick Towne is the first person to come to Nathaniel's rescue. While driving north on Whitewood, Towne spots Nathaniel. With all the traffic, Towne's afraid turning around to assist the child might cause an accident. So Towne zips around the corner to his house and calls 911.

Now it's Linda Cole's turn to help. Driving south on Whitewood, she spies Nathaniel and comes up slowly on him. She stops the car to also dial 911.

A curious Linda Mejia is right behind her. A Murrieta code enforcement officer, Mejia tries to not meddle in other people's affairs unless it's official business. But why has this woman stopped her car by the little boy? Is she trying to abduct him?

Once Mejia sees that Cole is trying to rescue Nathaniel, they try to corral the feisty kid, who's having the time of his life. Just then Officer Steve Lang arrives, responding to Towne's call.

Mejia and Lang send Cole on her way with a hearty thanks, and then walk up Whitewood to Blackthorne Drive to see if they can find the little guy's house. A neighbor steers them toward the Hondas' home, where the screen door is still wide open.

Needless to say, Francy Honda is shocked to find out what's happened. While Mejia, a fellow mom who's lost a son to cancer, is sympathetic, Honda can tell Lang is perturbed, thinking he's having to deal with another negligent parent.

That couldn't be further from the truth. I've been a neighbor of Honda's for 11 years and know she's as dedicated as any mother I've ever met. Her four wonderful children are proof.

Honda expresses gratitude for their efforts, but she doesn't stop there. She checks with the police to see who helped, then delivers fruit baskets with teddy bears and pictures of Nathaniel to all four heroes.

"Everybody was doing their job. People who didn't have to do their job were right there, and I just feel like, 'Wow,'" Honda says.

A touched Officer Lang knows his first impression of Honda was wrong. He says her teddy bear sits in a place of honor on his dining room table. "That thing means more to me than any commendation," the 19-year police veteran says. "That little stuffed bear is the cutest thing."

Towne, the firefighter, has his picture of Nathaniel taped to his refrigerator door. "That's way more than I expected," he says. "I would just want someone to do the same thing for my kids."

Cole is touched in another way. She'd been meaning to call a former roommate of hers for months. By the time Cole finally did last spring, she learned the woman had died two weeks before.

Since then, she's determined to react more quickly to things she felt she had to do. While dozens of other motorists whizzed by Nathaniel that terrifying afternoon, Cole leaped into action.

The line between tragedy and celebration is thin.

Francy Honda has now written something else on the computer, "I will be forever grateful. Once again, Nathaniel and mommy were able to cuddle together on the couch as he drifted off to sleep. Our morning prayer, that the kids and I had recited that very morning, was heard and answered."

CHAPTER 12

2000 - Passions for religion and candy

Lifestyles issues were big, including a profile of a child-care business, an operation at the core of much of what we do. I also wrote about the quiet backbone of our Southwest Riverside County, the commuters, the folks who often leave home when it's dark and return when it's the same. Their treks are what the phenomenal growth of the past quarter century is founded on.

Then there is one of my all-time favorites when it comes to quirky, Ron Wickerd of Murrieta, and all the history he experienced, dating back to the origins of his community. There was talk about Ralph Love, Temecula's most famous painter. If you've never seen his work, check it out; he's really good. And no, for the umpteenth time, we're not related!

There was a lot going on with my family that year. We debated whether to invest a bunch of money in elective surgery for one of our dogs, Midnight, and I reflected on how pet owners of an earlier era handled such matters. Let's just say today's pets have it good.

My family discussed religion, something many a clan considers in our area that is home to so many churches. Speaking of religion, there is the destruction of Halloween candy and the parent who can't stop at just one when it comes to sneaking something from the kid's stash. Let's just say some penance is long overdue. Forgive me my children, for I have sinned.

Commuters pay a price to live here
Publication Date: January 4, 2000

Everybody was telling Richard Cook how much they liked the new paint job on his house. There was just one problem: He hadn't seen it yet.

"I didn't get to see it until the weekend," Cook says.

This time of year, Cook misses out on a lot of things in his hometown of Temecula. He doesn't see the place in daylight on weekdays because he's driving three or four hours a day to work, depending on traffic.

During the winter months, the sun rises about 6:45 a.m. and sets around 4:45 p.m. Ten hours of daylight -- not much when you're gone 12, 14, 16 hours a day.

In the early '90s, I wrote about commuters who had given up on these exhausting drives. They were moving back to the coast. No house was worth the time spent on the freeways. Among the frustrations they described, never being able to see your town in daylight in the dead of winter.

Cook, who's commuted from Temecula for seven years, isn't about to say this is the ideal way to live. In fact, he's tried repeatedly over the years to get a job locally.

Those trying to look on the bright side tell him that driving home at night must be a great way to unwind from the stress of a job. Yeah right, he says, that 91 Freeway at rush hour is sure relaxing.

One way he deals with it is humor. Asked what's the worst thing about never seeing your town in daylight, he deadpans, "I never get a tan."

The best way to cope is to remind himself how great it is to raise a family in Southwest Riverside County. The housing is more affordable, which means his wife Rowena can stay home with the kids. The benefits for their boys, Daniel, David, and Mark, are priceless.

"If daddy has to suffer and go out on the range and kill buffalo for three days, then daddy will," Cook says of his commuting sacrifice.

Jim Chance seems to feel the same way. Like Cook, he's usually on the road by 4:30 a.m., dead of night this time of year. They often pass each other at the 76 gas station on Rancho California Road and Old Town Front Street in Temecula.

The difference is that Chance has to schlep to a manufacturing job in Northridge, an amazing 115 miles away. He gets home anywhere from 6:30 p.m. to 8 p.m.

That's 230 miles a day, 1,150 miles a week, more than 50,000 miles a year. Yet Cook can't say enough about the good things of living in Temecula. What's four, five, even six hours a day on the road compared to those benefits?

Hanging out at the 76 station from 4:15 a.m. to 5 a.m. one recent day, watching these guys load up on caffeine and sugar for the long haul -- affable clerk Dwight Hazel says the commuters buy the same things day after day -- you hear a lot of positive comments from these road warriors.

They love to tease each other about "getting a life," they obviously would rather work locally, but somehow, in some strange way that's hard to figure, they think it's worth it.

"This is a cool little town," says electrical contractor Mike Salvadore on his way to Westminster. "I just never see it in daylight."

It gets me to thinking that our local booster types have it all wrong. They don't need to talk about the physical attributes our communities have to offer to lure businesses, they need to talk up these guys. People willing to endure ridiculous commutes to live here -- what better endorsement could any community have.

On my way back up Interstate 15 to Murrieta that recent morning, I'm reminded by something Cook tells me. Look at the headlights on the freeway, he says. Look how many there are, thousands upon thousands, wave after wave. Morning after morning, night after night, the commuters behind those numbing headlights endure.

As we enter our first work week of the new millennium, my hat's off to you folks. Even though you're not around much, you're the backbone of our towns, the ones making the ultimate sacrifice for your families. As for me, I appreciate my one-mile commute even more.

Murrietan seeks heir to history
Publication Date: January 18, 2000

Ron Wickerd suffers from any number of ailments, but that doesn't keep him from having plenty of self-confidence.

"I am, whether I like it or not, Mr. Murrieta."

Wickerd was born here. Not many 86-year-old Murrietans can lay claim to that. His grandfather opened Murrieta's first store in the late 1880s. When school district officials went looking for local Indian names for their new facilities (such as Shivela, Avaxat and Tovashal), Wickerd says they turned to him, the guy with the Cherokee father.

Then there is his oddest claim to local stature, his home in old Murrieta. The self-proclaimed museum is referred to by Wickerd as both "Compost Manor" and "Murrieta Ethnohistorical Research Center." There's truth in both.

Throughout his yard are makeshift historical displays with hand-painted signs explaining various stages of the world's development: Indian artifacts, "History of the Ages," "One Cosmic Instant" and "500 Luiseno Indian names."

Mostly though, there are rocks -- ancient stones or ones that are just plain interesting. Wickerd and his late wife Fran collected them over 20 years.

But my interest in recently visiting Wickerd recently was the change in the millennium. What better person to put this in a local perspective, I figured.

While he didn't disappoint -- fondly describing the Southwest Riverside County of a thousand years ago as a lush paradise inhabited only by Indians while deriding what he considers the polluted and crowded conditions of the present -- I left with a concern of his that needs to be addressed.

Wickerd isn't in the best of health. In the past three months he's endured a stroke and prostate surgery. He is still alive and kicking -- Oh, is he ever -- but he is confined to a wheelchair.

At 86 and with a lifetime of poor health in him (he weighed only 3 pounds at birth and somehow survived in a town without a doctor), one can't help but wonder how much more his body can endure.

"I'm hurting right now," he says. "There's no fun about hurting."

Without surviving relatives to look after his fascinating stuff, Wickerd's afraid it will be hauled off to the dump after he's gone. "It makes me sad," he says. "I've got enough here to make one heck of a museum. But how the hell do you save it? I can't because I can't get around. Why the hell don't you do something?"

Wickerd is refreshingly blunt, something you don't find much of anymore in our politically correct world. He can curse a blue streak, doesn't mind boasting about himself and is more than happy to demand.

Of course, what would you expect from a guy who's seen so much, who's traveled the world as a writer, a photographer, a merchant marine and even a hobo.

Wickerd returned from his adventures to Murrieta in 1970 to explore his hometown. "It was the Indian in me," he says. "Indians always want to come home."

He tracked down the Shoshone Indian elders he'd known as a boy. They took him into the hills, showing him the ancient spots. The eager Wickerd brought back grinding stones, stone carvings and took thousands of pictures.

He's knows much about his hometown. "Do you know how many volcanoes are up there ready to explode any minute?" he asks, pointing to the Santa Rosa Plateau. "Four."

It's easy to see Wickerd could go on all day sharing his stories. But after 90 minutes, I've got to go, the world of work and parenthood calling me.

I help him lock up the place, but he insists on putting away his wheelchair by himself.

"I have to do it on my own because what in the hell will I do when you leave?" he notes, cantankerous to the end.

On the way out he makes me promise I'll do something about saving his stuff. If you can help out in some fashion, give me a buzz. Our valley's history depends on it.

Solving today's child-care conundrum
Publication Date: February 15, 2000

The pairs of kids' shoes on the front porch are the first sign that Dawn McDonald runs an unconventional business.

Six children snack on apples, oranges, chips and dried fruit at her Murrieta home. A children's video is on the tube. Two preschoolers affectionately cling to McDonald as if she's their mommy.

McDonald runs a child-care business. She has as many as eight kids at a time in her house five days a week from 4:30 a.m. until 5:30 p.m. And you thought you had long hours.

You might have the impression that McDonald's business is trivial, one our community could easily get by without. But parents who can't get their children placed in satisfactory day care cannot work and so, can't contribute to the economy.

A statewide study finds that the shortage of child care in California is at "near crisis proportions." In Riverside County, for every child-care slot there are more than 6.3 children waiting.

That poses important questions for parents here in Commuter Country. Do you take a chance on putting your darling with a stranger for most of the day? Or do you try to get by on much less so one parent can stay home and be with the kids?

McDonald knows all about it. She used to drive to Corona every day to work as a nursing assistant. In one year, she placed her kids, Derek and Adam, in three different child-care settings. Frustrated with the quality of care her kids were receiving, she took matters into her own hands to start her business in summer 1997.

Since then, McDonald gets to see her own kids more, has a steady paycheck and knows she's an important part of a society seemingly dependent on two-income families.

Speaking of which, meet Jackie and Marco Batey of Lake Elsinore. They are the working parents of Marc, 8; Jaycee, 7; Ashley, 6; and Matthew, 3. They drop their kids off at McDonald's home at 4:30 every morning on their way to work in Temecula.

The Batey kids troop in bleary-eyed and quickly go back to bed in their home away from home. Their parents pick them up almost 12 hours later.

To the kids, McDonald is "Auntie Dawn." Judging by how much they smooch with her, it's easy to see why they consider her family.

Jackie Batey knows she's fortunate because she leaves her children with someone who she believes provides quality care. It's every worried working parent's dream come true.

"I don't know what I'd do without her," Batey says of McDonald. "She sees the kids more than I do during the week. She's like a sister to me."

The two women exchange high-fives with each other.

We all know the horror stories of day care. Adults who scream at kids more than they hug them. Places where the entertainment amounts to a TV marathon and not much else. Homes where the food is more junk than healthy. Providers who are more interested in making a buck than helping to raise a child.

McDonald's approach is different, right down to the fact she's only taken four days of vacation since she started her business. "I know how hard it is to find other day care," the licensed child-care provider says. "I don't like to make my parents have to find other arrangements."

There's a commotion at the front door. McDonald's part-time helper, Sharon Clark, has arrived with three kids she took to the library. Another round of snacks and homework quickly commences.

On my way out I see another mom pull up to pick up her kids. Our area's system of child care, seemingly chaotic at times, somehow meets our needs.

Aneurysm turns lives inside out
Publication Date: March 14, 2000

It can be a fine line between a good life and a hard life.
Consider Paul Hogan's fate.

Six weeks ago, Hogan was preparing to take his first vacation in years. He and his family were going to drive to Wyoming to visit his elderly parents, who'd never met his younger daughter, Sara. Co-workers said he was so excited.

His world turned upside down Feb. 3. His wife Maria had a seizure that morning. Maria, only 41, was airlifted to Loma Linda University Medical Center with a brain aneurysm.

She's been hospitalized ever since. Even though she was moved from the intensive care unit last week, doctors don't have a long-term prognosis for her.

Here's a typical day for her husband, a 43-year-old Sun City resident: Up at 4:30 a.m., he readies himself for work and his three kids for school. Logan drops them off at a friend's house -- it varies from day to day, depending on what he can arrange -- then makes the commute to Temecula to work at an airplane-parts repair shop.

Off at 3 p.m., he races over to pick up the kids, then swings by the house to let them unwind for a little bit. Next it's off to the hospital 45 minutes away for his nightly visit with Maria.

Sometimes he swings by Riverside to drop the kids off at a relative's, tacking another 45 minutes onto his journey. He doesn't return home until 9:30 or 10:30 at night, depending on whether he has to fetch the kids in Riverside.

Even then, he doesn't get to bed until after midnight because he needs to tend to the housework and the mounting medical bills, $320,000 and counting. He'll have to come up with 20 percent; his insurance will get the rest.

Logan typically gets three to four hours of sleep a night. Two nights recently, he couldn't sleep at all and had to call in sick because he was so exhausted. But he doesn't want to burn any more vacation or sick time because he wants to save it for when Maria gets home, whenever that is.

"It's just so hard," he says of his existence. "I go and look at her and get no response at all, and I just get dragged down."

That vacation they were going on this month seems so far away now.

I learned about him from a concerned co-worker, Sophia Hogan, who's checking everywhere for help. "He wants to be with them (his children) since they really need a parent with them now," she says in her e-mail. "He also wants to spend as much time as possible with his beloved wife. He needs to bring home a paycheck. How does someone in this situation cope?"

Like a lot of people, the Logans live paycheck to paycheck. Maria decided to be a stay-at-home mom shortly after their eldest child, Paul Jr., was born 13 years ago. She's been there ever since for Crystal, now 10, and Sara, now 4.

Being a one-income family, the Logans have had to make plenty of financial sacrifices. Their rewards came in a different form: knowing they were doing everything they could to raise their children right. Now they're having to pay an unfortunate price because Maria didn't work and doesn't qualify for disability payments.

Then there is the emotional toll of watching a loved one suffer. Crystal is a delightful child, a kid who laughs a lot and is so eager to please. While her father and I wrestle with how to spell aneurysm, she runs into the other room, drags out a heavy dictionary and looks it up for us.

Her smile fades when I delicately ask how it's been since her mom got sick. "It's a little sad," she says quietly. "I cry some times."

Her mom's fate is so uncertain. Maria is making progress but remains in a deep sleep and rarely wakes.

For now, her husband relies on the faith Maria displayed just before she was wheeled into surgery for the first time six weeks ago. Still coherent, she looked into her husband's eyes and told him, "I have no fear."

Paul Logan tells me, "That's helped me along so much. It keeps me going."

In a world with so little between happiness and despair, something has to.

Penning letters is an almost forgotten art
Publication Date: June 20, 2000

"First of all Mr. Love let me apologize for writing on this lined paper," Norman Taylor starts. "I guess I'm one of the very few seniors who have no computer printer or even a typewriter." No apologies necessary. Taylor, a Temecula retiree, practices a lost art: He writes letters. He even uses cursive.

He corresponds with seven friends and relatives from across the country on a regular basis, writing a couple a week. He's written a 95-year-old woman, the mother of his best man, for 47 years. He writes every two months and she's saved everyone.

Taylor's two sons, Temeculans Bob and Chris Taylor, encourage him to send e-mail from their computers, and he has from time to time. But it's just not the same.

"E-mail is cold," he says. "It's fast and it's nice. But a letter that's handwritten is personal."

In the spirit of full disclosure, Taylor, a retired postal worker, has a self-interest at stake. Letters require stamps, which help fund his retirement, he says with a chuckle.

In a more serious vein, Taylor says everybody likes to get mail, even the junk variety. It shows that somebody -- or some machine in the case of most junk mail -- is thinking of you. And a personal handwritten letter is as good as it gets.

I know, having corresponded with the best man from my wedding for the past 12 years. Every other weekend I write him a letter, he returns a postcard every 10 days or so. I began e-mail last fall and we debated whether to start communicating that route. After exchanging two short notes, we decided it's just not the same.

My friend, Ron Dicker, has moved from San Francisco to New York in the time we've corresponded. I've seen Ron twice in that time and maybe talked to him a dozen times on the phone. Yet in many ways I feel as close to him as when we worked in the same newspaper office 17 years ago, thanks to the miracle of letters.

The letter I wrote four years ago during the week my mom was dying moved Ron's own mother to tears when he read it to her. The card in which he told me this made me cry as well.

Like Taylor says, there's something about sitting down with a piece of paper to communicate your thoughts, and this time he was writing as a fan of the Temecula Valley High School junior varsity softball team. Letter writing brings out special things, painful as the process can be sometimes.

E-mail is quick and flippant; letter writing is slow and meaningful. The rise of the former and the fall of the latter says a lot about how the world is changing.

It's not easy finding letter writers. I went by the Parkside Apartments in Lake Elsinore, a place with mostly retirees, and had a hard time tracking down any current practitioners. The only one I found, Leatrice Douglas Young, trades letters monthly with former local George Gonzales, who moved to La Quinta last summer.

She only does that because he doesn't have e-mail. Besides writing an occasional letter to a brother in Arizona, everybody else gets e-mails or calls.

"It's so much more fun," she says. "Writing letters is hard to do."

Another of the Parkside retirees, Tommy Thompkins, left home in Mississippi at the age of 14 to go to work in the big city of New Orleans. He faithfully wrote his mom every two weeks for 42 years.

"If I waited a month, my mom would get all over me," he recalls. Now that she's passed away, he doesn't correspond with anybody. Too bad.

One hope I have for letter writing's future is Kalie Schaal. She was in my third-grade class last year -- I'm a teacher as well as a newspaper guy -- and sent me a beautiful letter a few months back inviting me to her fourth-grade awards assembly at the school she's now at.

There was no way I could pass up such a heartfelt invitation.

After the event I sent her a letter thanking her. She wrote me back two weeks ago, explaining that she'd found my old letter while cleaning out her room.

"I was very touched, so I wanted to write," she explained.

I was moved that she'd thought to write me again. I'm sorry, e-mail just can't compete.

Religion begins to grow on you as time goes by
Publication Date: June 27, 2000

"Hey, mommy, is it true that I don't have the Holy Spirit because I haven't been baptized?" my 11-year-old daughter Julia asks.

Now there's a loaded question. And it's only breakfast.

Our family is asking a lot of loaded questions these days. The dicey proposition of instilling spirituality in two kids, the fact my wife Joanne and I are well into our 40s, and the passing of her dad and my mom in recent years has combined to make religion a keen interest.

This is a radical change for me. I went to church when I was a kid, but usually had to be dragged kicking and screaming.

That influenced me all right: From the time I was 18 until I was 35, I can count on one hand the number of times I set foot in a church of my own free will.

Joanne broke this pattern about six years ago. She started taking our kids to a local church. I followed, more out of a sense of duty than desire. Now I'm a Sunday school teacher, of all things.

We're not alone either. It's with good reason some people refer to Southwest Riverside County as the Bible Belt of Southern California. It seems every local school is rented out by congregations Sunday mornings. Numerous business parks also house places of worship.

Joanne and I find even our social gatherings are dominated by religion. One Friday night over pizza at another family's house, we discussed what God has to say about homosexuality and abortion. The next night with a different clan, the conversation turned to what Holy Communion signifies.

My focus isn't just Christianity. I had a long talk about Buddhism with my sister a couple weeks ago. I was so fascinated by a recent article on how other religions view Jesus that I read it several times. Growing up, I lived in India for a year and attended numerous Hindu ceremonies.

Still, it's with considerable trepidation that I approach people in downtown Lake Elsinore to see if they too find themselves more fascinated by religion as they age. Unless you're looking for trouble, politics and religion are matters you try to steer clear of.

Fortunately, I start with Gil Rasmussen who could talk religion for days. Rasmussen's dad, a Pentecostal minister, collapsed at the pulpit while claiming to see an angel, then died later that day.

Rasmussen knew by the age of 12 he too wanted to be a minister, and worked as one in Los Angeles for 10 years.

Today, Rasmussen, 53, characterizes himself as a "recovering Fundamentalist" who hasn't set foot in a church in eight years. He still considers himself Christian and still loves to discuss religion; he just can't handle a church anymore. "I get ticked off when I go."

Dolores Mayhall, who runs a downtown print shop, also isn't a regular churchgoer. She stopped going 30 years ago because she was working seven days a week. However, she watches a TV minister every Sunday morning and says she's as religious as ever.

"I've never not been interested. I just don't discuss it with people. It's led to too many disagreements among friends."

Alice Jackson, 66, prefers to discuss philosophies, not religion.

"Everybody has their own theory," she says. "It's a very personal belief. It's very difficult to get into the hearts of other people."

Jackson and I are joined by Cecilia Black, 48, who has good reason to think more about religion, having endured every parent's worst nightmare: the loss of 17-year-old daughter Cecilia in a car accident 18 months ago.

"My faith has never altered," she says. "It's how I survived."

Jackson had her own brush with death 18 months ago after a bout with pneumonia. Since then she's found herself looking at her past, wondering how she could have helped people more.

"We're all on a journey. The journey is to love and grow and benefit other people."

I leave feeling really good about the people I've discussed religion with. Sure, the topic can drive us apart, even ignite wars. But it can also bring us together.

Dependable pet care and burial service
Publication Date: August 8, 2000

Look to see you've got the plane tickets. Check to see if the hotels and the rental car are still reserved. Last but hardly least, make sure the folks watching your pets know what they're doing.

It's summertime when people take vacations. Think of all the pets dealing with strangers this time of year, be it in a kennel, somebody else's house or, if they're lucky, their own home. Either a pet-sitting service -- there are a dozen in the Yellow Pages -- or the master's friends handle the chores then.

Watching pets is a big responsibility, which is why our friends, Steve Harding (the former Murrieta city manager), his wife, Nancy, and their kids, Sarah and John, turn to our family.

They have quite the menagerie, including two dogs, two rats and a bird. But we're up to the challenge, considering we're dependable, honest, caring and, most important of all, we don't have a criminal background. With us around, what harm could possibly come to their beloved home and animals?

The Hardings put the dogs in a kennel anyway, partly because it'll be easier on us and partly because the dogs might make a meal out of the rats. Hard to argue with that logic.

Our first visit goes well enough. My daughter, Julia, tends to the bird, my son, David, helps with the rats, and I sit on their leather couch and watch a ball game. I can even see making some extra cash with a pet-sitting service. The trouble starts on our second trip two days later, when we notice that a piece of that comfortable couch has been consumed by Patches the rat, who's escaped from the cage that we hadn't properly locked up.

Oh-oh.

To make matters worse, the other rat, Princess, has taken a turn for the worse. She'd suffered a stroke the week before our watch and now looks near death. Sarah had left detailed burial instructions in the event of you-know-what; at least we didn't have to cremate the animal.

I also notice a trickle of ants coming in a kitchen window and made a mental note to bring pesticides next time to nuke 'em.

It's a shame we don't have a movie camera for our third visit because it could qualify for America's funniest home videos. Princess is dead, or at least appears so. While I investigate her status -- how do you check the vital signs of a rat? -- my wife, Joanne, lets out a horror-movie-type scream because the other rat, Patches, is crawling up her dress. Her shriek sets off the bird, who flies over to the kitchen sink, narrowly avoiding a moving ceiling fan that could have chopped it to bits. This is news to me because I thought the bird couldn't fly.

While Joanne curses the living rat, I drop the dead rat and try to retrieve the freaked-out bird. Coaxing her onto my hand, I notice that the trickle of ants is now a flood. I make yet another mental note to bring those pesticides.

The bird back in her cage, we next try to figure out what to do with the dead rat. It's dark, so we can't bury it in the back yard per Sarah's instructions. We can't leave it out because the ants might eat it. We also can't leave it in the refrigerator because the cleaning lady is due the next day, and what happens if she finds it there? For some reason we stuff it in the freezer.

Our last visit is rather poignant. Princess' death moves my kids to write beautiful messages in her honor. We also place the now-frozen Princess into a shoe box that Sarah had turned into a casket. My kids decorate the box with flowers while I dig a hole in the back yard. We gently place the casket there and mark it with an American flag. Julia reads her eulogy while David fights back tears. It reminds me of when I was 9 and how I cried when my turtle died.

We troop inside to finish our last day of chores and write a note chronicling all that's happened. The ants are still there, and I've forgotten again to bring my pesticides. Oh well.

Our saga is the source of considerable amusement among friends. One sent an e-mail titled "pet cemetery" to say he had a couple cats he wanted to get rid of and perhaps we could pet-sit sometime. I advised another to make sure the homeowner's insurance was paid up before calling on us to watch pets. Thanks, but they'll use another neighbor instead.

At least the Hardings haven't disowned us. They say the sofa was old and they were thinking of getting a new one. (Yeah, right.) They also are touched by Julia and David's letters and plan to save them.

As for me, I've ditched that planned pet-sitting service. It's too much stress.

Overcoming Halloween's temptations
Publication Date: October 31, 2000

After the kids are in bed tonight, it'll be sitting there in a bucket, bag or old pillowcase. You told yourself you wouldn't dive into it, but that was before you saw the haul the kids brought back. Every year it seems to be more.

So you have one piece, figuring you've earned it, what with having to cart your kids around all night when you would rather have been sitting at home watching TV. But nobody can eat just one, so you have two or three more. Surely the kids won't notice that. Now you're out of control though, putting the stuff away faster than your dog goes through dinner. Before you know it, half the loot is gone. Oh my gosh, how are you going to explain that to your kids?

That was me nine years ago, before I got help. Yes, I was one of those Parents Who Can't Control Themselves Around Their Kid's Halloween Candy.

I remember it as if it were yesterday. My daughter, Julia, was only 2, her brother, David, wasn't even born. My wife, Joanne, and I had been taking Julia trick-or-treating since before she even had teeth, using her as a ruse to get what we really wanted -- CANDY!

Sure, everybody thought it was so cute when we would show up at their door, Julia sitting in a stroller dressed in an adorable leopard costume. The suckers, I mean our neighbors, were so touched that they often would give us extra candy. Yes, more for us, my wife and I would whisper gleefully to ourselves.

Our scheme got out of control by the time Julia was 2. She'd figured out the wonder of Halloween by then, i. e., FREE CANDY! It was hard to get her to bed that trick-or-treat night because she couldn't stop eating candy. "JUST ONE MORE!" she cried herself to sleep.

Peace and quiet finally restored, I remember sitting down to have a piece. Before I knew it, half was gone. Oh, the shame I felt that night. I've avoided Halloween candy ever since, knowing I cannot restrain myself. Sad, but true.

Cash wedges between man, dog friendship
Publication Date: November 14, 2000

Let's see, the property taxes are due, the car needs some work, Christmas is coming up and the vet bill has to be covered.

Yes, these days animal care ranks right up there with the big ticket items when it comes to expense.

Our family is going through this big time with one of our dogs, Midnight. He's had a small growth near his eye for about a year, but it isn't getting any bigger, it isn't affecting his vision, and it doesn't irritate him.

I'm dreading his annual checkup because I know the vet will want to take it off. Sure enough, the doc says it could be cancerous; it'll hurt him cosmetically if it gets any bigger, and, by the way, it'll be $500 to remove it.

My wife, Joanne, who takes him in, knows I won't want to pay for it. She carefully marshals her forces before telling me the news, enlisting the support of our two children. My 11-year-old daughter,

Julia, is particularly effective, all but bursting out in tears as she strokes the dog, turns on her "Daddy's Girl" charm, and says she'll forgo her allowance for years if we'll just take care of her poor, sick, Midnight.

Give me a break, I want to scream. But I know I'll never hear the end of this, so I cut my losses and agree to the rip-off, I mean, expense.

I'm now convinced this is one of those Male-Female Great Divide issues. The morning I drop Midnight off at the vet, a fellow teacher sees me striding through the parking lot with him. She asks me about it later at school, prompting a tirade from me about what a waste of money the procedure is. I make the mistake of saying this in front of about a half-dozen women, meaning I get really reamed.

"What is it with men and animals?" one of the more hostile ones fumes.

Looking for some male bonding, I tell my dad the story. Now this is a guy who grew up bounding around on Midwestern farms in The Great Depression. One time the grownups take the family dog out into a field and shoot it because the animal is dying. Then they go to town and find a new dog. No big deal.

Naturally, my dad says he'd never shell out $500 to remove some harmless bump. It's nice to know your dad is there when you need him.

It could always be worse. A teacher I know, Joanne Seufer, spent about $2,800 at a specialist's hospital a couple years ago trying to keep their dog Jenny alive. The animal dies anyway, meaning Seufer and her husband, Tim, also feel obligated to dole out more money for cremation and a special cedar box for the dog's remains.

Another dog of theirs, Hank, is also a major cash drain. He has a burr stuck in his nose, so he tries to sneeze and snort the thing out. (Sounds pleasant.) On another occasion his stomach becomes infected after he eats a wood chip. Then there is the time his paw is inflamed between his toes, possibly due to a foxtail.

All of these instances require expensive vet visits.

"All in all, we really believe the doctor knows best, so we follow advice on all tests and blood workups," Seufer explains. "I'd hate myself if I didn't do what was prescribed and something bad happened to one of them."

Looking for some middle ground on this issue -- somewhere between shooting your pet in your back yard because you can't afford its annual physical, or taking out a second to cover the expense of cosmetic surgery for a beloved animal -- we turn to Anne Washington, executive director of Animal Friends of the Valley, our local shelter.

When it comes to keeping pets alive at any expense, Washington exercises caution. With all the advances in medicine, vets can keep animals going much longer today. But quality of life is what matters most to Washington, not longevity.

This is an issue for her recently when her 13-year-old Doberman has bone cancer that's spread to his lungs. A vet can do an amputation and other things to keep the animal alive longer, but Washington doesn't want the dog to suffer. She makes the hard decision to put him to sleep.

"Let nature take its course," she advises.

A post script. We get the tests back on Midnight's bump and it isn't cancerous. But hey, for 500 bucks he looks great cosmetically.

CHAPTER 13

2001 - An inspiring painter and teacher

Growth was heating up again this year, with folks even camping out for tract homes. Shades of the late 1980s.

On the dreadful day of 9-11, my column appeared about a Murrieta man who one day woke up with 90 percent of his vision gone. His refusal to not give up in the face of profound adversity mirrored the strength our country showed following that horrific day, our generation's Pearl Harbor.

I also experienced personal loss when fellow teacher Joanne Seufer died. She and I shared a classroom when I was hired as a teacher a couple years before. The time we spent together was so much fun. Now she's gone.

Inspiration came from Nicolai Billy, a painter in the mountains who was living the simple life many of us only dream about. Then there was the baby shower I unfortunately attended. Too much adorable, darling, cute and whatever adjective you want to slap on for a bunch of women going on about babies.

My family acquired our third dog, a stray we named Happy. My wife rescued her off busy Whitewood Road, a development I wasn't "happy" about at the time. Today, with both of our kids grown and gone, our other two dogs passed away, I'm grateful for my only remaining four-legged friend's constant companionship.

Murrieta blessed by faithful fans
Publication Date: January 30, 2001

Certain things are automatic in Murrieta. The summers are hot. The Santa Rosa Plateau is gorgeous. Murrieta Hot Springs Road is a mess. And Dick Sherman and Joe Sehorn are at Murrieta Valley High School games.

These guys are as faithful as Hillary Clinton. Sherman, a member of the boys' basketball boosters, spends eight hours at the school on game days, setting up the snack stand, then cheering on the junior varsity girls, junior varsity boys, varsity girls and varsity boys' teams, before finally breaking down the snack stand.

Sehorn hasn't missed a varsity football game in the school's history, meaning he's seen about a hundred straight games.

He's also a basketball fanatic. He sits in the same spot at every home game, stomping his black boots and loudly leading cheers. The paint on the bleachers below his feet has been worn away.

"DEFENSE!!!," he shouts, slamming his boots down on the poor bleachers during a recent game. "DEFENSE!!! (Stomp! Stomp!), DEFENSE!!!" (Stomp! Stomp!).

Within moments the school cheerleaders and many other fans pick up the chant.

They know who their leader is.

Sehorn and Sherman are also regulars at the school's baseball games. The funny thing is that neither has a kid on the teams.

They simply love getting to know the players, they enjoy cheering them on, it helps them to feel a part of the community, and they appreciate the purity of high school sports. How quaint is that.

Each wears a school letter jacket to games and they usually sit together. The silver-haired, mild-mannered Sherman, a 73-year-old retired plumbing contractor, has the number "45" stitched on his jacket, the year he graduated from high school.

Sehorn, a 51-year-old security officer, has his nickname, "Superfan," etched on his jacket. Sherman's as quiet as Sehorn is loud at the games.

Each connects with the kids off the courts and fields as well. Sherman is teaming up with coach Steve Tarabilda and school board member Austin Linsley to carpool varsity players this year.

But Sherman just does it because he wants to spend time with the players and help out.

"I get more out of them than they get out of me," Sherman says of the team.

Sehorn, whose wife, Shirley, is a Murrieta elementary school teacher, stresses what's really important by never failing to ask players if they're keeping their grades up. He says his devotion to the Murrieta teams sends a message to the kids as well. "Eighty-five percent of supporting the child is just showing up for them," he said. "Consistency and stability are important to them, seeing the same faces all the time."

Varsity basketball players C. J. Richardson and Dan Larsen appreciate the backing. Larsen says Sherman could be likened to the team's faithful grandfather, a guy who's always there when you need him. "I like him a lot. You feel like you can talk with him about anything."

Richardson says no matter how packed the stands might be for games, Sehorn's booming voice stands out. "He's always the first one to cheer and the last one to finish."

Coach Tarabilda can't say enough about the contributions Sherman and Sehorn make. "Anytime you have supporters that don't have kids in the program you know you have something special ... These men are here to serve others. That is a quality that is being lost in our society today. More people should follow their example. This is a trait that I hope our players pick up on and apply to their own lives."

Sherman and Sehorn go to great lengths to be there for the kids. The basketball team took a 536-mile round trip to Arroyo Grande last year and the pair sat side by side on the team bus. "I travel with them no matter how far it is," Sherman says. "It was a privilege to be asked to go. It was one of the best experiences I've ever had."

Sehorn says he feels rewarded for his efforts when kids he sees around town tell him how much they appreciate him. One kid had it right when he shouted at Sehorn, "You the man, Superfan, you the man!"

"That's why I keep coming back," Sehorn says. "It's important to them and that's why I need it."

Too bad Sherman and Sehorn can't cheer all of us on.

Nicolai Billy puts his life in simpler order
Publication Date: March 20, 2001

There are the folks running as fast as they can on the career tread-mill to keep pace with the bills and stress of modern-day life. That would be most of us.

Then there is the rare individual such as Nicolai Billy, a moun-tain man who for a quarter-century now has somehow carved out a life of peace and tranquility amid the hustle-bustle of Southern California.

His job -- if you want to call it that -- is to paint. He's what's called an expressionist painter. Wrote one Orange County art critic, "Using combinations of unusual color tones and creating feelings that engender a classic primitive overture, Nicolai's oils cause the eye to stop and re-examine the very basis of art reality."

Art isn't the only reality Nicolai causes the eye to re-examine. After spending an afternoon on his idyllic two-acre retreat nestled in El Cariso Village in the Cleveland National Forest above Lake Elsinore, I'm left to wonder what the heck I'm doing in suburbia.

Nicolai hears that all the time from visitors. But when it comes right down to it, he doesn't think most people have what it takes to survive in the mountains without a strip mall down the corner and neighbors next door. And you know what, he's right.

Still, you cannot help but wonder what it must be like to (A) do abstract art for a living; (B) take secluded walks on property that includes gently sloping hillsides, towering trees, a trickling creek and a spiritual retreat; (C) have to drive 20 minutes down a windy Ortega Highway to find the nearest strip mall in Lake Elsinore; and (D) build your own house.

He's a man who believes in reincarnation, a man who has re-invented himself many times in this lifetime alone. He's served in the military, taught high school English, sold real estate, worked in construction, written newspaper stories, been a sailor, and run a popular dinner show house for more than a decade, Nicolai's El Cariso. His silver hair in a small ponytail, he was once part of the Laguna Beach hippie scene as well.

He was good friends with famed artist Jon Serl, who pleaded with him for years to pursue his art more seriously. Nicolai kept saying the time wasn't right and he didn't get serious until after his friend died a decade ago.

The timing also was right when he moved to El Cariso Village a quarter of a century ago. He was sitting in a bathtub in Orange County when something told him he needed to go by the country market in El Cariso. He dried himself off, jumped in his car, and drove the Ortega to a place that had a foot of snow on the ground in April.

The market wasn't for sale anymore but a real estate agent across the street was pounding a for-sale sign into another property. She said she was psychic and he was destined to buy the land. He wasn't about to ignore her because he considers himself psychic as well.

Clearly, unconventional is a way of life for Nicolai. He has hitch-hiked through Europe, visited India four times, and plans a fifth trip there this spring. I lived in that country for a year when I was a kid and we talk about the place at great length. During the discussion he offers me a dab of gray powder to put in my mouth, a mixture that's called vibhuti, a sacred ash from India.

"I give you these ashes to let you know that life is illusionary at best," he says. Our egos, vanities, material needs -- all will result in ashes, he advises. "All that survives is love."

He can be conventional and old-fashioned as well. Don't get him started on what's being done to the English language, for instance. "You don't say, 'Just between you and I,' you say, 'you and me,'" he fumes.

He came up with the moniker for the CLOUT community group, citizens who banded together in the '90s to disband the Ortega park district because they didn't think they were getting enough services for their tax dollars.

Frustrated by the growing number of people who don't remember Pearl Harbor, he posted a billboard last December on his property that fronts the Ortega to remind passing drivers of the event.

Psychic, abstract painter, mountain man, world traveler, proud veteran, tax critic, former high school English teacher, and business-man -- we should all be as lucky as Nicolai to jump off the treadmill and explore our many talents.

Injured dog finds town full of best friends
Publication Date: March 27, 2001

Twelve-year-old Samantha "Sami" Otte is doing what she does every day after school -- walking her dog, Roxanne, down to Whitewood Park in Murrieta to meet her friends.

Sami is holding Roxanne's leash, but the dog isn't attached to it because she's been minding so well recently. Suddenly Roxanne sees another dog on the other side of Whitewood Road and darts across the busy street.

This sets off a chain of events that is both miraculous and heart-warming. At a time when it seems so many people couldn't care less about anybody but themselves, some Murrieta neighbors prove otherwise.

Mike Zeldin is heading north on Whitewood with his son, David, when Roxanne races into the street. Unfortunately, he doesn't see the dog before it bounces off the back side of his vehicle.

Zeldin, who's never hit a dog before, pulls over as soon as he realizes what's happened. "I felt so bad," he says. "The little girl was crying and screaming. In a way I felt responsible."

Sami, who'd just met up with her friend Cori Freeland at the park, hadn't seen Roxanne cross into the road. All she notices is her dog rolling across the street after the impact. In shock and terrified at what she'll see, she can't even go look at her beloved 6-year-old Roxanne, an animal she's had since she was a puppy.

An old man, nobody gets his name, pulls over and jumps out of his car to direct traffic. His good deed keeps other motorists from running over Roxanne.

Others also jump into action.

A teen-age girl lets Sami use her cell phone to call her dad, George, who fortunately is just a couple minutes away.

George phones his wife, Kim, at work. She calls a neighbor, Nancy Leavitt, whose heart stops when she first thinks Sami, whom she's known since she was a baby, has been hit. She drives down to help.

Within minutes, a dozen people are there. Some try to console Zeldin, who feels awful about something he couldn't have prevented. A woman, nobody gets her name either, gives George some money.

"I know it isn't much, but it'll help pay for the vet bill," she says. It turns out to be $20.

Allison Gorman, the mother of another of Sami's friends, delicately puts Roxanne in a blanket and places the small bleeding dog in her van. A sobbing Sami rides with her dog to the vet, trying to keep the animal calm. At one point, Roxanne stops breathing.

Valley Veterinary Clinic has people in the parking lot ready to help Roxanne when they get there.

Vet Gary White figures it doesn't look good. The dog has broken ribs and is suffocating from a ruptured lung. Another 90 seconds without medical help and Roxanne would die.

The dog is hooked up to oxygen and an IV while the vet works furiously to save her. The neighbor sits with Sami in the lobby and prays with her.

About a dozen people are at the vet's now and the small lobby is packed. Another six people call to check on Roxanne's condition. All for a mutt most have never met.

At one point the vet allows Sami to see Roxanne -- it looks like the dog might not make it. Watching her leave the room in tears after just a few moments, he realizes it's a mistake.

Meanwhile, the distraught driver of the car has arrived and tells Sami's father he's trying to arrange to get another puppy in case Roxanne dies.

"My kids have had dogs," he says. "I know how much they mean to them."

A short while later, the miracle everybody is pleading for happens. Somehow, someway, Roxanne starts breathing on her own. "I was dumbfounded," the vet said.

A few days later, I'm sitting with Sami in her back yard, choking back tears as she tells her moving story. Roxanne, a keeshond mix, is still recovering from her wounds. It's hard to imagine a sweeter animal: She nuzzles up against me, a total stranger.

The value of walking a dog on a leash isn't the only discovery Sami has made.

"I didn't know there were so many good people out there," she says with a big smile.

Zeldin, who has lived here since 1976 and has watched the place grow from just a couple thousand to 50,000 today, says the story shows there's still a lot of small town in Murrieta.

"It was nice that everybody cared so much. That's definitely the most popular dog in Murrieta."

Times, like babies, are changed

Publication Date: May 1, 2001

The presents, all wrapped in frilly paper, are placed in the entryway. The delicate finger sandwiches are neatly aligned on a handsome tiered serving tray. Everybody is going on about how lovely the decor is.

The punch is tasty, but unfortunately it's not spiked. The games include trying to guess the maker of various infant products and tossing lettered dice made out of sugar cubes, hoping to spell the word "baby."

So this is what women do when men aren't around.

I'm attending my first baby shower. Fortunately it's not my spouse who is pregnant. The shower is for Kevin Nickoloff, a third-grade teaching colleague of mine, and his wife Melody. Rail Ranch Elementary School's third-grade teachers are hosting the affair.

The worst thing about the event is that several other men, including my father, phone me while I'm out. My wife Joanne dutifully reports the truth -- that I'm at a baby shower. Why couldn't she say I was at a wet T-shirt contest or some other raunchy male thing?

Needless to say, I'm in for a fair amount of teasing when I return the calls. You'd have thought I'd hosted the dang thing and wore a dress to the shower.

Times have changed in terms of baby products. My kids are 12 and 8, so it's been a while since I've been around infant things. Among the presents accumulated by the Nickoloffs is a baby-wipe warmer. All the women are cooing about how hard it must be for their precious bundles of joy to get a cold wipe slapped on their bottom. My attitude: Get used to it, kid. It's a cold world out there.

This is the fifth shower for the Nickoloffs. They're having a son named Mark and they've accumulated some 70 outfits for the kid, all apparently in blue. (Who says women aren't sexist?) While 70 may seem excessive, teacher Mary Mikolich, mother of three, says it's not.

"You need a lot of outfits. They poop all over the place." Thanks for sharing that.

In hopes of re-establishing my manhood and sanity, I head to the ET Sports Lounge in Temecula for some male bonding.

Talk about extremes. About 15 guys huddle around their drinks. There's a ball game on a couple of TVs. Smoke fills the room. The decor is your basic dark and dreary. There's not a woman in the place. You couldn't be any further from a baby shower.

The friendly bartender, Jim Bisbocci, asks if anybody has ever been to a baby shower hosted by women. One hand goes up, but that guy doesn't want his name in the newspaper. Who wants to be publicly branded with such a thing?

One patron, "Avocado Mike" Hobson, says he's been invited to several women's baby showers, but he's always declined.

"It didn't seem like a good place to be. A bunch of women talking about babies. Besides, they didn't have any booze."

Here comes the shocker. Bisbocci says he and Andy Hudig hosted a baby shower for a friend, Windell Smith, about six or seven years ago.

It involved the crowd that used to hang at the Shakespeare's bar in the old Murrieta Hot Springs resort.

Smith and his wife already had one baby, but now they had triplets on the way. The guys figured it was the least they could do for a buddy. They fondly recall how Smith practically needed a truck to haul away all the disposable diapers that the boys provided.

Maybe the world's not such a cold place after all.

Special teacher had a big heart, sense of humor
Publication Date: May 29, 2001

I'm wearing a new shirt, a blue- and-white number with a western look, as I pass one of my fellow teachers, Joanne Seufer.

"Hey Seufer," I shout at her because we always call each other by our last names.

"Hey Love. When's the rodeo?"

I try to come back with some weak rejoinder, but there's no way I'm topping that one. Seufer's the master when it comes to one-liners.

She ribs me Monday morning. Tuesday night she suffers a heart attack. Wednesday afternoon she dies.

An elementary school may be filled with books and pencils and tests, but most important are its people, both adults and children. At Rail Ranch School in Murrieta, 48-year-old Joanne Seufer was the biggest of people, both in stature and in heart.

She was one of those rare people who filled a room with her presence. You could be having the most serious meeting, with the principal making some monumental point, and Seufer would break up the room with a wisecrack.

Guaranteed.

She was more, so much more. It's a cliché that teachers care about kids. There are more than 50 teachers at Rail Ranch, so there's a whole lot of loving going on. Nobody cared more than the one with the jokes.

I sat in a meeting once with her and some parents to discuss why their kid was having so much trouble in school. At the end of the meeting, as we walked back to her classroom, Seufer started bawling. She cared so much about that kid.

It wasn't just the students either. She was legendary for the kind notes and gifts she left in other teachers' boxes. Whatever the occasion, be it happy or sad, you could count on Seufer to remember it. It was like clockwork -- just like the laughs.

Our school was like a mortuary. There was hardly a dry eye in the room as our principal, Pat Kelley, struggled to announce that Seufer has died within the hour. You don't lose the class clown and the teacher's pet all at once and not feel it.

I'm fighting back tears myself as I write this. For me, Seufer was more than a colleague, more than a friend. She was my mentor, not to mention the reason I ended up at such a wonderful school in the first place.

In the fall of 1997, when the Murrieta district went to class-size reduction in third grade, a lot of teachers had to be hired ASAP. It was going to be an unusual situation for the rest of the school year because two teachers were going to share a class of 32 kids. Those teachers better like each other.

I interviewed for those jobs; Seufer was one of the people asking the questions. Kelley fondly reminded me last week how she told him after my appearance that she wanted me as her partner. Fortunately for me she was the teacher of the year; she got what she wanted.

We spent six months working together five days a week in a room with 8- and 9-year olds. It was a difficult class, but one of the best times of my life because it was so real. We laughed, we cried, we laughed some more. God it was fun.

It turns out Seufer had one more lesson plan to show me. Last Thursday morning, as I struggle to share with my class of 20 third graders what Seufer meant to me, I can tell a lot of the kids feel my

pain. Who cares about reading and writing and math -- we're talking life here! The learning doesn't get any better than that.

And somewhere Joanne Seufer's laughing. She got me again.

Wife and kids win battle of the strays
Publication Date: June 12, 2001

"There's a lost dog standing in the middle of Whitewood Road,"
my wife, Joanne, announces breathlessly. "I'm going out to
rescue it."

"No, you're not," I insist.

Too late.

Another couple, out for a walk as Joanne performs her search and
rescue operation, helps bring the dog back to our home. The wife
commends Joanne for doing the right thing, then adds that she's
taken in five dogs and cats the same way, always over the objections
of her husband. The helpless look on the guy's face confirms it.

But I'm not giving up without a fight. While my kids, Julia and
David, plot names for the new dog -- "Happy," for how we're making
her feel; and "Dawn," to contrast with the name of one of our two
other dogs, "Midnight" -- I'm on the horn to the animal shelter.

The place is closed for the night except for emergencies, which
unfortunately this doesn't qualify as. By morning Joanne and the
kids will be bonded with the dog, which means I'm doomed.

A stray dog says a lot about a person. I can't tell you how many
times I've been driving down some busy street when we'll see some
lost dog wandering in the middle of the road. While my kids plead
with me to stop and save the creature, I contend that the animal's
fate rests with a power greater than ours, then step on the gas. It's
rare that I feel so ruthless.

At the same time, I've seen people stop and try to rescue a stray.
I say good for them, just don't make me take in the stray.

Which brings us to Christa Kaminski of Lake Elsinore and
Elaine Hernandez of the Perris area. These kind souls make a habit
of picking up animals from the Animal Friends of the Valley, for-
merly known as Lake Elsinore Animal Friends or LEAF.

Kaminski has adopted two dogs from the organization. One,
named Kasia, she kept; the other she gave back to the shelter because
it didn't get along with the first dog. However, Kaminski plans to
try a third dog in the next few months.

"We've heard of how it's so populated," she says of the number of strays in our midst. "We wanted to keep at least one off the streets."

Considering how upset I was about my wife's taking in one stray, it's a good thing I'm not married to Hernandez. She's adopted 10 animals from the shelter in the past decade alone. The retiree, who is widowed, has four cats and two dogs to keep her company.

As a kid, Hernandez took care of birds, dogs and cats. When she moved to Perris from Los Angeles 14 years ago, she brought with her three dogs and two cats, all once strays. Rescuing strays is a part of her, as much as driving past them is in my makeup.

"I don't go looking for them," she insists. "But when you see them bad off, you can't help yourself."

As for our stray, we're adjusting. Happy escaped three times in the first week, so we're learning to be more careful. The kids like her, the other dogs tolerate her, and my wife's announced Happy's her favorite dog.

I will say this: The other day I was barreling down Interstate 215 in the Perris area when I noticed a dead dog alongside the road. Before I wouldn't have given it a second thought; this time I felt sorry for the animal, even thinking that could have been Happy's fate if not for Joanne's actions.

Did I get sentimental contemplating this? Nah.

Class of 1976 was wild, but now we're old
Publication Date: July 17, 2001

It's a Saturday night in a hotel banquet room in Iowa, the deejay's playing rancid '70s disco music, the dance floor's empty, and I'm feeling really old.

It's my 25-year high school reunion, so everyone in the room is 43 or thereabouts. To a stranger stumbling onto the scene, it might look more like a company party with a group of 30- to 50-somethings.

Receding hairlines, shocking amounts of gray hair, extra pounds galore -- and that's just with the 85 who show up. Imagine what's happening to the 365 who didn't have the nerve to come.

Everybody has high school reunions; everyone treats them differently.

Some can't be bothered; others wouldn't miss them for the world. A psychologist would have a field day figuring out why.

This is the third Betterndorf High School class of 1976 reunion I've attended, and the experience is going downhill fast.

The 10-year gathering, my first, was one of the best weekends I'd had. I saw good friends I hadn't seen in a decade and I got to know a lot of people for the first time.

The festivities ended with us all twisting and shouting on a crowded floor to some Stones classic.

The 20-year event was more of a mixed bag. The Friday night icebreaker at the local bowling alley was a blast; the formal dinner the following night was a dud. It's like we weren't sure whether to act 18 or 38. I like 18 better.

Which brings us to the empty dance floor at the quarter-century gathering. A friend I'm sitting with likens it to a scene from a "Saturday Night Live" skit.

The music's awful, one of those ancient disco mirror balls is spinning lamely, and the deejays are pleading with the fuddy-duddies in the crowd to dance. It's truly pathetic because we're the fuddy-duddies now.

It's hard to believe this was the same bunch that had so much fun 25 years ago. A number of us swap stories from those bizarre days -- the big parties, our experimentation, and our recreation league basketball teams with the suggestive nicknames.

I want to go up to the deejay and scream, "We really were wild and crazy!"

Once.

Now we sit and pray that our kids -- many of them now high school age -- don't do the same things.

We rail against the drinking age in Iowa, which was 18 in 1976, and marvel that many of our escapades were perfectly legal.

We swap stories about the ones who didn't know when to grow up and let the good times go.

I learn a high school buddy has been in and out of drug rehab so many times his front teeth are rotted out.

A girl I had a crush on at 18 got hooked on cocaine. Another party animal was killed by the local police a few years back during a drug-induced rampage.

The vibes from that weekend of time travel to a town like the one where I live now leave my head spinning.

Part of me feels sad that I'm getting old and don't know how to have a good time anymore; that I don't want my kids doing the same idiotic things I did.

Another part feels lucky to be alive, no matter how much I've aged or changed. What revenge my kids have in store for me!

In the end, it's hard to have it both ways.

Losing sight, but not hope

Publication Date: September 11, 2001

Craig Schneider enjoys taking power walks with his dog every day, working on a career change and cruising the Internet.

Altogether a fairly normal life except for one thing: Schneider is blind. He went to bed one night in December 1995 with normal vision. He woke up the next morning with 90 percent of it gone. Now his world is complete darkness.

"Sometimes I feel like I'm dreaming," the 47-year-old Murrieta man says with a rueful chuckle, "that I'm going to wake up and this nightmare is going to be over."

It's hard to say what caused him to go blind at the age of 41. Perhaps it was the radiation treatments he took for eight years to beat back cancer.

Maybe it's the radon gas found in a Los Angeles home after he'd lived there for 18 months. A number of people encouraged him to sue the person who owned the home. He refused.

"It's not going to get my eyesight back," he says. "What good will money do me?"

Schneider understands why seeing people would want to sue, because he thought the same way when he had vision. He made great money as a general contractor, enough to afford three boats and a collection of 27 muscle cars. He needed a warehouse just to store all his toys.

He got rid of it all when he lost his sight.

"All that stuff doesn't mean anything to me anymore," Schneider says. "Before, it was like being in hell. I was never satisfied. I'm a more spiritual person now. I judge people more on what's inside, not how they look. I also have more peace of mind. I have less to worry about. My life isn't as complicated"

He hasn't always been so content with his fate. Initially he was in denial as he looked desperately for a cure. He figures he spent $100,000 on experimental therapies in Mexico.

Then he was angry when he realized the doctors couldn't provide the miracle he so desperately sought. Next he battled a brutal bout of depression. Finally, about three years ago, he decided he had to integrate himself back into the seeing world, to be there for his wife, Laura, and son, Garry.

They moved to Murrieta from San Diego in 1999. He acquired his affectionate seeing-eye dog, Luster, last year. They're a fixture on busy Whitewood Road where they take long walks together daily.

Schneider has to be very careful to avoid straying into traffic. Even so, Luster once led him into a low-hanging tree branch, and his master had to be taken to an emergency room.

Ginelle Dexter, a Rail Ranch Elementary School crossing guard at Whitewood and Los Alamos roads, sees Schneider several times a week.

"It's amazing to see what he's able to do on the walks," she says. "He's really been able to get on with his life."

He built an office in his garage himself. He even did the electrical work, with son Garry helping him properly line up the different-colored wires. An electrician who inspected the work couldn't believe a blind man did it.

Now he's starting Charities for the Blind, a group that donates computers to people without sight. He's become so proficient on computers that he feels he can work as a construction project coordinator, if someone will just give him a chance.

"I work hard," he says. "That's the only reason I'm where I'm at. You can't be lazy and be blind, not if you want to get anywhere."

CHAPTER 14

2002 - No more tractor races for you, Temecula!

It was the surest sign yet that Southwest Riverside County's rural roots are just about a thing of the past. The death of the Great Temecula Tractor Race moved us one step closer to being like the rest of Southern California suburbia. We haven't been the same since.

The Little Professor bookstore's demise in Temecula was another sad event, though for a different reason. What's it say about an area that can't support an independent bookstore? So we can't tolerate a grimy tractor race and don't buy enough books either? Who in the heck are we?

While we grappled with those issues, Irving Kasow was daring to be public about his atheist beliefs. You can imagine the reaction in a place that's inundated with churches.

Religion came into play a lot in my life that year. At home, my son David was questioning why he had to go to church, something his own father wrestled with decades before. And in the realm of local sports, there was the issue of leagues holding games on Sundays, when some local kids won't play because of their religious beliefs. Why does life have to be so complicated?

On to less weighty matters, such as Ray Borel, a longtime land-owner in French Valley looking at all that growth headed his way, a piece on Larry Markham, a local development consultant who we can credit – or blame – for so much of the change; and finally, a mere tract house in Murrieta where 15 children were being raised. And you thought your kids were loud!

Religion and sports collide

Publication Date: February 12, 2002

Eight-year-old Nathan Matson of Murrieta really wanted to play the last game of his soccer season. It was a big out-of-town tournament, he wanted to be there for his teammates because they'd been together for five months and he loves to compete.

There was one catch: His Mormon religion advises followers to abstain from games on Sunday, the day his soccer season ended. The church recommends parishioners spend the day with family and religious activities.

So Nathan didn't play. "I was so mad," he says. "I really wanted to be there."

The good news is that Nathan will be able to play the final Murrieta Youth Basketball League game. The league is juggling its schedule so that for the first time, no games are played on Sundays, including the critical playoffs this weekend.

League President Bob Stiles knows all about the issue. A fourth-grade team he coached last year had the best record during the regular season. But the team lost the championship game on Sunday when its best player, Jake Tarabilda, didn't play because he's Mormon.

Sunday playoff games left teams not playing at full strength, which wasn't fair to anyone, Stiles says. "It really wasn't a hard decision at all for the board to make the change."

It could be for other leagues. Sports fields are at a premium in rapidly growing Southwest Riverside County. League officials say sometimes the only way to squeeze in tournaments is to spread them over two days.

Mormon parents such as Cindy Sanders are glad at least one league is changing its ways. "It's a big relief not to have the coaches saying to your child, "Can't you play just this once?' "

Her husband Raoul has coached a lot of the basketball teams that their five kids have played on. Raoul has also had to skip a few big games because they were on Sundays. Cindy says, "Of course, it is difficult for the coaches to play one man short and I know they don't want to get a lot of LDS (Mormon) kids on their teams because of this."

No kidding. I know of several coaches who'd rather not have Mormon kids because of the Sunday issue. I've coached four teams the past two years and there have been Mormon players on each squad. Nathan Matson was one of three Mormon kids on my soccer team this year and we had to play two playoff games without them, meaning we had no substitutes.

But there's an issue here that's bigger than wins and losses. The other players and parents on the team accepted that the Mormon kids weren't going to be there, and I think the children learned something huge from it.

Standing up for what you believe is important.

Says Sanders: "It takes a lot of understanding and conviction to follow through when there is a championship game to be played, but we feel our kids have benefited from living this commandment. It has helped them to polish their characters and to be a better person for it."

Local dentist Larry Hoyt had to deal with the issue when his son Spencer was invited to try out for an all-star soccer team. At first Hoyt decided not to let his son take part because of the Sunday games. Then the coach called and said she didn't mind if he skipped the games. Spencer made the team and played Saturday.

If Hoyt's forced to choose between his church and a team, the church wins. What's unfortunate is that he's forced to choose at all.

House filled with love

Publication Date: January 29, 2002

The numbers themselves are mindboggling: Fifteen kids packed in a five-bedroom Murrieta tract home, seven vehicles parked out front and 14 loaves of bread piled on the kitchen table.

What's even more amazing is what's brought them all together: A sense of family that you don't often find in our transient, divorce-prone, two-income, home-alone society.

The best place to start is with the parents, Tammy and Donal Pearce, who have 11 children, ages 18 years to 21 months: Donny, Sallianne, Veronica, Jessica, Sammy, Ian, Sean, Judy, Brian, Suzanne and Elizabeth.

Dad's a computer designer, Mom's a homemaker. And with 11 kids, that's a lot of home to make. They live in a 3,010-square-foot home, one of the few families who actually needs one of those large tract homes they build these days.

Then there's grandmother, Jean Pearce, who was living in Perris with four children of her own, all adopted. Grandmother, now 60, had her first baby when she was just 16. She's already raised four of her own, as well as two other children she adopted as babies. The four adopted children she's currently responsible for are Keriann, Kadilyn, Kimisu and Tony.

Jean was diagnosed with breast cancer last fall, a hard thing to tackle in the best of circumstances, let alone when you're a grandmother whose husband has passed away.

Donal, a faithful son if there ever was one, offered to let his mom's family move in with his, the one that already had 11 kids. Jean accepted, and arrived with her brood in early December, which is why you now have 18 people living in one tract home.

Tammy, already the mother of 11 children, says the more the merrier. "It's been such a blessing and a joy to get these other children. Otherwise you don't know what would happen to them."

It's a clan that never stops making sacrifices. Seven girls sleep in a "bonus room" packed with three sets of bunk beds. Donny, Tammy and Donal's oldest son at 18, agreed to give up his own bedroom -- quite a luxury in a home of 15 kids -- so his grandmother who's battling cancer could have a room of her own.

Now Donny sleeps with Ian and Brian, ages 11 and 5. Not exactly cool for a kid a year removed from high school, but very noble.

"It doesn't bother me," Donny insists. "He (5-year-old Brian) knows his boundaries."

So it goes with the Pearces, a family that just deals with things. It's hard enough to feed a regular family when only one parent works, now imagine having to keep a household of 18 well-nourished on a single income. Donal, who dutifully clips coupons, carefully tracks newspaper specials, never buys anything that's not on sale or that he has a coupon for, and spends $500 a month on groceries, or about $25 a person.

The Pearces stretch their food dollars by cooking a lot of casseroles, soups and stews, the latter two meals in a hard-to-find 22-quart pot. Life with 18 people is a constant juggling act. A lot of the kids know to take their showers at night to avoid the morning congestion.

Jean and Tammy carefully map out their errands each afternoon, taking kids here, there and everywhere. They try to do everything in one trip, quite a feat with their brood.

They gather as a family every evening for scripture readings and prayer. They say they have a lot to be thankful for when it comes to family. The numbers prove it.

Rural image no longer fits

Publication Date: February 26, 2002

Now what -- the Great Temecula Van Olympics? A huge part of us dies with the news that the Great Temecula Tractor Race is kaput. The notion that we're somehow different from the suburban sprawl that's swallowing up most of Southern California is fading fast.

All that's left to do is to come up with a replacement competition for the tractor race, something in line with what everybody else has. The more we blend in the better. Perhaps the Great Temecula Lexus Pull would be appropriate.

Attendance at the 25-year-old tractor race dropped like a rock due to the town's changing demographics. Longtime race official Bill Harker says the peak crowds were in the late 1980s with 12,000 in for the weekend. Two years ago, 5,000 showed. Last year was even worse.

The tractor race's appeal -- dirty, quaint and silly fun -- just didn't fit the town's sophisticated ways anymore.

Bill Harker, who's lived here 28 years, recalls a time when locals lived the country life that the tractor race reflected. Everybody wore Western clothes back then, even business people. "I knew it was going to change once I started seeing a bunch of neckties around town."

I'm not saying the change is a bad thing because I've lived here 14 years and I'm not going anywhere. Besides, the people who made Temecula what it is today -- and Murrieta to a lesser extent -- got exactly what they wanted. The goal of the Powers That Be has been to make Temecula an Orange County East.

Mission accomplished, judging by the fancy retail, expensive housing and upscale incomes of today's Temecula.

Now if we could just enclose the whole city and air condition the place in the summer, we'd be Irvine year-round.

Some will disagree with my argument, contending Temecula's roots are still preserved in Old Town. Problem is it's a gussied-up Old Town, thanks to the fancy sidewalks, streetlights and monuments that the city put in a couple years ago. It looks nice, but it's not authentic.

Rick Busenkell knows what I'm talking about. The vice president of the local museum board says it's practically false advertising to label it part of the Old West. "There's nothing there that fits its real history."

For starters, somebody could restore the Ramona Inn saloon that used to be at Front and Main in Old Town. The lore of the place includes the two guys who were shot and killed in 1907.

"Talk about Western history, a saloon shootout," Busenkell says.

Newcomers today know nothing of that event. Just like most are ignorant about the fact Temecula was once a stagecoach stop, a railroad stop and a cow town. Most signs of our past are gone, trampled by the rapid growth that's seen the Temecula-Murrieta area go from a population of 2,200 when Harker moved here in 1974 to well over 100,000 today.

Busenkell says the demise of the tractor race is just the latest sign that Temecula's country life is gone. "I'm sorry to see it go," he says.

"If there's anything that Temecula could call its own, it's the tractor race."

But who else will have the Great Temecula SUV Challenge?

The sad loss of a bookstore
Publication Date: March 12, 2002

This being a bookstore, there's no shortage of metaphors for the closing of Little Professor.

There's the fireplace that's now extinguished, not unlike the loss of the store's profits. There are the empty shelves, which could be likened to the lack of customers. There are the hushed tones of the people there on its last day Saturday, more reminiscent of a funeral parlor than a store.

In a sense, the death of Little Professor is like the loss of a loved one.

When it opened six years ago, there wasn't a bookstore in Southwest Riverside County. It's a sad commentary on any community, especially one as affluent as ours. Sandy Dodson, the store's jolly owner, likened the initial business surge to a feeding frenzy, so hungry were we for books. Those days of robust sales are long gone for Little Professor.

A combination of things did it in. There's the obvious, the gigantic chain book store, Barnes & Noble, that opened a few years ago on Winchester Road. There's the not-so-obvious, the closing of the movie theater in the Target shopping center that Little Professor was located in. Traffic at the store dropped dramatically after that.

But the biggest factor of all was the opening of The Promenade mall. That giant sucking sound you hear in Temecula these days is every business scrambling to situate itself next to the mall. Even our kids' dentist and our eye doctor, people we've gone to for more than a decade, are moving near there. It's where the action is right now.

The effects are obvious on Dodson's west side of the Target center. On a Saturday afternoon when the place should be packed, the parking lot is half empty. Not good.

Appropriately enough, Dodson, a former minister who's not sure what he's going to do next, went out with a fund-raiser, this time for the local Boys & Girls Club. Books were being donated to the organization, an event organized by Jon Laskin of the nonprofit Musicians Workshop education center.

Over the years Dodson was named Rookie Rotarian of the Year, served on the chamber board of directors and helped out the library, local schools, The Komen Foundation, Aspiring Angels and much, much more.

Laskin says it feels like Little Professor has been here 60 years, not just six, so powerful was the store's impact on our area. "He's (Dodson) a fixture in the community," Laskin says. "We wanted to celebrate his involvement."

Laskin is afraid we're losing some identity with the large number of chain stores invading, lured by our upscale demographics. We recall with a laugh the long-gone Jimmy's coffee shop, a place operated by locals and so full of quirks. It was so Temecula. Now we're inundated with big chain Starbucks, where once you've seen one, you've seen 'em all. Whether it's Seattle or Temecula (or now even Murrieta), everything's the same.

While Laskin and Dodson say chains have their place -- there's a reason they're successful -- they also tend to be less involved in the community.

"With a chain, the profits all go outside of the community and it cuts down on the money multiplier," Dodson says. "As a whole, it is a disaster for the community when the independents are all wiped out."

It's a book that doesn't have a happy ending.

Food not sold at Ray's Café

Publication Date: May 14, 2002

The first sign that Ray's Cafe in Murrieta isn't what it seems is the phone number that's not listed. What profit-orientated business isn't listed?

"There is a phone but I don't want to give it out," says the owner, Skip Bezanson. "There's no one I want to call. It's just for emergencies."

Just then, as if by divine intervention, the phone rings. A potential customer perhaps. "Now what?" Bezanson growls through his thick beard before answering. The caller hangs up.

Then there's the matter of the establishment's name, "cafe" implying that food is served. Wrong. Hasn't happened for years. It's just a bar now.

Of course, if you want to bring your own food and have Bezanson heat it for you, no problem. Randall Wharton does just that, plopping his canned food on the counter. A few minutes later, Bezanson returns with a bowl of steaming hot chili.

"It's BYOF," Wharton cackles. "Bring your own food."

So it is with Ray's Cafe, going on its 52nd year now on Washington Avenue in old Murrieta. It occupies a building that was put up in 1912, a country store at the time. In many respects not much has changed today in the building, the oldest in town to still house a business.

Just like his building, Bezanson oozes local history. His great grandfather leased land from Juan Murrieta for farming. It doesn't get any more original than that in these parts. No wonder Bezanson likes to say, "I was here before I was born."

His mom basically lived here her whole life. His father, a jazz musician, arrived in 1935 to work as a waiter during the day and play music at night at what was then the Murrieta Hot Springs Resort. (Today it's Calvary Chapel Conference Center in case you just arrived.)

Bezanson's parents bought the cafe in 1950. At the time Washington Avenue was Highway 395, the main route through Southwest Riverside County, a prime spot for a restaurant.

Times have changed. The afternoon I'm there just four people pass through. "It's been slow, not as good as it used to be," Bezanson says of his traffic.

Not that the place isn't entertaining. It's a local museum of sorts, with a 1930s juke box and a painting of what once was the center of Murrieta, the old Fountain House hotel and train depot. A shelf above the front door is packed with antiques such as an old scooter.

Then there are the stuffed animals Bezanson keeps behind the bar and the mechanical singing fish he has on the walls. Clearly, this 60-year-old man likes toys.

Bezanson is an educated man who quotes John Steinbeck.

He keeps the chemical makeup of alcohol posted behind the bar, as well as the exact latitude, longitude and elevation of Murrieta. It's as if Bezanson is trying to educate as well as entertain.

Whatever Ray's is, the clientele is fond of it. Last summer, one of the towering eucalyptus trees on Washington Avenue crashed into the bar, taking out one of the white pillars that makes the place look so distinctive.

Bezanson's friends put on a fund-raiser to raise about $2,000 to pay for the damage. Bezanson was touched. "I truly appreciated it. People I hadn't seen for years showed up."

Regular patron Fred West says the feeling is mutual. "It'll be a sad day in hell when Skipper goes," West says. "They'll probably bulldoze it and put in another condo."

It'll be sad.

Convenience, but more folks
Publication Date: May 28, 2002

It's another late night for Larry Markham. He isn't out carousing, he is out campaigning -- for the developer he represents.

This time it is past midnight before the Murrieta City Council finally approves the project he's lobbying for, a U-Haul complex at Whitewood and Los Alamos roads.

Late nights have been a way of life for more than 20 years for Markham, the guy who's surely represented more development projects in Southwest Riverside County than anybody.

California Oaks, Bear Creek, Copper Canyon, most of Temecula's apartments, tons of gas stations, strip centers galore -- you name a local land use, Markham has peddled it.

With Riverside County working on its growth plan for the future, Markham is a good guy to talk to. For the residents who feel growth has hit the southwestern county like a baseball bat upside the head, Markham is the guy with the black hat, the developer's hired gun who's shooting up their dreams of the quiet country life.

Markham knows all about that. He first showed up here in 1978 to represent ARCO and its land that is now Bear Creek. That was back when Temecula and Murrieta had a couple thousand folks between them.

Back when you had to go to Fallbrook to find a real grocery store, when you had to go to Corona to see a movie.

Now Markham can find all that and more within a five-minute drive from his home in Temecula. It's development that's made the convenience possible. Yup, those rotten developers.

But even Markham has been surprised at the pace. Locals suspected the place would take off when Interstate 15 was punched through in the mid-1980s. It's just hard to imagine it would climb so rapidly to the heights of more than 150,000 that it has today.

Ironically, it's a project that didn't happen that helped launch the growth. In the early '80s, Markham and others tried to lure a giant Hewlett-Packard plant to the northwestern side of Temecula. One key reason the company didn't come was because southwestern county didn't have enough housing for its workers. Imagine that.

It made the powers that be such as Markham realize what the area needed if it wanted to attract top-flight industry. The first major tract of that era, Starlight Ridge, was soon started in Temecula. When the project was a hit, developers knew the area was a gold mine.

We're not tapped out either. Temecula is expected to wind up near 200,000, Murrieta at around 100,000. At the rate we're going, that could happen in less than 20 years.

Given the battle over growth, it's clear not everybody wants it. Markham likens the objections to "social engineering" and says it's dangerous to try to put limits on the people who can move here. "Who do you exclude?" he asks.

A better approach is to minimize the effects newcomers have on the rest of us, Markham contends. Like his critics, he's worried about the traffic the growth will bring, which is why it's critical to build more east-west routes, to add another I-15 interchange between Temecula and Murrieta, and to keep widening our freeways. Given that he feels we've already successfully absorbed 150,000 people, Markham is confident we can handle another 150,000.

And having lived here almost a quarter century, Markham the planner projects he'll still be here another quarter century from now to watch it happen. The question is how many of his critics will still be here.

It has that Vegas feeling
Publication Date: July 2, 2002

The feeling hits me as soon as I walk in the front door: "This is Vegas."

There's the steady hum of slot machines, the lights that are dim around the clock, the shouts of the winners, the groans of the losers, the long lines at the buffet, the smokers everywhere, and the guys having a beer in the middle of the afternoon.

Of course, as most of us know by now after an avalanche of publicity, it's not Vegas. It's just supposed to feel like it. It's actually Temecula, home to the largest Indian casino in the Western United States, $262 million worth to be exact.

That's what Temecula will be known as now, a gambling town. What would you expect after more than 20,000 people storm the Pechanga Indian casino the first night it's open. Oddly, that 20,000 also happened to be Temecula's population the year I moved here, 1988.

That was back when Temecula was truly a small town; back when locals would picket a video store that dared to rent adult videos. Now, the day after the casino opens, the Temecula City Council renames the street in front of the casino after the Pechangas.

It's all about business, which is what everything seems to be about these days in Temecula. The previous name, Pala Road, promoted the name of a nearby gaming tribe that competes with the Pechangas. Can't have that, the Temecula Powers That Be decreed, not if we want our casino to be the biggest. So it'll be Pechanga Parkway. At least it's not Casino Court, Slot Street or Wager Way.

Most of Temecula doesn't seem to mind. Nobody's picketing the casino. There was a time when Pechangas made a big deal out of the fact they didn't serve liquor at their old casino, but nobody's squawking now that the tribe has raised the gambling age from 18 to 21 to be able to serve alcohol. What's a casino if you can't have a drink while you play, if you can't get so sloshed that you don't care how much money you lose. Not a Vegas one, that's for sure.

Temecula has basically evolved into a live and let live kind of town, which is fine. A community doesn't more than triple in size in less than 15 years and not change.

Even the prudes have to concede there are a few benefits. The casino's created 2,200 jobs in a region that needs every job it can get. The showroom will host Broadway-style shows and concerts, so no more whining that there's nothing to do around here. There are also seven new restaurants that are decently priced. Heck, even kids are welcome in those places. Is this a family town or what?

None of this decadence would be possible without the avalanche of gamblers who somehow have endless money to blow. (Don't these people know there's a recession going on?) The ones I talk to mostly give our casino a thumbs up.

Rene Aguirre of Downey likes any place that gives him $305 on a $20 bet, and he also thinks the Pechangas will divert a lot of traffic, including himself, that would otherwise go to Vegas. While Charles Schreiber of Murrieta wishes the Pechangas had lower betting minimums, he likes the new place. The most discord I heard was from Ladd Schweitzer and Beth Carrington of Antelope Valley. Besides the fact she dropped $300, Carrington says the joint doesn't have enough action for her.

Give us time, lady. The way things are going in Temecula, there's Bound to be more "action" on the way, whether we want it or not.

French Valley roots run deep
Publication Date: September 17, 2002

Not many business tycoons drove a tractor when they were 10. Or farmed land from Wildomar to Vail Lake just 20 years ago. Or today dip into chewing tobacco while talking in their offices.

Ray Borel has about as many pretensions as a dog has wings. He's as country boy as it gets, even if he's the point man for the family that has the most land in French Valley, which right now is changing faster than any other community in Southwest Riverside County.

Giant earthmovers cruise the land Borel once farmed, turning French Valley into another slice of suburbia. Borel watches with a smile because he's about to cash in like you wouldn't believe.

He shows me an offer for a piece of land his great-grandfather first acquired. Don't print it, he cautions, just think about the kind of money these developers are tossing around.

If only my great-grandfather had bought some land here in the late 1800s. Yup, the Borels go way back. Great-Grandfather Alex first came across the place in 1886 while running cattle from LA to Mexico. There was water from springs here for the cattle. Water being more valuable than land then, Borel started scooping up the acreage.

Borel had come from France because he didn't want to fight in the wars going on in Europe. There were three other French families in the area as well: Pourroy, Nicolas and Auld. Thus the name of the place.

Most of the family's holdings, which at one time amounted to about 2,400 acres, were acquired in the 1930s and 1940s. At the time the family grew grapes and made wine, even when something called Prohibition was going on. One thing about the Borels, they're survivors.

In 1923, Ray Borel's grandfather, another Alex, convinced his dad that they needed to invest in a wheel tractor if they wanted to keep farming. Fine, Dad says, but only if you run it. I'm sticking to my horses.

Never mind that the son was only an Elsinore High School freshman at the time. And had to quit school to farm. Borels had to adapt. Or else.

The family has brought that same spirit to this business of developing. While a lot of old-timers either: (A) stay put and curse the arrival of all them city folk, or (B) sell their ranches to builders and get the heck out of here ASAP, the Borels have chosen to adjust. The county got the land for French Valley Airport from the Borels, but the family hung on to the acreage around it. Their dream of a giant airpark development on almost 900 acres is now taking off.

One thing Ray Borel's aiming for is quality. He's almost proud to say his land isn't just being sold off to mere housing developers ("We're not into building puppy mills," he says.). He's planning to bring jobs and industry here. "I want a really good commercial and industrial development, nicer than Temecula or Murrieta has ever seen," he says. "I'm taking my time."

Borel is able to take the long view, considering the picture in his real estate office of the one-room schoolhouse in which he was educated. The photo of Los Alamos School was taken in 1966, Borel's fifth-grade year.

Fifteen kids, grades one through six, attended the school, and taught by the aptly named -- this being a farming community -- Miss Fields. Heck, Borel even walked 2 1/2 miles to school. "You do not fight progress if you came from where we came from," he says.

You make do, something the Borel clan has done for more than a century now.

Religion war in the home
Publication Date: September 24, 2002

It's Sunday morning and there's a war going on in our house.

It's over my 10-year-old son David's reluctance to go to church. He said he's already learned everything he needs to know about it. "Jesus is the son of God and I'm supposed to live like him. I hear the same thing over and over," he insists.

It's not like he's some juvenile delinquent in training. He's got good grades, he cares about others, and his friends are nice kids. He just doesn't want to go to church.

Complicating matters is my own experience: I dreaded going to church when I was a kid. I always promised myself I wouldn't put my own kids through this torture. The only reason I reluctantly started going again is that my wife persuaded me our two kids needed a religious education.

I know we're not alone in this battle. Considering Southwest Riverside County is teeming with churches looking to attract young families, religious education is a big issue. Ministers tell me the Sunday school program can make or break a church. Children who don't want to go sometimes force parents to try another venue.

Nobody knows this better than Steve Struikmans, who's been ministering at Rancho Community Church in Temecula for 33 years. It's not just his longevity either; he went through the same battle over church school with his son Neil some 25 years ago.

Struikmans compares church school to regular school. Although there are certainly plenty of kids who don't want to go to regular school, they go regardless. Church school needs to be considered in the same light, Struikmans says.

At the same time, parents need to practice what's being preached and lead righteous lives. "You've got to walk your talk" is how Struikmans puts it. Otherwise, kids see church as an exercise in hypocrisy. Once that happens, forget it.

Sean Cox, pastor at St. Thomas of Canterbury Episcopal Church in Temecula, also was bored by church when he was 10. His parents worked with him, opting to go to shorter Saturday night services. What really turned him on to church as a teen was a great youth pastor.

Cox suggests letting my kid stay to hear the minister's sermon, then discussing the message with him afterward. In effect, his parents can help be his Sunday school teachers.

Then there's Tony March of Murrieta, who considers himself an agnostic, a person who disclaims any knowledge of God. He was raised in Spain in a Catholic school that required him to attend church regularly, a ritual he despised. "The things they try to indoctrinate you on never made sense to me," he says.

A few weeks ago he went with a friend to a local parochial pre-school graduation. He says he was appalled at how much school officials connected their curriculum to Christianity. "I felt like these kids were just like trained parrots. They don't have a chance to make up their own minds."

March doesn't take his own kids, ages 5 and 8, to church, though he won't object if they decide to go on their own with friends.

"I want my kids to be open-minded about church," he says. "I want them to figure it out on their own, to be able to think for themselves."

In the end, dealing with my son's resistance to church is like a lot of matters pertaining to the spirit: There are no easy answers.

He stands up for non-beliefs
Publication Date: October 29, 2002

Atheist Irving Kasow is not bashful about his view on religion. It's there on two bumper stickers on his car: "Religions are just cults with more members" and "Freedom is the distance between church and state." Or the message on his T-shirt: "Freedom from religion."

The funny thing is that Kasow looks a lot like Santa Claus, a character associated with Christmas, that most celebrated religious holiday of all. He's got the jolly disposition, the paunch and the white hair. Lucifer he's not.

"Contrary to popular opinion we don't have horns and tails," says Kasow, 73. "I'm not a monster who evicts widows and burns down orphanages."

He is a guy willing to stand up for what he believes. For that he's to be commended, regardless of your take on religion.

Kasow created a stink this month when his lobbying helped convince the Lake Elsinore City Council to remove references to religious figures such as Jesus Christ from invocations. Besides speaking out against the practice at council meetings, Kasow contacted the ACLU, which fired off a letter to the city threatening legal action over its invocation.

Kasow has been heckled at council meetings for his stand. He's received 10 angry phone calls since the council revised its rules on invocations. One diehard even followed him home after seeing his bumper stickers, advising him he was going to hell and it was his duty to save Kasow from his fate.

A liberal for as long as he can remember, Kasow knows he's out of step with the conservative, Christian views of Southwest Riverside County. But he likes our warm weather and the fact he can play poker at the nearby Pechanga casino in Temecula. (Heavens to Betsy, more sinning on his part.) Bottom line, he's not moving.

He readily concedes he likes to stir the pot, but it's more than that. He says he feels obligated to stand up for what he believes in, the separation of church and state, even if he's ridiculed in the process. "You have to get up on your hind legs and roar every once in a while."

He's been what he calls a "free thinker" for as long as he can remember. Raised in a Jewish family, he decided on his own to be an atheist at 13. At UCLA, he attended meetings of a group that was considered to have communist leanings. He fought in the Korean War, but regrets he didn't stand up for what he believes in -- he had doubts about the United States' fighting there -- and moved to Canada instead of serving in the military.

In Japan he met his wife, a Buddhist who rarely attended religious services. He made his living owning restaurants and working in L.A. card clubs. His wife died in 1986, and he moved to Lake Elsinore five years ago when he got a job at Pechanga.

He's been in church a few times over the years for weddings and he enjoys the music of religion.

As for the message, he's not buying.

Of Jesus Christ, who Christians believe is the Savior, he says, "He was probably a philosopher trying to do some good. Maybe he was a teacher. He was a spellbinding speaker and probably a nice guy. But nothing more."

Of the Bible, the book many consider the word of God, he says: "It's a bunch of stories, some probably historically valid. I can't believe it's the word of God. I think Karl Marx was right. Religion is the opiate of the masses. It's a way to control people and I think it's done more harm than good."

No doubt many locals feel the same way about Kasow.

A tense time for the coaches
Publication Date: November 26, 2002

The coach scans his evaluation sheets and notes, hoping to find the best available player while avoiding the kind of uncoordinated player who can kill a team. Meanwhile the tension mounts because the clock is ticking down and coaches only have a minute per pick in this league.

A high-stakes professional league it's not. It's a Murrieta Youth Basketball League draft, and grown men are in agony over the selection of 10-year-old kids. Does it sound demented? Don't these guys have something better to do, like mow a lawn?

You're asking the wrong guy because I'm one of the dozen coaches sitting in that room. And I spent an hour preparing for the thing. Forget the lawn, honey, draft night's this week. It's not a sickness confined to Murrieta either; it goes on all over Southwest Riverside County, wherever there are rec leagues designed for the kids just to have "fun." Yeah, right.

There's a reason these adults -- oversized boys if you will -- are so intense about this stuff.

League president Bob Stiles says the most important event in any rec league is draft night. It doesn't matter how good a coach you are if you don't have talent. Blow a draft night and you're blowing a season. The pressure's on, baby!

Stiles, who has sat through some 20 drafts in basketball, soccer and baseball, says, "People would die if they knew what goes on in those rooms." There's the guy who's stalling while pouring over his draft notes, hoping to buy time to find the 10-year-old equivalent of Kobe Bryant in a lower round. Come on, buddy, this is rec league, not the NBA Finals.

Then there's the dad who's been advised by his wife to pick their son's best friend at all costs. The problem is the coach passed on the friend in the early rounds, figuring he could pick him up later. That loud moan you hear is the best friend being picked by another coach.

It's a night of exhilaration, agony, calculations and cruelty all in one. It's better than TV.

Leagues conduct drafts in a couple of basic formats. One is the "blind draft" in which coaches are allowed to freeze a player or two or three, such as their child, their best friend's, or players that have been together for many years.

All the other players are selected at random with coaches drawing from stacks of players ranked by all-star status and years of experience. This is easier on coaches' blood pressure because it involves some luck of the draw.

Still, this seemingly mellow method of drafting can lead to extreme behavior. Brent Dobson of Murrieta says one coach offered him $100 if he could freeze Dobson's son Noah for his under-12 coed soccer team. Dobson passed, keeping his son with the coach he's played with for the past three years.

The other method of dividing up players is an actual draft where tryouts are held. Nervous players do a couple of basic drills while coaches take notes. League officials rank the players from best to worst, slot players in rounds, and distribute rankings at the draft. The one player the coach is assured of getting is his child in the round he or she is assigned to.

As cutthroat as it seems, there is something humane: Ranking sheets are usually taken from coaches by league officials once a draft is done, assuring that parents of the lowest ranked players won't know what's been said about their kids.

Who says aggressive, competitive, macho coaches don't have a soft side?

CHAPTER 15

2003 - Going to war in lots of ways

The war in Iraq played out big-time in military minded Southwest Riverside County.

I wrote about a Murrieta father who thankfully returned from combat. It's hard for a dad to leave his children behind, never knowing if he'll come back alive. Just ask my dad.

I had my third graders write letters to a Marine in Iraq, the cousin of a kid in our class. As I put it in the piece, "It gives the kids a way to express what they're feeling, something we all need."

Then there was the peace vigil at the California Oaks Sports Park in Murrieta. Let's just say we're not San Francisco.

I wrote about a Murrieta family that has been plotting their child's sports career since the day before he was born (When it comes to college scholarships in athletics, one can't start soon enough.), and an immigrant's struggle to learn to read so he can better chase the American dream.

And what a sad sign it was that a "for sale" sign was posted on a storied Murrieta horse arena, another nail in the coffin of the rural lifestyle here.

Learning lingo truly gritty

Publication Date: March 25, 2003

Carl Kwang Yong Ahn is watching an American classic, "True Grit," on his big-screen TV.

There's just one problem, he can't figure out what grit means. He's looked in the dictionary but he doesn't understand the definition. "Vocabulary, this is hard," he says.

He tried the first entry, small pieces of hard material, but that doesn't make sense in the context of a John Wayne Western. Look at the second definition, I tell him, determination.

"True determination," he says, beaming with the look of "now I get it."

"Like you with the English language," I tell him.

Of his struggle, Ahn replies with a laugh, "Until I die."

Most people with Ahn's background would be in cruise control by now. He owns 51 percent of a successful Korean publishing firm that has 20 full-time employees. He's 56 and his three daughters, a classical music group known as The Ahn Trio, are very successful. It would seem to be time to kick back and enjoy the fruits of his labor.

There's just one thing. Ever since he was a boy, it's been Ahn's dream to live in America and speak English.

He's living his dream here in Southwest Riverside County, but it sure is a lot of work.

He's taking five English classes at Mt. San Jacinto College in Menifee as well as attending two morning English sessions a week in Murrieta. His dining room table is covered with study aids, including three dictionaries, two writing books and a grammar book. He spends at least 20 hours a week on homework, not to mention the time trying to decipher TV shows and newspaper stories. Hardly the life of luxury.

That day's paper, for example, has several headlines circled; a sign Ahn doesn't understand what they mean. One calls Lake Elsinore "a no-prayer zone." With a perplexed look, Ahn wonders if this means people can't pray at the dinner table or before they got to bed. No, I explain, it means invocations with religious references can't be given at City Council meetings.

With a weary look, he says it can take him half an hour to comprehend a newspaper story because of the words he has to look up. "Now I realize English is the hardest language," he says.

There is one part of Ahn's life that's relaxing. A good golfer, he'd also dreamed of coming to America to learn to play even better. He came to southwest county because of the Professional Golfers Career College in Temecula. His home in the Golf Knolls community in east Murrieta also is connected to the game, considering he was putting on the 14th green of a nearby course when he noticed a for sale sign. He made a deal that afternoon.

"This is my garden," he says, pointing to the scenic view he has of the course. "Nobody has big garden like me."

There's one dream left to accomplish: sailing around the world with an American bride. An accomplished boatman, his plan is to relocate to San Diego in a couple of years to buy a craft, hire a crew, and prepare for the big trip. He's also dating somebody. "I like her and I think she likes me," he says with a shy smile.

Before I leave, he asks for help with a grammar worksheet on plural nouns. I'm willing to do more, but he makes it apparent he doesn't want it. He feels he needs to learn on his own. It's the true grit thing again. It's what dreams are made of.

Peace vigil glows quietly

Publication Date: April 1, 2003

Some guys are playing a pickup game at the California Oaks Sports Park hoops. A couple is sitting on a park bench. Some people are on the swings.

And an encounter of sorts between pro-war and pro-peace forces -- albeit a stealth one -- is playing out as well. Yes, these are strange times.

I'm here to write about a Murrieta candlelight peace vigil, something that's been going on since the Sunday before the war with Iraq was launched. Supporters of peace, about 15, are sitting under the park's gazebo, singing songs and making quiet speeches backing said cause.

Somebody comes up and says there's another group down on Cal Oaks Road also in favor of the cause. This was a place the pro-peace group had gathered the previous Sunday evening as well. Let's go join them, they decide.

On the busy street, there is a gathering of about a half-dozen, most waving American flags. They're shouting and some passing motorists are honking back their support.

It dawns on the group of peace supporters that these folks represent the other side, the ones supporting war. The backers of peace decide to head back to the gazebo.

"I don't think we need to clash," Jamie Barnett, the group's song leader, says.

So it goes in Southwest Riverside County, a politically conservative region if there ever was one. It's hard to even hold a peace vigil without somebody nearby backing war.

One of the war supporters, Murrieta resident Debbie Walker, says she'd read about the other group's meeting in the newspaper. She was under the impression that it was a rally to support the troops and President Bush. "He is the commander in chief."

Impressions notwithstanding, nobody from the peace group is there to criticize Bush, at least Sunday evening. "We're hopeful," the unofficial organizer, Kynn Bartlett, says. "We're saddened. We're also scared."

They've met three times now, their numbers dwindling each time, from about 75 to about 35 to about the dozen now. Bartlett says a friend of his asked what was the point of holding a peace vigil now that there's war going on.

"If we decided to stop, I don't know what it says about our commitment to the troops, to the people of Iraq, to peace," Bartlett contends.

So they carry on with their candles and songs. One is Amanda Rines, a 65-year-old woman from Lake Elsinore who dubs herself "a grandma for peace." She went to an anti-war demonstration in San Francisco and sports a T-shirt she picked up there, "War is not the answer." She's even dared to place a sign in her yard that reads, "War is not healthy for children and other living things." So far so good, nobody's vandalized the sign yet.

Sure, she knows she's outnumbered in these parts, but she's not about to bite her tongue. "We need to protest because this is an unjust war and we need to speak out."

After some debate -- should we or shouldn't we? -- the group opts to return to Cal Oaks Road, but stand apart from the folks backing the war. In contrast to their boisterous cheers, the peace people stand quietly with candles and hold aloft the universal sign for peace. A truck of shouting teen-agers races by. "Support the president," they bark.

The peace folks promise to be there again this Sunday evening at 7, theirs a quiet voice in a loud valley of war supporters.

Kids have write stuff

Publication Date: April 8, 2003

I'm praising Drew Obeso for how much he's written in a letter to a Marine in Iraq.

"Hey, I play war with my toys all the time," he says, indicating he knows plenty about the topic.

Kids across America such as Drew are being educated about war and it's not just because of toy soldiers. Credit our invasion of Iraq for the lesson plans.

I teach third grade at Rail Ranch School in Murrieta and about a month ago the 20 kids in my class wrote to Matt Smith, a Marine in Iraq. His cousin Josh Companion is in our class. Josh's mom, Megan, thought the letters would cheer Matt up.

Although we haven't heard back from Matt (he's been a little busy), I thought it would be a good idea to write another letter now that the war is actually happening. It gives the kids a way to express what they're feeling, something we all need.

Violence is a big issue for children. Jourdan Wren tells Matt that his mom won't let him watch the war on TV, "even when I have seen tons of guns movies." Moms know there is a difference between movies and real life.

The kids also know that violence brings sadness. "I wish it was over because I don't want you guys and girls to get hurt," Adriana Salas writes.

Like a lot of us, kids have questions about the war. While Colby Cordova wonders if Matt wants America to win the war (Let's hope he does, for our sake.), Kevin Tong asks what Matt's favorite guns and bombs are. Ariana Smyth has another question kids can relate to, "Do you get screamed at a lot?"

Amanda Medina, one of the sweetest kids in our class, also talks in terms kids can understand. "I want the people in Iraq to be nice. But they just won't be nice to us. Do you think the people in Iraq are nice or mean? I think they are mean."

These being 8- and 9-year-olds, most can't write a letter without including a picture to go with it. Alexa Sohail draws someone saluting the flag, Kelsey Rendon makes a big flag with the caption "God Bless America," Shawn Chidester depicts a tank pointed at another flag, while Riley Leming's flag looks more French than American. I suppose the irony isn't intended.

Nicole Carr has the best caption for her picture: "Time to boom Saddam."

These being children, there's also competition. While watching Drew draw a battle scene, one kid tells him he can make a better helicopter. Quin Woolsey, who may have a future as a diplomat, puts the skirmish in perspective: "It doesn't matter who draws the best one."

There are the optimistic, such as Eric Longnecker who hopes Americans win so "we can spend a lot of money to redo Iraqi schools," and the cheerleaders, such as Jacob McCormick, who tells Matt, "Yo! Yo! America Rools!" (Isn't that kid's teacher teaching him how to spell?)

While Kyle Logan wonders what the troops want kids to do ("Do you want us to cancel sports and keep our lives normal?"), U.S. intelligence experts might want to confer with Laura Gow. "I think that Saddam is not talking on the news," she argues. "They don't even look the same."

More than anything else, kids are concerned. "I am extremely worried for everyone that is fighting over in Iraq," Nick Flores writes movingly. "In fact, my neighbors are fighting in the war too. I hope with all my heart that my neighbors and you return safely."

Papa pilot at the palace
Publication Date: May 27, 2003

Michael Parkyn is back in his palace, which must mean all is right in his world.

He's spent the past three months in the Persian Gulf, serving his country in the war against Iraq and enduring 12-hour shifts every day without a single day off. Not to mention living in a tent without air conditioning and temperatures into the 120s. No wonder he considers his five-bedroom Murrieta tract home -- did I mention it was air conditioned? -- a palace.

Of course, Parkyn had it good by some measures. A Marine Corps pilot, he planned bombing runs this time and didn't carry them out like he'd done in earlier tours in Kuwait and Afghanistan. He also got to take showers, quite the luxury compared to infantry troops he knows who didn't take one the entire war.

I last checked in with Parkyn in February just before he took off into the great unknown of combat. He was nervous, so much so that he increased his life insurance. It's called confronting your own mortality.

It's one thing to go to war as a thrill-seeking single guy like he was in the first Gulf War, it's quite another to leave a wife and four young kids behind like he did this time. Now it's a thrill he can do without.

The final night with his wife and kids was the worst. What can you say to kids who are so young: Kate, 1; Lauren, 3; Jillian, 4; and Madison, 9? It's why words aren't enough at times.

His absence was hardest on Madison. It meant a lot more chores, helping her mom care for three younger sisters and keeping a big house clean. It's a ton of responsibility for any kid, let alone one worried about her father away at war.

Madison insists it was no big deal having her dad gone because she believed him when he told her everything would be OK.

Her mom, Amy, would beg to differ. What about those nights when you would lie awake crying because your father wasn't there to tuck you in, she asks her daughter.

It reminds me of my own childhood, when my own father, a 25-year Army veteran, spent two years in Vietnam. The nights were the hardest, trying to fall asleep while praying for his safe return. Now that their dad's back safely, things are different for the Parkyns.

There's a new appreciation for what's important: family and health.

Dad, the old thrill-seeker who couldn't wait to go into combat in the first Gulf War, now says proudly, "My wife and kids are the most exotic things I've ever seen."

Parkyn and his colleagues in the desert spent a lot of time talking about the "stuff" Americans like to accumulate: the cars, the gadgets, the clothes. The list goes on and on. In combat, everything he had fit underneath his bed. He didn't miss any of his "stuff" because, he came to realize, it doesn't matter that much.

What matters is taking his girls to the dentist like he did the afternoon I saw him. To see his baby Kate marvel at the toothbrush she's been given to play with while they wait. "Just seeing that learning, the growth, it's amazing," Parkyn notes.

Parkyn holds Kate while we talk. His other girls are upstairs making a ruckus. Just then a doorbell rings. It's two neighborhood kids wondering if the Parkyn girls can play.

Sure they can, Dad says with a smile. It's good to be home.

Upscale Temecula

Publication Date: July 22, 2003

There was a time when the Winchester Collection homes were in the middle of nowhere, as recently as the late 1980s when they were built.

There wasn't much but empty fields from here to Interstate 15. Heck, Margarita Road, a busy street the houses branch off from now, was just a dirt trail in these parts then.

Today there's a mall, a high school and a Lowe's, and that's just the major stuff. No wonder a home developer is able to argue that being here means you "live in town."

That developer's project is Harveston, Temecula's latest development blitzkrieg. Planned are 1,921 homes on 550 acres on the west side of Margarita, across the street from now ancient Winchester Collection. The two projects reflect how far Temecula has come since the development rush started some 15 years ago when the town was about 15,000.

Winchester Collection's homes are small, from 924 to 1,458 square feet, which is what young families were looking for back then. Many of the homes are single story, unusual in today's market. The old-fashioned mailboxes placed in front of the homes aren't locked, hearkening back to a time when Temecula really was a small town.

While most of the homes are still well-maintained, more than a few have yards of brown grass and weeds. Many of the houses, which originally started at $88,900, are rented out today. Two residents I try to talk to speak only Spanish. Most neighbors say they still feel safe, but some worry about crime. A number of homes have security doors out front.

By contrast, Harveston reflects the upscale side of today's Temecula. The goodies include a lake, boathouse, amphitheater, 20-acre sports park, shops and restaurants. No wonder one prospective home buyer at this month's opening labeled the place a "mini Newport Beach."

These aren't mini homes, not with floor plans of 1,991 to 3,720 square feet. Homes range from the low $300,000s to the mid-$400,000s, about four times what Winchester Collection first fetched.

Despite the many attractions across the street, Winchester Collection residents I talk to say they're happy with the simple pleasures they have.

Guido Schulte, a real estate agent who sold the Winchester Collection for the developer, likes his 9,000-square-foot lot and mature trees, amenities you don't often find in new projects that tend to have smaller parcels and twigs for trees.

Schulte estimates 95 percent of the project's original buyers are gone now, most having moved to bigger houses. So many are rented because the original owners hung on to them.

The area's crime is a matter of perspective. Tile worker Joe McCluney moved here from Hemet eight years ago for the better schools and lower crime that Temecula offers by comparison. "This is a good neighborhood," he says. "I feel safe here."

While Marine Doug Lindamood, just back from Iraq, is happy with his home, he's reluctant to let his three young kids play out front by themselves. He's from Oregon, a place he considers safer than here.

He sees himself moving eventually, but like so many before him, he'd like to hang on to his Winchester Collection home as an investment. What once represented the first piece of the American Dream for young families is now a mere asset to be rented out. So much for the romance.

Wonder how Harveston will be viewed 15 years from now?

Something to remember
Publication Date: August 5, 2003

The business of turning a boy into a man being a dicey proposition at best -- think of how many guys you know who've never grown up -- it's time for summer camp.

My 11-year-old son David is on his first such male bonding outing, the Mataguay Scout Reservation near Warner Springs, with 20 other boys from Troop 526 of Murrieta.

Besides creating memories to last to the next Ice Age, the boys are learning to be more independent. If that means starting a trip by gathering sleepy-eyed in a church parking lot at 4 a.m. for a caravan to a camp about 60 miles away, then so be it.

The operating principle here is to get up with the sun every morning to jump into a pool of freezing cold water, to work your fanny off earning as many merit badges as possible, (some of these kids thought only regular school could be hard), and to sever all ties with mommy.

Of course, when three moms show up one afternoon with homemade chocolate chip cookies for everybody, well, so much for the best-laid plans of mice and men makers.

Those duties fall primarily to Brian Nash, a 47-year-old local financial planner who doubles as scoutmaster for this trip.

Nash, who's here with his son Brady, says the job can be a hard juggling act, trying to push the kids to earn as many merit badges as possible, while at the same time not going overboard, considering it's the first chance to be away from home for many.

That parental support can be terrific, which helps account for why Murrieta and Temecula have such great schools, Nash notes. But at some point, the kids need to be weaned from it. "You can get a lot of pampering. The reason these towns are so special is because we have parents who love their kids. But it's also time for the kids to start growing up."

A. J. Briggs is one of the beneficiaries of that process. The seventh grader says the first day at camp was the hardest because he wasn't that organized. By day 2 he had things wired and the rest was easy. "I like being independent," he says proudly.

Of course, not every boy is ready to fast forward to manhood, such as the one who alternates between having a blast and bugging Nash to call his mom so she can pick him up.

There are the guys who lose things, including, Jacob Nowlin, a 12-year-old whose merit badge cards are gone. Imagine his delight when I walk into camp with said cards, having found them outside the craft shop. "Thank you," he shouts, giving me a big hug.

There's the 11-year-old boy who's crying because his chips, cookies, and candy are confiscated by Darrel Payne, a local tile business owner and our assistant scoutmaster.

"Why did my mommy pack them?" the sobbing boy asks.

"Because she loves you," Payne gently explains, towering over the lad with his 6-foot-5 frame. "And we love you too, which is why we don't want you to have them."

Ultimately, my son David says, there are the memories. Hanging out with his buddy Spencer Rushton and his new pal Matthew Payne, riding a makeshift swing that's fashioned by some eager kids and one mischievous adult, yelling when a raccoon wanders through camp, recalling the distinctive fragrance of our latrine after a week, and doing the "Hokey Pokey" late at night, boys both young and old wiggling and giggling long past their mommy's bedtime.

The kinds of memories you'll look back on as an old man and smile.

'For sale' sign is bad omen
Publication Date: August 26, 2003

The horse poop in the dirt parking lot is the first sign this isn't your basic urban land use. It's the Murrieta Arena, a place where horse people have gathered for 23 years.

While friends compete, many folks sit in the bed of their pickup trucks, a few pulling on beers, all of them talking horses. As one girl tries to steer a cow in the right direction, a supporter shouts, "Come on Cheyenne."

Cheyenne, now there's a horse person's name.

There's just one problem with this quaint picture: That "for sale" sign on the front of the property off Juniper Street in old Murrieta. Lee Anderson, who's run the place since it started, figures it'll be gone by winter. With Murrieta's new police station across the street, and a big condo project and a Lowe's nearby, it's obvious what's about to trample the arena to death.

This doesn't sit well with Anderson, who leases the site and wishes now he'd bought it when he could have afforded it. "I hate to see it stop," he says. "Got a lot of good friends in the area. But everything has to end some time."

Anderson, who lists his occupation as cowboy, isn't giving up just yet, even if he's 65. He's planning to run some cattle in French Valley. Of course, that land too is slated for houses in a few years. (He must feel a little like Saddam Hussein, except in his case it's development that's closing in on him, not American troops.)

Mimi Glassman of Wildomar and Alejandro Munoz of Perris can relate. Glassman, who runs The Tack of the Town horse shop, remembers when she could ride a horse to the local Jack In The Box and go through the drive-thru.

No way now, not with the traffic, the four-wheeled kind.

"People are very disrespectful of people on horses," she says. "It's getting harder and harder to find places to ride."

She came from L.A. 11 years ago for the country living we had; now she's fixing to move to Sage, east of Temecula. Good luck, it probably won't be long before it too is rooftops.

Asked what they think of the development, Glassman and Munoz in unison say, "I hate it." It's clear they've addressed the topic before. What old-timer hasn't?

They knew the arena's days were numbered. There were times years ago when there were 120 riders on a Friday night and the competition would go past midnight. Tonight there are 30 and that's a good night, considering there were just 15 a week before.

Jeremy Sackett also makes a living off horses; he shoes 'em. The Temecula resident bought his first horse when he was a Marine stationed at Camp Pendleton. He's known Anderson for years, helped him with several projects, and thinks it's a shame his place has to go.

"It's progress," he says. "You can't slow it down, can't stop it."

Trying to find a glimmer of hope in this stampede of development, he says he has plenty of business because a lot of newcomers buy horses. They board them because a horse isn't exactly compatible with a subdivision. They're weekend cowboys, not the full-time ones we once specialized in.

The consensus of the arena crowd is that it's a shame Murrieta or Temecula didn't make itself into a Norco, a town that caters to horses with lots of trails and rules. It's too late now.

"Temecula is supposed to be the last frontier town," Sackett says with an extra helping of irony. "It's not. It's just Orange County."

Family crosses generations
Publication Date: October 14, 2003

Ashley and Kara Matkins of Murrieta don't just have a great family life; they have a great-great family life.

The girls have a 97-year-old great-great grandmother, Violet Edmiston of Wildomar; a 75-year-old great grandmother, Mary Austin of Wildomar; a 52-year-old grandmother, Linda Matkins of Murrieta; as well as their mom and dad, Ronnie and Melissa Matkins.

Add in the girls and you've got five generations living in Southwest Riverside County, an amazing feat in an age when far-flung families are often more splintered than a piece of lumber in a saw mill.

They get together at least once a week to eat, drink, be merry and share experiences that are as varied as the near century their lives span.

Edmiston, born in Missouri in 1906, attended a one-room schoolhouse, grades one to eight learning all at once. Her daughter, Austin, also went to a one-room school in a small Missouri town, basically because things didn't change too fast back then.

Contrast that to Ashley, 8, and Kara, 5, growing up in a school district growing so fast that it opened a new elementary school and high school this year alone.

Then there's the minor matter of utilities, such as electricity and indoor plumbing, things Ashley and Kara take for granted. Edmiston didn't have the luxury of either.

Advised that she'd have to get through a summer without air conditioning if she'd grown up with her great-great grandmother, Ashley says she'd move to Alaska. Sorry, they didn't have very good indoor heating back then either.

Her parents say Ashley and Kara are mature beyond their years and it's easy to see why. Besides having wisdom passed down from four generations, the girls see a lot of what their elderly relatives go through because their family is so close knit.

When Edmiston, "Granny Vi" to the girls, broke her hip, it meant she had to move in with her daughter and give up living by herself, a traumatic experience for someone so independent.

Ashley often visited while her great-great grandma was recuperating, watching Anaheim Angels games with her, and a passion they both share. The family even snuck Edmiston out of her rehab facility last spring so she could watch her great-great granddaughter pitch in a Little League game. It was history in the making, considering Ashley was the only girl in the league that year.

In case you're keeping score at home, Kara and Ashley are two of Edmiston's 15 great-great grandchildren. She also has 26 great grandchildren and 14 grandchildren.

Edmiston can name every one of them, as well as rattle off most of their birthdays.

"I can't even begin to keep it all straight," says Ronnie Matkins, one of the great grandchildren.

Ronnie and his great grandmother have something else in common. Edmiston worked in a sporting goods store in Missouri in the 1940s, Ronnie owns one in Murrieta today, R & M's Locker Room.

His wife Melissa, the M in that local store's name, appreciates the close family ties she married into.

"I didn't have the luxury of what you see here," she says, sitting in a local pizza place surrounded by the five generations. "They are here as friends, as parents, as confidantes. I can't express to you how lucky my girls (Kara and Ashley) are to grow up with this. It's a blessing. This is one in a million."

Following hoop dreams
Publication Date: November 4, 2003

Allison Roldan needed to have labor induced in late summer 10 years ago, so the doctors asked her and her husband, Frank, when they'd like to have it done.

Frank said any time after Aug. 31 would be fine, that being a deadline birthdate that many youth sports organizations use in deciding in which age group to place a kid.

So it was that Garrett Roldan of Murrieta was born Sept. 6, 1993. He wasn't delivered with a basketball in his hand.

Ten years old now, Garrett is only 4-foot-7 and 65 pounds. But he's quick, shoots the ball with either hand and nails long, outside shots consistently. Which explains why he's running around a gym in Perris with kids from this town, Murrieta, Moreno Valley and Rancho Cucamonga. They're the Perris Ballers, a 10-year-old team that last summer spent five days in Las Vegas. They weren't vacationing; they were taking care of business at a basketball tournament.

Garrett's story is not unusual in Southwest Riverside County, given that our local sports pages are filled with stories about travel teams looking for stud athletes, primarily basketball, soccer and baseball players.

As the father of an 11-year-old boy who's dying to play high school basketball or soccer, there's a sense that if I don't get my son, David, on a travel team, he'll fall behind.

Frank Roldan is taking it a step further -- or "the next level" as sports people gush these days -- by driving Garrett twice a week to Perris for practice.

This isn't just a Murrieta Youth Basketball League all-star team that Garrett's with now; he's with what his dad says amounts to a Southern California all-star team. And if Roldan can get this other kid to join, he says it could be one of the top 10-year-old teams in the West.

If this all seems farfetched -- since when are 10-year-old teams ranked? -- there's also method to Roldan's zeal.

"It's extreme," he readily concedes. "But all I want is for my kid is to be able to compete at the highest level. This is an education for my son in real life."

For him, that highest level isn't to be found in Temecula or Murrieta.

"This is a different level of intensity. It brings out the best," the 49-year-old real estate broker and former high school basketball player says.

As we talk, Garrett and nine other kids -- including the gigantic 5-foot-6, 176-pound Lance Mungia of Murrieta -- are racing around the old gym screaming, "I got ball, I got ball, I got ball," in a defense drill. The kids are quick and handle the ball well, and all appear to be good shooters -- something you don't see on a typical rec team.

It's intense all right.

Garrett, who says he thrives on the energy, loves it more than the slower-paced rec ball he was playing last year.

"You get knocked around more in this. You have to think more. Everybody on defense is up on you."

Elaine Mungia, the mother of his teammate Lance, is another big fan of the travel team. In Murrieta, her son was considered a spectacle because of his size; here, his dimensions are considered an asset. In travel ball, everything is looked at in a different light.

"He's having the funnest time of his life right now because of the acceptance," Mungia says. "He loves this. He wakes up breathing basketball now."

He's not alone in this driven crowd.

CHAPTER 16

2004 - A tree and a pastor keep going

Soon-to-be Riverside County supervisor Jeff Stone emerged as the most powerful politician ever in the Temecula-Murrieta area. This would prove to be important for tons of local issues, most notably the proposed Liberty Quarry south of Temecula, a matter we'll get to in time.

A notable Murrieta couple, Rod and Barbara Spriggs, moved away, signaling a growing trend in the area. Many people who arrived here with young families now found their kids grown and gone. So some like this pair moved on themselves.

Another sign of the changing times was a local gay support group's decision to hold a public meeting. While folks had to call to get the location – we're talking baby steps with this volatile issue in this conservative community– it was further evidence that our area's gay population was growing. Good for them.

The majestic tree behind the name of Great Oak High School in Temecula was discussed, a local bicyclist was injured in a crash a shortly after riding past me and notable pastor Steve Struikmans celebrated 35 years with his now gigantic congregation, Rancho Community Church.

There's also Rob Hawkes, who heads up a Murrieta soccer league and all the hours he puts in running such an outfit. And did I mention it's all for no pay? Finally, I taught a session of high school summer school in Murrieta. Oh the things both teacher and students learned. If only the kids would read about it. Come on guys!

Dad fights culture wars

Publication Date: March 9, 2004

Bob Tyler is a busy man these days, but not busy enough to skip his kid's soccer game.

First things first with a family man, which brings us to Tyler's job: serving on the front lines of the culture wars, defending traditional families and marriage against what he considers to be the threat of gay marriage.

The Temecula-based lawyer has appeared on CNN and Fox News and been quoted in newspapers across the land. Needless to say, it's a heady experience for a guy who also gets his kicks coaching his kid's local soccer teams.

Here's a day in the life of Tyler, at least in the past month: Pulling an all-nighter working on a legal challenge to the avalanche of gay marriages in San Francisco, he suddenly gets a call saying he needs to get to the Bay Area ASAP. He showers, jumps on a plane, races to the courthouse and is greeted by an onslaught of reporters excited that he - Bob Tyler, 36, happily married, doting father of four, church-going man and a small-town lawyer if there ever was one - is on the scene.

"I realize, all of a sudden, `Oh my gosh, what am I doing?'"Tyler recalls with a laugh. "It's kind of fun I guess."

It's not the media attention he craves - a mutual friend of ours had to tip me off to his role in the case, ("You mean that Bob Tyler, the soccer coach," I say when I first hear of his 15 minutes of fame). It's the battle to defend traditional family values that's got him enjoying living life at a fast-forward pace right now.

Not that the fast lane doesn't have its hazards. All the publicity means he's well-known in the Bay Area homosexual community, which means he's had to walk the streets of San Francisco with police protection.

"These people would walk up to me and say, `You idiot! You jerk!' It could have been ugly," he notes.

The job that's brought all this on is his work for Alliance Defense Fund, a nonprofit organization that's evolved into the conservative equivalent of the ACLU. Tyler has worked with the group since 1999, and the group's California office is in Temecula because, well, not because it's a bastion of conservative politics, but because Tyler lives locally, and he sure as heck isn't going to commute.

The odd thing is he once wanted nothing to do with Southwest Riverside County. His parents moved here in 1989, and his brother Bill, a Temecula police sergeant and another soccer coach, was also here, but he swore he would "never, ever" join them. Bob was the big city guy at the time - Diamond Bar, to be exact - and there wasn't even a mall here then. Talk about the sticks.

Then the commercial real estate market he worked in tanked, he started law school in San Diego, and he had to spend time at his parents' house. All of a sudden, the area started to grow on him.

Now he says he can't imagine living anywhere else.

"I don't know of any other place in California that I'd want to raise my kids," he says.

Which brings us to the politics of the moment, gay marriage, something Tyler feels threatens the traditional family life he so cherishes. While we talk in his living room, the talking heads on MSNBC are ranting while this message sits on the bottom of the screen, "Gay Weddings Flaunt Law."

"I've got to catch up on the latest," Tyler says, turning to the TV.

There's no rest for the weary on the front lines of the culture wars.

Touched by tragedy
Publication Date: March 23, 2004

Gerry Marinucci emerged from the early-morning darkness on his bicycle, something I'd seen hundreds of times.

"Hey Carl!" he shouted, waving at me as he passed on the other side of Whitewood Road.

"Hey Gerry!" I yelled back.

"Have a good day," he said, gliding off into the darkness.

"You, too, buddy!"

About a half-hour later, Gerry, 47, was run down by a vehicle on California Oaks Road. The driver then went on for at least a mile with Gerry's bike stuck to his vehicle, according to police.

Victorville-area resident Federico Baltazar was arrested on suspicion of running down the bicyclist.

Gerry is in the hospital in serious condition. His wife, Laura, says doctors believe he has brain damage.

This incident has been front-page news in Southwest Riverside County, the kind of tragedy that reminds us how delicate our lives are. One minute, a guy's riding his bicycle as he does every morning. The next minute, he's fighting for his life. It's been haunting for me because Gerry and I are friends.

It's an unusual friendship in the sense that we basically would meet only on the street. He would be on his bicycle at about 5 a.m., when I was walking my three dogs. We would see each almost every day because we're creatures of habit and early morning is an incredible time to be out and about.

Once a week or so, usually on weekends, Gerry would stop when he had time to talk. Ours wasn't just small talk either, it was big picture stuff. Over the past four or five years, we settled most of the world's major issues -- terrorism, the economy, unions, health care, gay marriage, religion, always religion when it involves Gerry - many times over.

Politically, Gerry is about as conservative as you can get; I'm about as liberal as they come. We would get quite animated, and I suppose it made for a rather strange scene: one guy sitting on his bike, the other clutching three dogs, going at each other with both barrels in the pitch-black. Bush and Kerry have nothing on us in extremes.

One of the many great things about Gerry is he practices what his strong Christian faith preaches. He and his wife recently adopted two Russian sisters, ages 7 and 10. He would describe in great detail how excited the kids were to be in America. It was Gerry and Laura who rescued them.

I also saw him several times at my mother-in-law's nursing home in Escondido. He would go there on Sunday afternoons with his guitar to sing religious songs to the elderly residents. Judging by the big crowd that always gathered around him, they got a lot from it.

As I said, I'm troubled by Gerry's fate. For starters, was I the last person to talk to him before he was hit? The day after the accident, I woke up in the middle of the night, haunted by an image of Gerry emerging from the darkness on his bike - something I may never see again.

The next morning, a bicyclist came toward me. Could it be, I thought for a moment, that a miracle's occurred? The stranger passed without a word.

I long for another debate with Gerry, this one about the Bible. How would he deal with the driver? Would he take the Old Testament approach, believing that justice is "an eye for an eye"? Or the New Testament's, turning the other cheek and loving our enemies?

I pray we'll have that talk someday.

He'll have the power

Publication Date: April 6, 2004

Those song lyrics used in "Bruce Almighty" - "I've got the power!" - come to mind when Jeff Stone is talking.

The words fit Stone because he arguably just became the most powerful politician in fast-growing Southwest Riverside County.

When he takes office in January, the longtime Temecula councilman will be the first area resident to serve on the county Board of Supervisors. It's going to be Stone who basically decides what happens to growth hot spots such as unincorporated Menifee, Winchester and French Valley, which in turn will affect all of us big time.

Whether we end up a decent place to live or another of those too-much-traffic-and-development armpits that Southern California seems to specialize in is very much up to Stone.

The good news is that Stone, a 48-year-old pharmacist/politician, knows the area as well as he knows medicine. He came to the old Murrieta Hot Springs resort often while growing up, before realizing his dream of opening a "country pharmacy" in Temecula in 1983.

It was back when Interstate 15 didn't punch through, when the only gridlock was tumbleweeds.

"I expected it to grow, but I never expected to see what's happened today," Stone says.

Managing the rest of that development - some would call it an avalanche - would seem to require creative thinking, which Stone has a history of.

Heck, he tells the story of being busted by his dad when he was 10 for running a business, of all things. He'd sneak behind a supermarket, retrieve expired potato chips destined for a food pantry and sell them.

At about the same time, a fifth-grade teacher was telling his parents that their son wouldn't make it past high school. He says he was bored in school then, and there's something to that - considering he eventually graduated from the USC School of Pharmacy.

Hard work and ingenuity helped him land his first pharmacy. Out of college, he worked four jobs, 70 to 80 hours a week, to save up for his own business. He bought his store's fixtures on the cheap, scooping up $75,000 of stuff for $3,000 from a bankrupt pharmacy. His Temecula pharmacy was profitable in three months, realizing his goal of being country pharmacist without being a bumpkin.

He's owned a total of six pharmacies - his current one is Innovative Compound Pharmacies in Murrieta, but his partners will soon assume his duties so he can focus full time on being supervisor - and helped make Temecula the economic powerhouse of the area.

That's not just Stone's idle boasting either, considering that he led the charge a decade ago against the council's offer of incentives to Wal-Mart to come to what's now the Temecula mall; a deal that would have resulted in the mall going to Murrieta, costing Temecula an estimated $4 million a year in sales tax.

Now to his biggest challenge, saving us from becoming an urban hellhole, something that may require divine intervention the way things are going.

Perhaps his - and our - best hope lies with the inspiration of his now-deceased mother, the person he got his amazing drive from. The longtime Murrieta Hot Springs resident once inscribed a book to her son: "Seek and you shall find." They're words he tries to live by.

Let's hope he finds what he's seeking one more time.

The flock is in flux
Publication Date: May 18, 2004

The belief that the Lord works in mysterious ways can be applied to Steve Struikmans' ministry.

Struikmans, 62, came 35 years ago this month to this town that was more cows than cars, more Wild West than suburbia.

The cows would be the dairy farms that dotted Ynez Road then, not the car dealers of now. As for the cowboy mentality and hard drinking some engaged in, nobody would much associate that with the upscale, family friendly version of Temecula today.

From a lifestyle standpoint - wide-open spaces vs. the conveniences of a fast-growing city - Struikmans has mixed feelings as to how 1969 compares with 2004. As Jack Liefer, who's been here even longer than Struikmans, once told him when the pastor suggested the town put up a drawbridge because it was getting too crowded, "I said the same thing when you came here."

From the perspective of the town's senior pastor, the growth is a no-brainer.

"I'm in the people business," he says with a smile. "I love people."

Besides, since when can you share the Gospel with an animal, Temecula's primary resident in 1969? Not that the amiable Struikmans wouldn't try.

As pastor of Rancho Community Church since then, Struikmans has seen his congregation morph from seven families to more than 2,000 people today. The growth is so monumental that the church is moving in the next year from its first and only home on Vallejo Road (built on land donated by a developer) to a much larger, more noticeable and, at $3.3 million just for the land, more expensive location on Highway 79 South.

It's all a big change for Struikmans, who still lives with his wife, RaeAnn, in the same Temecula house he paid $25,000 for, located in the city's original subdivision on Rancho Vista Road, a place known as Hill 27 because that's how many houses were built there. They now build that many a day here.

The Ynez Road dairy connection - not the auto mall - brought Struikmans here. Raised in Artesia in a Dutch dairy farming family, he went off to college in Iowa and seminary school in Michigan. By then, dairies were being squeezed out of the coastal counties, and John Bekendam and Al Fikse, once Struikmans' Sunday school teacher, were shifting their cattle to Temecula.

Oops, that would be Rancho California, the name slapped on the area by a developer that bought the legendary Vail Ranch. An old development ad proudly framed in Struikmans' office even advertises him as the community's preacher.

That was back in the days when he wore a lot of hats. He was the town's Mr. Welcome Wagon, greeting the occasional newcomer to the place. He served on the volunteer fire department, responding to accidents at all times of the day, and even delivering a baby once.

"It's been a neat, a unique experience," he says of his ride.

His ministry was a one-man show in 1969; today, he has a staff of nine. Back then, he had to help more than a few people with their drinking problems; now his flock's issues are more of the family variety, such as divorce and raising kids in a culture that doesn't always promote the values he extols. Talk about swimming upstream.

But swim he must, surely thinking the Lord's work is never done, not even after 35 years.

Wondering what's next
Publication Date: June 8, 2004

It's something I look at almost every day, now that I'm 46. If the cause isn't listed, I wonder what it was. Increasingly, one of the people on the page is my age; occasionally it's even somebody I know. That's when it gets really chilling.

I'm talking about my increasing fascination with the obituary page, apparently a taboo topic for some, based on the reaction of people when I ask if they, too, read it.

I'm in a shopping center of the Sun City retirement community, figuring this is the best place to find folks who share my interest. It would seem to be a generation thing, seniors and obituaries. Sort of like teens and video games, kids and candy.

I'm surprised at how many seniors brush me off when I bring up the topic, as if I'm asking them for their ATM number. One guy just walks away; another says he's too busy for such stuff.

In his Sun City Barber Shop, 61-year-old owner Ken Browning is at least receptive to my question.

"The only time I read it is to see if my name is there," he jokes. "If it's not, I can relax."

Sitting in the stool next to him, Mark Matkin, 50, says he never looks at obituaries.

"I have a friend who always looks and I say, `Why would you look at that?'" Matkin says. "It doesn't interest me. I'm more interested in life. Why would I want to read that, so I can focus on death?"

Well, uh, yeah. A couple of months ago I read that the father of a kid who played on my son's first soccer team had died. A guy I used to stand on the sidelines with, a guy younger than me. It got me thinking (always a good thing).

I'm especially into the tributes, the ones that ramble on about the deceased's family, work and passions. Of the 41-year-old man who died in a car accident in Palm Springs last month - once again somebody about my age - it said, "He was a very happy man, and a very kind, sensitive, generous, loving son."

Beyond the fact that everybody is always talked about in glowing terms on the obits page (How often does that happen in life?), imagine the agony the surviving mother must feel. It makes me appreciate what I have, which also explains why I like reading these things.

Talking while waiting for his bus, Travis Harp, 29, offers a younger perspective. Not surprisingly, he never looks at the obituary page.

"It's real depressing," he notes. "It's talking about dying and whatever. When it's your time to go, it's your time to go."

Walking out of a health food store, youthful looking Casey Clarke, 73, says he's never looked at the obituary page either. No particular reason, he says. "It's irrelevant unless it's somebody I know. At our age, you learn real quick if it's a funeral."

Out of the eight people I talk to, the only one who shares my interest is Nelma Irvine, 82. She's looked at them for a long time, especially in the small town in Utah that she used to live in, a place where there was more of a sense of community, where everybody knew everybody.

"It's a way of keeping track of people," she says.

Irvine, whose husband Arnold died five years ago, says she's not afraid of death.

"My belief is very firm," she says of what will happen when she dies. "I believe it's going to be a great adventure."

Another reason I'm so fascinated: What's next for the people on the obituaries page?

Finding the time
Publication Date: June 15, 2004

Don't mind me, I'm just busy taking a break from the hustle and bustle the rest of the world's caught up in.

I'm waiting for my daughter Julia and her sidekick Nicolette Jonkhoff to take what's supposed to be a 60-minute college prep test at Temecula Valley High School.

I'm alone in this endeavor.

Everybody else, I'm talking several hundred teens, has either driven themselves here or been dropped off. No other parents could be bothered to wait around and contemplate things.

It's not easy taking a timeout from our fast-paced world. You know the drill: things to do, people to see, blah, blah, blah, even on a Saturday.

I'm doing that, too, just nothing planned. I'm being spontaneous, as bizarre as that sounds.

The test is starting at 8 a.m. and finishing at 9 a.m. so I walk to the Rancho California Sports Park, a place I don't get to much these days.

It was different when we came here in 1988, back when the big playground at the sports park was just one of a couple places in all of Southwest Riverside County to take your kids. I'm serious.

We came here a lot; my wife, Joanne, and me, watching Julia the preschooler run around. Now she's across the street testing for college. Kind of sad.

Next I walk to a Little League game. The kids are little, so small that adults do the pitching. It takes forever to get three outs and you'd need a calculator to keep score, but nobody seems to mind.

Across the way, I hear loud rock 'n' roll coming from a skateboard competition warming up. The kids in the makeshift attire of extreme sports make for an interesting contrast with the uniform regimentation of the nearby Little League. Temecula's version of Melting Pot.

I head back to the school, figuring the hour's mostly over. I look in on my daughter's classroom and hear the test proctor finish reading directions, meaning they're just now starting. Grrr. So that's why people leave and have kids call when it's over.

I stroll around the old campus, long a favorite, in part because of the inspiring arches that the kids pass through with messages such as "The Quest For Knowledge Doesn't Stop Here."

Neither does the quest for cash. I see an old lady digging in a trashcan, pulling out recyclable cans.

Another guy strides by, Jess Anderson. He got a call from his kid, who couldn't take the test because he'd forgotten to bring his student ID when his mom drove him in. So Dad's delivering it, having come from Anza, 40 minutes away. The things parents do.

We talk about how Anza, a place he's been since 1989, is still a small town. But even there, you can feel the growth coming, speculators moving in like buffalo stampeding the plains.

I report my finding that the world's changing because nobody will wait an hour while their kids take a test. Anderson, 47, agrees, noting his parents would have waited for him. It's a big change he says - and just in our lifetimes.

He leaves, and I'm the only one sitting in the student quad, listening to the birds sing and the old lady smash cans. Soon, the first dozen kids come out, done with the test. Eight are on cell phones the moment they emerge, calling for rides. It's time to hustle and bustle again.

No time for limits

Publication Date: June 29, 2004

Rick Hayden cruises in the front door, hot on the heels of his middle-schooler, Jenna.

"Is this yours?" he asks, grabbing a pile of clothes in the living room.

Yes it is, Jenna sheepishly says.

"Pick it up," Hayden barks.

It could be any parent getting on his kid about cleaning up, which is how Hayden wants it to be. His spinal cord injured, Hayden has been in a wheelchair for 27 years. Yet he gets around as much as anybody.

He runs a rehabilitation-technology-supply business.

He's a full-time father, so much so that he stayed at home with his twins, Kyle and Aimee, when they were babies, juggling diapers and work.

He's active in youth sports, coaching Murrieta Youth Basketball League teams the past four years, serving on the board and volunteering for Southwest Soccer Association.

One way to look at Hayden is from the perspective of his faithful dog, Ben. The Haydens rescued him from the shelter as a puppy 12 years ago. Now he has diabetes and is blinded by glaucoma.

Yet Ben keeps on trucking, greeting me with a wagging tail, then faithfully parking himself at Hayden's side with the grace of a dog without health problems. Credit the shots he gets twice a day and a determination not to let his handicap slow him down.

Just like his master.

And just like his dog, Hayden, now 48, was once totally healthy. He played high school basketball and liked to ride friends' motorcycles. He bought his own when he was 21, figuring it would be more economical than a car.

Crossing a bridge one day in his native Massachusetts, he clipped a car, was tossed from his bike and hit in mid-air by a vehicle coming the other way. The other driver sped off, leaving Hayden with injuries that landed him in a hospital for more than three months.

Hayden's first wife gave birth to their second child just four days after he was released. A New England winter was looming, and the marriage was collapsing.

"That was a tough one," Hayden says of the stress at the time. "We're going to test Rick. Has he found God?"

He found something to keep going. He definitely didn't let his wheelchair slow him down, working with a disabled friend to make people more aware of what handicapped people had to endure while at the same time teaching them not to pity them.

They rode hand-powered tricycles across Cape Cod, worked at summer camps, gave speeches and played tennis and basketball.

Their first team, Western Mass Mean Machine, lost its debut game 80-10. Obviously, the opposition didn't pity anybody.

Which is what Hayden wants. He's rebuilt his personal life, having been happily married to Karen, a local kindergarten teacher, for 17 years.

His two older kids, Rick and Rachelle, are adults now, successfully reared despite that stressful launch more than a quarter-century ago.

What Hayden despises more than anything else is limits.

He met a little girl in a wheelchair in a local store recently, and she was telling him that her mom wouldn't let her play a sport because she was handicapped.

It was hard, but Hayden restrained himself from hunting down the mom to tell her: "How dare you!"

Lazy days of summer
Publication Date: August 3, 2004

Supposedly, being the wise one in the bunch (as opposed to the wise guys in the room), I remind the high schoolers the first day that this class is just three weeks, a mere moment in their lifetimes.

This being summer school - when all their friends are sleeping in and homework is the last thing on their minds - it's more like an eternity to them.

A third-grade teacher by trade, I step up temporarily to the big time to teach ninth-grade English at Vista Murrieta High School to a group who didn't do well the first time because they didn't get it, i.e. they're not good at reading and writing; or they didn't do it, i.e. they're lazy.

This being the system, which says you have to pass this class to graduate, these folks have no choice if they want that most basic of tools in the fast-paced global economy of our century: a high school degree.

Lessons abound this summer, both in textbook and in life, both for student (hopefully) and teacher (most definitely).

Let's consider how transient Murrieta is. After telling them the grade I normally teach, I ask how many of the students attended third grade locally. Of the 21 students in the class, three hands go up. That means more than 85 percent of the class has moved here in the past six years, primarily from San Diego County, by the way.

Next I ask how many of the kids hate to read. Thirteen answer affirmatively to that, about two-thirds. We read "To Kill A Mockingbird," and their attitude is captured by a girl writing in her summary of the book: "I did not like it a lot because I don't like to read. I don't understand some of the words. My favorite scene is none because I don't have one because I don't like to read ..."

We get the point. By the way, she failed summer school.

Considering it's a class full of kids who didn't do well the first time, it's no shock most hate to read. Now consider my follow-up: How many of you want to go to college? Seventeen want to, more than 80 percent.

Guys, how can you go to college if you don't want to read?

"You don't need to read and write to be an engineer," one kid pops up.

There's a certain disconnect with these kids, one that can be infuriating. For example, when a few talk while I'm lecturing, I stop to ask them if they know what they're doing to me. Before I launch into my tirade about disrespect, they answer: "We're disrespecting you." So they've heard it before. Next I ask how they'll hold a job if they talk while the boss does.

"This isn't a job," one says. "This is school. We can talk."

As infuriating as they can be, there's something wonderful about these kids. A few, Alex Girardot in particular, are incredible readers who write with powerful insights. Another, Ezequiel "Zeke" Rivera, says he wants to be a writer and really takes my praise and criticism to heart. There's nothing more inspiring for a teacher.

They call me "Mr. L" and laugh at my jokes, at least most of them. Many hang out in the room before school and at break, some even deigning to swap stories with me. When I tell them about my high school days with long hair in the 1970s, they laugh, wondering whether I wore bell bottoms and was a hippy.

I wore bell bottoms - who didn't? - but wasn't a hippy.

Did I mention I loved to read? Hint, hint.

THE SHAQ OF OAKS
Publication Date: August 17, 2004

Towns and presidents, those are the things they name high schools after.

But a tree? Come on. What are they handing out as diplomas? Branches? Are the young students, still not adults, to be called twigs?

All yucks aside, there's much to be said for the name of Great Oak High School, Temecula's third high school, which opens later this month in the southern end of the community.

Clearly, this isn't just any tree. Considered the world's largest coastal live oak, it stands a staggering 96 feet tall, and its branches extend to a circumference of about 590 feet. With a trunk 20 feet around, it's the Shaq of oak trees.

There are all kinds of estimates as to how old it is. Butch Murphy of the Pechangas, which bought the tree and its surrounding 750 acres a couple years ago because they are considered part of the tribe's traditional lands, says it could be as much as 1,500 years.

Impressive indeed. Still, it's a tree. What's the school mascot to be? The Fighting Leaves? (Actually, the Wolf Pack.)

Tim Ritter, the new school's principal, says his first reaction was, "How do we turn it into something that's a positive symbol, rather than a punch line?"

He says the tree has attributes that kids can aspire to, such as strength, nobility and longevity. No joking matter there. When it comes to creating a positive school culture, you can't ask for anything more.

The tree is visible to the west of the campus, meaning students won't have to look far to be reminded of its assets. Looks can deceive. The tree's many low-lying branches have growth that starts up to the sky, creating the illusion of a stand of trees. Nope, it's one amazing specimen.

School board member Stewart Morris gets credit for the name, tossing it out during a meeting about what to call the school. Morris has been to the tree tons of times because his four sons, all Boy Scouts, did lots of campouts and other things near the tree.

Morris hopes the name will make locals more aware of the natural surroundings of Temecula. "We've got this wonderful symbolic tie between the history and us," he says. "We're so new, compared to 1,000 or 1,500 years. And yet it's stood there, in droughts and in floods, and now the modern era."

Nobody appreciates the tree more than Jeff Loefke, its caretaker for a quarter-century. When he started, the property was owned by Edward Vosker, who sold it to the Pechanga.

He lived about a quarter-mile from the tree in a house once the residence of Sam Hicks, a longtime Temecula character.

The property also once belonged to Erle Stanley Gardner. The Perry Mason author has a middle school named after him.

That tree has seen it all.

Loefke, who now runs a Boy Scout camp in Idyllwild, compares standing under the tree to being in a cathedral. Church services and weddings have been held under the tree, including the marriage of his daughter, Adrianna.

Loefke, who will be at the school's dedication at 5:30 p.m. Thursday, says he hopes the name will give the kids more respect for the environment. "It makes you take pause and realize you're just one of God's little creatures. It makes you feel special because you're with this very special thing of Mother Nature," he said.

The school's name is an inspiration, not a joke.

Leaving Murrieta
Publication Date: September 14, 2004

The "sold" sign in the front yard says it all; Rod and Barbara Spriggs are moving.

This is significant because of the Murrieta that they represent (and Temecula, for that matter). They represent the folks who moved here in the late 1980s because these were small towns - neither was even incorporated then - and they wanted to raise their kids here.

Now the kids are grown and so are the towns. Murrieta and Temecula are booming cities today, just what the Spriggs - and many like them - were trying to avoid 15 years ago.

So Rod, 64, and Barbara, 55, are moving, most likely to Sun City because they want to stay near their three children (Nye, 28;

Anais, 20; and Lanelle, 18), who still live in Southwest Riverside County. They know what they don't want: Murrieta today. Too big, too congested.

They are significant for another reason. On the Saturday I find them cleaning out the garage with the help of friend Judi Husband - oh, the joys of moving - I also come across folks collecting signatures for an election to recall Murrieta City Council members Jack van Haaster, Kelly Seyarto and Doug McAllister.

What's interesting is the recall group's literature, the stuff that talks about "out-of-control growth" and "responsible managed growth for Murrieta."

The Spriggses spearheaded a group seven years ago that qualified a ballot measure that purported to have some of the same growth-related goals.

That measure went down to defeat back when they feel it could have had a real impact on Murrieta. Barbara says it would have capped the population at 74,000, which the city has already surpassed.

So they're moving on, leaving memories connected with raising three kids in a small town.

There's the new-home sales agent who sold them their first house, the guy who told them that Alta Murrieta School across the street - then just portables and dirt - was going to be a permanent school with grass and big trees in six months! The Spriggses nodded, bobblehead-like, Barbara says with a laugh, believing every word the salesman had to say.

Imagine their surprise when the permanent school didn't come for five years. In the meantime, Alta Murrieta didn't have dictionaries, globes or maps. And it was shared by two schools - Rail Ranch and Alta - running double sessions in the portables, Alta from 7 a.m. to noon, Rail from noon to 5 p.m.

"I was shocked," Barbara says. "That's what got me so involved."

She was active, big time, in the Alta PTA, then moved on to be PTA president for Shivela Middle and Murrieta Valley High schools.

Rod got busy too, running for the City Council in the early 1990s before bowing out when he thought he was being relocated by his employer.

Now they're leaving, and there's no turning back. Their house that they had paid $200,000 for sold for $450,000 the first day it was on the market. Murrieta's sure booming.

Five of the 18 houses in their neighborhood have gone on the market this year, many owners moving because their kids are grown and the town's changed.

Barbara Spriggs says it's sad: "Murrieta has just become a sea of tile roofs. The qualities that made us move here to begin with aren't here anymore."

So it goes in the bustling Murrieta and Temecula of 2004.

All This for No Pay

Publication Date: October 26, 2004

Former rec soccer coach Carlos Cordova knows the grief involved in running just one team.

When I tell him that Rob Hawkes coaches his two kids' soccer teams, then runs an entire league on top of that, Cordova just shakes his head.

"I'd rather not imagine that," he says of the stress that life must entail.

In one sense, Hawkes, president of the Murrieta Youth Soccer League, and the other folks who run local sports leagues have the world's worst jobs: long hours (in Hawkes' case, 20 to 25 hours a week on top of his own coaching duties), stress (we all know how volatile some parents can be) and many hats to wear (in the two hours I'm with him, he runs a field, answers questions, sells raffle tickets, puts out a few fires that come to him via his constantly ringing cell phone and prepares a team for its game).

Oh, lest I forget, all this and more for no pay.

In another sense, it's a high that money can't buy. Walking around the busy California Oaks soccer fields on a recent Saturday, Hawkes waves at kids he used to coach, shares laughs with parents and fellow board members, and swaps barbs with rival teams ("Good luck boys," he says to the team he's about to play, "just not too much luck.").

It must be quite the rush to know all these good vibes, as well as the wonderful things being taught to more than 1,300 kids - including teamwork, good sportsmanship and exercise - are happening in no small part because of him.

"Saturdays, when you're out here seeing all the kids playing, it's just great," he marvels. "If everything else was bad about this job; that would be enough to recharge the batteries."

Hawkes could use an occasional jump-start. The extent of most parents' involvement in youth sports is hauling the kids to games and dropping them off at practices. For them, the leagues run seamlessly without much of their help. It's as if the tooth fairy or Santa Claus was managing the show.

Instead it's dedicated volunteers such as Hawkes and hundreds (or perhaps thousands, considering the youth sports going on in Southwest Riverside County) of others who make it all happen.

And it's not as though Hawkes, 41, operations manager for Temecula-based Northstar Tools and husband to Cynthia and father to Austin and Sierra, doesn't have a life outside of running a sports league.

He does it in part because he loves soccer, having played through high school and continuing in an adult league now.

He started coaching local soccer in 1999. He joined the board in 2002 after longtime local soccer guy Vic Griganavicius recruited him, noting that the league could always use help. He became vice president earlier this year with the understanding that he'd run the show eventually. That happened in May, sooner than expected, when president Lynn Culver left because she was moving.

He and about 20 other board members handle things. There have been just a few glitches, this being for many their first season in their positions.

Hawkes compares his president's job to running a company, which means he has to deal with finances, planning (he has lots of ideas about how to better teach kids about soccer) and the never-ending concerns of board members, coaches and parents.

Then there are the days that make it worthwhile: Saturdays.

A Tale of Two Parks
Publication Date: November 2, 2004

In one spot, kids wear what they want, say what they want (cursing isn't out of the norm) and do what they want, the law be damned.

Nearby, kids all wear the same clothes (uniforms), say what the coaches want them to say on the field and do what they're ordered to do, free choice be damned.

It's a tale of two ways of growing up. One is the Murrieta skate park, where kids often make the rules, with a little help from the cops. The other is the surrounding sports fields at the Cal Oaks

Sports Park, where my son's soccer team and others play; the place where grownups make the rules and the cops aren't involved.

Some of the sports parents who sit to watch their kids practice can't help but judge what's going on just a few feet away at the skate park. The language, the smoking, the trash some leave behind, even the activity itself - name me one good thing that comes from a skateboard, some must think - all add up to one thing for them: trouble.

I've seen some in the two months I've watched this saga play out. Skateboarders get hurt from time to time, in part because there isn't much official supervision at the park. It's definitely the law of the jungle there.

For instance, the posted rules say you need to be accompanied by an adult if you're under 14, yet there's often kids there flying solo who clearly aren't teens. You're not supposed to ride bikes there, but kids do. You're supposed to wear safety equipment, but a lot of kids don't.

Joanne Alba watches her son Jared, 9, whirl around on a skateboard. She drives him here twice a week, but he'd come every day if he could. She does worry about Jared hurting himself, and she agrees the cursing is bad.

But she's sure he knows right from wrong and won't be damaged by the scene.

"The good ones are good, and the bad ones the police usually take care of," she says.

After talking with two other boys, Montay Price and Jared Rios, about what they get from skateboarding, I see a cop talking to some kids on bikes. One asks if the officer will let him make one run through the skate park.

"One ride equals one ticket," the officer says. End of discussion.

Now I'm surrounded by a bunch of high school kids on bikes, including Nathan Martinez, Calvin Kuchinsky, Andrew Peterson and others. They feel the cops pick on them ("If you ride bikes, you're a criminal," Andrew says) and how they just might get up a petition to take to the City Council to get a park for themselves.

Besides admiring their interest in civic involvement, I'm struck by the casual way that these kids talk about dealings with the police, like no big deal.

Part of me wants to say they should consider it a big deal; part of me also admires the street smarts. I know my 12-year-old son isn't as wise to the world. It's what happens when the adults run things.

Another adult, Shawn Peck, says the skateboarders are misunderstood, that there's not much difference between them and the kids in the sports uniforms.

"The only thing they get is more recognition," Peck says of the sports kids. "Here, they're on their own."

Which appears to be just how they like it.

CHAPTER 17

2005 - Recall what that kid said

Murrieta's momentous City Council recall campaign dominated the news here. Once again growth was a big part of the discussion. Like it has been for the whole time I've lived here.

Temecula was showcasing its financial clout in many ways. A new study showed just how affluent the city's residents are. Later that year, the city debuted its gorgeous $11 million community theater that was once again the envy of every other community in Southwest County. Luxury never gets old.

There was a Buddhist meditation center in Wildomar and a Temecula civic group informing folks about medical marijuana. Both were further evidence that we're becoming more diverse, always a good thing.

In the always interesting world of the third graders I teach, I wrote about the sweet girl whose father died in Iraq just before she joined our class, plus the ever volatile topic of sex in the classroom. One young boy suggested that his female classmate could give me a lap dance after getting a drink. I think I'll pass. And keep my job!

MURRIETA `HOOSIERS'

Publication Date: February 22, 2005

In this corner, weighing in with five state championships, 17 CIF titles, 21 league crowns, and nine CIF players of the year, one of the most legendary high school basketball powers in Southern California: the Mater Dei Monarchs.

In this corner, with barely a winning season in its first varsity season and without a senior because the school is only in its second year of existence, yet with hearts as big as a 7-footer's legs: the Vista Murrieta Broncos.

If Friday's Vista Murrieta-Mater Dei matchup in the CIF boys basketball playoffs were boxing, it would have been heavyweight versus flyweight. Instead, it's high school basketball, meaning it's "Hoosiers."

Before the game, more than 100 parents and fans of the Broncos talked hopefully of at least keeping the game competitive. Vista Murrieta player Justin Attebery told his mom that somebody would make a movie if his team beat basketball machine Mater Dei.

Murrieta basketball junkie Frank Roldan, a scout for Irvine Valley College, said before the game that the team has more heart than any team he's seen, and if anybody could pull off the upset, it would be Vista Murrieta's wily coach, Kurt Ruth.

"They're probably going to get (beat) tonight, but it'll be a great learning experience," Roldan said.

If a game can be over in the player introductions, this game is. The first announced Mater Dei player is a 7-foot-1 center; the next is the superstar who's supposedly already been promised a UCLA scholarship.

Twelve seconds into the game, a Monarch makes a layup. Ballgame.

Then somehow, Bronco Carlos Palmerin steals an outlet pass and scores inside, and the game is tied.

With 6:25 left in the first quarter, apparently frustrated that the game's not already over, legendary Mater Dei coach Gary McKnight takes a timeout, the scoreboard reading 4-3 Broncos. Remember that famous Al Michaels line after the U.S. hockey team beat the Russians in the Olympics: "Do you believe in miracles?"

A minute later, Palmerin hits a long jumper, putting the Broncos team ahead at 7-6.

With 2:49 to go in the quarter, Attebery, the man with the movie plan, drains a three-point shot, and the Broncos are down only 14-12. Vista fans, who braved Orange County traffic on a rainy Friday night, are beside themselves.

Then before you can punch up Spielberg on speed dial with the movie idea, it is 33-17 Monarchs after an avalanche of steals, lobs, dunks and threes.

The rest of the game is real life, not Hollywood. Mater Dei is clearly the dominant team, steadily building its lead into the 20s and eventually the 30s.

Yet there is no quit in these Broncos, with Kyle Theret flying all over the court, Adrian Dixon steaming fearlessly into the lane and Vista's lean center J.D. Stiles epitomizing the team's heart, drawing three charging fouls as burly Monarchs plow into him.

The end at least is perfect: Little-used Bronco Trevor Hussman nails a long bomb at the buzzer. In a movie, it would count for 33. Reality, Mater Dei wins, 95-66.

Having dressed, the Broncos file by solemnly as the Monarchs stay on the court to entertain their fans with a dunking contest. Determination is still in the Broncos' eyes. If this were a boxing flick, it would be the "Rocky" series.

They'll be back.

Political Shock

Publication Date: May 10, 2005

Here at ground zero for the political earthquake rolling through Murrieta, people are speechless.

Moments before, they are giddy at the election night party, with City Council members Jack van Haaster, Kelly Seyarto and Doug McAllister beating back a recall in early returns.

Now Riverside County Supervisor Jeff Stone is taking a call with the final results of the recall election against the three incumbents. The room of more than 50 quiets, eager to erupt with joy.

But by the somber tone in Stone's voice, it's apparent the news isn't all good. He gets off the phone to announce what many seem to already know: Mayor van Haaster is history.

The party's over in more ways than one.

Most everybody at the bash at McAllister's home - which includes many members of Southwest County Taxpayers for Responsible

Government, the pro-business group that spent a breathtaking $317,000 on the anti-recall campaign - seems to know it won't be business as usual at City Hall.

Time after time on controversial projects, they pass by 3-2 votes, with Warnie Enochs and Dick Ostling on the short end.

Now it's anybody's guess. The most powerful person in Murrieta is suddenly van Haaster's replacement, Rick Gibbs, who's endorsed by the pro-recall group Rescue Murrieta.

With Stone's grim announcement still reverberating through the now-hushed partygoers, a few talk of the need to "educate" Gibbs about running a city.

Another mentions Temecula City Councilman Mike Naggar, considered a maverick when elected in 1999. He's turned out just fine, a few note approvingly.

Stone, a former Temecula councilman, is optimistic as well about Gibbs. "He's a team player."

Only time will tell what team he's on.

Many at the party can't explain how their team ever got in the fix it's in. Phil Dominguez, longtime leader of the local firefighters union, which opposed the recall, says Murrieta is a better place because of growth that's swelled the town's population from about 25,000 to some 80,000 in the nearly 15 years he's been in town.

There are more restaurants, more places to shop, more places to go. Remember when that was people's biggest complaint, there was nothing to do, Dominguez recalls. Not anymore.

Stone, who's lived in the area since 1983, recalls when Temecula residents, furious about too much building, launched their own recall against then-incumbents Ron Parks, Pat Birdsall and Peg Moore, a campaign that fizzled before making the ballot.

"Growth can be painful," Stone concedes. "Coping with it hasn't been easy."

Then again, Stone says it's not fair to blame van Haaster, Seyarto and McAllister for Murrieta's problems, not at a time when the state and the feds can't help cities like they used to, not at a time when Murrieta is still struggling to build a tax base that can provide quality services such as what Temecula, with all of its financial clout, can offer residents.

McAllister elaborates in his victory speech, noting it's builders who put up much of the money for better roads and parks. "Dan

(Stephenson, one of Murrieta's most influential builders) and his `evil' developer friends are here tonight," he jokes.

Not everybody in Murrieta is laughing, not by a long shot.

Lesson on Dad

Publication Date: June 21, 2005

Susan Bertolino comes in before the first day of school with the news: Her husband, Tony, was killed in Iraq in November 2003 and their daughter Karina is going to be in your third-grade class this year.

She's also really behind in school because she had a tough time in second grade, with her teacher leaving in the middle of the year and her dad dying.

The first week of school, Karina wears a shirt with her dad's picture on it: "My soldier, my hero, my dad."

It's all I can do not to cry.

It's something Karina didn't do all year, except the time some kids supposedly said they were better than her because they had a father. Nobody can be meaner than little kids.

Heroes come in all shapes and sizes and, for me, this school year it was Karina, the long-haired girl with the mischievous smile. While a lot of kids would use their father's death as an excuse to not try in school Karina never once used it as a crutch.

She just kept plugging along, day by day, until she could read lengthy chapter books by the end of third grade and be at grade level. Her brother, second-grader Jason, did well this school year too, having been helped by the same Title 1 reading assistance program at my school, Rail Ranch Elementary; that Karina went through.

And his brother Daniel, a middle schooler, grew by leaps and bounds as a basketball player, something I also know firsthand because he was on my son David's team. As for the oldest kid, high school student Tony, he plays the saxophone like you wouldn't believe. I've heard him because he's in the band with my daughter Julia at Vista Murrieta High School.

The Bertolinos are local celebrities. A haunting, two-page photo of them standing in a vacant lot near Los Alamos Road ran in Newsweek with a story headlined "Children of the Fallen." A CBS News crew spent a day with them last month and they've been quoted in many newspapers.

The Bertolinos made local news last Veterans Day when the "Letters Home" memorial sculpture was unveiled at the Temecula Duck Pond. It features 16 letters from soldiers, including one sent by an Army platoon leader to the Bertolinos after Tony was killed.

"I could go on with stories of people whose lives Tony changed for the better but that would not diminish your grief," Eric Olson writes to the family. "I could tell of how Tony took the tough missions because he wasn't going to let anything happen to `his kids,' his `second family,' his platoon. But that would not change the fact that a wonderful man was taken from us way too early."

The Bertolinos skipped the Duck Pond ceremony, preferring a free day at an area amusement park for military families.

"We did that instead of cry," Susan says.

Sitting in their tract home in Murrieta, she says she's proud of how well her children have held up since their dad died in November 2003 when his convoy was attacked. She credits her oldest sons, Daniel and Tony, for being especially strong.

On the last day of school this month, my class signs autograph pages for third grade. When Karina hands me hers, I write about how much I admire her courage and what she's done this year. I hand the page back to her and she's smiling, her father's face staring back at me on her favorite T-shirt, "My soldier, my hero, my dad."

Updating History

Publication Date: November 8, 2005

You don't have to be a historian to know Temecula has changed since 1969.

That was when Sam Hicks put together the "They Passed This Way" monument, which sits in the park in Old Town named after him.

Sketched on the giant granite slab are the notable people who passed through Temecula to that point. They include folks recognized throughout the state such as Kit Carson and Pio Pico. Also there are the guys with local communities named after them - Juan Murrieta, Frederick Thomas Perris and J.P.M. Rainbow.

And there are the people with streets named after them: Felix Valdez, Juan Santiago, Juan Moreno, Vincente Moraga and Mercedes Pujol.

Hicks, writing in a small book about the monument that can be found at our local museum, says it was erected "to honor the passing parade of devoted frontier people who suffered to bring this town its proud and wealthy heritage and who, in some measure, personally contributed to the development of this historic valley."

There are 56 names on the monument, built at a time when Temecula had perhaps 500 people.

Today, Temecula is more than 90,000 people and the number of notables who've passed through might fill many monuments.

Is it time for an update?

Mayor Jeff Comerchero and former longtime school board member Joan Sparkman think it's an interesting proposition.

Consider the famous people who've passed through here to entertain at the Pechanga casino in recent years. Musicians such as Ray Charles, Tom Jones, B.B. King, Tony Bennett, Julio Iglesias, Wynonna Judd, Paul Anka, Dennis Quaid, Pat Benetar and Clint Black.

You want funny, we got funny, including Bill Cosby, Ray Romano, Jerry Seinfeld, Jeff Foxworthy, Tim Conway, Harvey Korman, Vicky Lawrence and Larry the Cable Guy. For good measure, magician David Copperfield also appeared at Pechanga.

I'll bet not a one had heard of Temecula in 1969. When I moved here in 1988, people howled that there was no local entertainment.

Then there are the community leaders, the ones who've brought Temecula so far, so fast (some might say too fast), since 1969. Comerchero came up with a dozen people he would list on a new monument: former council members Karel Lindemans, Pat Birdsall and Jeff Stone; current council member Ron Roberts, wine country pioneers John Moramarco and Vincente and Audrey Cilurzo; active citizens such as Jeff and Martha Minkler and Carol Niles, and developer/philanthropist Dan Stephenson.

He says his 12th would be himself. Given the time he devotes to the city, he's earned it.

Sparkman, who's been here since 1969 and has an elementary school named after her, adds a couple of others: Tony Tobin, a Mr. History of Temecula if there ever was one, and Lilian Vasquez, a local tribal member long active in the community.

A couple of other names to mind: Bob Taylor, a town prankster who once ran a comical city council campaign and was best known as Santa Claus. He didn't even have to dress up much, so close did he resemble St. Nick. And Sam Pratt, the quirky former councilman who epitomized Temecula's slow-growth effort, such as it was. Given what's happened here since 1969, slow growth it's not.

Sex in the Class

Publication Date: November 22, 2005

The kids troop into my third-grade classroom after recess asking for drinks, just like they always do on a hot day.

After I give one girl the OK, the boy behind her comes up to me very matter-of-factly, like he does this all the time, and says: "You know, Mr. Love, after she's done, maybe she could give you a lap dance."

There are times teachers pull a kid aside because they don't want the rest of the class to hear what's going on. This would be one of those times.

I end up talking to dad, who's dumbfounded as to where his child could pick up such a term. "I have to keep an eye on what he's watching on TV," he says.

The story comes to mind with a study this month that shows 70 percent of TV shows include some sexual content, with an average of five sex scenes an hour. On the top teen shows, the number is a staggering 6.7 scenes per hour.

The rate has nearly doubled since 1998, about the time most of my third-graders were born. It's multiplied exponentially since when I was a third-grader in the 1960s and a racy scene was Ginger looking seductive on "Gilligan's Island."

Other examples of what the Kaiser Family Foundation considers sexual conduct in today's salacious TV fare include discussions of sex on the WB's "Gilmore Girls," depictions of oral sex on NBC's "Law and Order," and sexual intercourse on Fox's "The O.C."

The lap dance isn't an isolated incident either. In the past couple of years, I've had enough sexual content in my third-grade classroom to make any TV executive salivate over the plot lines.

Let's see, where do I start? There's the boy in my class found rolling around in the grass at recess with his so-called "girlfriend."

Probably like something they saw on TV the night before.

There's the year the local Republican women are kind enough to donate dictionaries to third-graders. Sounds great until I pass out the gifts and some boys in the class start looking up sex words.

Still disgusted with these clowns, I start walking my class down to lunch and overhear another third-grade teacher chewing out her kids for the same thing.

But hey, at least dictionary skills are a state standard.

My most shocking story is the sexual-predator ring my administrators help me break up a few years back. A couple of these jokers were walking up to girls and asking them to lift their shirts so they could see what's underneath. Another kid was literally stalking a girl around school, even following her home for a couple of blocks. The girl was in tears, she was so traumatized.

What's different today is what kids are exposed to on TV. In my first couple of years of teaching - I've been doing it for eight- I didn't have any issues with kids and sex. The same can't be said since then.

I'll close with the thoughts of Sen. Barack Obama, D-Ill., who appeared at the Kaiser Family Foundation's press conference: "We don't teach our children that healthy relationships involve drunken, naked parties in a hot tub with strangers- but that's what they see on `The Real World,'" he says, citing an MTV show. "When they're fed a steady diet of these depictions over and over again from the time they're very young, this behavior becomes acceptable, even normal."

Which is how a third-grader ends up asking his teacher if he'd like a lap dance.

CHAPTER 18

2006 - Random violence is so not us

The issue that would dominate the headlines like no other – Granite Construction's proposed quarry south of Temecula – emerged this year as residents stepped up their opposition. The irony was not lost on me – quarries produce the concrete that feeds all the construction in Southwest Riverside County.

There was a less dramatic protest as well, one arising against an adult entertainment business in Murrieta. Given our area's historic opposition to all things porn, it was no surprise.

A more serious matter was the pedestrian gunned down on Whitewood Road in Murrieta in the middle of the night, I've walked the street about 25 years. It's the kind of random violence we don't associate with our area. Fortunately it hasn't become common.

And who can forget Floyd Landis, the world class bicyclist. Murrieta did not know whether to celebrate his feats after he was accused of doping. In a community that prides itself on being squeaky clean, it was quite the conundrum.

Other moments included the passing of Pat Birdsall, the Old Town Temecula activist who went on to become mayor; my profile of Grace Mellman, who has done so much to boost local libraries, and my daughter Julia learning how to drive and all the thrills and chills that entailed.

Driving Drama
Publication Date: April 11, 2006

It's still a shock to my system, akin to the first step or the first word. My 16-year-old daughter Julia is driving. Granted, she takes turns too wide ("Look out for that brick wall!"), she doesn't start to brake soon enough ("You're going to rear end that guy!"), and she doesn't always pay attention ("You just drove up the curb while giggling with your friend in the back seat!"), but she does fit the dictionary definition of operating a motor vehicle.

Take a recent family outing to dinner just a mile from our house. On the way we hear a cop hurtling up from behind us. All of us, that is, except the driver, Julia. As she blithely weaves down the road, the cop swerves to miss us, apparently racing to an emergency while narrowly avoiding another.

As my wife Joanne freaks out in the back seat and screams at Julia to pull over, here comes another officer in hot pursuit, also weaving to avoid us.

Wait, it gets better. On the way after dinner to get ice cream, she does one of her turns where it looks like she's headed up the curb, I start to hyperventilate and Joanne is freaking out anew in the back, saying she can't take it anymore. Bear in mind she's the one who was so insistent that Julia learn how to drive when she really didn't want to. Grrrr!!!

As Julia parks the car and practically takes up three spaces in the process, my 13-year-old son David deadpans, "Driving with Julia sure is a rush."

Finally, as we debate whether to let her drive home, we see an accident across the street, complete with a fire engine, an ambulance and three police cars.

Opting not to add to the carnage, I take the keys.

Actually, Julia's doing OK for the most part. The day before she'd done her best driving so far. And while tooling around with one of her driver friends in the back, he proudly says he's already got his license and has only had like 10 near-miss collisions. So we're coming along just fine, I guess.

Protests, Publicity
Publication Date: April 18, 2006

Life can sometimes be bests described as strange, such as when two women storm into a Murrieta adult entertainment store and immediately ask two guys if their mothers know they are here.

They follow the men into the Dream Box store parking lot, shouting "Praise God." Neither responds, trying to get out ASAP. Meanwhile store clerk Matthew Guerrero is in hot pursuit.

Debate ensues about the morality of it all. You're just adding to the perversion, the women tell him.

Then the pair jump in their cars, declining to give me their names because they're afraid of what their husbands may think if they are here. But they can't resist asking me, "Does your mother know you're here?"

Guerrero, who's worked here since the store opened March 1, says this is the first time such people have actually confronted customers.

"I just don't understand why people can't mind their own business," he said. "If they're religious, why can't they just leave people alone?"

Dream Box is a popular punching bag: pastors, that would be a lot of them in Murrieta; nervous parents, of which there are plenty in this family-friendly place; and politicians, the city having filed a lawsuit, contending Dream Box's operators break the law by selling items such as lingerie, adult videos and sex toys within 1,000 feet of a youth organization.

Guerrero hopes they keep it coming.

"The publicity is awesome," he said, noting that business is great and the store has expanded its hours by four on Sunday nights just to keep up with the demand.

Imagine that, on the Lord's Day, people can now get porn videos in Murrieta until 10 p.m. I'm not sure that's what the pastors have in mind.

Ironies abound here, such as the store's entrance, which, Guerrero says with a straight face, is designed to be conservative.

Lingerie and other clothes are in the front of the store, giving it the feel of, say, Victoria's Secret in the mall. Further inside are the sex toys, water pipes and videos that have the virtuous folks so worked up. Politically, that is, not sexually.

Guerrero, who's lived in Temecula 20 years, can't figure out what all the fuss is about. He says several liquor stores sell porn videos and magazines, businesses in the mall offer lingerie, and water pipes and sex toys can be found in other shops.

Why isn't anybody confronting customers in those places? he wonders.

Then again, things could be worse for such outlets. Nine years ago Ed Elder, once a Temecula school board member, and others picketed a Temecula store selling adult videos. Lenny Pechner, who ran the store, even planned to bring in porn star Sunset Thomas for autographs.

Pechner eventually closed his store.

He says it was because of a new Blockbuster that opened down the street, not the protesters, which he says actually helped his business. Almost a decade later Guerrero says the same thing.

The moral here?

If the goal is to hurt these establishments, maybe the protesters should just shut up.

A Vocal Opposition

Publication Date: May 9, 2006

Ellen Lemieux stands at the corner of Margarita and Rancho Vista roads with a painter's mask ominously draped over her mouth.

"I don't want to have to wear this permanently," she says as she takes her place with about 1,000 other marchers Sunday.

There's no shortage of theatrics from the folks who oppose Granite Construction Co.'s proposal to open a gravel mine south of Temecula.

Marching from Temecula Valley High School to the Ronald Reagan Sports Park, high school band kids wearing bright orange shirts play the classic college fight song "Go Big Blue." This time, it's "Save our hills, no quarry" that they chant.

Little kids such as third-grader Allison Ryan get involved too, carrying folksy homemade signs bashing the project. Then there's the placard of the day, crafted by senior Ken Johnson: "Give Me Death, Not Liberty," referring to the project's proposed name, Liberty Quarry.

Kathleen Hamilton, a founder of Save Our Southwest Hills (SOS), the group that organizes the protest, is confident her side will ultimately prevail.

"They will never put a quarry in here," she says defiantly.

The drama and feistiness are all well and good. But it's Big Bucks that often carry the day in such battles. Big Bucks in this case are the construction industry, which says it needs the building supplies the quarry will churn out to keep the local economy in turn churning. Oh the horrors if the local growth pipeline is somehow plugged up!

Major powers such as local Assemblyman Ray Haynes and state Sen. Dennis Hollingsworth are backing the project. And Liberty spokesman Gary Johnson pooh-poohs the notion that the quarry will be an ecological disaster, predicting the project's environmental impact report will show the quarry is no big deal.

That's a battle for another day as far as the protesters in orange are concerned. (Organizers say more than 650 people put up the $10 donation needed to acquire the orange shirts many people are sporting.)

It's a sophisticated bunch. And it's clear that these people know their marketing. Some examples from Sunday's march:

Many wear very official-looking placards with the words "SOS Hills Event Staff."

It's announced that SOS has its own media director, a luxury that most grass-roots groups can only dream about.

They think ahead to have an SOS-Hills Kids Petition that's ready to be signed.

Organizers set up "Kids Corner," a stand stocked with anti-quarry pictures to color and the aforementioned petition.

"We want to be able to play outside without having to worry about breathing in yucky air," the petition pleads. "We also want the animals to be able to live in a peaceful place."

Manufactured cute is one thing. The real thing is more media-friendly. A girl of about 9 has a homemade sign with this memorable phrase: "Help Mother Earth With Her Heavy Load."

Ross Mowrey, a freshman band member at Great Oak High School, provides the closing act, albeit impromptu. Standing under a tree, he watches the crowd file out after a series of speeches. He plays "Amazing Grace" on his trumpet.

No real reason, he says. Just felt like it.

Amazing it will be if these people beat Big Bucks.

A Special Parent
Publication Date: June 13, 2006

Ginelle Dexter is in her element.

Kids are pouring into her home, girls from the elementary school dance team her daughter Rachel is on. Their parents haul in food for a potluck, all shouting greetings to Dexter.

It's her life, at least for the past 12 years.

All five of Dexter's kids spent their elementary school years at Rail Ranch in Murrieta. Dexter, 42, has been involved at Rail since 1994, when son Zach, now a high school senior, started kindergarten.

She's what every elementary-school parent should be.

She has been really active in the school PTA for nine years, including the past two as president - a thankless job if there ever was one. This year alone, she spent 20 to 30 hours a week on planning events, setting up, cleaning up, fundraising and then more fundraising.

She faithfully helps in her children's classrooms, including mine when her son Ben, now ready to start high school, was a third-grader. I still use the laminated letters she made for me for a spelling game every week. I know it took her many hours, and I didn't even have to ask.

She gets plenty in return.

She knows all the teachers, a plus when it comes to picking the right one for her kids' personalities. Then there are all the warm, fuzzy feelings she gets from helping those little darlings and from being at a place where everybody knows her name.

And now it's over.

Rachel, her youngest, graduated Friday from fifth-grade teacher Matt Owens' class - three of her kids had him - and is headed for Shivela Middle School next.

Her mom, as much a fixture at Rail as the school's red tail hawk mascot, won't be around anymore.

The good news is she won't have to make the drive to Rail, a bonus when she had to get kids to an elementary school, a middle school, and a high school this year. She moved out of the Rail Ranch attendance boundaries six years ago but couldn't bring herself to shift to another elementary school, not after all the friends she made and the sense of community she found.

In fast-changing Murrieta, those are things people cling to, even if it's inconvenient. "It's strange knowing I don't have any more elementary kids," she says, standing in her kitchen as, what else, Rail Ranch kids run up to greet her for one of the last times.

Her own children know they were lucky to have their mom around so much, especially in a commuter town where so many parents can't find the time to be more involved in their child's education. "They liked the fact I was always in the school," she says proudly.

There were some issues, Ben says jokingly.

First off, Mom would always volunteer them for PTA events, which meant they'd be setting up and cleaning up all the time, even though they no longer went to Rail.

Then there's the downside to having your mom know all the teachers. "I could never get away with anything," he says, grinning mischievously.

Every kid should have such problems. And every school should have such parents.

Coaching Run Ends
Publication Date: June 20, 2006

His team has won the championship again.

But coach John Leavitt isn't smiling. He's fighting back tears.

His career of coaching his three kids, Jill, Thomas and Adam, is over. It's an amazing 46 teams since 1994, spanning basketball (his true passion), soccer (an acquired taste) and baseball (only a couple of times because his kids weren't into it).

Hillary Clinton says it takes a village to raise a child. In sports-crazed Southwest Riverside County, our village includes recreation coaches. Leavitt has probably coached some 300 local kids, making him a mayor of the village of Murrieta.

Having coached 16 teams involving my son David (including three as an assistant with Leavitt), I know of the big-time commitment with running practices, coaching games, calling parents and dealing with the politics that creep up.

Now multiply that by 46, and you get an idea of what Leavitt, a 49-year-old salesman, has dealt with.

And he relished it. First, he's competitive. There's a reason a Vermont newspaper referred to a 4-foot-11 eighth-grader as the little bundle of John Leavitt dynamite.

Or as former Vista Murrieta High School starting guard Andy Hall, a member of numerous Leavitt teams, told Thomas: "Your dad is the Bobby Knight of Murrieta basketball."

Knight, the legendary college hoops coach, is known for winning, longevity and intensity. While Leavitt never has thrown a chair as Knight did, he certainly has yelled at refs and exchanged words with coaches, though he has mellowed.

And he has had only one losing season - the first he coached, daughter Jill's in fifth grade. It was a team mostly of her friends, often a kiss of death in youth sports. He lost the first game something like 45-2, and the team accidentally scored that lone basket.

His team didn't win a game.

Along the way, Leavitt made history, helping convince Murrieta Youth Basketball League officials to start a girls division, something many opposed. He and wife Nancy passed out fliers at middle schools. Jill played in that first group of four girls teams. Now there are girl teams at all levels.

Leavitt could make a movie with his memories. There's the fourth-grade basketball tournament in Fullerton when he drew up a play, his players ran it perfectly, the kid still missed the shot, and Mohammed Khidir - another longtime Vista Murrieta athlete - tipped it in at the buzzer to win.

Then there's Adam, now planning to play sports in high school, who stepped up in the last game his dad coached this month and made two clutch free throws to secure the Warm Springs eighth-grade team's title win over longtime rival Shivela.

Or when he coached Adam and Thomas this year on the same basketball team. A team picture hangs proudly in his living room.

As for trivia, Scott Terrazas played on the most teams (10), Linfield School star Chuck Wilson was the best, and incoming Vista freshman Julius Anderson has the most potential (Remember the name, folks).

Leavitt still plays in an adult hoops league, but now with kids he coached: Hall, Khidir, J.D. Stiles, Aaron Gagnon and son Thomas. He also hopes to referee games with Adam next year, mixing sports with family, just like he always has.

Murrieta's Moment

Publication Date: August 15, 2006

Acouple of months ago, the vast majority of Murrieta residents had no idea who Floyd Landis was.

Today, he's Murrieta's most famous resident. Or is it infamous?

In case you've been hanging out under a rock, Landis last month won the Tour de France, the Super Bowl of bicycling.

Something worth celebrating, which is what the city was planning until tests found elevated testosterone levels in his urine sample, prompting tour officials to announce he's no longer the winner as far as they're concerned.

Landis is protesting like crazy, contending he's innocent of any doping. But with the Babe Ruth of cycling now looking more like the Barry Bonds of the sport (Coincidentally, Bonds also once called Murrieta home.), local officials are understandably struggling with what to do.

Plans for a big public event at a local high school? On hold for now, depending on what he wants to do, City Manager Lori Moss says.

Celebrate his win on the official city Web site? Hmm, they're handling that like a hot potato.

The latest version, the third so far since he initially won, says, "Despite recent disappointing news, friend and neighbors of Murrietan Floyd Landis want him to know his extended local family still admires what's he's accomplished in racing. Landis remains one of the world's premier bicycle racers. That he could mount a bike at all with a bad hip and push himself to such limits deserves admiration."

Besides the bad grammar (it should be "what," not "what's.") and the bad hip (he's due to have surgery soon, and whether he was doping or not, Landis deserves kudos for his grit), note that there's nothing about the race.

Banners welcoming him home and proclaiming him the winner? Four are up, despite the doping evidence. What kind of mixed message is that sending to kids when they pass by them at two local sports parks? That you win no matter the costs and your hometown will recognize it even if there's a cloud bigger than Jupiter hanging over you?

While Moss declines to comment, Councilman Warnie Enochs says of the banners: "I can see where it could send a mixed message. We don't want role models as drug addicts."

Mayor Kelly Seyarto says the banners are "a testament to the support that we, as a community, want to offer to Floyd."

In keeping with the city's more uncertain message on the Web site, perhaps revised banners are in order: "Welcome Home Floyd Landis, Bad Hip And All."

Of course, if any local can relate to Landis' press, it's Enochs, who's facing 14 felony charges in a criminal case unconnected to his office and a city ethics investigation.

"I stand behind the guy until everything pans out," says Enochs, who has lived here 35 years and says the Landis firestorm is the most publicity yet for a local.

Seyarto, who often clashes with Enochs, joins with him in backing Landis, saying, "Whether or not he is ever vindicated, it has still ruined the moment for him, his family and his very proud community."

How big a moment? A Google search of Murrieta and Floyd Landis yields 54,200 hits, including the major networks and newspapers across the world.

An irony in these 15 minutes of fame for Murrieta: Landis' Web site lists his hometown as San Diego.

Last Link To Old City

Publication Date: September 6, 2006

Before there were almost 100,000 people, a giant mall, and shopping centers galore in Temecula, there was a Sears catalog store. Pat Birdsall, whose memorial service is set for later this month, and her husband Dick ran the place. Everybody from Southwest Riverside County shopped there. "It was the only store in town," explains old-timer Irene Hotchkiss.

It was also a store that helps explain Pat Birdsall's unusual political success.

She was elected to the City Council in 1989 when the city incorporated and Temecula was still a relatively small town. She was a numbers cruncher by trade and voluntarily did the books for the tractor race, the balloon and wine festival, the rodeo, you name it.

"I'm sure we knew almost 99 percent of the people," Dick says.

She was the last political link to an era that's fading fast in Temecula, a community then known for its slow pace and western traditions. She came here in 1971 to work for Kaiser, then the major developer in town. She and Dick bought the Sears store five years later.

She was big in the Temecula Town Association, the closest thing to a local governing body. It was her idea to start the bingo games that made the money that kept the community center running; then the major public building in town.

"She was so up on everything," Hotchkiss says. "Every time you turned around, Pat was there."

Despite her name recognition, she initially wasn't interested in a political career. Politics just didn't seem to suit her just-the-facts-ma'am approach to life. "She had to be talked into it," Dick recalls.

It was a given that she'd be elected, because if anybody had the respect of folks to set the city on the straight-and-narrow path, it was her. Once she got in she worked like crazy to understand her new career. "At that point I started college all over again," she told Dick.

A couple years later, Ron Roberts, now mayor, joined her on the council. "Pat was a leader from day one," he said. "She had the ability to let you know she had an opinion. Normally her opinions were right."

She served two different times on the council, a total of almost seven years, including two as the city's first woman mayor.

The park and rec system for which the city is famous, the overflowing cash coffers that allow Temecula to do so much for its citizens, are both byproducts of Birdsall's approach to politics.

It's easy to see why the City Council broke with tradition before she died and named its second sports park in the south end of town after a living person - Birdsall.

Bill Harker, another friend from the old days, says he so admired how Birdsall kept going despite her health problems, zipping around town in an electric scooter equipped with an oxygen tank, nothing stopping her.

It's how she approached everything.

Thanks, RIP

Publication Date: November 7, 2006

Eavesdropping is tacky, but I can't help myself when it comes to Erle Stanley Gardner.

The guy wrote tens of thousands of words a month, spoken into a dictation machine. His army of five secretaries would type his words into books, Temecula Museum Manager Wendell Ott told some guy while I listened in.

"He was like Mozart," Ott said. "He had the whole thing in his head."

He wrote 90 bestselling novels, each more than one million copies sold. The books became 271 top-rated TV shows, six movies and 3,221 radio episodes.

Many of you have no idea who I'm talking about.

Maybe you've heard of the Temecula middle school named after him, but James L. Day has his moniker on one too and you don't know who he is.

Gardner's claim to fame is that he created the mystery guru Perry Mason. He did most of his work on a gigantic Temecula ranch - he owned as much as 10,000 acres - land near Great Oak High School, tons of houses and other stuff. He's Temecula's most famous resident.

Last weekend kept his memory alive with mystery events centered in Old Town. About 40 people gathered Friday night for the kickoff, dining and listening to a theatrical re-enactment of "The Court of Last Resort," another TV show with which Gardner was involved.

Gardner, an attorney, gathered experts to look into the cases of people who felt they were wrongly accused. It was a predecessor to shows such as "CSI."

Ott is filled with information about Gardner, including the whimsical story of how he came across Temecula. He was passing by on Highway 395 - the Interstate 15 of its day - on one of his many trips to the desert, when his dog Rip started barking. Gardner pulled over, thinking the guy needed a nature break.

Instead, Rip leaped out, sat under a tree and basically said, "I'm here to stay." Gardner paused, took a look around and said, "You know what, Rip, I think you're right." It was Temecula, it was away from it all, it was the 1930s, and Gardner bought some land.

He had lots of homes but spent most of his time in Temecula until he died in 1970. He loved this place, but would he have enjoyed it at 100,000 people, today's population?

No, Ott, answered. He would have moved on.

"Not that Temecula isn't a great place to be," Ott said, "but it's not what he would have wanted."

Mysteries always attract interesting folks, which brings us Steve and Gerrie Jantzen, textbook publishers who moved from Rancho Palos Verdes a month ago. They're fascinated by Gardner and intrigued by their new town.

"I'm interested in the 21st century because I don't understand it," Steve explained, pointing to how much the world has changed in his 65 years. To him, Temecula is a 21st century community.

Also there was Kathy Lentine, a Murrieta resident and museum docent. She loves Perry Mason, watches him on TV, and figures she has seen every episode like 20 times.

Sounds like she's into mysteries, just like Gardner. Now if we can just figure out whom that James L. Day was.

Not So Safe
Publication Date: December 5, 2006

A random act of violence. It's, like, so not Murrieta.
It's something out of, oh I don't know, Baghdad or some insane place like that. Not Murrieta. Not the place that brags it's the safest city in Riverside County.

People aren't just gunned down for the heck of it on Whitewood Road like Daunte Mercado-Bates, 18, was late last month. A good kid by all accounts, the kind in which wholesome Murrieta specializes.

It was done on a street I walk every day and have for the past 18 years. I've seen joggers, bicyclists, dogs and cats, even a few wayward coyotes and skunks cruising in the early morning. But a random act of violence? Not unless you count the occasional road kill on the busy street.

Now I get the creeps every time I walk on Whitewood. Is this motorist going to shoot me? That one?

Is this any way to live in what's supposed to be the county's safest city?

The good news is that two men have been named suspects in the shooting, one a former Murrieta resident. These guys were arrested in connection with the slaying of a 7-Eleven clerk in the San Diego area. A sheriff's lieutenant there called that shooting "particularly violent," with no indication demands were made.

Looking to make some sense of the senseless, as well as to honor his much-too-short life, more than 100 gathered at a memorial service Saturday for Mercado-Bates.

Trying to explain the madness, there was a stab at spirituality, that somehow it was the Lord's plan to call Mercado-Bates at this time. Death is only the end of his life on this earth; now he has a new beginning with the Lord, a pastor said.

Maybe it was as good an explanation as any. How do you explain a suicide bomber? What happened to Mercado-Bates could be considered just as maddening.

The pastor reminded us that we're not promised tomorrow, not even the next five minutes. Don't live with grudges, settle your differences, and make peace, because you never know when it could happen to you.

Now, even in Murrieta.

Through much of the two-hour service, Alex Mercado-Shilati quietly wept. As Daunte's younger brother, he struggled to speak about what he meant to him.

"He is very special to me because we grew up together," he told the crowd. "I miss my brother from the bottom of my heart."

Family members such as his older brother, Emmanuel Mercado, talked of the teen's life, the kind heart he had, the charm, the wit, the drive, the passion and the potential, lots of it. The teen talked of going into medicine or making clothes. He loved to read and write and already was a philosopher, talking about the meaning of life and what happens next. Now he knows.

A slide show of his life was presented. Images of a childhood, baby pictures, sitting by a pool, dressed in a Halloween costume and family gatherings. The boy aged before our eyes. It ended with a photo of a smiling kid, somebody you'd like to know.

The program notes the shock to the family and the community. Explaining the trust fund in his name, it states, "Please donate any amount so we can help protect the community and bring justice to Daunte." It also thanks "all who have helped prepare this unexpected event."

A Friend Indeed
Publication Date: December 27, 2006

Grace Mellman is about the last person to toot her own horn. If for some reason she did, she'd need a full symphony to tout her attributes as president of the Friends of the Temecula Library the past 16 years.

For starters, she's helped raise more than $1 million to support local libraries. That's right, a seven-figure income in donations.

Still, she's not pleased when she realizes she'll be the focus of this column. When it's explained it's for a good cause - and they don't get better than libraries - well, then, all right.

"I'm just thrilled you want to give the Friends the credit," she says, sitting next to a window in the new library, which overlooks a gorgeous sports park.

Asked why she's devoted almost 40 hours a week for well over a decade to local readers, Mellman, a retired business executive, pauses for several moments before answering.

"I think libraries are very important," she finally says. "I think reading is very important. I think teaching reading to children is very important."

She has a story to illustrate her point. Her husband, Carl, told her he was taking her to India in 1993, but she said she was too busy with the library and didn't have time.

"What about if I said you can meet Mother Teresa?" he asked.

Mellman couldn't get on the plane fast enough.

Once there, she and seven others met with Mother Teresa for about an hour. The nun asked what Mellman did, and she said she was so humbled being in her presence that it didn't matter.

"What do you do?" Mother Teresa insisted.

Mellman explained how she supports libraries.

Duly impressed, Mother Teresa told her, "I'll keep them alive. You teach them to read."

Inspired, Mellman says she gets no greater joy than watching kids in the local library check out a big pile of books. "To me, a stack of books is tantamount to a literary ice cream cone," she says.

In a sense, she's the one driving the ice cream truck, at least locally. Back in 1985, then Riverside County Supervisor Walt Abraham told her that Temecula was like No. 38 on the list for new libraries.

To give you an idea of how badly the town needed one, when Mellman moved here in 1981, the library was 750 square feet in what is now the Tower Plaza.

Mellman asked, "What would you say if we raised $500,000 to help pay for a new library?"

Abraham said he'd have Temecula bumped to No. 2. Which is how Temecula got its first big library in 1992.

Not to be outdone, Mellman led the way and raised another $500,000 for Temecula's second library, which opened a few weeks ago.

She's had tons of helpers along the way. About 400 members are part of the Friends group, led by a busy board of directors that includes Janet Regier, Stan Williams, Michael Shirley, Betty Hugaert, Sharon Cooney, Harriet Egerston and Don Myren.

"It wouldn't be right to give too much credit to me because you and I know that no one does anything worth doing without a lot of help from many, many people," she says.

On my way out, after our talk, I notice something she fails to mention, the "Grace Mellman Heritage Room."

There she goes again, not tooting her own horn.

CHAPTER 19

2007 - The moments that still bring me to tears

The housing collapse ratcheted up this year. In one local neighborhood, there were a dozen foreclosures among just 35 homes. I wrote about a rather dubious "open house" for a home that was up for auction.

It was another sad day when Bob Taylor of Temecula died. Among his many roles, he played Santa Claus and literally looked the part year-round, he was the folksiest of greeters in the Old Town Temecula before it boomed, and he was the ultimate when it came to making jokes and bad puns.

Murrieta was raided by a "fight club," a group of local troublemakers who became a fixture in the news. I watched the movie by the same name and wrote about it. Also in Murrieta, a survey of local employees found the lengths people were willing to drive to make more money. No wonder we have so many commuters.

It was a hard year for our family. We had to put our oldest dog Smiley to sleep. We comforted ourselves with the notion that she was in a better place, given how hard her last days were. Making the decision to play God with a pet is hard.

Then there was the departure of our daughter Julia, who first graduated from Vista Murrieta High School, having gone to local schools all 13 years. Watching her board a plane to go to college across the country was my toughest moment as a parent. Thinking back on that day, I still come to tears.

Fighting Mundane

Publication Date: March 13, 2007

Amid the intrigue swirling around the Fight Club gang police say was formed by former Murrieta Valley High School football players is this question: Why would kids raised in a safe, upper-middle class community turn to the kind of bizarre behavior described by authorities?

In search of an answer, I rented the 1999 film "Fight Club" (starring Brad Pitt), after which police believe the gang named itself.

As odd as this group's alleged behavior was (fighting each other, burglary while armed with a Taser, arson, assault, selling steroids and armed robbery, according to police) this film is even more whacked.

In a nutshell, it's rated R for "disturbing and graphic depiction of violent anti-social behavior, sexuality and language."

I'm sure "disturbing" came to mind when many locals heard about the allegations.

A movie review Web site says the movie concerns the "mundane existence of a product liability evaluator and insomniac who meets up with a sadomasochistic arsonist (that's Pitt) who is plotting to overthrow civilization."

I suppose we're fortunate that, according to police, the local gang didn't take it to those extremes.

There are certain parallels between the movie and what it could be like growing up in the "mundane existence" of a place such as Murrieta, Temecula and other Southwest Riverside County communities.

Eerily, I saw a number of these guys, who are now in their late teens and early 20s, play in local recreation leagues and high school sports.

While the film is about a guy looking to escape his dull career, I've heard parents and other local residents wonder if our local suspects were looking to bust out of their safe, boring childhoods.

If indeed they patterned themselves after the movie (where a bunch of guys get together regularly to beat each other to a pulp before graduating to a crime spree) it's easy to see how watching this movie a bunch of times (besides being interesting, I can see how it would be addictive) could lead to a warped sense of reality.

As the movie's lead character, the product liability evaluator says after one of the initial brawls: "After fighting, everything else in your life got the volume turned down."

Another parallel between the movie and the real life is the religion angle, especially considering Murrieta is a big church town.

After the suspects' first court appearance, parents defended the boys and said there was no gang. Anne Unmacht, mom of suspect William "B.J." Unmacht, arrived at a courthouse carrying a Bible, and talked about ministering to the homeless and attending anti-gang summits in which her son participated.

The movie's main character compares the brawls to a religious experience where observers shout so fervently that it's like they're speaking in tongues. "Afterwards, we all felt saved," he says. I've heard similar comments from many Murrieta faithful over the years.

Perhaps the best way to conclude is with the last line of the movie, delivered with numerous skyscrapers dropping, compliments of the Fight Club.

The main character announces to his love interest, "I'm at a very strange time in my life."

That about sums up the state of what police are calling our Fight Club.

Smiley's Time
Publication Date: April 10, 2007

I'm here scratching my dog's head while she's being put to sleep.

It's taken some 17 years for Smiley to reach this point, a remarkable run for a medium-sized mutt.

It's a testament to her tenacity, one of many things she taught us. We had her 12 of those years. She was our first of three dogs. We got her from friends who rescued her from the local pound. They thought she was too much work. We are forever grateful.

They had been told by the pound that she had puppies and somebody drowned them. Can you imagine? Supposedly she also had been beaten. She didn't bark, a possible sign of abuse, somebody told us.

If any creature deserved to give up on life, it was Smiley.

Yet she carried on with grace. Both of our other dogs bossed her around, but she ignored them.

She prized her independence. Often she would sit in the back-yard by herself. She loved being outside and taking daily half-hour walks on Whitewood Road, our other dogs steaming ahead while she tried to savor the good smells. She always had good taste.

Even after her cancer surgery 18 months ago, still wrapped in a bandage, she demanded to go walking with the other dogs. She didn't give up the group walks until five months ago, the first of many sad days to come.

We started walking Smiley by herself on our block. She struggled to make it, often stumbled, but never gave up. One neighbor cried when she saw Smiley, reminded of her own dog's passing. Several kids marveled at her, wondering how any animal could look so old.

The last couple weeks I had to carry her for much of the walk. At first she struggled mightily against it, like it was beneath her to accept such help. The last few times she rested peacefully in my arms, finally acknowledging that yes, she was starting to die.

Her last walk was 10 days ago and all she did was cross the street, falling several times. Yet she made it.

We turned to that most difficult of decisions for a pet owner: when to play God. After we took her to the vet for a urinary tract infection, we were told the cancer might have returned, but there was nothing to be done now. She still wants to eat, she can still stand, she's getting lots of TLC, just let her continue, the vet advised.

All her food was made in a blender at this point because she couldn't chew. A week ago she started throwing up in the backyard and shaking for a half hour. We thought she might die then. She also stopped being able to stand on her own that day, a sign for many people that it's time. We called the vet but couldn't bring ourselves to take her in.

I held her while she walked a few steps the next few days, still willing herself. But she got violently sick again late one night and stopped eating. Our conscience finally said it was time.

We took a final picture in the backyard with her resting in our arms while all of us cried. Next, trying to compose ourselves in the lobby of the vet's office, a woman walked out of a room weeping, having just put her dog to sleep. The receptionist said it's one of those days.

I lay Smiley down for the last time and Dr. Gary White and his assistant administer the lethal injection. I ask White to say a prayer and he graciously does. Now she's with the other angels.

Psychos Just Won

Publication Date: April 24, 2007

They're so predictable now: days when violence is threatened at a local school. Police are out in force, cruising the parking lot, patrolling the campus. Officials from the district office are there en masse, watching closely.

And hardly anybody's in school that day.

Two-thirds of Vista Murrieta High School's 3,400 students didn't go Friday after graffiti on campus warned that everybody was going to die. My two kids, freshman David and senior Julia, went. In David's photography class, there are supposed to be about 35 kids. Friday there were four.

It capped a bizarre week.

There was a rampage at Virginia Tech you might have heard about, in which a student gunned down 32 people. Locally, wild rumors flew around campus and the My Space Internet site: Authorities know who wrote the threatening graffiti and a bomb was found on top of a Vista Murrieta building Thursday night!

Wait, it gets more bizarre. Friday also happened to be the eight-year anniversary of the infamous Columbine High School shootings in Colorado. It's also the 118-year anniversary of Adolph Hitler's birthday. With all that going on, it's a wonder a gigantic meteor didn't smash into the Earth that day and blow up the whole planet.

Yes, somehow we're all still around to talk about it. The next question seems to be where we go from here? We all know there's going to be a next time when a local campus is threatened with violence. And many more, the way things are going.

For starters, consider my son's soccer team filled with Vista Murrieta kids. They talked about it after practice Thursday and only two were going to school the next day. I know a lot of those kids, and some struggle in class. They need every minute of school they can get and then some. It's a shame they didn't go.

Talking to other parents following a long history of school days that have been threatened with violence in Murrieta - I can think of at least five - three reasons are offered for not sending their children:

"I'm afraid my kid is going to be hurt" or "My kid is too scared." Fine, don't send them. But did you send your kid to school yesterday, when the place wasn't crawling with cops?

Second, "My kid needs a day off." I've heard many parents say it through the years, including this time. By the way, last week was the first one back to school after 16 days off. What will your kids do when they have a job?

Last, and this is the most common reason I hear: "It's a waste of time because nobody else is going to be there." I don't know about your teens, but here's what mine would have done if they'd stayed home: My Space, video games and a "Grey's Anatomy" marathon.

What did they get out of school that day? Both got to do a lot of their homework and, in a few classes, they actually learned stuff. Do you think they got a lot of attention from the teacher? It also was a day they'll never forget because it was so strange being in school.

But here's the most important reason to send your kid to school: If you don't, the psychos win. I guarantee you the idiots who sprayed that graffiti couldn't stop laughing when they saw what they created.

Guess what? They won. Now it's more likely to happen again. Don't let them win next time.

From K through 12

Publication Date: June 12, 2007

While getting ready for a show, kindergartner Kyle Weaver looked really spiffy in his black shirt, pants and top hat.

"Mr. Love, everybody keeps saying I'm cute," he said with a look of true anguish.

Fast forward 12 years to a recent Vista Murrieta High School awards ceremony. Weaver came running up excitedly to tell me he would be driving an ambulance soon, meaning the 18-year-old is on his way to his dream job: firefighter.

What's happened in between - Weaver's childhood - dovetails with my oldest child, Julia. Both graduate from high school Friday, along with hopefully the rest of Lorrie McKenzie's Alta Murrieta Elementary School's class of 1995 kindergartners.

They mean something to me because I volunteered at least half the school days that year. We cut, we pasted, we played tag at recess, we hugged and we bonded like you wouldn't believe.

Over the years I'd see many at schools and joke with them about kindergarten. Kenny Ulrich has been part of the Vista Murrieta band with Julia. Derek Finke is friends with band kids.

According to last year's Vista Murrieta yearbook, Matt McCutchan, Armando Aguirre and Taylor Spurgeon attend that school. I know that Nicole Jacobs, A.J. Agnello and Timmy Sebreros - I'm friends with his parents now - went to Murrieta Valley High School.

Some moved away because 12 years is a long time. Julia's best friend, Gina Munoz, went to Temecula. Other pals, such as Shasta Doty and Kodi Timpano headed out of state.

The one I probably know the best is Kyle, because I'd see his parents around town a lot (his dad coached soccer like I did) and Kyle is just one of those excitable kids who always says hi.

Consequently he spent much of kindergarten in McKenzie's doghouse. Asked what he recalls about that year, he said, laughing: "I remember getting in trouble a lot."

He said it continued that way through elementary school before he settled down at Shivela Middle School and focused on his career goal.

He does fine academically now, but said: "I'm not really a big school guy."

He's glad he hasn't moved away like others and hopes to get a job locally and live here.

"It's like the safest place in the world," he said. "Murrieta is just like a little bubble."

While he can't wait to start life after school, this is always a bittersweet time for McKenzie, who has taught 22 years, including 15 in kindergarten, currently at Buchanan Elementary School.

Every once in a while she gets a graduation invitation.

"I'm happy for their success, yet a bit nostalgic and saddened about the rude awakening and realization that time really does fly."

She spoke for all teachers when she said: "I hope to instill in them a love of learning that will carry them through their school years and into life beyond the playground fence."

Looking back at what I wrote about the kindergarten class' 1995 graduation, I was pretty emotional, thinking that a special time was ending for these kids and that their lives were about to get more hectic. Now that their high school graduation is here, I feel it even more.

One other thing hasn't changed - I'll bet Kyle Weaver will look really spiffy in his cap and gown. It's just too bad it happened so fast.

Rude Awakening
Publication Date: June 19, 2007

In the newspaper it was a short story, a "brief" in journalism vernacular: "Police arrest 2 Hemet teens after chase."

Most of us move on to the next story, but living through it is another matter.

It was about 2:30 a.m. on a weeknight and my dogs were barking. Half awake, I staggered out my bedroom door to shush them before the kids woke up. I noticed a giant flashlight shining in our window.

Yikes, I thought, scurrying back to bed, pulling up the covers. A moment later, the doorbell rang. Then there was a loud pounding on the door, meaning somebody was about to knock it down.

Realizing the covers probably weren't much protection, I bolted downstairs to dial 911. I screwed up the first time because it was dark, I was scared, and I had never done it before. Watching some frantic guy do it on "Law & Order" wasn't much help in real life.

The operator, who knew instantly where I was, said "that's the Murrieta police at your door. Let them in." It turned out they were looking for a couple guys who could be in our backyard. Oh joy.

They advised us to stay inside while they handled it. I thought: "'Have at it guys, I'm going back to sleep."

But of course I couldn't, and apparently neither could many others in our neighborhood near Blackthorne Drive and Whitewood Road in seemingly safe east Murrieta.

In the next hour, the six officers and a police dog went through people's houses. Police got on a loudspeaker to tell everybody to stay inside, even using Spanish. Hey, this is Southern California.

Finally two cops asked to go into our backyard. They pulled out those big flashlights again. Good thing, considering I forgot to scoop after the dogs the day before.

A few minutes later a suspect was found in an adjoining yard. All's well that ends well in Mayberry, uh . . . Murrieta.

Not so fast. One neighbor, her husband already gone to work and not knowing the suspects were caught, headed to Banning for the day with her two kids.

At least we got to be famous: News 27, our local channel, filmed in our neighborhood in the afternoon.

Sgt. Bob Landwehr said two teenagers from Hemet stole car-stereo equipment from a truck on Wild Flower Drive, took off when cops arrived, then ditched their car in our neighborhood.

The officers established a perimeter to corral the suspects, something they do about once a month. By comparison, in South Gate, an LA County community of similar size - about 100,000 - where Landwehr worked before helping start the Murrieta P.D. 15 years ago, had such searches weekly.

Murrieta brags it's one of the county's safest cities. That and our affluence make us attractive targets, considering people often leave their cars and garages unlocked. Area bad guys know this; witness the two clowns accused of "commuting" from Hemet to ply their trade. Our naïveté is evident in this: Two-thirds of Murrieta burglaries were unforced entry in one recent month.

"We could do a better job of crime prevention," Landwehr says.

So, just when you thought it was safe to leave your door unlocked, who's that pounding on your door at 2:30 a.m.?

Activists' Legacy
Publication Date: July 10, 2007

Phil Hoxsey headed south until he got out of the smog. Temecula was where he moved 20 years ago this month.

At the time, it was a city of little more than 10,000 people. He said there wasn't a traffic light in the place. Perfect for a family man looking to raise two young boys in clean air.

It also was a place where you could make a difference. Don't care for apartments planned on Pauba Road overlooking the Rancho California Sports Park? Go to meetings with fellow resident activists such as Marcia Slaven, make tons of phone calls and just like that, the land is instead zoned for houses.

Today, it's Temecula's new library, in part because Hoxsey got involved for the first of many times.

How Temecula has changed. Sure, the air's still clean thanks to the prevailing winds. But now there are about 100,000 people and, it seems, almost as many traffic lights. As for the notion that an activist can still make a difference, well, it's a lot harder when the city is approaching build-out.

"Things were developing, and now they're developed," he said of yesterday and today.

As a result, many of Hoxsey's old allies - former Councilman Sam Pratt, Old Town lobbyist Therese McLeod and one-time Planning Commissioner Slaven - now live out of state.

They left behind tactics that included passing around petitions and creating clever acronyms, such as STOP (short for Save the Only Pond, the notable city duck pond at Rancho California and Ynez roads that could have been devoured by development).

Their most effective tactic was standing at what was then the center of town, Rancho California and Ynez, waving signs at passing motorists for whatever was the latest cause.

It seemed everybody had an opinion on the issues: Opposition to a proposed Wal-Mart in the area of what's now The Promenade mall (had it gone through, the mall today could be in Murrieta), former Broadway producer Zev Buffman's massive Western-themed entertainment project to remake Old Town, the need for more parks, the battle to save the duck pond and the constant that ran through everything in Southwest Riverside County at the time - unrelenting growth that seemed to trample everything in its path.

Hoxsey and George Buhler, an 85-year-old retiree once known for churning out tons of letters to the editor, are among the few rabble-rousers left from those days. Buhler still watches City Council meetings on TV, but he hasn't been to one in at least five years.

"I'm too old, and we've got younger and smarter people running the place," he said, mentioning City Manager Shawn Nelson in particular.

Hoxsey, who also said it's been about five years since he's been to a council meeting, isn't quite as enamored of Temecula, noting that traffic is still bad.

His main regret is that he and his allies didn't focus more on residential development, trying to get developers to build more roads and fewer houses.

"We were off focus," he said.

Now 58 and a retired firefighter, Hoxsey makes sure to take his trips around town when traffic is lighter. He likes his neighborhood and is comfortable here, so he's staying put. He considered moving to a Hemet retirement community.

"But it's Hemet," he said.

Meaning it's not Temecula, even with all the change.

Murrieta's War

Publication Date: July 17, 2007

For the ultimate political effect, you have to be heading north on Washington Avenue at the post office in Historic Downtown Murrieta between 4 and 5 on a Friday afternoon.

On "the right" are Iraq war supporters; on "the left" are peace boosters.

You occupy the center (of the road and political spectrum), each side trying to woo you with signs. Maybe you'll honk or wave at the group you support. Maybe you'll stare straight ahead wondering, "Who are these nuts anyway?"

Regardless, it's what America is all about: the baseball, hot dog and apple pie stuff.

In an age of political cynicism and voter apathy, it's refreshing to see people who care enough about an issue to go out on a hot afternoon to express an opinion. The Founding Fathers would leap out of their cars and high-five both sides.

Peace backers took up their position last October, when local Beverly Perkins got the idea after seeing a similar gathering in a small Northern California town. The pro-war side moved in last April.

As might be expected given the nature of their cause, the war boosters are more aggressive about their views.

Former Murrieta Council candidate Casey Evans and his cohort Bob Kowell said they're winning based on motorists' honks of support, 10 or 15 to 1 in their favor.

On the other side, former Murrieta Valley school board member Austin Linsley and his wife, Kathy, said they could care less.

"There is no score," she said. "This is a witness for peace."

One recent day, there were about a dozen peace boosters, outnumbering the war backers 2 to 1.

Many sat on chairs quietly holding hand-painted signs. The pro-war crowd stood and many hoisted signs printed off a Web site.

Shuttle diplomacy occurs.

Retiree Don Lambert crossed the divide to gently persuade peace boosters of the error in their ways.

And after Evans created bad vibes with his "Liberalism Is A Mental Disorder" sign, a rival brought him cookies as a peace offering.

A bit of a stir occurred when state Sen. Dennis Hollingsworth, R-Murrieta, moved in on the pro-war side. Home from Sacramento, he had to get his mail and figured he'd check out the discourse.

He contended that most Murrietans "don't want to see us cut and run" from the war, which he said only can lead to mass chaos.

"We're there and we have to win it," Hollingsworth said.

A 17-year Murrietan, he said the town always has been political.

On the other side, peace backers such as retiree Sharon Golden and World War II veteran Dick Sherman said they also care about our troops and don't want to see any more die for the mess they think President Bush created.

"This is not a war; this is a personal vendetta," Sherman said.

Golden joked that she has to be careful of what she says in conservative Murrieta.

"Most of my friends, I don't mention it to," she said of her appearance here.

Peace demonstrator Jamie Barnett joked that the weekly skirmish was about over.

"We're a minute away from ending the war."

Until hostilities resume next week.

Jokester To The Grave
Publication Date: July 31, 2007

The words "hysterical" and "entertaining" are printed on a video of Old Town Temecula put together by Bob Taylor.

They sum up his life as well.

Whether it was playing Santa Claus (he looked the part year-round), Old Town Temecula greeter with wife Bea, facetious City Council candidate, comedy club proprietor, founder of the B.O. Frat. (it's not what you think), or lots of other outrageous roles, good times were always being had by Taylor.

No wonder the mood was light at Taylor's memorial service Sunday afternoon at the Temecula Community Center. Taylor, 84, wouldn't have had it any other way.

So how goofy could he be? Talking about his role as Santa, he once deadpanned, "Every year the IRS calls and wants to know about the $6 billion in stuff that we've given away."

Then there was the council campaign he ran in 1989, when the community incorporated as a city and when everybody else was taking themselves too seriously because that's what real politicians do. His slogan: "Cast a vote 4 Taylor & look for the silver lining! Cast several votes & look for the sheriff!"

Taylor distributed more than 1,000 pieces of his campaign literature and Pat Birdsall, a fellow candidate and later the mayor, said she worried some might take him seriously.

Taylor agreed: "I've had so many people, they read this junk and say, `I'm going to vote for you.'"

For once he wasn't laughing. But that didn't keep him from continuing his comical campaign. For Taylor, the show always had to go on.

The B.O. bunch actually was the Bib Overall Fraternity. Taylor loved to wear them, having acquired the habit in his native Kansas. He printed up certificates of authenticity that were a joke. Of course.

There was another side to Taylor that shows how he was treasured by the community he called home for 30 years. It goes beyond the lifetime achievement award the Temecula chamber gave him and his spot in the Temecula Wall of Fame.

The Taylors moved from Torrance to a local mobile-home park because Bob liked the small town, the West and the history, Bea said.

They lived in the same unit and money was usually tight. Over time their mobile home fell into disrepair. Word got to some Rotary Club of Temecula guys. Led by Jeff Gavitt, they fixed up the place last year, spending more than $6,000 and tons of hours.

"The Taylors have done so much for Temecula and the valley," Gavitt said. "It seemed everybody kind of forgot about them."

There's a reason.

Bea said Bob also suffered from dementia. A doctor told her that, in effect, her husband's brain didn't have a filter. He just said whatever popped into his mind, even if it was inappropriate.

Bob played Santa for 16 Christmases but Bea said he should have stopped at 15. That's how bad the last year was. The couple stopped going to Chamber of Commerce mixers for the same reason. They couldn't even eat at sit-down restaurants.

"He'd embarrass me by the things he would say," she said.

Bob actually had the dementia more than 20 years but was able to function in public much of that time, Bea said. "He was good at acting; good at covering."

Now he's taken his act elsewhere. Lucky them.

Letting Go

Publication Date: August 21, 2007

It's a moment I've been dreading for 18 years, three months, and 13 days.

That would be how old my firstborn, Julia, is. From the moment I first held her in the delivery room and cut the umbilical cord, I've been thinking: I never want to let go.

Recently we were in a terminal at Ontario International Airport because she was about to get on a plane for some college across the country.

This parenting business is never easy, but this was the worst because now I had to let go.

The good thing is she was excited about where she was going: Duke University in North Carolina, her first college choice. She's already got three friends there too, fellow freshmen Nick Altemose, Zach Fuller and Ryan Potts, recent Chaparral High School of Temecula grads.

So I'm happy for her and isn't that what parents are supposed to want for their kids?

I guess, but why do I feel like a character in those children's books I used to read to her? Like the old guy or the tree or whatever the source of wisdom was, and I've given and I've given and I've given for her whole life and now the child is ready to take off - in her case literally - and I want to keep on giving. Like the storybook character, I'm left behind feeling old and sad. (Even her younger brother David, with whom she never passed up an opportunity to argue, said he can't believe how much he misses her.)

I could go on and on with these morbid references, but I've belabored that point. Instead I'm trying to look at this as a celebration of her life, as our child and as a product of Southwest Riverside County.

Like a lot of parents, my wife Joanne and I made a calculated choice moving here at the end of 1988 when Julia was still in her mom's womb. Young families arrived in droves then, like today. The difference was the place was so remote, before another 200,000 people arrived. We felt like pioneers, albeit with covered patios, not covered wagons.

On our way out of Murrieta for the final time of her childhood, Julia said it was like the community grew up with her. We talked about how her mom pushed her up Los Alamos Road in a stroller to the first McDonald's in Murrieta, that there wasn't a traffic light in town when she was born, and that we got her baby stuff at what passed for our mall at the time, the Target on Rancho California Road in Temecula. (Inadvertently coming full circle, we did our last-minute college shopping the night before at the same store. What I wouldn't give to have it be for baby clothes again.)

Julia got to be on the ground floor of so much cool stuff, such as the fledgling church that she went to most of her childhood, the community parades that now are much larger but still provide the small-town feel, the many wonderful teachers she's had and still sees around town, and her memorable years at Vista Murrieta High School, where she began as a freshman the year the school opened.

"As I leave, there's the sense that the face of Murrieta won't be waiting, frozen in time, for me," Julia said. "Murrieta will continue to grow and develop as I do."

These thoughts were with me an hour later as I let go and watched Julia pass through airport security and travel so, so far away. She'll grow and develop and that's all her teary-eyed family can ask.

Open House

Publication Date: September 18, 2007

It's an all too familiar - and depressing - sight in Southwest Riverside County.

The lawn is as dead as a corpse, the grass crunches beneath your feet. The hot tub in the back is filled with slimy water. And the house inside is emptier than a carcass picked over by vultures.

Speaking of which, I'm talking about a Murrieta house that's up for auction, i.e., the buzzards are circling. Getting here was like following a real-estate Yellow Brick Road of sorts, the yellow auction signs luring you in from busy Whitewood Road.

Finally an arrow in front of a home on quiet Camino Mancho pointed to the grand prize: "Coming soon," the sign all but shouts.

You have to wonder why the excitement, given it's for a house that's dropped in value by at least 25 percent in a market that's heading south faster than a snowbird for winter.

This home is more than a real-estate forecast. This is about lives. Going through the house - amazingly, it was open - signs were everywhere of what was once a family.

There were little kids because the child-safety latches were still on many of the cupboards. There was a pet, which explains the doggy door on the garage door. The family must have liked Hawaii. Why else would there be a "Maui" sticker on a closet door? Besides the aforementioned hot tub, there were hardwood floors in much of the home. And the family was well off enough to afford security service, though it couldn't protect them from the real-estate market.

The home looks repainted. Boxes for a microwave and stove indicated those appliances are new. A giant white paper in the living room outlined the legalities of an auction. That gives any home a warm, fuzzy feel.

Unhappy neighbors said the place has been empty at least a year. Wait, it gets worse. Next door to the auction house is another in foreclosure that's been vacant for three months.

Tom Thompson keeps that place looking decent because he maintains the yard and called code enforcement about a pool, which - with mosquitoes, dead rodents and water as green as Jell-O filling it - was beyond gross.

Thompson has lived here since the early 1990s and in that time has seen the neighborhood turn from mostly homeowners to renters, which he said occupy 85 percent of the street's homes. Then again three of the homes are vacant, including one in which no one has ever lived.

He's lived in Southwest Riverside County since 1975 and seen it overrun by growth. He's considered moving to the Southeast to get away from it all.

"It's not like it used to be," Thompson said. "California properties have been overvalued for 20 years. You don't have to be a genius to figure that out."

He knows from personal experience. Thompson figures his 2,150-square-foot home has plummeted from $440,000 to $325,000 in the past year.

"And it's still dropping."

Linda Williams, visiting a relative who lives next to the house up for auction, said the whole thing was sad. "People are losing their homes and that's pitiful."

All this seems to be creating a panic of sorts. For instance, a couple neighbors I talked to decline to give their names, saying they didn't want to get involved. It was as if they were afraid their home would be next.

CHAPTER 20

2008 - Talking vaginas and new cities

Menifee and Wildomar joined the ranks of incorporated cities, giving Southwest Riverside County five such places, further diminishing Riverside County's influence. When I started this column in 1989 there was just one, Lake Elsinore. Home rule is now the norm, not the exception.

Temecula continued its transformation from prude to well, I'm not sure what, as the community celebrated the performance of Vagina Monologues. Whatever conclusion you want to draw from the name of the production is fine by me, but it was further proof that Temecula was no longer so closed minded.

In Murrieta, I looked at the fascinating history of the old Murrieta Hot Springs resort. Too bad it's not as accessible as it used to be. There also was the consistency of a Murrieta kid who received accolades for not missing a day of elementary school.

And my ears are still ringing from the battle-of-the-bands show where my son David's band played.

Keep On Interacting

Publication Date: January 15, 2008

Last July 4th at the annual parade, I ran into a bunch of Temecula City Council members. Ron Roberts and I chatted, and I exchanged pleasantries with several others.

Good thing I saw them then, before the council last week discussed a policy of taking only questions in writing from members of The Press-Enterprise.

Had it been adopted, I suppose I could have handed out fliers with standard queries, such as "How are you?" and "How's the family?" But that wouldn't be real neighborly or efficient; given how long I'd have to wait for them to respond in writing before jotting down more questions, such as "Are you hot? I am." and "Doesn't it make you wonder if there's something to global warming?"

Besides, imagine what other people at the parade are going to think when they see us interacting like that. Heck, they might follow my lead and start writing their own questions for the council members. Then the politicians wouldn't have time to wave at us while riding in the parade because they'd be too busy writing stuff down. What would America have come to?

Instead of approving the rules, the council has instructed City Manager Shawn Nelson to set up a meeting with the newspaper's editor to discuss ways of improving communication between Temecula and The Press-Enterprise.

If you can spare a few minutes between Britney Spears updates (Trust me, I know those are hard to find.), check out the council's riveting discussion on the video at the city Web site. It features the press, the government, a siege mentality, lies, truth and speeding cars.

And while there is no mention of a sex scandal, that Richard Nixon dude comes up. For you Britney buffs, he's a former president who had "issues" with the media and that thing called the Constitution and ultimately resigned in disgrace. Just what every politician aspires to do.

The policy was proposed by Councilman Ron Roberts, who missed the meeting because he was recovering from back surgery. Sorry conspiracy theorists, he wasn't stabbed in the back by the press, at least literally.

While a staff report outlining the policy makes no specific mention of Press-Enterprise errors, Nelson in a letter to the newspaper criticized the accuracy and tone of a Dec. 2 article detailing the business dealings with developer Dan Stephenson and council members. The newspaper responded and found no basis for any correction.

The policy could have started the council down the proverbial slippery slope. Today it could have been the press; tomorrow it might have been citizen watchdogs, who might have been required to submit their stuff in writing to the council. Instead of a mere slope, the council could have been falling off a First Amendment cliff.

Now I can get back to writing about fun stuff instead of serious pieces like this, of which I know both the politicians and my bosses are scrutinizing EVERY SINGLE WORD. From now on, I'm covering only the Easter Bunny. I figure he (or she, if you prefer) can't read and won't need everything in writing.

It also means that at the next Fourth of July parade, the council members and I can chitchat and not have to put everything in writing. Maybe we can even watch the fireworks together, instead of making our own.

Off Limits: V-Word
Publication Date: February 20, 2008

Vaginas.

How's that for shock value? Ranks right up there with the impact of a certain play the other night in Temecula.

It's the "Vagina Monologues," the production that marked a changing of the guard in the town, known far and wide for its conservative, Christian family values.

Those views still exist here, but finally (or at least publicly) so do other views, which everybody here seems to celebrate as they watch the powerful production in the Old Town Temecula Community Theater.

(And to think a taxpayer-supported venue would allow such trash! What will happen next, the old dominant way of thinking must be thinking, A GAY PRIDE PARADE!)

Sure the play is obscene and it bashes men, though somehow this man doesn't feel any pain. Instead I feel pain for the women who have been abused, raped, mutilated - and all the other awful things members of my sex have done to them over the centuries.

Appropriately, proceeds from the sold-out performance - Thank you very much, critics of the play who complained to the Temecula City Council a couple weeks ago, thus drawing Super Bowl-like attention to the production. - are going to Safe Alternatives for Everyone, a local group that helps domestic-violence victims.

In the program, Melissa Donaldson, SAFE's executive director, says, "We need to be outraged and outspoken, but not at the word vagina and not at the First Amendment right of these women to speak their piece this night, but at domestic violence and the children it leaves motherless and fatherless and the families it leaves utterly devastated."

The play's focus is right there on center stage next to director Patti Drew, who was inspired to make the production happen after a murder-suicide occurred in her neighborhood last year.

At the start, two cutout black feminine figures stand ominously next to Drew with five names written on them of local women who lost their lives to domestic violence. Enough said.

The effervescent Drew practically leads us in cheers as she describes the play's background. Then she takes a photo of all the people who dared to attend and crowd members make the "V sign" with their hands. On this night it has a new meaning.

From the opening piece with Hope Davidson, Ellen Watkins and Rebecca Reber, the play is obsessed with vaginas. The play has seemingly hundreds of jokes made in the next 90 minutes about the heretofore off-limits (at least locally) topic.

There are lots of laughs from the audience about bizarre stuff chiefly centered on the female capacity for sexual pleasure. Given how graphic it was, I won't even try to provide more details.

Contrast that rollicking atmosphere to the you-can-hear-a-pin-drop moments as the pain and suffering of women abused by men are conveyed. "I live someplace else," says one victim of rape. "I do not know where that place is."

The woman I sat next to, longtime local Bev Hoffman, noted afterward that she previously had seen the play in Los Angeles and that the local production was much racier. (Take that LA).

Yet she says the local production was also more significant because of the additional statistics of violence against women. And in the end that's why this matters and why I'm writing about vaginas.

Must-See Meetings
Publication Date: April 15, 2008

Go hang out at a city council meeting? What are you, crazy? No paint to watch drying?

Oh ye of little bureaucratic faith. There is something wonderfully refreshing going on in Wildomar these days: People go in droves to watch their City Council meetings. Why? Because they can.

Wildomar is our first newborn city since Murrieta 17 years ago. There is a certain glow among civic-minded Wildomar residents. They have wanted to be a city for the longest time to fend off ravenous advances of surrounding municipalities such as Murrieta and Lake Elsinore.

Wildomar will be official July 1 but, in the meantime, the council is meeting to gear up. The first gathering last month drew some 200 people. And nobody had an ax to grind, unlike the typical council meeting that is only packed when somebody's ox is about to be gored. People were there because they are proud of their community.

A more recent meeting was held at Cornerstone Community Church. And since when does a council meet at a house of worship? (i.e. the dreaded church and state conflict.) Since it is a new council, it will meet any place that will have it, insurance requirements notwithstanding.

Yes, when the discussion turned to the need for insurance, until the politicians find a permanent home, Councilman Bob Cashman said they had better be careful, given the lawsuit-happy times.

"Amen," somebody shouted from the audience, though we don't know if he was moved by the sentiment or the location.

No matter, in case the politicians decided to break out in song, (maybe "Kumbaya" considering how excited everybody is in Wildomar these days), set behind them were musical instruments from a previous worship service. Heck, think of how much better Congress would get along if it would just harmonize about Iraq or whatever members are ticked off about. Wildomar could be revolutionizing the way we do government.

In the audience of about 50 was Bob Wheeler, a retiree from Murrieta, who is so fascinated by the new government that he had to see it in person. Take it from an outsider, folks, Wildomar right now is better than TV.

Also there was Sharon Heil, of Wildomar, a local of 12 years. She has long been active in the Wildomar community and practically sprints to the front when copies of some document are offered to the public.

At another point when the agenda turned to public comments, several people dashed to the podium, apparently not aware they first needed to be called by name. It is refreshing to see such excitement when people elsewhere are so bored by their government.

Even the new city staff members (the crowd seated in the front row, conspicuous in their suits and ties) got a round of applause when introduced. Since when are people cheering on bureaucrats?

Cashman pushed the envelope even further when he talked about how the new council needed to stay in close contact with its residents. Regular town hall meetings could be a way to achieve that, his colleagues happily chimed in. Fancy that, politicians who want to hear from the public. What exactly are they smoking over there in Wildomar?

Always There
Publication Date: June 20, 2008

When the topic of today's youth comes up, old-timers want to snarl, "All those kids do is play video games and watch TV. Why if it were up to them, they probably wouldn't even go to school!"

Then there is Marcus Gow, the antithesis of what kids may appear to be today.

He's not into video games or TV. And he just proudly graduated from elementary school, a place he attended every single day since kindergarten, 1,080 days over six years.

Trying to do that multiplication problem in his head while I do it on paper, Marcus is off by one number. Asked to account for his rare mistake, he said, "I'm not at school."

It only seems like he lives there. When he was in my class in third grade at Rail Ranch in Murrieta, he broke his nose before a baseball game. A doctor told him he needed a few days off, something that would make most kids think, "A broken nose isn't so bad."

When Marcus got upset instead, his mom, Lenore, told the doctor she didn't understand and he really needed to go to school. The doctor suggested Marcus attend half days in order to rest.

"Who needs rest?" Marcus said, noting he went the whole day anyway.

So how do you account for such dedication and determination, traits that seem to be in short supply with kids today?

Well, the plaques don't hurt. After a second consecutive year of perfect attendance at Rail Ranch, kids get a plaque. Marcus has now earned five red-and-black plaques, reflecting the school colors.

But it's more than just the stuff. He talks of commitment the way other kids talk about SpongeBob. Having finished elementary school; now he wants to go every day to Shivela Middle School and Vista Murrieta High School after that.

Even his sister, Laura, about to enter high school, can't understand why her brother is so obsessed. "You don't get a plaque in middle school," she advised. "So what's the point?"

His friends - the ones who "miss days of school," Marcus said with a grin - told him they had heard of some kid who went every day from kindergarten into ninth grade. Although the kids didn't know his name - sounds like an urban legend among perfect attendance circles - Marcus still wants to top this mystery idol. "I want the record," he said.

Marcus, a polite, blond-haired boy, says most everything with an infectious smile. When he talks about how he would rather be outside playing instead inside with electronics, it's understandable. A kid with his enthusiasm has to be out and about.

While Laura jokes that he likes to go vandalize the city, Marcus says he's into riding his scooter, his bike, or his friends' skateboards. Video games, smideo games.

His mom says perfect attendance runs in the family. Laura earned plaques for being in school every day for three years. Lenore Gow also always made sure that her older children, James, a college sophomore, and Christine, a high school senior, went every day unless they were really sick.

As for life after school, Marcus one day handed me a business card with his name and "attorney of law" typed on it. While that seems within reach, he's also thinking about the Navy or being a doctor.

Whatever he does, one thing is for sure: He'll be there every day.

Future Shock

Publication Date: August 19, 2008

One thing has been a constant in Paul Babb's 18 years in Old Town Temecula: Change.

Babb has a front row seat for Old Town's transformation from a dusty, small town, dim lights kind of place, to a sleek, urban, bright lights kind of place - something never seen in suburban, sprawling Southwest Riverside County.

Granted, it has a ways to go to be finished, but it is happening. Babb is Exhibit A, having once operated On The Farm Antiques with his wife, Cheryl, on Old Town Front Street near Fifth Street. Today that space is long gone, the gigantic Old Town Center going up in its place.

Babb says On The Farm was in two dressed-up modular buildings, the kind of set up that typified the previous Old Town. The new center, to be finished later this year, is the future. Call it New Town for our purposes.

Now Babb is across the street in Cheryl's Antiques. On Friday night, many hundreds of people strolled around the area. Babb practically had to pinch himself. Gone are the days when Old Town was about 80 percent antiques stores, by Babb's estimate. New Town is less than half antiques stores, and that is decreasing fast. A wave of gift shops, specialty stores, offices, and restaurants is arriving.

Speaking of being in shock, I was sipping a glass of wine on that same Friday night with friends on the outdoor patio at Palumbo's Ristorante, also on Fifth Street. Just the fact there is something calling itself a "ristorante" ought to show something profound is going on in an area that once specialized in Western casual.

The couple we're with used to live in San Diego and we're pretending we're not in Temecula for a moment. Instead, we're in some urban setting, say the Gaslamp Quarter.

Now before you laugh - Old Town is no more the Gaslamp Quarter than John McCain is Miley Cyrus - I'm asking you to take a leap of faith to New Town. There's a trendy looking café, a spice shop, and big-city looking apartments nearby.

Temecula City Hall is going up, two other classy buildings have just been finished, some 227,000 square feet of commercial space is in the development pipeline according to the city, and several other old structures like the one Babb used to occupy have "For Sale" signs. Now give this five, maybe 10 years, and an economy that will mend eventually. New Town isn't so farfetched, huh, Miley McCain?

With his Dallas drawl and folksy charm, the 61-year-old Babb was a perfect fit for Old Town. And if he had a dollar for every time he has heard somebody say "My mother used to have one of those" while marveling at antiques, he would be a rich man.

It is a changing clientele though. There are more young families in Old Town, not as many antiques hunters. It is still mostly out of towners, about 65 percent Babb estimates.

He says some people don't care for the transformation - the loss of antiques stores and the big buildings going up - and he basically says, Get over it! Of course with his country charm, he is much too polite to actually say it so brusquely.

"If you do business today the way you did business yesterday, you will be out of business tomorrow," he says of his philosophy of keeping up with the change, not trying to fight it.

Smart man, given the New Town that is coming. And coming fast.

Play it Smart, Still Lose Out
Publication Date: September 26, 2008

The house a block from me sits in weeds, some close to a foot high. Tons of business fliers are strewn on the front doorstep. Broken tiles lay on the front sidewalk that once looked nice. There is a forlorn real estate sign in the front yard, even if it's been months since any buyer traffic.

Let's see. Is it (A) one of Bill Gates' houses, (B) a model home or (C) a foreclosure? Sadly we all know the answer.

Sadly is used lightly because of what this house off busy Whitewood Road in east Murrieta (and its companion foreclosed property across the street) has come to represent in the past two weeks: The end of our economy as we know it, if not the whole global system as well.

That's because the federal government is talking of a bailout of $700 billion for the financial institutions that got caught up in this whole mess of no-money-down, who-cares-if-you-don't-have-a-job, just take-this-teaser-rate-adjustable-interest-rate-loan-that's- going-to-go-through-the-roof-the second-you-sign-on-the-dotted-line- of-this-paperwork-you-don't-understand.

While I still feel bad for those people, I'm also starting to feel angry. We all know of somebody in Southwest Riverside County who latched on to one of those silly loans. For well over a year now we've seen foreclosures pop up like pimples on a kid with bad acne.

While it was obviously horrible - there was once a family that called that abandoned wreck "home" - it seemed to be just their problem, not a trigger for the next Great Depression.

Not anymore. Our 401ks are being slaughtered in the stock market, our equity is a thing of the past, and even our jobs could be at risk as unemployment soars. All because some guys on Wall Street got greedy (OK, that's a given) and in part because some folks you know in Temecula, Murrieta, Lake Elsinore, Menifee and Perris - we're all afflicted with this stuff - either got greedy too, or were so desperate to buy a house that they'd accept any loan, no matter how goofy.

Three years ago our property values topped off a dizzying climb. My Murrieta house that I paid $182,000 for in 1998 was worth about $450,000 in 2005. It made no sense, it seemed too good to be true, and I should have cashed out and moved to an empty field - but I did nothing.

Not that I wasn't tempted. My wife dragged me into a house on the west side of Murrieta that was on the market for just more than $500,000, having dropped $50,000 at that point. It seemed like a great deal, and I actually ran some numbers. Today you'd be lucky to get $250,000 for it. And we'd have a loan of about $450,000 if we'd moved.

In the meantime, I know of one guy who used his equity to buy land and somebody else who put in a pool, bought a truck, picked up an RV and took trips. Now the first guy is about to lose his house and, while I don't know about the other's finances, they can't be good.

This happened other places too, but it was a way of life here. In Murrieta there are an estimated 2,500 foreclosures and another 2,500 coming in the next year. Now the feds want to bail out the big guys (another given) and maybe some little guys, perhaps some you know. Meanwhile, those of us who didn't take the bait look on and want to scream.

Monumental Meeting
Publication Date: October 3, 2008

Jameela Atooli leans over at the historic first Menifee City Council meeting and asks, "Do you know if Arnold is going to be here?"

By Arnold she can only mean Schwarzenegger. And while this is the biggest night ever in the new city's history - granted, it's the only one at this point - it's not that epic.

That's Arnold's problem. He missed a blockbuster of a meeting as these bureaucratic functions go - complete with a standing ovation (hold on to that moment, Menifee politicians, because you never know when that will come around again), stirring speeches (Mayor Wallace Edgerton knows how to deliver one) and a terrific souvenir - gorgeous city medallions for everybody.

Sorry, good citizens of the city of Menifee - doesn't that feel good to write - but unless your officials plan to cater future sessions and dole out World Series tickets, subsequent meetings can only go downhill from Wednesday's smashing debut.

Babies resting in mothers' tender arms, elderly residents walking with canes, two residents with seeing-eye dogs, dignitaries in dark suits and black dresses, casual folks in flip flops and shorts - they come from all walks of Menifee's life to see history in the making.

Typical of the reaction is folksy 85-year-old volunteer Eileen Parnell. She's glad the city incorporated before other neighboring cities, such as Perris, Canyon Lake, Murrieta and Wildomar, started annexing pieces. "We're good to gobble up," she says with a laugh, referring to Menifee's desirable qualities.

Another dedicated helper, Margarita Acosta, has been here eight hours helping to set up the big event. She moved here in 1989 and notes how her two kids, Sandra and Michael, didn't want to relocate at the time.

Now they're both grown but they still live in Menifee and plan to raise families here, just like their mom. "Now they can appreciate what we have," she says.

Atooli, a 17-year-old Paloma Valley High School student, is here to earn extra credit for her government class. "It's cool," she says of the gathering, quite the endorsement from a teen. Who cares if Arnold didn't show?

A standing-room-only crowd of more than 800 people crams into the Bell Mountain Middle School auditorium. The show starts with a video of the community's history, from black and white pictures of the agricultural past to today's bumper crop of chain stores to serve the needs of newcomers arriving day and night. The trick will be balancing the two. May Menifee learn from the mistakes of their overbuilt neighbors, Murrieta and Temecula.

That's a skirmish for another time. Tonight is only stirring fellowship, concluding with Edgerton's feel-good remarks that put everything into perspective. He talks of a hill he likes to walk up at dusk, one that provides a sweeping view of a town he's watched change in 12 years: "What you see is what we are celebrating tonight."

More important is what's inside the rooftops: Families that moved here in waves. Kids are being put down for the night by parents with dreams of what their children can achieve. It's hard not to get emotional at times like these, the new mayor says. The possibilities seem endless.

The same can be said for baby Menifee for at least the first night. The possibilities seem endless.

Music To Our Earplugs
Publication Date: October 7, 2008

Officially it's known as the sixth annual Battle of the Bands. Unofficially, at least among weary parents, it's the Battle of the Earplugs.

It's bad enough when a bunch of teenagers in a garage make loud music and call it a "band."

Now imagine seven of these bands in one place for almost three hours of noise. I know the name of that tune - migraine!

My son David's band, Goodnight and Good Luck, was among the entries at the concert Saturday night at the Murrieta Community Center. And a tip of the headache medicine to fellow dad Chris Talbot who lets the teenagers practice at his house. The way he sees it, his son Tyler is growing up fast and he wants to spend as much time as possible with him. Good for him - and his ears.

There's actually a decent crowd - well over 100 - and the music is high quality, according to Matt Buffington, who's doing sound and logistics.

Buffington does teenage band shows about once a month, and he says the bands are solid. He recalls one recent show where he had to sit through 15 bands. "We won't discuss the names in order to protect the guilty," he deadpans.

Buffington, 28, was in a high school band. He says the difference today is it's easier for bands to promote themselves. With a video camera and access to the Internet, they can wreak havoc on eardrums all over the world.

There's also the value of the experience. His band sparked an interest in the industry and while he's not performing today, he is making a living at music. And given the economic climate, whatever you can do to make ends meet is music to anybody's ears.

Another great thing about bands is their names. The lineup here is Doulos, Soul Missive, Aesthetic Is Love, Diminishtry, Sepherin and Spared. Here is how the program describes the thinking behind Diminishtry: "They came up with their name after a long process of elimination and desperation."

Among Diminshtry's fans - do I sound ancient if I call them groupies - are Cody Antolowitz, Jack Clifford and Travis Chrest. Clifford has been to four band battles and admires the collective courage of the groups. "You've got to give them credit for getting up there."

Clifford himself is in a band that only practices sporadically. "We are tossing around a name but I don't think it would be appropriate for a newspaper," he says, laughing.

Ryan Bilton, whom I've known since he was a third-grader, and Tara Honda, who's a neighbor of ours, are part of Soul Missive. I've heard them occasionally practicing in Tara's house, and they've been in shows in LA and Orange County. The group is different because it has three girls. Ryan, sporting a big grin, swears he's there just to make music.

Mary Loyd, one of the singers, teases him, "He loves us."

As for my son's band - with Tyler Talbot on guitar and vocals, Garret Stratford on drums, Spencer Rushton on piano and vocals, Dallin Proffitt on guitar, and David on bass - they've played three times. After their first show about a month ago, a guy in the industry told them to be more animated, not just stand there like musical statues. So Saturday they hop all over like they've got disco fever. (There I go being ancient again.)

It worked because they won. First prize includes $500 courtesy of Murrieta Valley Foundation and a $100 gift certificate.

That'll buy a lot of earplugs.

Hot Springs History

Publication Date: November 28, 2008

Irony abounds with the history of what used to be the Murrieta Hot Springs resort.

It was a place known for a good party, one area even dubbed "Whiskey Row." When asked why, tour director Malcolm Barnett notes sheepishly, "Probably Whiskey Row because they did a lot of drinking in those days."

Today the area at Murrieta Hot Springs and Margarita roads is a Christian conference center and Calvary Chapel Bible College. Somehow I doubt drinking is part of the curriculum.

Back in its heyday, seemingly everybody in town worked at the resort. "The town of Murrieta existed because of Murrieta Hot Springs, it wasn't the other way around," notes old-timer Les Dunham.

Today one has to pass through a guard station in order to try to see the once legendary resort. With Murrieta's population at 100,000, it's a good bet that many locals have no idea of its famous past or seen the beauty here.

A shame, considering these are perhaps the most scenic and historic grounds in our area.

A public tour was given because of an authors' signing for a book about the history, "Images of America: Murrieta Hot Springs." The four authors - Marvin Curran, Rebecca Farnbach, Tony Guenther (grandson of the owner who first made the resort famous) and Loretta Barnett (wife of Malcolm) - sold about 100 books.

The tour showcases an area that is in pristine condition. Many of the older buildings have been restored or torn down and rebuilt to look like the original. Flowing fountains are everywhere and mineral water with a pungent smell runs along meandering walkways. A stunning vista offers a gorgeous view of a giant pond.

Barnett, who worked here 16 years, says, "They (Calvary Chapel people) have done a magnificent job of restoring it."

The church's imprint extends beyond the landscaping. One sign on the tour advises: "Female Dorms No Men Beyond This Point."

Calvary acquired the property in 1995 and Annette Jennings, who worked here in the 1970s, says limited access has been good for the resort's well-being. "I'm glad they've kept it nice. It's like walking back in time again."

The book features an advertisement from the 1950s that advertises Murrieta Hot Springs as "California's Greatest Health Resort." It was popular with Jewish people from Los Angeles and Hollywood celebrities such as John Wayne.

The resort fell into bankruptcy in the 1970s and was rescued in the early 1980s by Alive Polarity, a vegetarian group that operated it like a retreat. The rules included vegetarian meals only, and no smoking, liquor, telephones or television.

What is it about the resort that attracts extremes?

The resort changed hands again in the late 1980s, and I remember buying monthly pool passes and swimming there the first summer we lived locally in 1989. At the time it was the only public pool in Murrieta, and it was like visiting Europe, what with all the languages I could hear from foreigners who vacationed there.

Now it's a place hardly even known by many locals. Oh well, at least we can read about it.

CHAPTER 21

2009 - A Super Bowl and a ritzy mall

While the economy continued to stink, Temecula's Promenade Mall finished its much anticipated expansion with a bunch of glitzy new stores opening. The center became even more of a destination, especially for the upscale crowd.

President Obama was inaugurated and the changing times were also reflected in a Southwest Riverside County that's become dramatically more diversified in the past quarter century.

Moving community moments drew my attention, including the Memorial Day service in Murrieta and the Good Friday walk with the cross in Temecula that has come to symbolize the power of the local Christian faith.

Our stunning lack of hospital beds made news unfortunately, as did a Murrieta church that proclaimed its open doors to the local gay community and a Vista Murrieta-Chaparral high school football championship that was our Super Bowl.

Finally, I profiled an autistic boy who spent the entire year in my third grade class. He taught us tons of things you can't find in textbooks. We all benefited.

Changing times reflected here
Publication Date: January 20, 2009

Today we inaugurate a black man as president, something I never thought I'd see in my lifetime.

Especially from the perspective of a Southwest Riverside County I've called home the past 20 years.

When I moved here, blacks were few and far between, something I felt was more by circumstance than design. It was a mantra with people moving here at the time: They wanted to escape the big city - which tends to be more racially diverse - and live in a small town, which in Southern California tends to be not as integrated. I honestly don't believe white people were moving here to escape minorities.

However, the first year we lived in Murrieta, I attended a party in the neighborhood of our new subdivision. At one point I heard one of the neighbors use the N-word in discussing a black person. For some insane reason I didn't challenge the guy about what he said. I wasn't the only coward either, considering he said it in front of a number of people.

Also at the time, noted white supremacist Tom Metzger lived in nearby Fallbrook. The TV repairman even did work up here. There were a few problems with skinheads, especially in Temecula. And occasionally in Murrieta there were newspaper stories of blacks feeling they were victims of racism.

Fortunately we've become more diverse as we've become more populated. Perhaps reflecting that, Chuck Washington, a black man who now serves on the Temecula City Council, was elected to the Murrieta City Council in 1995.

According to a 2005 study of the city's ethnicity, 6.3 percent of Murrieta's population was black. In Riverside County as a whole that year, 5.5 percent were black; meaning Murrieta had more African-Americans than many county cities. And in the 2000 census, just to show how the number has grown, just 3.3 percent of Murrieta was black.

Five years ago I was an assistant coach for a Warm Springs team my son played on in a local middle school basketball league. Warm Springs is in the more racially mixed east side of Murrieta and six of 11 kids on the team were black. A Shivela team in central Murrieta had a similar mix of black and white players. By contrast, hardly any of the kids from the Thompson team on the more affluent west side were black.

My son now attends Vista Murrieta High School and in a mock election among students last fall, Barack Obama beat John McCain by a whopping 55 percent to 34 percent. While Murrieta voters still went overwhelmingly for McCain in the real election, it's clear times are changing among local kids.

I've taught third grade at Rail Ranch Elementary in east Murrieta for 11 years and have seen the racial mix of the campus change dramatically. I went more than five years without a black student in my class. In recent times I've had black students more often, including four out of my 20 this year.

During the presidential election campaign last fall, the kids in the class - black, white, Hispanic and Asian - often talked about Obama and I could tell he was a favorite of many. We sometimes write fictional stories with famous people and cartoon characters that they suggest, and Obama was often nominated. (Sorry Republican boosters, John McCain was only proposed a few times.) And it was amazing the superhuman feats they'd have Obama do. Fixing the economy will be easy by comparison.

Last Friday before our three-day holiday weekend - celebrating Martin Luther King's birthday, of all things - I asked my kids what would be the big news when they come back to school. Surprisingly, almost in unison their hands shot up: Obama will be president! Looking out over this excited sea of ethnicity that reflects the Murrieta and America of today, I thought, what a great country!

Council Holds City's Attention
Publication Date: March 20, 2009

City councils aren't the most exciting groups. They'll build roads, OK some houses, try to keep the local economy humming and, if they really want to get wild and crazy, raise taxes.

Then there is the crew in Canyon Lake, which is to humdrum city councils what octuplet mom is to birth control.

There is the ongoing ruckus with one of the area's most controversial housing projects, Goetz Hill, or Goat Hill as it's known to locals.

Then former Councilman Frank Kessler pleaded guilty last month to embezzlement in connection with misusing his city-issued credit card. He and his wife, Suzanne, were accused of using the card to pay for $6,239 of charges made on a Hawaii cruise, including $3,000 for alcoholic drinks and casino tokens. It's apparently easy to be a high roller at the public's expense.

Not to be outdone, City Councilman Martin Gibson this month used his business, Pepe's Mexican Restaurant, to host "Seduction: The Exotic Men of Magic."

Unfortunately, I suppose your typical politician would steer clear of such an event. Not in Canyon Lake, where an undercover deputy from the sheriff's department confirmed that performers "simulated sex acts, displayed their buttocks and touched and fondled patrons and themselves."

This is why most public officials just stick to mundane stuff such as fixing potholes. Anything sexier can only lead to trouble.

A state Department of Alcoholic Beverage Control rep quickly shut down the not-so-subtle seduction, and Gibson is being fined $100 by his own city. The ABC also is investigating a complaint of lewd conduct at the performance. His fellow council members may publicly reprimand Gibson. Gee, I wonder why.

This is quite the turn of events for Canyon Lake, a city of more than 11,000 previously best known for its gated status and its pristine lake. Incorporated in 1990, controversy used to be as alien to Canyon Lake as a stripper performing in a church. Only with Canyon Lake's sexier-than-thou politics can one get away with such an analogy.

Right Time for Sophistication?
Publication Date: April 3, 2009

In need of a $12 bottle of ketchup, I'm at the newly expanded Promenade mall in Temecula.

This place isn't just high end; it's skyscraper high - or at least the price of the spicy ketchup is.

There is no doubt that the expansion is a home run. Stepping back in the old mall after walking through the spiffy outdoors expansion, it feels like stepping back in a place that's seen better days.

So kudos to The Promenade's owner, Forest City Enterprises of Cleveland, for making a posh - there's a word that's never been associated with us - expansion.

It's supposed to be a Main Street setting, with many of the buildings sporting fake storefront paintings reminiscent of yesteryear. Among the depictions are a drug store with a soda fountain, an old-time diner, Jimmy's Bicycle shop, and a business with a Chevrolet out front. You know it's ancient when somebody actually bought an American car.

Plenty of people are "oohing" and "aahing" over the new tenants. Pottery Barn, the Sephora cosmetics chain, and Williams-Sonoma are among the many stores crowded with customers.

Walking out of Williams-Sonoma, a store greeter offers me a cup of jellybeans. Wow, when's the last time the Wal-Mart greeter did that?

When I decline, she asks, "Would you like a vitamin instead?"

"Are you serious?" I reply.

Just joking, she says with a smile. Greeters with a sense of humor - now that's classy.

Dick and Garnet Sherman, of Murrieta, are among the new shoppers. Dick isn't a mall man himself. "If I had my choice of anything I wanted at a mall, it would be to go home," he says with a wink. But this place has him impressed. "We like it very much," he says. "They did a good job."

But Dick agrees the timing could be better, given this little problem we have with the economy these days.

Supposedly this couldn't be helped, given that the expansion started in 2007 just as the economy started to tank. General Manager Jeff Kurtz says no expansion tenants have pulled out, and he's hopeful the economy is about to recover.

Then again, what's he supposed to say?

Assuming the economy moves forward again, what the mall expansion really means is we've moved into a different shopping dimension. It appears the chain stores that run our retail lives previously considered us beneath the high end. You can have Sears and JC Penney, but Nordstrom? No.

While that legendary store isn't here yet, the retail powers-that-be have deemed us (with our La Cresta, De Luz, Temecula Wine Country, west Murrieta, and Bear Creek homes) worthy of similar shops. The mall expansion amounts to our version of Rodeo Drive, with prices to match. Williams-Sonoma also has the upscale ketchup. And it has beer mustard for the same price. A bottle of bourbon BBQ sauce is even more at $12.95. Jim Beam is in the ingredients. Sophisticated, I guess.

Can you live without this stuff in this economy? Time will tell. Then there's the Yard House restaurant and its $10.45 cheeseburger.

I'll pass. It says it has the "world's largest selection of draft beer," and when have we had such bragging rights before? It's a different dimension.

Anyway, I have to leave the mall, but I'll stop on my way home at WinCo, the only place I can afford to buy groceries on my teacher salary these days. Pulling up, I see a limo in the parking lot. Don't tell me times are tough even for the high-end crowd?

The ketchup is on sale for 97 cents. That I can afford. The mall expansion I can't.

Walk Shows Faith, Pride
Publication Date: April 10, 2009

Think of long running annual Temecula events and the Balloon & Wine Festival and the Rod Run come to mind right away.

Then there is a less publicized gathering happening today that in a way says more about our area than those more widely known events: It's the 23rd annual Good Friday Cross Walk.

It's a walk to commemorate Jesus Christ's crucifixion and death. Christians remember Good Friday as the day Jesus died on the cross and believe that three days later Jesus rose from the dead on Easter Sunday.

There's a reason this area is known as the Bible Belt of Southern California, and the size of this event is one big reason why.

A crowd between 1,500 and 2,500 is expected to gather at 11 a.m. at the Temeku Theater on Ynez Road. They'll carry crosses about two miles to Sam Hicks Park in Old Town Temecula, where a worship service will be held. Pastor Brent Yim of Temecula Community Church will lead that moment.

There will be babies in strollers, older people using walkers, and everybody in between. There will be lots of honks from supportive motorists.

Some will park their cars and join in the fervent display. Many denominations of Christianity - Calvary Chapel worshipers, Catholics, Methodists, Baptists, and others - will be represented.

Regardless of your beliefs, it's amazing to watch this public procession of faith marching down major streets in the middle of the day, something you'd expect to see in perhaps conservative Oklahoma, not racy Southern California.

Big cities have gay pride parades; this is our Christian pride parade. Today's event reminds us that Southwest Riverside County is still a place with a strong fundamental Christian influence.

Longtime local resident Monty Sharp, 58, started the march. He moved here in the late 1970s and wryly notes that Temecula at the time had a large number of bars for a few number of residents.

"I wasn't walking with the Lord myself," he says, contending he was Christian in name only. That changed in the early 1980s when he walked into a local church, Valley Christian Fellowship. "It was the first time I ever heard the Bible taught," he says.

About five years later he started the Cross Walk after hearing of Arthur Blessitt, who has been walking around the world for about 40 years carrying a cross for Jesus.

"The Lord said, `You need to do it,'" Sharp said of his inspiration. He speaks matter-of-factly of that moment, something you often hear in talking to local Christians about their faith. Compare that to big cities such as New York, Washington and Los Angeles where I once lived and rarely heard such testimonials.

That first walk included about 70 people and ended at what was once the site of a hardware store and is now The Stampede, a huge country-western bar. Not exactly hallowed ground for conservative Christians anymore.

Sharp, who started the local Student Venture, a national Christian ministry group, says the first year was a blast, just like everyone since then. "It's like a giant family reunion."

That first event people just showed up and Sharp didn't bother getting any prior approvals. Temecula at the time wasn't even an incorporated city.

Today he has to meet with city officials and get a permit for such a big crowd. Not that he's complaining.

"The city is just incredibly gracious," he says.

Besides, the last thing a group of devout Christians would want to do is break any laws, especially on Good Friday.

What Matters In Murrieta

Publication Date: May 27, 2009

Boy Scout Gage Ruppert, 10, is standing out front of Murrieta's Laurel Cemetery with his colleagues Aaron Baggest, 11, and Trevor Daniels, 10.

"Good morning, sir," he says while handing me a program to the Memorial Day service.

Sir. Not often I get called that. Like something out of the military, this is what the day, and to a certain extent the community, are about.

Like a rose bursts with blooms this time of year, Murrieta bursts with patriotism on national holidays. Lots of people have flags on their houses. Red, white and blue is a frequent fashion statement. The holiday is known for its purpose, not just an excuse for a long weekend.

Gage reflects that sentiment. He talks about Decoration Day, which is what the occasion was originally called when it was started.

"I read a lot of books," he says of his knowledge, so much so that he sometimes gets in trouble for doing it while the teacher is talking. We should all be blessed with such faults.

His great-grandfather was in World War II and his grandfather was in Vietnam. "I have a lot of service in my family," he says proudly.

When we're done talking, the boys all offer handshakes. "Thank you very much, sir," Gage says. There's that respect again.

Walking into the cemetery and the hundreds of headstones, it's easy to pick out white crosses and American flags that stand next to a lot of them. And I mean a lot.

They're next to the veterans who are buried here, including a few from the Civil War. One such headstone belongs to Lyman Ashley, though I have to rely on the cemetery district's helpful secretary, Patti D'Andrea, for the name. It's mostly faded from the grave marker now, given he lived so long ago.

Of the approximately 1,200 people buried here, about 140 were veterans. Seven are from the Civil War, six from Vietnam. "Thank God I don't have any from Iraq," D'Andrea says.

This is the 10th year the local American Legion Post 852 has hosted a Memorial Day service. The post is also responsible for the cemetery flagpole.

D'Andrea gives me a history from Joe Grammatico, the post's former commander, about how he met with the cemetery board in 2000 and asked why there wasn't a flagpole. "They responded that they had thought about it, but there was no one that seemed to care," he noted. He replied that he cared, which is why there's a flagpole.

That's often the case with such matters - somebody just has to do it. Murrieta City Councilman Rick Gibbs, who served in the Air Force 32 years, talks movingly about a guy he knew who died on his first combat mission in Vietnam and about another man who never returned from what was supposed to be his final mission. "The freedom we have is because of those men," he says.

Arlean Garrison is here; just like she's been to most big community events in the 69 years she's proudly called Murrieta home. She says her favorite community has always been a patriotic place. "It's because we like each other," she says. "We're interested in each other."

Pete Ramos, another American Legion guy, talks about how excited people get when they see contestants returning from "American Idol." Yet when people killed in battle return in caskets, nobody makes such a fuss. He wonders what that says about our values as a society.

But sir, on this day in an ancient cemetery on the rural southwest end of a city that's otherwise changed so much, people still know what matters most.

'Andrew Is Sooooo Cool'
Publication Date: June 6, 2009

As a third-grade teacher, it's easy to help kids in reading, writing and math. That's what textbooks are for.

But how do you teach empathy?

Thanks to Andrew Grimes, my students this year have PhDs.

Andrew is a boy with autism who has been fully included in our class this year at Rail Ranch Elementary School in Murrieta, with the help of his wonderful aide, Diane Haly.

We laugh with him when he blurts out Chicken Little at the strangest times, we commiserate with him if he gets frustrated, we are proud of him when he displays his amazing spelling skills and we high-five him a ton because he loves it so much.

"Andrew is a good guy," says Justin Thomas. "Even though he cries sometime, he's not a bad guy."

No doubt, at times Andrew has been a disruption. But he's not alone in that department, as any teacher can tell you.

At the start of the year you could feel the tension in the room when he started crying while the other kids were trying to concentrate. But after about a month the kids learned to adjust and keep working. They definitely weren't mad at Andrew; they seemed to understand it was just how he coped.

See what I mean about empathy.

Tina Pattison, a kindergarten teacher at Rail, has a son, Bob, a Vista Murrieta High School student with autism. One of his friends, Brian Tolle, has hung out with him since their days at Rail.

Pattison, a teacher for more than 30 years, says children with autism benefit immensely from sitting in a regular education classroom. "The constant immersion in a classroom of wonderful children is a full immersion in language and culture, much like one experiences in a foreign country."

They also gain from the kindness of others. "But in the end, what I have discovered is that others have benefited from, and seek out his companionship for, the way it makes them feel," Pattison says. "Really, that is what friendship and love are."

My third-graders love to hold hands with Andrew when we walk to recess. They jockey to sit with him at lunch, especially the girls.

One recent lunch we talk about what everybody's favorite food is. While everybody else lists the usual pizza or burgers, Andrew says, "penguin food." Everybody cracks up.

He calls a kid named Nick "Nickelodeon." The other kids who often sit with him, Maria Reyes, Andrea Gonzalez, Jason Ward and Amaiya Shell, are laughing with him.

Some will follow Andrew to the playground. He loves to swing, but Heather Long (the aide who supervises him while Haly takes a break) tries to get him to play games such as handball. When he messes up, they let him try again. And if you've ever seen how cutthroat elementary kids can be when they play handball, you know that's a big concession.

In the classroom, Haly says she has to pay close attention to what motivates Andrew that day. When she figures it out, the rest falls right into place.

She enjoys seeing Andrew make friends, including a girl in another third-grade class. At recess they love to talk about Disney stuff. "They both laugh and it is a joy to see this interaction," Haly says.

Here's something that says it all about our year with Andrew: Sorting through his homework last week, I came across a beautiful picture he made with his spelling words, an assignment we call "Words in shape."

Inside his colorful picture, he wrote in big bold letters, "Andrew is soooo cool."

Soooo true.

Southwest's Super Bowl

Publication Date: December 11, 2009

A hot ticket is something you don't associate with Southwest Riverside County.

Hot weather, sure. But a hot ticket? What do you think this is, the Super Bowl?

Well, tonight's Vista Murrieta-Chaparral game for the gigantic Inland Division football championship amounts to just that. And I didn't list Vista Murrieta first because my son is a senior there and my daughter is a graduate. No, I'm strictly neutral on this one.

Anyway, high school sports here are huge. And you know how mayors of cities of pro teams in the real Super Bowl make bets? If Temecula Mayor Maryann Edwards and Murrieta's Kelly Bennett were to wager on valley supremacy, now is the time.

Maybe Edwards could put up a bottle of wine and Bennett could put up, oh, I don't know, a stop sign to help with Temecula's traffic.

The Super Bowl is familiar turf for Chaparral, which has been to the big game three of the past four years, previously against teams outside the area.

Its program is so huge that Sports Illustrated wrote about the team a couple years ago, detailing how well Chaparral was playing while players' homes were ravaged by the foreclosure crisis. Chaparral players don't figure to be fazed by the packed stadium a hot ticket generates.

Vista Murrieta, which will host the game, has a seating capacity of 4,200, Athletic Director Ray Moore says. Additional seats will be hauled in for tonight that could bring the total to 5,500. When a big game such as the annual one with rival Murrieta Valley happens, about 8,000 people have been there, thanks to standing-room only space. That many and more figure to be there tonight, fire marshal permitting.

Ryan Tukua, Chaparral's defensive coordinator, says players from both schools have known each other since Pop Warner and middle school days. Playing in the biggest game of their lives against kids they've competed against tons of times will be a thrill, he says.

"We couldn't ask for anything more."

It's hard to believe basically young men will take the field, especially since I've watched so many grow up. I'm a third-grade teacher in Murrieta and one of Vista's starters, Ben Dexter, was in my class nine years ago.

I coached a number of the Vista kids in recreation sports over the years, including Hollis Jones, who's caught many a big TD pass, defensive stud John Hardy, and Ben Madison, Aaron Duenas, Scott Terrazas, Curtis Speed and Emil Mejares. One reason Vista football is probably so good is that I coached basketball and soccer.

Then there are Shane Hunter and his mom, Roxanne. She's been a school nurse in Temecula for 20 years, including 18 at Temecula Valley High School. Shane plays for Vista and is one of the nicest kids you'll ever meet. He's been a great athlete since third grade, and I helped coach him on two middle school basketball teams.

As much as she loves her job in Temecula, Roxanne says her allegiance tonight is clear: Go Vista! Shane has an inspiration that goes beyond winning a mere Super Bowl - he's playing in memory of his dad, John, one of the nicest dads I've ever met.

He died about a year ago, and Shane recalls how he and his father would get together after a game and break down the good and the bad, just like a lot of parents have done for players on both of these great teams.

Sure, Shane says he's going to be nervous tonight, but his dad's memory is there to inspire him.

"Everything I do, I always think of him."

Enjoy the game. And the moment.

CHAPTER 22

2010 - After all this time, empty nesters

It was a time of passion in Southwest Riverside County, most notably the titanic debate over a mosque proposed in Temecula. It was a holy war of words as folks debated everything from terrorism to world domination, all in the name of religion.

Temecula residents were also passionate about their new Civic Center that debuted in Old Town. While some complained it was an expensive Taj Mahal, supporters said it would help attract more business to the community. One thing everybody agreed on – it was beautiful enough to be a resort, not a mere government building.

Some folks in the Menifee schools were worked up about dictionaries, of all things. In the not so glorious history of innocent books creating massive controversy in Southwest Riverside County, not even a simple dictionary was spared.

The Murrieta Valley High School boys' basketball team made a run for the ages, advancing further in the state playoffs than any other local outfit in history. Three of the team's star players grew up competing against my son David in local recreation basketball leagues. From those humble beginnings they went all the way.

Finally, it was a time of strong emotions for my family as well. We had to put our beloved dog Midnight down to sleep. Later, my son David graduated from Vista Murrieta High School in June and my wife Joanne and I took him to college in Santa Barbara, leaving us empty nesters. We moved here to raise our children and after 21 years of life with kids, it was, unfortunately, time to move on to new passions.

When the game is over
Publication Date: January 1, 2010

It's as much a part of the parent gig as changing diapers, packing lunches and helping with homework.

You do it because you think it's going to help, though at times you wonder how - especially after a tough loss when your kid's fighting back tears.

The goal is to keep your children engaged so they don't end up ditching school and smoking weed, which you somehow presume is going to happen if you don't haul them around to endless activities.

It's a cottage industry of sorts in Southwest Riverside County, a place where so many people come to raise their young free from the perceived ills of big cities. Usually the activity is a sport, but it could be piano lessons, a youth group, the theater or, in the case of my daughter Julia, ballet.

She's in college now so we don't haul her around anymore. Now it's just my son David and he's playing his last out of town sports tournament, the Upland High School boys' soccer event.

He's a Vista Murrieta High School senior and I'm standing on the sidelines with parents I've been with for years, some well over a decade.

Nita Born has been hauling her Robert to soccer games since he was 4. His first Murrieta Youth Soccer League coaches were Will Gainer, later a high school teacher of his, and Henry Diaz, a coach I happily competed against many times.

Through all those late practices and out-of-town games, Robert's goal was to play high school soccer, especially his senior year when he'd presumably be peaking.

But after injuring his knee he's stuck on the sidelines, hoping to play again before the season ends. Dreams don't always come true, one of many lessons you learn in sports.

"He wants to play so bad," Nita says, feeling her son's pain like only a parent can.

Ryan Vanderpool has been hauling around kids for about 15 years. First it was baseball player Casey, a college student today. Now it's Vista soccer player Cory, who dreams of playing in college.

Ryan laughs about the drill parents go through with out-of-town weekend tournaments: The first game Saturday morning often means getting up before dawn to drive like a maniac or getting a costly hotel room the night before.

Of course everybody wants to be in the championship game, which is played late on a Sunday, thus wrecking the workweek. All for a little medal and a T-shirt they quickly outgrow.

"As crazy as it sounds, it's our lives," he says. "Fortunately," he says he has one more year with Cory, a junior.

On the way to Upland, my son David and I talk wistfully about all the tournaments we've been to in the past 13 years, perhaps 30, from Vegas to Temecula. While we chat, a kid I coached in fourth grade, A.J. Lee, speeds by us, now able to drive himself to games.

We recall the first tournament, a Commissioner's Cup for the best teams when David was 8.

It was the first of 15 soccer and basketball teams I coached. We made it to that championship late on a Sunday, only to lose to a squad from Temecula.

After the game I remember all the players from both teams standing in a circle while those silly medals were passed out, David crying when I gave him his.

Standing on the sideline watching his last tournament wind down, I see so many kids he's played with, some since preschool - A.J., Cory, Robert, Adam Leavitt, Aaron Duenas, Julio Lopez, Tyler Holt, Armando Vasquez, J.C. Orozco and Curtis Speed - and I think back to what Ryan Vanderpool felt after Casey's last out-of-town baseball tournament: It's just really sad.

Censoring school books is no way to protect kids

Publication Date: January 27, 2010

Naked. Sex. Breast. Gay. Urine.
Before you start thinking I'm a weirdo, all I'm doing is looking up words in a third-grade dictionary where I teach, Rail Ranch Elementary in Murrieta.

Good thing those dictionaries aren't in Menifee - they might be pulled from kids.

The well-intentioned folks there did just that after a parent complained about an elementary school kid coming across "oral sex" in a classroom Merriam-Webster's Collegiate Dictionary.

The reason the folks there mean well is that if kids see "oral sex" in a classroom dictionary, they'll no doubt drop everything they're doing and act it out.

Oh, please.

Tuesday, the district announced the dictionaries would return and an "alternate" dictionary would be available.

Still, why do some people in Southwest Riverside County continue to think they can shield their kids from everything bad the grown-up world has to offer? In the past 20 years I can think of several great works of literature that area school officials considered controversial - "Bridge to Terabithia" and "Speak" come to mind - because somebody thought their child might be scarred by the work.

The Puritan Police in Menifee formed a committee to determine whether the dictionary supported curriculum.

Here's a thought: If a dictionary doesn't support curriculum, what does?

According to a Menifee Union School District memo last week, officials with apparently nothing else better to do poured through this supposedly lurid dictionary and found that "a number of referenced words are age-inappropriate."

Given that somebody with the same mindset could make the same argument about the words I mentioned from the third-grade dictionary, where do you draw the line on this madness? Do we ban books that mention the word "war" because kids might start one?

I've taught third grade for 12 years at Rail Ranch and I can think of tons of times when kids, usually at recess, use age-inappropriate words. Hey Puritan Police, have you ever heard of the things kids find on TV and the Internet and then drag to school? Better pull all the televisions and computers. Better yet, move to China.

As far as stuff found in the classroom, there is the book "James and the Giant Peach." At my school we read it together as a class annually. It's a wonderful story and a joy to see many kids start reading other books by British author Roald Dahl because they love his work. It's one thing great literature is supposed to do: spark a passion for reading.

Yet one of the insect characters a few times uses a three-letter word that starts with "a" and refers to a donkey. Immediately, the third-graders say, "Mr. Love, it says a bad word." I tell them to say "beep" instead. They giggle and move on, fascinated with the story, not the word. Thank God that book hasn't been pulled.

Another time, about five years ago, a generous community group donated paperback dictionaries to all third-graders at school. A couple of weeks later a joker found a sexual term and, of course, had to show everybody where it was, which got them all yukking it up. I told the kids if they didn't knock it off their parents would get a call. End of problem.

Three years ago, Friends of the Temecula Libraries sponsored a community read of "Fahrenheit 411," Ray Bradbury's legendary tale of a futuristic society that has banned books. A crowd came to Temecula to hear the author discuss the important work.

Friends official Janet Regier said at the time: "The book reminds us how lucky we are to be able to pick up any book and read it."

Too bad kids in Menifee didn't have the same luck.

Family bids a final good night to beloved pet
Publication Date: February 7, 2010

When my wife Joanne first thrust him into my arms, my reaction was an emphatic "No!"

We already had one dog and that was enough. Despite my most strenuous objections - and if you know me, you know I can be strenuous - Midnight became a part of our family.

His first reaction to me? He peed on my shirt.

It was love at first sight, at least for him. When we went to bed that night, the 8-week-old pup cried nonstop from the kids' port-a-crib where we had him corralled. Unable to sleep, I finally gave in and let him lay next to me.

For almost 15 years, Midnight was my No. 1 fan. My bosses might demand too much. My kids Julia and David might drive me crazy. And my wife might test my patience. But Midnight always lit up the moment he saw me. And, like he did that first night, he just had to be with me wherever I went.

By now you may have noticed I'm writing about Midnight in the past tense. We had to put him to sleep recently because he couldn't stand or walk anymore. He wasn't even wagging his tail the last couple days.

Hard as it was, it was time. Oh my God, it was hard.

David had to carry Midnight into the vet's office while I parked the car. He noted the irony: When we first got Midnight, 3-year-old David loved to carry him around even as he quickly outgrew his ability to hold him. The last couple days, our friend was reduced to depending totally on us. Now 17-year-old David, a strapping 6-footer, carried him one last time. Funny how life comes full circle.

Most of his life, it was hard for anybody but Arnold Schwarzenegger to lift Midnight. A black lab and German shepherd mix, he stretched almost five feet from head to tail and had an appetite to match. He was the perfect watchdog because people coming to the door were terrified of him - until he started licking them to death.

Anybody who came across Midnight noted what a gentle creature he was. While we'd like to take credit, he seemed to be born with it. When Julia picked him out of a litter, he was sitting there peacefully while the others bounced around like puppy maniacs. Of course, it was one of the few times he was calm his first couple of years.

When I took him to a dog obedience class at Cal Oaks Sports Park in Murrieta, the instructor asked me to excuse myself from the group because Midnight was so out of control. Some master I was.

Another time in preparation for David's fourth birthday party, I'd stashed a couple of bags of chocolate kisses under the bed for safekeeping. While I was out mowing the yard, Joanne came out frantically waving the now-empty bags. Midnight had inhaled the candy, foil and all. While she insisted that we needed to take him to the vet to have his stomach pumped, I said no way could we afford it and his fate was in God's hands. The vet won out.

Midnight had the heart of a warrior. The day after Christmas 2008 he had a brutal stroke and the vet said we might have to put him down if his condition didn't improve. We jacked him up with steroids and he amazingly recovered to live another 13 months, long outlasting most dogs his size.

He insisted on going on his morning walk up until the last couple of weeks, when he collapsed after a block or so. By then he would whimper in the middle of the night and I'd have to come downstairs and lay with him on the floor. Bad for my beauty sleep, great for my soul.

His last night, he gave one meek whimper, and I trudged downstairs to sleep with him one final time. Words can't describe how much I miss that.

Murrieta parents have hoop dreams, too
Publication Date: March 17, 2010

Year after year Nancy Duffy, Leonard Garcia and Tim Hurley sat in gym after gym.

Their kids Jake, Ryan and Shane, respectively, were gym rats of the best kind, forever chasing the dream of playing high school basketball. For every gym rat there have to be gym rat parents, who dutifully haul their kids to practice after practice, game after game.

Every late night, every long drive, every floor burn the dedicated parents endured was rewarded this month as the Murrieta Valley High School basketball team made the kind of run nobody has ever made in Southwest Riverside County. The team became the first area squad to win a CIF Southern Section hoops title, and advanced to the second round of the state tournament before its improbable march ended in overtime last week.

It wasn't just March Madness, it was a March miracle as the Nighthawks triumphed without one of the best players, Austin Quick, who was out with an injury.

I've known these parents since elementary school and Murrieta Youth Basketball League days. My son David chased the same dream. Today there are area kids - in gyms from Menifee to Temecula and every backyard hoop in between - praying that someday they'll do the same thing as these Murrieta miracle makers.

LeBron, Kobe, come on, those guys are freaks of nature. But everybody thinks they can hit an open shot like Jake, box out on rebounds like Ryan or play tough defense like Shane. The three seniors did just that, helping their team make a run for the ages.

"I had a front row seat for the best ride of my life," a grateful Nancy Duffy said the day after the Nighthawks finally lost.

Shane Hurley played on two teams I coached in elementary school. I matched wits against Leonard Garcia many times when he coached Ryan back then. And with her raucous cheers and jeers, everybody always knew when Nancy Duffy was in the gym.

So it was with a lot of nostalgia that I caught up with them at the team's last game before a packed house of 2,600 fans in one final gym.

Hurley proudly noted how Shane never lost a championship game, winning three straight titles in recreation days with his older brother Wes coaching him. With such a championship pedigree, he knew the Nighthawks were in good shape in the CIF championship game at the famous Honda Center. And so they were.

Garcia talked about how chunky Ryan was as a kid, yet he could always play and always knew the game. He slimmed down with the growth spurts and now look where he's at.

Duffy, an all-CIF player herself in her own hoop days, noted how her calm son Jake found tenacity in basketball.

"He has learned to listen and focus. He has learned to be encouraged and to encourage."

All those things local parents pray for with the endless extracurricular activities they engage their kids with came to pass with this trio. The title is icing on the cake.

A team is more than three players, though, and this team's star was Justin Gudger, another kid my son played with, albeit soccer. His modest dad Jim says it was local basketball gurus such as Mark Nielsen and Ulysses Ruffin who helped develop his son and many others on this memorable team.

Then there's Nighthawk coach Steve Tarabilda, who gave annual talks to the Murrieta recreation coaches such as myself about the right way to play the game. He knows what he's talking about.

The stands this final night were teeming with tons of parents I know from those grade-school basketball years, all there to witness history. And don't forget Dick Sherman, the 83-year-old guy who's watched Nighthawk sports for 14 years, taking in as many as 80 games annually.

The purity of high school sports, rooting for your hometown, it doesn't get any better, Sherman swore. He clutched a bag of candy bars, something he always passes out to each Nighthawk after the game, win or lose.

The candy will still be sweet as this glorious march closes; the memories even sweeter.

Councilman in personal struggle with autism
Publication Date: April 18, 2010

As a longtime Temecula City Councilman, Mike Naggar is one of the most powerful people in Temecula.

Yet a mere 4-year-old boy can bring him to his knees.

The boy is his autistic son Liam Michael.

Like any devoted father, the councilman closely watched him playing recently at a local park. "There's an ordinary boy there," he said proudly. "He's just got some quirks."

Those quirks are a disorder that affects the ability to communicate and interact with others.

Liam was diagnosed about 15 months ago, a development that prompted the 10-year council veteran to, at the time, seriously consider stepping down from the council seat he so clearly relishes.

"He comes first," Naggar said while pushing Liam in a swing.

What convinced him to stay is that he could do something with his position to help Liam and other autistic children. Power never meant so much to him.

Naggar got his fellow council members last month to authorize a task force to look at the needs of autistic kids and their families in Southwest Riverside County. It's modeled after another panel Naggar serves on, one formed earlier to look at the area's health care needs.

Mary Mollway, who runs a nonprofit autism support center in Temecula, said that 20 years ago the autism diagnosis rate was one in 10,000 children. It's one in 91 today and one in 58 for boys under 8.

Which brings us to Liam, who was hitting all his developmental milestones until he was 18 months old. Then he started having terrible tantrums and wouldn't talk.

Naggar, his wife Mylah, and their teen-age daughter Sienna were in agony.

"Our boy just disappeared," Naggar recalled. "He went away."

He was finally diagnosed with autism.

"Our world came crashing down," Naggar said. "I was depressed."

If one word could describe Naggar, it might be passion. On the day I met his son, Naggar sported a T-shirt that said he doesn't need your opinion because he's always right. He shows the same fire on the council dais when addressing political issues he cares about.

He's dived into the issue of autism with typical intensity. He can rattle off statistics and research like he goes on about what a great city he thinks Temecula is. The Naggars doggedly solved Liam's earlier troubles by figuring out he was allergic to wheat and dairy.

Naggar was obviously moved when he described how Liam emerged from this difficult phase with his first words: "Mommy, I love you."

His passion also comes out when discussing a time the family was eating in a local restaurant and Liam was having a tough moment. Reluctantly, the Naggars decided to leave, but not before a woman complained to them about the boy.

"She could not have a clue of what we've been through," Naggar insisted.

He hopes his task force can raise public awareness about the issue, making such protests less likely to happen. He also wants to talk about what can be done locally for autistic kids once they finish public schooling.

"It's a social health care crisis in the making," he said.

And in typical fashion, he's thinking the sky's the limit with his new panel. Why not see if we can get TV star Jenny McCarthy, whose son has autism, to talk to us, he asked. With Naggar's charisma and drive, the possibilities are endless.

While he still has nights when he's up with a frustrated Liam for many hours, it's clear Naggar has found reason for hope for Liam and so many others like him locally.

"It's not the end of the world," he said he's come to realize. "It's the beginning of a wonderful world."

Graduation day brings joy and tears
Publication Date: June 9, 2010

I won't be packing brown bag lunches anymore. Nor will I be driving kids to school, watching them perform, or helping with homework, even though I haven't really done that for a while. Sadly.

After almost 16 years of watching two kids educated in local schools, my youngest, David, graduates Friday from Vista Murrieta High School.

There's definitely a sense of mission accomplished, given that our two kids are the primary reason why my wife Joanne and I moved here 22 years ago, even if our oldest, Julia, wasn't born until four months after we arrived.

It's like a mantra with most of the quarter million people who've swarmed Southwest Riverside County in the past quarter century: We want to raise our kids in a safe place with good schools.

And so Joanne and I have. And now that phase of our lives is over for us Friday. Sadly. (If you haven't figured it out by now, that's going to be a recurring theme in this piece.)

We're not the only ones enduring this bummer. Neighboring families my kids grew up with will have children in that same graduating class, Adam Leavitt and Tara Honda. I can remember watching David and Tara playing together as babies, David and Adam playing together and against each other on countless soccer and basketball teams.

Fittingly, the last team David played on included Adam, a championship team I might add. And Tara and David shared an Advanced Placement English class together this year. To think they've been friends from before they could talk to when they could discuss the great works of literature.

Growing up together goes on in neighborhoods across Southwest Riverside County, an area populated by families piling into subdivisions that seemingly spring up overnight. After we moved to Murrieta in 1988, it seemed the kids would forever be little, swinging in parks, making messes at dinner time, playing together in the bathtub, countless - and I mean countless - sleepovers, oh my God where did the time go?

The things we do for our kids year after year after year. From Perris south to Temecula, from Lake Elsinore east to Menifee, commuters pour out of subdivisions in massive waves in the early-morning hours, heading to jobs in far off San Diego, Orange, and even Los Angeles counties.

They trudge home wearily after 10-hour, 12-hour, even longer days, often after the sun is down: All because they want an affordable home in a community where they feel safe. To someone in, say, Montana it may seem like madness, this working so far from your home. And on some level maybe it is. But not to parents here.

And so all the hard work moms and dads endure to try to raise their kids right ends for us Friday at the graduation ceremony. I remember Julia's three years ago, the one where I got teary eyed as soon as I saw the graduates in their caps and gowns marching far off in the distance toward the rest of us packed in the football stadium.

This time I'll remember that each of my kids was blessed with the same kindergarten teacher at Alta Murrieta Elementary School, Lorrie McKenzie. They didn't share a teacher again until high school, when they both had Kurt Olson, Jean Hoppe, Denise Williams, Corey Quinn, Chad Atwood, Randy Johnson, and Ellen Filar, who they each had multiple years for journalism. Hmmm, why would they take that class?

Next the graduates will file onto the field and I'll pick out David, who's now taller than I am. There will be speeches, some of them pretty good actually. Then the graduates will be handed their diplomas, somebody reading off David's name, 13 years of school boiled down to one moment.

And then both of my kids will be raised. And I'll be glad I'm wearing sunglasses in the late afternoon to hide my tears.

Vail Ranch exhibit reminds us of our past
Publication Date: September 1, 2010

So just how big was the Vail Ranch?

About three times the size of San Francisco is one way to look at it. And the developer who bought the place in 1964 envisioned a half-million people would live here 20 years later.

Fortunately he was wrong, way wrong. For if he'd been right, local traffic today would be like the Golden Gate Bridge.

Instead, 46 years later the Temecula and Murrieta area, which Vail Ranch mostly covered, has more than 200,000 people. So much for that developer correctly forecasting market trends.

It's just one of the many things that gets you thinking in the impressive Temecula Valley Museum exhibit of photos and items from the Vail Ranch.

Newspaper articles from the mid-1960s predicted we'll end up being an "urban pastoral complex," which is a contradiction in terms.

You can't have it both ways. Either you're going to be urban or you're going to be country, something we've wrestled with ever since. All of us have seen model brochures that say we can have it both ways, the peace and quiet of rural living combined with the conveniences of city life. Dream on, folks.

Vail Ranch was country living at its finest and (sorry to say this) its worst. In the mid-1960s, Temecula was about 400. That's it.

A photo in the exhibit of a popular car from the days of ranch life, a Ford Model T, has this caption: "Fortunately, it had a high enough profile to clear the chaparral and ford the streams on the Vail Ranch, because at that time, you could not find much of anything that you might call a road."

That's the reality of rural life. No malls to idle away your weekends, no interstates to whisk you to jobs 50 miles away, no schools to walk your kids to, no public safety to speak of.

Those are the conveniences of city life, which most of us essentially want. Go stand at the corner of Winchester and Ynez roads if you don't believe me.

The value of the Vail Ranch photos is to remind us of where we came from, even if there's no turning back. Cattle really used to be driven through the streets of Old Town to the railroad depot there. Crops such as potatoes really were grown here. The photos prove it.

Sandy Wilkinson, who died in 2006, gathered the exhibit. His son, Whitney, donated the materials to Temecula.

Whitney, now 50 and a San Diego resident, grew up on the ranch. His dad kept about 180 acres toward Vail Lake after the sale in 1964. He recalls the house he grew up in didn't have a phone line when it was built in 1957 and how he learned to drive a tractor at 8.

He passes through the Vail Ranch of today about every six weeks. He calls it "overcrowded" and wishes we somehow had houses with bigger lots.

He's not the only one.

Memories fill empty nest

Publication Date: September 22, 2010

It almost goes without saying that a big reason people move to Southwest Riverside County is to raise a family.

With our good schools, quiet neighborhoods, ample sports leagues and wholesome lifestyle, people feel it's the perfect place for kids.

But what if your kids are all gone?

That's what my wife, Joanne, and I are dealing with after taking our youngest child, David, to college in Santa Barbara last weekend.

For more than 21 years we've raised kids here. I lost track of how many sports teams I coached - I think it was 15 - and there is no way I'll ever be able to catalog all the performances, awards ceremonies and other events I attended.

So now what?

On the way out of town Saturday morning, I mentioned to David what we did on other Saturday mornings for more than a decade: Drive to a sporting event, usually in our hometown of Murrieta. A part of me wants to swing by one last soccer field or gym and see if somehow we'll be miraculously transported back in time.

That's impossible and perhaps even selfish on my part. Instead I'll have to console myself with the Southwest Riverside County that is built for kids. Who can forget thumbing through model brochures while deciding whether to actually move here: Those iconic images of kids playing in a park or running through an open field, of which there were many when we came here so long ago.

Those same brochures never featured empty nesters mourning the loss of their kids who've grown up. But I am too sad about this. No matter how much I envisioned a funeral procession and "Amazing Grace" playing as we headed out of Santa Barbara after dropping David off, it isn't that way at all.

We feel happy that he's achieved his dream, because isn't that all any parent can ask? Sitting in the student center for our last supper together - it was pizza, an appropriate sendoff given that it's the primary dining experience of Southwest Riverside County families - we talked about the many great things in Santa Barbara.

Out of the blue, as we got up to head to our car and he returned to his dorm, David said, "I'm going to miss Murrieta."

It reminded me of what our oldest kid, Julia, said when we drove her to the airport to go to college in North Carolina three years ago. She felt Murrieta changed as much as she had in her time here, developing from a small town to a mature community before she departed.

And so as Joanne and I got off the 15 at California Oaks Road after the drive back Saturday night, we felt happy to be returning to what we still call home. It'll be different for sure with no kid things to do. But all the while it still feels right, and it's not like there aren't any Saturday sports going on if I ever feel a need for nostalgia.

Who knows? Someday this could even be a great place to baby-sit grandkids. As long as it's far, and I mean very far, off in the future.

Temecula's war over mosque rages on

Publication Date: December 5, 2010

The first sign that it was a Temecula Planning Commission meeting for the ages was the numerous Los Angeles TV news vans outside.

"The mosque" - that's all you have to say and locals know what you're talking about - lured them here.

Inside, piano player Earlene Bundy made beautiful, calming music as the audience filed in. It was the last time many there would be calm.

The Islamic Center of Temecula Valley's imam, jovial Mahmoud Harmoush, came prepared, sporting the badge "God Bless America." He knew his audience.

Not even the Pledge of Allegiance was safe from politics. When the crowd recited it to open the meeting, a number of folks added extra emphasis to the words "under God." Did they mean their God? Your God? My God? Our God?

In a sense, the whole meeting boiled down to that.

Sure, there was the planning staff recommending approval on technical grounds, meaning the project appeared to meet all city requirements for traffic, parking and building sizes.

If that was all this was about, there wouldn't have been much of a crowd.

But we all know this was really about terrorism, religion, 9/11, the Constitution, Islamic law, stereotypes, racism, favoritism, equal rights, world domination, what makes America great and not so great, the president's religion, etc.

Bracing for the storm that was sure to come, city planners constantly reminded people to stick to technical issues such as traffic. Nothing else mattered, people were told.

There were 87 folks signed up to speak and at least 350 people (that's what a cop told me) packed into every nook and cranny of City Hall, most watching a TV feed of the proceedings in the council chambers.

The first two speakers in the public hearing, Suzanne St. John Rombach and Margaret Jones, stuck to the criteria, bringing up concerns they had with traffic. Meanwhile, it was as if everybody else was sitting on the edge of their seats, knowing this wasn't what we came for.

Mosque supporter Sylvester Scott didn't disappoint. With his talk about justice and fairness, we knew right away his point wasn't about traffic jams.

As Scott continued, others in the crowd barked "off topic" and "political," and Planning Commission Chairman Carl Carey for the first of many times pleaded with folks to let him finish.

After about five hours of passionate back-and-forth never seen before in a Temecula public meeting, the Planning Commission did what most expected: It OK'd the mosque.

A spokesman for an anti-mosque group calling itself Concerned American Citizens (does that mean that supporters of the mosque are not concerned Americans?) is vowing to appeal to the City Council, which means this drama that Mayor Jeff Comerchero worries is giving Temecula's image a black eye has legs.

The holy war rages on.

CHAPTER 23

2011- Good night and no, we can't all get along

We said goodbye to one controversy – the mosque was approved by the Temecula City Council after much debate – and hello once more to a contentious old friend, the quarry planned south of the city.

A dispute some six years in the making finally was played out before Riverside County planning commissioners. The heated debate left some wondering if Temecula really was such a tranquil place. To paraphrase a sentiment from a much larger city, Can't we all just get along? When it comes to Temecula and the quarry, No we can't!

More local politicians went on social media and yours truly sent out a bunch of Facebook friend requests to the elected officials on that site. Some were accepted, others ignored. Fine, be that way.

At home, my daughter Julia graduated from college and immediately decided to move anywhere but here. Ditto for her three friends from Chaparral High School in Temecula who also finished up at Duke University. Oh well.

My son's high school band played one final time in a rousing concert in somebody else's living room. The band gave them something wholesome, fun and productive to do, an activity all parents hope their high school kids can find. We were lucky our son David did.

Teenage band says a final Good Night
Publication Date: January 2, 2011

Garret Stratford looked sharp in his white dress shirt and dark blue tie.

"It's our last show. We wanted to dress up," he said.

It was the finale for Good Night and Good Luck, though probably the first you've heard of them.

It was my son David's teenage band that played together about three years, an eternity for such groups.

They recorded a CD; won a Murrieta Battle of the Bands competition; played at the mall, The Merc and Mulligan's several times each; performed out of town a bunch; and did tons of makeshift locales like last week's at somebody's house.

The five guys - Tyler Talbot, Dallin Proffit and Spencer Rushton are the others - grew up and grew apart as three headed to college last fall.

It was a rite of passage parents can live with. They didn't do drugs or lie around in their free time doing nothing. Instead they made music and memories.

They shared their last show with Step Stevie Step, a group of older friends including Garret and Spencer's brothers, Ryan and Mike, respectively. Music runs in their families.

They went out with a bang, given Murrieta cops arrived as the show wrapped up. Two squad cars responded to loud noise about 10 o'clock last Monday night. No wonder Murrieta is such a safe place.

It was your classic teenage band space, Mark Fernberg's living and dining rooms on the west side of town. The willing dad cleared all the furniture and the crowd of probably 100 packed the two rooms and family room, and lined the stairs.

David went off to college last fall, and my daughter Julia, now a college senior, was there, too. Besides her affinity for her brother, she shared an Alta Murrieta fifth-grade classroom with Mike and Ryan, the guys from the older band.

The place was filled with kids - excuse me, young adults - I watched grow up. Many I haven't seen in years. Julia's friends such as Jeremy Ogul dropped by. John Matson, a guy she's known since middle school, filled me in on brother Nathan, a kid I taught in third grade too long ago. Then there were dozens of my son's friends there for the final show.

Don't forget the parents who make such things possible. Tyler's dad, Chris, the band's unofficial manager - the guy who hauled their stuff in his truck from show to show - stood in a corner with a wistful smile. Garret's dad, Randy, the multimedia guy who always took photos and videos and posted them on the web - was busy recording.

They played their new songs, they played their old songs and they played their favorite covers. My favorite was their next-to-last piece, when Step Stevie Step joined them. Ten guys shared the stage jamming on instruments, bongo drums and cymbals, tapping speakers with drum sticks, whatever they could find to keep the rhythm going one final time.

Together they sang the stirring lyrics in unison, "Joy, Where Have You Been?"

I know where.

Growing up gay in Temecula
was tough life for student

Publication Date: January 16, 2011

There is the Nick Altemose many locals know. The guy who was valedictorian of Chaparral High School in 2007, had perfect scores on the SATs and earned a full-ride scholarship to Duke University, one of America's top schools.

Then there is the Nick Altemose many locals don't know: The guy who is gay.

He hid this while growing up in Southwest Riverside County, first in Menifee, then Temecula. Ever since becoming aware of his sexuality, he's felt that way.

His was a tortured childhood, for he attended a conservative Christian church in one of the most conservative Christian communities.

Often he heard pastors condemn homosexuality.

"I came to despise myself because of my sexual orientation," Altemose said.

He prayed about it, in the hope he'd be cured. He kept a journal, the one place he could speak truth about who he was. He felt depressed, even suicidal.

He carried this burden all through the glory of being the top student at a top local high school, all the while hoping he'd change. He sure tried, even dating girls. And yet he still knew he was gay.

He finally came to terms with it in college, telling close friends and family.

"I was tired of leading a double life," he said.

He felt grateful for their support.

"It was incredibly relieving that all the fears I had built up, turned out to not be a big deal," he said. "In college I've realized the importance of coming out publicly to reduce hostility toward gays and to provide hope for young teens like I was who are struggling to come to terms with their sexual orientation."

Today, motivated by the It Gets Better Project, a worldwide movement to inspire young gay people facing harassment that there is hope, Altemose hopes his experience will connect with local teens wrestling with these issues.

"Learn to love yourself for who you are, no matter how much people in your community might try to diminish your humanity and worth," he said. To those looking to come out, he suggests seeking the guidance of the few local groups that support gay teens.

Ultimately, he says, realize it does get better, that you can achieve your dreams.

Now 21 and embarking on his last semester of college, Altemose already has earned a scholarship to legendary Oxford University in England to continue his studies of the human genome. His goal is to be a university professor and research scientist.

Last, to local church leaders, Altemose said, "Know that we are normal people and not monsters. Know that by invoking a god who shares your animosity toward gays, even if you claim to 'love the sinner but hate the sin,' you're sending teens to the streets, to the hospital and to the grave. At the very least, you're driving these tortured teens away from your churches and away from your god altogether."

Mosque debate was diversity on display
Publication Date: January 30, 2011

A long line of people lined up outside hoping to get in. You'd think it was a door-buster sale on Black Friday at some bargain hunter's paradise.

Would you believe it was a Temecula City Council meeting instead?

Only one issue could prompt 112 people to sign up to speak at a public hearing, a council meeting to run until past 3:30 in the morning and so many people to prepare speeches like so many potential politicians.

It could only be the proposed mosque, the issue that reveals how much more diverse Temecula has become in the 23 years I've lived in Southwest Riverside County.

People bashing a religion that's not Christianity, questioning whether foreign-born residents might impose their own law on our country, wondering if people attending the mosque could be part of a terrorist network - those are comments being made now (they were at the dramatic meeting last week when the council allowed the mosque's approval to stand). These comments also would have been made back then if such an intense issue had erupted.

What's changed so dramatically is the level of support for such a facility, proving once and for all that Southwest Riverside County, and Temecula in particular, is a more diverse place than when the area first started to grow. Then, it was primarily populated by white Christians escaping the ills of the big city.

Now locals in droves dare to go to a council meeting and counter the other viewpoints that have been here all along. It's the ultimate indicator that the various ethnic restaurants now here, the wide variety of religions practiced locally and the vast number of nationalities in area schools are as real as the affordable housing we're best known for.

When the ultimate in hot-button issues comes along, a mosque that dredges up all the worst stereotypes of Muslims in a post 9-11 world, there is not just one side to be heard from. There are so many views to be expressed that a council meeting can run far, far, into the night.

Councilwoman Maryann Edwards agrees the area is more diverse.

"As Temecula has grown, we more closely reflect the demographic of the state, or at least a conservative part of the state like Orange or San Diego counties."

Yes, Temecula is definitely getting more liberal to a degree, but Santa Monica it's still most definitely not.

Councilman Mike Naggar relishes the debate.

"The dialogue, which should continue in my opinion on a higher level than the City Council, should continue. We should not be afraid of it. It is the essence of what has made our nation great. When we stop the dialogue is when we need to worry."

This is one issue where nobody is about to stop talking. What's so great is that so many kinds of locals are talking about it. On the night of the State of the Union speech, Temecula's union never appeared so colorful.

Facebook changes local politics
Publication Date: March 6, 2011

How active are local politicians in social media? Even Juan Murrieta, the long deceased founder of said city, is communicating from the grave.

Murrieta the man and now the invincible, confirmed one of many friend requests I've bombarded Southwest Riverside County officials with.

I'm about as advanced as Murrieta when it comes to technology - the guy died in 1936 - so it took me a while to figure out the feature where you can find others on Facebook, which I joined a few years ago after my kids forced me.

I'd mention all the local politicians I found there, but not all of them have accepted me as friends. Let's say I'm not feeling very popular.

I can say this: Murrieta, Rick Gibbs (Murrieta city councilman), Maryann Edwards, Jeff Comerchero, Chuck Washington (Temecula council members), Darcy Kuenzi, Wally Edgerton (Menifee council members), Jeff Stone (Riverside County supervisor), Kevin Jeffries (local Assemblyman) and Robin Crist (Murrieta school board member) are now online buddies.

But Darrell Issa isn't. I tried to friend request the local congressman, but received this advisory instead: "If you send a request to a stranger, it will be considered spam and your friend request will be blocked temporarily. Please only send this user request if you know this user."

I don't know Issa, but does he have to be so abrupt? Some friend.

Given how people in the Middle East have used social media to help foster revolutions, I wondered if local politicians are using it to better communicate with constituents, if not actually foment uprisings in their town. One never knows, given how worked up people are about that proposed Wal-Mart in Menifee, for example.

Edgerton seems to share my sentiments, considering his kids also put him on there.

"When someone asks to be my friend I usually just delete it and hope they understand," he said.

It sounds like he's had it with Twitter too.

"Today I have observed that so many people obsessively tweet that they have become twits," he says.

Kuenzi, his Menifee colleague, is more into it. She has close to 1,000 Facebook friends, considerably more than my meager couple hundred.

Has it helped her stay connected with constituents?

"It is like a relationship," Kuenzi said. "It takes work for it to be meaningful. I am still working at it and it has certainly caused me to pause before I post. I enjoy reading posts that give me insight to community issues and the perception that people have on a variety of topics."

Murrieta's Gibbs signed up last summer and already has about 200 friends. And he doesn't confirm every friend request.

As to the growth potential of social media, Gibbs says, "If you can predict where this is all heading, I want your stock pick."

Better yet, let's ask Juan Murrieta.

Temecula, top boss shine

Publication Date: July 10, 2011

If it's possible for one person to symbolize a city, Shawn Nelson just might do for Temecula.

He's a good-looking guy, just like his city. He came here when he was a young man, just like his town was then. His bosses came to see him as the best at what he does, just like many Temeculans think of theirs as the best city in Southwest Riverside County.

Now he's in middle age and so is his maturing city. Temecula thinks of itself as cutting edge and so Nelson is doing something out-of-the-box when it comes to an ambitious guy.

He's retiring.

Nelson is leaving his city manager's post at year's end at just 51. He is high-energy, which a city manager's job requires. A news release for the occasion of course trumpeted Temecula's many accomplishments: The Promenade mall expansion, the Old Town revival, the countless new roads and the crown jewel of the community: the new City Hall.

Nelson's quote says it all: "The thing that I am most proud of is that I gave the city of Temecula 100 percent of my best efforts every day for more than 20 years."

That's what comes to mind with Nelson - effort. I remember the first time I met him at some parks commission meeting too long ago. He was all enthusiasm, just like now. It was easy to see why he'd been a successful two-sport player in college. He all but led the meeting in a cheer.

Temecula had one park when he was named director of that area. Today it has 39. That says it all about how Temecula has developed as a city in Nelson's more than two decades of service there, including a dozen as city manager.

Beyond the energy, the financial success (in 2009 he was the sixth highest paid city manager in California), and the accomplishments (Mayor Ron Roberts calls Nelson the finest city manager he's ever seen), Nelson is family.

Temecula first and foremost bills itself as a family place. Nelson epitomized that spirit with his wife, Stephanie, and his children.

Nelson wears his emotions on his sleeve, his pants, his shoes, you name it. When his family suffered tragedies, it was like the rest of us were there sharing his agony. First his oldest daughter Jennifer was badly injured in a 1997 car crash on her way to an out-of-town soccer tournament. Then his oldest son Jacob died in a crash five years ago.

So when Nelson says he's retiring to spend more time with his family and to work on the foundation he's established in his son's memory, it's easy to see why he's leaving such a great job.

He's just like the city he symbolizes.

Temecula is Not so tranquil
Publication Date: August 14, 2011

Think of Temecula and a bucolic wine country might come to mind. Or the quaint pleasures of a historic old town. Perhaps the safe streets and great schools the community is so proud of.

This is not what comes to mind: A man screaming about a proposed quarry he says will destroy the local environment as he is escorted by a sheriff's deputy from a public meeting in a church.

Or people at another public meeting angrily bashing a religion that's not Christianity, questioning whether foreign-born residents might impose their law on our country, wondering whether people attending a mosque could be part of a terrorist network. This was all picked up by the national media. What happened to the Temecula of chardonnay-sipping yuppies?

Yes, those 1980s upscale types who moved here in great quantities might seem a distant memory as two recent projects - the mosque and quarry - have brought out extremes in the city.

Is the chardonnay spiked now?

Temecula has changed with the growth that rocketed the community from less than 20,000 a quarter century ago to more than 100,000 today. More people, more diversity, more opinions.

Phil Hoxey, who's lived here since 1987, has seen it all. He spearheaded one of the city's first protests, a march to protest talk of turning the now famous duck pond into a parking lot.

"It wasn't like the cops had to be called out," he said of the sedate gathering of the late 1980s.

There was constant debate about growth through the 1990s, especially promoter Zev Buffman's plan to plop a mammoth western entertainment center in Old Town Temecula. The project eventually died, but not before it divided the community over what to do with the historic area.

Hoxey led the charge in that campaign, too. While the group had its share of characters, he recalls the public meetings as being generally civil affairs.

"We were only doing what Americans are supposed to do: Try to make sense."

Mike Naggar has served on the Temecula City Council since 1999. He says lots of things have people worked up today, but they can't exactly go to Sacramento or Washington on a moment's notice. Venting in a local public meeting is a way to release.

"It seems to be the only level in which the people have a voice anymore," Naggar says.

Naggar also doesn't think the recent outbursts represent a different Temecula.

"This is a conservative enclave," he says. "And by conservative, I mean that everyone, no matter what their political ideologies, still want to raise their family in a clean, safe, friendly environment."

And with the Riverside County Planning Commission set to hold its fifth public hearing on the proposed Liberty Quarry in Temecula on Monday, one other thing is certain: It's going to be passionate.

Remembering a Temecula icon
Publication Date: August 28, 2011

Things happen for a reason.

And a reason the Temecula arts scene is so happening is Eve Craig.

She did so much for her hometown. Her list of accomplishments could easily fill up the rest of this space. Yet that's not what people who know her best remember.

For the nearly 100 gathered at her recent memorial service it was the smile that came to mind. It was like her lips were permanently creased so that whenever she walked into a room, happiness followed.

When asked how she was doing in the final days of her 88 years, after what surely had been so much pain and suffering, she'd simply say, "I'm fine."

And so she was.

I knew Craig for more than 20 years, even visited her house many times. Yet I never knew she had such a life of heartache. She found her mom murdered, a case that never was solved. Her child preceded her to death. Her husband died the day after she bought a house in Temecula.

Yet Craig never stopped smiling, never stopped giving, and never stopped trying.

What she did to bring sophistication to Temecula is nothing short of the miracles that are so often discussed in the church her service was held.

Craig was eulogized as a woman of strength, the kind that kept going after the hardest of life's tragedies, the kind that wouldn't take no for an answer when it came to dragging culture into a small town, the kind that allowed her to be the best player on her college tennis team - the men's squad.

I remember sitting on the first Temecula film festival board with Craig back in the early 1990s and thinking, this is silly. Nobody's going to come to a film festival in this Podunk place.

So how can you explain how Jo Moulton - the festival's other prime creator along with Craig - is planning to name an award for Craig next month during the festival's 17th year?

Apparently the film festival had a future after all.

It should come as no surprise when longtime local pastor Steve Struikmans told us that Craig picked all the music for the service. What, you think she would have left it to somebody else? It's the music, of all things!

There were stories and more stories: how she couldn't tell a lie but could sure stretch the truth if it meant something good for Temecula.

How she was a middle child and so had to be the most competitive. And how she had to correct somebody happily humming the most innocuous of tunes. How dare you!

Hopefully, Temecula's powers-that-be will see fit to name something after her. A street perhaps, one that passes by an Old Town public place. Eve Craig Way sounds about right.

For, what better way to live?

CHAPTER 24

2012 - Katy Perry didn't build a quarry either

It was a year of highs and lows. The quarry south of Temecula was dead once and for all. The Pechanga tribe rode to the rescue, buying the property, and killing the project. The longest, costliest and most tumultuous development battle in Southwest County history ended.

There was sadness too this year. Former Temecula city councilman Karel Lindemans – the loudest, funniest and most loquacious politician in the quarter century I've written about Southwest Riverside County – passed away. Temecula loves to think of itself as a one-of-a-kind place and nobody promoted that idea more than this one-of-a-kind public figure.

A man known more for his sweet tongue, "Papa Joe the Ice Cream Man," also died. Known locally as the best ice cream man ever, he distributed the sweet stuff here for well over 20 years.

There was the tale of whether famous singer Katy Perry went to Chaparral High School; the return of local firebrand Ed Elder, who rivaled Lindemans with provocative things to say; and the frequent comings and goings of local city managers, a position typically known for stability.

Personally, a former third grade student of mine, Tyler Hughes, returned from a tour as a proud Marine in war-torn Afghanistan, proving that kids really do grow up and some go on to do great things.

The Temecula quarry dispute is about to be settled?

Publication Date: February 3, 2012

Say it ain't so.

As an issue, this has been our Watergate, our 9-11 and our Kardashians rolled into one. It has been a source of controversy and gossip for almost seven years now. And now it's ending?

What will more than 1,000 people – the approximate number that showed for last week's Riverside County Board of Supervisors' hearing -- do without you, my quarry friend? What to do with all the orange shirts the quarry opponents wear, the green attire the backers prefer? Upcoming garage sales will be well stocked for sure.

I know the quarry's critics are worried about the foul air they believe will result if the quarry is built. But what of all the hot air in those seemingly zillions of hours of public hearing debate over the issue? Talk about global warming. And to think the last scheduled one is Monday in Riverside. Where will we vent after that?

Opposition to the quarry has made such strange bedfellows: Environmentalists, the Pechangas, the Temecula chamber and the city of Temecula. After decades of fighting over growth, the effects of busy casino traffic and the brawl over Zev Buffman's massive western entertainment center proposed for Old Town Temecula, it seemed those folks would never find common ground.

The quarry united them for once, especially odd given that the project's supporters cite the economics the thing would bring; a mantra of city and chamber officials for more than 20 years.

Yes, I can hear these same folks saying, "But it's about how the quarry will wreck our tourist economy and our pristine environment, you fool!" But where was that concern before 100,000 people moved to Temecula in the past quarter century? Back then a quarry would have been a slam-dunk OK because coyotes can't vote.

It's also exposed our elitism. We've always considered ourselves better than the rest of Riverside County. We've got a wine country (said with eyebrows arched appropriately) and we don't have the crime of Moreno Valley, the smog of Riverside, the heat of Palm Springs, the economy of Hemet.

So when quarry booster John Husing dared to suggest a similar one in Corona hasn't hammered economic activity or property values in that upper-end community, a local letter-to-the-editor writer huffed, "But we're better than Corona! How dare you compare us to them!" Temecula, the land of the smug.

It's hard to find much new to talk about after so much debate. We almost could have taken the words right out of the critics' mouths in last week's hearing (Temecula's pristine air will be fouled, the truck traffic will be horrific, the health effects will be catastrophic and our tourism will collapse) while backers used their same song and dance (our air will be fine, trucks won't be a problem, the medical issues are overblown and the nearly 300 jobs the quarry will support are a boom, not a bust).

Stuck in the middle, having to delicately settle this most cataclysmic issue of Temecula's times are the supervisors: local Jeff Stone and outsiders Bob Buster, John Tavaglione, John Benoit and Marion Ashley.

No matter their verdict, masses will be irate. Lucky them.

Quality-of-life issue killed quarry

Publication Date: February 18, 2012

Quality of life.

When it comes to the Temecula-area quarry, those three words boil down far too many years of studies, lobbyists, protests, public hearings, speeches, orange shirts, green shirts, sacred grounds, campaign contributions, news releases, politics, politics and more politics.

Those three words — what the modern-day community of Temecula was founded upon — triumphed yet again when Riverside County supervisors momentously rejected the Liberty Quarry.

Temeculans didn't move here by the hundred thousand in the past quarter century to create just another Southern California suburb crammed with tract homes and strip malls. No, they're better than that, haughty and misguided as it may seem to some. Sure, other communities have quarries that haven't thrashed their property values (i.e. high-end Corona), but they're not the all-mighty Temecula.

To paraphrase their hero Ronald Reagan, Temecula residents are that shining city upon a hill he spoke of. To the zillions of quarry critics, all of its dust, noise and congestion wouldn't have just blurred that idyllic image, it would have destroyed it.

And so the supervisors voted 3-2 to preserve Temecula and all of its glory. And it was no accident that the two guys who most speak for us — Bob Buster and Jeff Stone — voted no. They know all too well what the quarry meant to local voters.

So what if Temecula, with its tract homes, massive commerce and congested freeway, is a sea of concrete, a quarry's sole reason for existence. So what if Temecula residents are more than happy to build themselves silly with aggregate from other people's quarries. They'll be damned if they're going to do their fair share. That's some other sappy community's headache, not Temecula's.

Yes, in a tough economy, with claims by quarry boosters that it would support about 300 jobs and generate $300 million in sales tax revenue over the life of the project, Temeculans en masse said no, it's not worth our — all together now — quality of life!

To them the quarry was the great unknown. Yes, the developer produced study after study after study after (OK, you get the point) that said those concerns were overblown, that other communities are doing just fine environmentally with a quarry in their midst. But Temecula residents weren't willing to take that risk.

The quarry's demise also was a rejection of Temecula's idol, San Diego County. We in Southwest Riverside County drool over all things San Diego, from the beaches to the sports teams to the big-city culture.

Yet when it came down to our precious quality of life, our county supervisors essentially told our neighbors to the south, "Take this quarry and shove it!"

Time after time supervisors hammered the point: If much of the aggregate mined from the quarry is going to be trucked down to San Diego, build the thing there. No matter their beaches, we're tired of being their whipping boy.

We close with this thought, compliments of the Temecula-area Pechanga Band of Luiseño Indians. They say the quarry would have obliterated a tribal site on par with the Bible's Garden of Eden.

To the typical Temeculans and their hallowed quality of life, that says it all.

Saluting A Unique Leader
Publication Date: April 29, 2012

Original. One-of-a-kind. What-in-the-heck-will-that-loud-mouth-say-next?

Temecula old-timers know I can mean only one politician: Karel Lindemans.

He was a reporter's go-to source, the guarantee of a great quote no matter how delicate the topic.

You may notice I'm talking about him in the past. Lindemans died last weekend at 80.

You know what? Sometimes life … well, I can't say the word I want to because I'm not Lindemans and the newspaper couldn't print it anyway. Let's just say he'll be missed. Words-can't-describe-kind-of missed.

Want proof of his outrageousness? Got a couple days? Weeks? Months? Here's one snippet.

At the dedication of the Temecula senior center about 20 years ago, the kind of event where folks only utter the most serious things, Lindemans noted he and legendary senior Mary Phillips got along because both were CPAs. In her case, he said, that means "Constant Pain in the A …."

Welcome to the world of Karel Lindemans.

It was a world of fun (On the stately day the city proclaimed in his honor, he said he wanted to spend the time in bed with his wife but she had to work.), a world of crazy (Who can ever forget the hot tub summits with former councilman Sal Muñoz?), and a world of ideas (The newspaper isn't big enough to print all those.)

As much as anybody else, Lindemans made the city of Temecula what it is today.

Yes, Jimmy Moore was the muscle behind the drive to create the city government. But once that heavy lifting was done, Lindemans was the big thinker who loudest said Temecula can be great.

And so it is.

Yes, he was as irreverent as a porn star in a church. But what people forget is it took a great mind to come up with all that outrageous material.

Elected to the city's first City Council in 1989, he started trashing the developers that were over-running the community at the time. And, you know what? He was right. He said Temecula could fix its hellacious traffic problems. And while he was hardly right on that score, he made it a heck of a lot better with his drive to build roads and bridges (Please city leaders, rename Overland Drive after Lindemans), and push public transportation.

Most important, he set a tone that persists to this day. Most city governments wouldn't have been so strident in opposing a proposed quarry; figuring environmental risks were worth the economic boost. Not Temecula, which made the defeat of the project a literal crusade.

The thinking was Temecula has a great thing going and a gigantic quarry would destroy that. Obviously, plenty of people disagreed, given how the project was narrowly defeated earlier this year by Riverside County supervisors in a decision of Titanic proportions.

Yet Temeculans stuck to their guns that theirs is a special place, no matter how elitist some outsiders consider their position. That thinking that Temecula is no ordinary town, that it's something utopian, was Lindemans' mantra.

So we miss you something fierce, my old friend. Yet you leave behind a community spirit as vibrant as yours.

A Sweet Man Lived The Sweet Life
Publication Date: June 10, 2012

Fame is usually associated with politics, entertainment, sports — stuff people care about passionately.

But ice cream?

Yes, Joseph John Tamborelli Sr., known far and wide as "Papa Joe the Ice Cream Man," had several newspaper stories written about him and was always recognized by adoring fans wherever he went in Southwest Riverside County.

Papa Joe passed away May 31 after a series of health issues. He was 82.

Why the fuss? It's just ice cream; where's the pizzazz in that?

While pastor Tom Burdick conceded he's never known a famous ice cream guy, he thinks he knows why Mr. Tamborelli achieved such lofty local status.

It's his character, the pastor said at Mr. Tamborelli's memorial service Friday, June 8. He didn't just take people's money and dispense a treat. No, he gave something more, kindness; a gentle spirit that those harshest of critics, kids, knew was genuine.

"It's such a lesson for us," Burdick, pastor of Blessed Teresa of Calcutta, said of the way Mr. Tamborelli lived. "Let's make sure he lives on."

He distributed ice cream locally from the late 1980s until just a couple years ago. He drove his truck 12 hours a day, five or six days a week, on a 35-mile route. That's passing out a lot of sweetness. And I'm not talking ice cream.

His service attracted about 70 people to England Family Mortuary in Temecula, including Connie McCay, of Temecula, whose sons Michael, now 34, and Jimmy, now 27, were faithful customers.

She recalls how Papa Joe would front kids an ice cream if they were a little short on money. Sure enough, the next day the kids would pay him in full. McCay said such transactions taught tons of local kids a valuable life lesson about being honest.

McCay later got to know him even better through her husband Dan. "He was nice, very giving," she said of the Ice Cream Man. "He made you feel at home as soon as you met him."

He's even become a Facebook sensation on the group called Murphy Canyon. Wrote Deborah Jones, "He was the BEST ice cream man ever!! Wish wherever he is he could read how he touched us all."

Added Rachael Kowalski-Milan, "Hearing that whistle after dinner. Those were the days, when $1 bought me so much happiness!!!"

Said Lisa Molvik Cline: "Papa Joe was awesome! It was like a candy store on wheels. Soo Cool. One of a kind!"

Mr. Tamborelli's widow, Deonna, said Papa Joe "was the best husband" and he adored children.

His son Tom noted Mr. Tamborelli was also a savvy business-man. If a rival ice cream guy tried to move in on his turf, Papa Joe would shadow him, knowing kids would always rally to their favorite celebrity.

He began his career in sales by going door- to-door hawking bread. He started up an ice cream truck in 1969 in the San Diego area before shifting his route to our area when he moved up here.

"My wife rode with me one time and said, 'you've got to be crazy,'" he was quoted in a newspaper story from 1991. "It's fun, it really is."

All of our lives should be so crazy.

Former Student Now A War Veteran
Publication Date: July 8, 2012

The strapping young man hops out of a vehicle and the first thing I notice is there's still some third grader in his face.

Tyler Hughes has been to war in Afghanistan, he's looked into the eyes of Taliban fighters, and he's slept outside on raw winter nights with merely his pack for a pillow and a bush for a mattress, often thinking this is a long way from safe and warm Murrieta.

He's 20 now, firm as a rock, a warrior for our country, but in some ways for me he'll always just be Tyler, the scrawny little third grader from my class 11 years ago at Rail Ranch Elementary in Murrieta, the sensitive kid with Coke bottle glasses.

After eight months in Afghanistan as a Marine lance corporal, he's far removed from those days.

He returned home last month and now is going to train in Hawaii. Trading Afghanistan for Hawaii?

Let's just say he's earned it.

Of course war has changed him. The small stuff doesn't matter, the petty conflicts he might have had with a fellow Marine while training for combat didn't mean a thing when you're depending on him in battle.

"It literally is a brotherhood," Tyler says of such moments. "He's got my back."

He signed up for the Marines right out of Vista Murrieta High School, heading for boot camp while other classmates headed off to college or jobs where you don't get shot at. Tyler was a smart enough kid, a guy who could easily go on to more education after high school.

But he wanted something different, a way to make a difference right now, and a way to continue his family's long military heritage.

So Afghanistan it was in October, Helmand Province if you follow the news. It was lots of patrols in a brutal winter; sleep was a challenge, especially having to take the shift on watch in the middle of the night. And yes, at times he wondered why he opted for this while his friends hung around Murrieta. The righteous life isn't the easiest.

He's happy to say none of his buddies died; he didn't even fire his gun in combat. Tyler doesn't expect to go back to Afghanistan; he'll spend much of his Marine time now in Southeast Asia seeing more of the world. When his commitment is up in 2015, he'll only re-enlist if there is a war going on.

"I would still like to get the job done," he says.

The time away has made him appreciate his family and friends all the more. He's glad he grew up in Murrieta, coming to realize it's the all-American city; especially after hearing about places his Marine buddies were raised. Murrieta was so much better for him.

We walk to his jeep and laugh about old third grade memories. As we part, he apologizes for his behavior. I smile because he was anything but a problem in my class.

On a behavior scale of 1 to 10, I tell him he was about a 7. Now another boy Tyler remembers, he was a 10. We both laugh.

I don't need to tell him that today it's Tyler who is a 10.

Singer Is Temecula's Urban Legend
August 19, 2012

Katy Perry went to Chaparral High School.

Stop the presses! You mean the famous singer went to our humble Temecula institution?

Why, it says so right here on the Internet. Just Google that combination and watch the links pop up faster than one of her hits climbing the charts.

On a top website it says, "Katy Perry graduated from Chaparral High School in Temecula, California and immediately moved to Los Angeles at the age of 17."

There you have it, case closed, Katy Perry is one of us. I knew I liked Temecula for a reason.

Wait a minute. The same search shows another site with this heading "Did Katy Perry go to high school?"

Hmm, let's hope she did because one can't get too far in life otherwise, even a singer. On this site, the first answer is from some anonymous person who says she went to Chaparral. Whew!

But then another post on the same site says "Wrong. She went to Dos Pueblos High School in Goleta, California. Got her GED halfway into her freshman year and dropped out."

The Internet also reveals that Katy Perry is her stage name. She previously went by Katheryn Hudson. The plot thickens.

I know, let's try her publicist. I get the name of her current one, who tells me she can't be identified. Huh? Who's ever heard of a publicist who can't be identified? She thinks she graduated from Dos Pueblos, but she doesn't know other details.

What about an interview with Perry to clear up this important matter? "She's not doing press right now," the publicist huffs.

OK, let's try the Temecula school district. There, spokeswoman Melanie Norton is at least willing to be identified, so that's progress.

She does a search in the district records under Katheryn Hudson. Nothing shows.

Turns out a person with her brother's name is in the district's database and is the same age as the one on a Google search. And he graduated from Chaparral. But Norton can't give out contact information.

So we're left with this: Maybe Perry's brother attended Chaparral. But the Katy Perry link appears to be another urban legend.

Oh well, look what she's missing out on by not being more public about her Temecula heritage or even dropping by here for a free concert. It's the least she could do if she's going to reject us.

World Series hero Allen Craig is more than happy to claim his Temecula roots. Heck, he even went to Chaparral. Super Bowl star Terrell Davis is a local, according to Internet stories. And my son David's friend has seen him shopping at a grocery store he works at. Longtime baseball player Reed Johnson also is from here.

TV's Jack Klugman and famous author Erle Stanley Garner each lived in Temecula. Then there is Larry Fortensky, best known as the last husband of Elizabeth Taylor. An Internet search shows he lived in Temecula after his divorce from the star, and then shifted to Menifee. Unfortunately, I can't find him in the phone book.

Fortensky's claim to fame is he married someone famous. Curiously, Katy Perry is famous. Maybe she could marry Fortensky and then there'd be no denying her local connection.

Somehow, someway, we're going to claim you yet, Katy Perry.

Sparkman Not Going To Fade Away
Publication Date: December 3, 2012

The question is whether Joan Sparkman – after almost 35 years as an education leader with a school named after her along the way – is a local institution.

"I should be in one," she says, laughing as always.

There you have her. She's been in Southwest Riverside County 43 years – first Temecula, now Murrieta -- and her accomplishments could easily fill up the rest of this column. Yet no matter how long the platitudes, she'll never take herself too seriously.

She's stepping down as a trustee for the Mt. San Jacinto Community College District, being replaced by Tom Ashley, who won her seat after she didn't run.

She was appointed to that board in 1999 after serving on the Temecula school board for 22 years starting in 1971.

At the time the Temecula district consisted of a K-8 school with about 300 kids. The school had just opened a new library, a project she worked on. What a surprise – Joan Sparkman doing something successfully.

She moved to Temecula in 1969 when her husband Will got a job locally. "I liked it from the minute I got here," she says. Yet she also remembers saying to Will at the time, "Nobody will move down here."

For once she was wrong.

Her daughter Margaret started at Elsinore High School, her younger son Steve went to the K-8 school in Temecula. Today Steve teaches history at Elsinore, more than 30 years and counting. Education is the family blood.

Sparkman worked at the local hardware store and knew everybody in town. "All 20 of them," she jokes.

She once told developer Dan Stephenson – a local legend in his own right -- she was going to write a book about all the area history she knows. "You're not going to use real names are you?" he asked.

No need to worry, Sparkman would never do anything to embarrass anybody. What comes to mind with her is class.

One bummer in her political career? She narrowly lost a county supervisor race to Bob Buster in 1992. She's happy Lake Elsinore's Kevin Jeffries finally beat Buster this year because it means more local representation.

As always she's got lots of opinions about how the local schools could improve. She loved leading the community college because she wants young adults to have a vocational skill, noting how important it is to have something to capitalize on.

Too many students show up in college not able to do reading, writing and math like they should. She'd like to see more of an emphasis in those areas in the K-12 schools. "If they've got the basics, they can do anything," she says.

She's seen her share of what she considers silly programs – math that didn't teach kids the fundamentals, reading programs that didn't stress enough phonics. She also worries that all the technology today's kids use could dull their basic skills.

And yes she's 78 and has two great grandchildren. But Sparkman isn't about to be a fuddy-duddy, arguing she has lots of hope for the future and what today's kids can accomplish.

She's not fading away either, promising to stay active with other community activities. Retiring is the last thing on her mind. As always.

Kerfuffle In Southwest

Publication Date: December 9, 2012

Certain things in life are a given. Santa Claus arrives on Christmas, not the first day of school. Vegetables are good for you, chips not so much. And Temecula is going to operate smoothly.

It's OK kids, Santa's still on schedule. Sorry, chips still aren't healthy. But somehow, someway, there's turmoil in Temecula.

City Manager Bob Johnson has been fired. Chief Finance Officer Genie Wilson is on paid administrative leave. And a Temecula union leader said city workers "were dreading come to work" under Johnson before he was canned.

What next, sprinklers at city parks going on strike?

Now granted, there's something weird going on with Southwest Riverside County city managers.

In Menifee they change top dogs faster than Kim Kardashian moves on to new boyfriends. Five in four and a half years — city managers, not boyfriends.

Wildomar City Manager Frank Oviedo resigned earlier this month. He left because he has family at his new job in the Santa Clarita Valley, not because it took forever for Wildomar just to pass one measly fee to keep a meager three parks open.

Lake Elsinore City Manager Bob Brady was given the heave-ho in March. Given that community's wild history, it's surprising there hasn't been another termination since then.

In Murrieta they seem happy enough with City Manager Rick Dudley, even renewing his contract at a pay rate that exceeds a salary cap on top city employees slapped on by Murrieta voters two years ago. So much for the will of the people, apparently.

Whatever happened to the days when bureaucrats were blissfully boring? Surely, a reality show is in the works, "Desperate City Managers of Southwest Riverside County." Imagine the drama. Sorry guys, I don't think we can get Brad Pitt to play anybody.

Almost as shocking as a movie star bureaucrat is what's happening in Temecula, a city known as our area's finest, with its wide array of parks, safe streets, ample shopping (the piggybank of southwest), a City Hall second to none (no wonder it's known derisively as "the Taj Mahal") and City Council members whose re-election is all but guaranteed.

Regarding the upheaval, mum's the word among council members, citing personnel issues.

Not even Riverside County Supervisor Jeff Stone, a longtime local resident and once a Temecula council member, is commenting about the controversy, according to a spokeswoman. And if you know the loquacious Stone at all, he declines comment about as often as a coyote passes on a rack of ribs.

This leaves us with Fred Bartz, a local who worked with city officials on that quarry dispute you might have heard of. He also heads up Morgan Hill homeowners talking about annexing into the city.

Bartz typically goes to every other council meeting and says he remains confident in how the city's being run.

"I'm not planning on moving out," he says, illustrating his point.

If he's the norm, it'll take more than Santa confusing the calendar to get Temecula residents to move on.

Reminiscing With A Firebrand

Publication Date: December 16, 2012

Writing down things as fast as Ed Elder can talk is not easy. You mean the guy who once filled up a newspaper with the provocative things he had to say?

The one and only, the retired Desert Storm Marine who took Temecula by storm after he moved here 20 some years ago. If he wasn't threatening to film people as they walked out of video stores with X-rated movies, he was shaking things up with local politics, earning a school board seat for four memorable years.

After that he disappeared from the news. So imagine my shock recently when I got an email from him. I'll never worry about stuff to write about again!

Elder is back in town briefly. He mostly lives in Australia — in effect, he did disappear — and comes back a few months a year, renting a room in a friend's house.

Now 60 and looking lively, he's got a retired military pension that allows him to travel the world.

He thinks Temecula is still a great place. Sure a porn place opened on Jefferson a few years ago without him there to protest, but he's keeping things in perspective. Look at the porn to be found on a phone now!

He dropped off the face of our local earth when he had cancer and tended to an out-of-town aunt on hospice care. He says he beat prostate cancer by radically changing his diet and exercise habits.

Consumed by this alternative lifestyle, he decided to check out New Zealand, a place where he heard "you can come up with some nutty idea and people will listen to you and see if it's true or not." Sounds perfect for him.

He flashes his current business card with the banner, "If you like antioxidants … You'll Love Our Water!" Then he whips out four books on his passion. As always, consumed.

Of course we have to talk about his local past, how he moved here while stationed at Camp Pendleton, went around to conservative Christian churches talking about "the miracles of Desert Storm," then being named grand marshal for a veteran's parade. He pushed to get Vietnam War guys included, a touch everybody loved.

There were crusades in the schools and a reading program that didn't use much phonics outraged him. It sparked a local campaign that drew statewide headlines.

Who can forget his protests of the NC-17 movie "Showgirls" and against Lenny Pechner, a local video storeowner who dared to rent adult videos. He and others prayed outside.

It culminated with his school board term for which he drew headlines I would need a book to cover. He says he still loves Temecula and its values (What other place could a Hooters come and go? he asks), though Elder can't fathom how city leaders could build what he calls "a Taj Mahal" of a City Hall and not have a permanent shelter for homeless people.

"Their snobbish elitism is very apparent," he says.

Until we meet again Ed Elder.

Let Our Sanctuary Be

Publication Date: December 20, 2012

All weekend I watched the talking heads go on about how to protect schools. Make sure there is somebody armed on campus at all times. Ratchet up the security. Every classroom needs a place where kids can go that can't be penetrated. In short, make schools a bubble.

To which I say: Stop!

My elementary school is a field of dreams, not an armed fortress, a chamber of horrors waiting to happen.

Yes, that's what happened when a gunman smashed into a Connecticut elementary school Friday, killing 26 people, including 20 little kids.

Among the heroes are teachers, the ones who did everything they could to shield their kids from this madman — including giving up their own lives.

Would I do the same? I've asked myself that more than you can imagine. I'm an elementary school teacher at Rail Ranch in Murrieta. I've been one for 15 years.

I know I mean the world to my kids the year I work with them. They call me Mommy and Daddy all the time. There is no higher praise.

There is innocence with little kids that can't be put into words. They crank out beautiful pictures at a moment's notice. They hug you nonstop. They cry, they frustrate, they love you.

Like a lot of parents, I spent the weekend with tears in my eyes. Tears of sorrow, tears of rage, tears of hope. It's an occupational hazard of teachers. This will get better, kids teach me every day.

Another thing I wrestled with is what I say to them. Before school Monday, we teachers debated it, ultimately deciding to pass the buck: Talk to your parents about it.

So when I pick up my kids a few minutes later, the first thing the first one said to me was, "What do you think about the shooting?"

I pretended I didn't hear him. So his friend asked the same question. And I said what I didn't want to, but felt I had no choice in these weird times where honesty isn't always the best policy: I told him to talk to you know who.

Oh, what I wanted to say: The world isn't crazy. It was one guy who went berserk at one school on one awful day. Yes, we need to do something about guns, and we sure as heck ought to look at all the violence that inundates my little kids in the video games they love more than me. And definitely we need to do more to help the other potential Adam Lanzas of the world who so desperately need help.

But whatever you do, don't ruin our schools; don't crush our spirits with all that outside world stuff of armed staff members and impenetrable walls. Let our sanctuary be.

I think of what we call "Friday Morning Sing" at our school. I'm sure the same thing goes on in some fashion at most schools across our land.

We walk down as one to our amphitheater, some 700 kids strong. We do the pledge, we sing a patriotic song, we hear the announcements, we watch little kids get up and bravely do their talents, be it some song, joke or dance. And we end with a school song about honesty, friendship and truth. We are eager to do our best, we sing, like everybody is supposed to do in life.

Our gates are open during this weekly ritual, as if to say, "Welcome, real world, come on in and join our innocence."

CHAPTER 25

2013 - What do you mean they can't go home again?

Our devotion to our children was highlighted when about a thousand people marched through rural Menifee for several days looking for an autistic boy who went missing. The search was called off after the boy was found dead in a shallow grave on his family's property, but it underscored our community standing as one when one of our own is in danger.

In odder news, some enterprising Chaparral High School students created a YouTube sensation with their video trying to motivate kids to go college; Menifee was mired in a debate about sludge, bunkers and City Council meeting etiquette; and I dug up a long-ago TV ad that introduced Temecula to the national stage.

In Murrieta, longtime community historian Arlean Garrison died at 97. Not only did she write a charming history of the community, she also ran the Chamber of Commerce from her machine shop back when the town first started to grow, dispensing information and folksy charm.

The town also introduced a fee for 911 medical calls that had people conflicted plenty. My family experienced this first hand when my wife Joanne fell off a ladder, broke her shoulder, and yours truly had to call 911. Fortunately she was OK; the same can't be said for our imperfect health care system.

Finally, a trip to San Francisco to see my 24-year-old daughter Julia brought me full circle. She lives in a big city in part because we don't have the same economic opportunities for people her age. Tons of people moved to Southwest Riverside County because it was an affordable place to raise children. Yet many of those children move elsewhere as adults because of our economy or because they feel it's too sheltered. So why exactly did we move here in the first place?

The American Dream
February 10, 2013

We all have people we depend on in a crisis, from parents to children to co-workers to a handyman.

Hang on. How can you include that guy?

Clearly you didn't know Domingo Hernandez, 39, who died a few weeks ago of a heart attack doing what he loved, helping somebody with a home repair and charging a fraction of what he could have.

A handyman was just part of his story for us and other families throughout Southwest Riverside County who relied on his work ethic, his talents, his honesty, his reliability, his, well, you get the point, Hernandez was an angel.

Not only was he all that, he represented much of the American dream.

There's irony in that because Hernandez was a Mexican national who wanted to be an American citizen in the worst way. And while I know many of you are bursting with objections as you read ("You mean he was here illegally?"), he also was the embodiment of the complicated debate over immigration once again on our nation's doorstep.

He, his wife and two children lived on the 20 acres owned by Reed and Mary Ann Webb of De Luz. They had a small home that Hernandez had expanded several times because he could do pretty much anything with his hands.

Like the rest of his life, there is a story behind how the Webbs came across Hernandez. They were planting avocado trees on their property in the late 1970s when two men stopped to ask them, "We work for you?" It was Domingo's father, Crescencio, who eventually lived on their land, later joined by his son in 1991.

Domingo's three sisters went to college in Mexico and became a doctor, an attorney and a banker. Domingo preferred to work with his hands, though everybody could tell he was intelligent and would have done well with the books, too.

"He very quickly learned English," Reed says. "He learned every skill and then perfected it with his ingenuity."

Here's one of many, many examples. We got these water-wise toilets from Eastern Municipal years ago. One of them went kaput so some company sent us a part to fix it. Yeah right, I can barely hammer in a nail.

So I called two plumbers and neither one could figure it out. So I tried Domingo. Thirty minutes later the toilet was fixed.

He did work for us tons of times since he was referred by fellow teacher Stephanie Ricci about five years ago. Mary Ann figures he had a client list of at least 50, many of whom she contacted about his funeral arrangements. Besides the 150 people at his memorial service at St. Catherine's in Temecula, Mary Ann says there has been tremendous support from the local Mexican-American community for Domingo's family.

No matter his immigration status, Domingo is somebody to be admired. He wanted to be an American in the worst way and was eager to take any steps that an immigration deal would have required, including paying fines.

He represented so much of what our country is about. And were he with us, Domingo would be honored to hear it — then he would go back to work.

George Alongi was born to make headlines
Publication Date: February 22, 2013

Saying George Alongi was controversial is like saying Johnny Appleseed had a thing for fruit.

Alongi was seemingly born to make headlines. And so it is in death too, his passing on the front page, under investigation by Riverside County sheriff's homicide officials.

The former Lake Elsinore city councilman, 77, was one of those rare people you either loved or hated, no in between with him.

Twice he was escorted from the council chambers by police. Then there was the time he had a fistfight after a meeting.

And you thought Congress was rough.

That was the side of Alongi that made all the headlines. Yet there really was a softer side, a guy who handed out food to the needy, a guy known to go all out to help constituents, a guy who loved playing Santa.

I interviewed him in a downtown Lake Elsinore restaurant in the middle of his council tenure from 1992 to 1999 and I remember our conversation being interrupted constantly by well-wishers. The guy was clearly liked by a lot of people and he seemed to have a heart as big as the lake. Such a kindhearted soul was a natural as Santa.

Whenever I called him about the matters of the day — there were a lot of them back then in Lake Elsinore — Alongi was perfectly polite. Of course, I wrote things about the constant uproars he created but he never complained. At least with me he seemed to accept I was just doing my job.

Others weren't as fortunate. Council meetings back then were always full of tension, one never sure how Alongi might square off against his rivals, be they on the dais — he feuded constantly with colleagues — or out in the audience. Clearly he had a temper as big as the lake, too.

His council tenure ended badly in 1999 — a judge ordered him removed from office after finding true 14 charges of misconduct.

He lost a bid to regain his council seat later that year. He rebounded quickly though, winning a seat on the Elsinore water district the following year. His political career finally ended in 2004 when he lost re-election. Lake Elsinore hasn't been the same since — which may or may not be a good thing, depending on your take on Alongi.

Chris Hyland was at his political side for almost a quarter century. She remembers those early years, back when the council was embroiled in controversies over the lake, the complicated financing of the Storm baseball stadium, police department issues and on and on and on. "It was a really bad time in Lake Elsinore," she says.

Here's how Hyland summed up Alongi's love-hate relationship in that era: "The people cared for him. The people leading the city didn't care for him."

She says her phone has been ringing off the hook since Alongi's death. "People are just traumatized by this whole thing. They can't believe it happened."

In death just as in life, George Alongi is making news.

A Roadside Ministry

Publication Date: March 16, 2013

Jerry Brown is asked what the future holds for his ministry. "How much time you got?" he replies with typical gusto.

That about says it all for the Murrieta retiree and his one-of-a-kind passion, a popup tent ministry that's been making the rounds in Southwest Riverside County for about five years.

He's at Kalmia Street and Washington Avenue in Murrieta right now, with his trusty signs such as "The Father Loves You" and "Stop for Prayer, Blessing and Healing."

Come on, you have to admit it's a tempting offer. Who among us, even agnostics and atheists, can't use a little healing?

On busy days he might get a dozen folks dropping by to see what exactly is going on during the six hours or so he's out there. Some days he doesn't get any and that's OK with Brown.

You get the sense most everything is OK with the jolly 57-year-old guy. Sporting a Dodger baseball cap and a physique as big as his smile, he's not about to be holier than thou. He is Christian but only one of his signs mentions Jesus, and he's not dispensing Bibles or soliciting donations; the point being he's more interested in talking about God's love.

"I'm not a religious weirdo fanatic," he cautions. "I'm a dude. I like the Dodgers."

This explains his prior life, a groundskeeper for The Diamond, the Lake Elsinore Storm's baseball field. Then he worked for the Elsinore schools where his football fields were usually rated the best in the area. It's that passion thing he's got going on, be it fields or faith.

After retiring and searching for a way to devote himself more to his faith, he saw a guy with a religious sign standing on California Oaks Road in Murrieta. He says he had an epiphany; he could do the same thing, but saying "Jesus Loves You," and trying to spread his Christian faith.

He started at the same corner he's at now, with the blessing of the property owner of the vacant lot, a Jewish man — a fact he appreciates that a man of a different faith could be so accommodating. He calls his program AgapeHeart Ministries.

He gets around, over to Murrieta Hot Springs Road between the two freeways, then Clinton Keith Road and the 15, over to the

Inland Valley Medical Center area, up to Menifee near Antelope Road, and finally back here.

He's had two run-ins of significance in his years of ministry — one guy trying to rip out his signs and tent; another man wanting to debate him about religion, something Brown isn't interested in. "It's all love," he says. "The whole ministry is God loves us."

Joining him the day I'm here are Jawaid Nasir and his wife, Tammy, of Temecula. Jawaid says he dropped by Brown's tent about three years ago, shortly after his father died. He found Brown could help him and he's been visiting him ever since.

"He's definitely changed my life," Jawaid says.

Brown's ultimate goal is to get a building where he can share his message of love in a more permanent place. For now he's happy where he's at, a minister on the road. Again.

First Contact with Murrieta's New Fire Fee
Publication Date: March 29

"Call 911," my wife Joanne says.

She's on the floor, holding her shoulder, breathing rapidly. Visions of a heart attack or stroke dancing in my head, I do as instructed.

Thus ensues a five-hour odyssey in our emergency health care system that leaves her in agony but OK, my wallet lighter and me cursing smoke detector batteries.

Yes something designed to protect instead led to an injury. Nothing like irony.

Joanne is upstairs on a ladder changing a battery while my son David and I watch a game, (I know, I know, men are evil.) when we hear her crying in pain. She missed a step on her way down, fell, and crashed into our very solid armoire.

So I call 911, which in Murrieta means we could deal with the fire department and the 911 medical call fee folks in town are conflicted about. Does politics have to infect everything?

A couple minutes later we hear the sirens. Soon three firefighters are in our messy bedroom (It's not like I was about to tidy up) assessing Joanne. Three ambulance guys arrive moments later.

Fortunately the worst isn't happening. After calming her vitals and zipping morphine into her, they decide Joanne's probably broken her arm. So into the ambulance she goes, preferably to local Loma Linda.

That's in a perfect world. In our imperfect health care system we get a call from the ambulance guys telling us to go to Inland Valley because our insurance doesn't cover the other. Crazy.

As David and I head out, a couple longtime neighbors, Nancy Leavitt and Larry Honda, are there asking what the heck is going on. After assuring them she's OK, we see many others lining our street. Later we hear one was even praying. Very Murrieta.

The hospital is its own drama. There's the guy moaning loudly while a sheriff deputy stands guard as docs work on him behind a curtain. Later it's pulled, he's doped up and by the looks of him you can see why a sheriff was there. We're not talking Boy Scout.

In our space it's a matter of waiting. Meanwhile the helpful male nurse asks how Joanne was hurt, and mentions he hasn't changed his dead smoke detector batteries in years. Smart man.

Three hours later we're told Joanne has a broken arm. The ER staff apply a splint and release us, advising we can hit any Murrieta pharmacy to get meds because they're all open until midnight. Of course the first one we visit is closed and a drug store worker says only one is open in Temecula.

Now it's 11:30 on a Tuesday night and I'm waiting for our region's lone pharmacist to fill the vital meds. Suddenly I hear a store manager threatening a creepy looking guy to get out before he calls the cops. Delightful.

We still can't see the orthopedic guy until Monday (and we go to Riverside at that because of our "affordable" health plan), who knows what the ambulance will cost (Is that neighbor praying for us on that one?), but at least those friendly Murrieta firefighters are knocking down their fee from $350 to $175 because it's still being rolled out.

A prayer answered.

Temecula's 15 Minutes of Commercial Fame
Publication Date: April 13, 2013

Temecula today is a growing metropolis known for its emerging wine country, thriving mall, booming casino and picturesque Old Town.

Temecula 40 years ago was known nationwide for its small town qualities.

Huh?

This contradiction — how can the same place be known for its growth and small town qualities can be explained by the city's first

15 minutes of fame (actually, it was 30 seconds): A Clorox TV commercial that ran across the land in the early 1970s.

San Francisco ad man Ron Berman had the brilliant idea of removing the stuff from a small town to see what would happen to its laundry and then making an ad out of it.

Thus was Temecula — a small town of 297, not the booming city of 100,000 plus now — first introduced to the nation in about 1973.

Local attorney Reed Webb recently recalled seeing the ad and after calls to the company, an old newspaper story about the commercial was forwarded. Included was a photo of Old Town Temecula at what looks to be the intersection of Front and Main.

Clorox launched its idea with a few phone calls to locals and word quickly spread.

"Somebody told somebody else about the calls and pretty soon everybody was coming in here buying Clorox so when the Clorox people called they could say they had it in their houses," said local market owner Jeannette Schroeder at the time.

Most locals signed an affidavit promising not to use the stuff and collected a whopping $10 fee for the inconvenience. The only holdout was Mary Talley who said the stuff was good for everything, even bee stings. And yet she didn't make the cut for ad.

Six lucky ladies did — apparently this was before the advent of house husbands — and camera crews came in to film them espousing the horrors of life without Clorox. A lucky three (Paula Franco, Mary Helen Murphy and Sue Dunagan) made the actual commercial.

All three said seeing themselves on TV was strange.

"My kids get all excited," Franco said. "They say, 'There's mom, she's a star.'"

They instantly became the town's only celebrities. Folks teasingly asked them for their autographs and local yokels loved to imitate the nervous laugh Dunagan showed on the commercial.

Some guy from up north saw the ad, was apparently smitten, and came through Temecula looking for Murphy. Told she was already spoken for, he picked up a post card instead.

Lots of others dropped by just to see what the real Temecula was like.

"They see the name and come in from other states saying, 'I hear you ran out of Clorox,'" Schroeder noted. "We've been discovered."

Yes and no. Soon enough, Temecula returned to its sleepy ways, laundry and all. It was about another 15 years before the place was discovered instead by commuters from the coast looking for a small town to raise their kids. Unlike its first go round with fame, there was no turning back. Temecula was discovered for good.

Arrest brings up memories

Publication Date: April 27, 2013

Flip-flops, that's what always comes to mind when I think of Murrieta community sports activist Bob Stiles.

It's what he often wears when out and about. They say plenty: His laid back nature (he also sports an earring), his finances (he drove around an old beat-up van for years) and maybe even his politics, which are liberal, something he doesn't exactly broadcast in a town known far and wide for its conservative views.

Wonder if he'll be able to wear his trademark flip flops if he's in custody?

Stiles, 61, has been arrested on suspicion of grand theft and other charges after local police say he embezzled more than $1.3 million from the business with his name, Bob's Murrieta Pizza Company on Kalmia Street.

If your kids were in youth sports in Murrieta over the past 15 years, there's a good chance you came across Stiles. I coached 15 soccer and basketball teams involving my son David, so I saw him plenty.

He ran the Murrieta Youth Basketball League for years. His son played in the league and refereed, too. He helped run local soccer as well, a sport his daughter excelled in. He was also active in baseball.

Saying youth sports are big in kid-friendly Murrieta is like saying country music is popular in Nashville. And Stiles was once the Dolly Parton of local youth sports, seemingly everywhere, running leagues, umping and refereeing games, coaching teams and always sitting in the stands.

Another big part of his world was pizza. His place on California Oaks Road was across from the sports park, at that time the primary sporting venue in town. Then he helped launch another restaurant near Wal-Mart with local teachers. Finally he started the business he's now in legal trouble over.

FROM TWO LANES TO THE FAST LANE/CARL LOVE

Leagues often held their registrations at his restaurants, and then the kids might see Stiles at their various games because he was a honcho with so many leagues, before ending their season with a team party and pizza, probably at his business.

Of course his places had sport themes. Not as much college and pro, but local high schools, the teams that mattered to him. His kids went to Vista Murrieta High School, but he was always careful to promote all the Murrieta high schools in his restaurant. Off the field, everybody was welcome at his place.

We'd always chat when we ran into each other, gossiping about local sports, maybe sharing our liberal politics, or catching up on our kids. I haven't seen him since the news first broke of his legal situation. Maybe that's for the best. What would I say?

Youth sports are ultimately about fair play. Stiles ran his leagues with an emphasis of just let the kids compete and have fun. There were minimum time requirements for even the worst players on the team and stud athletes could only score a set amount of points before they were removed from a game. It gave everybody a chance to be the star, something that doesn't always happen in the real world.

After an arrest and facing multiple criminal charges, the transcendent joy of the youth sports Stiles so immersed himself in must seem a lifetime ago to Stiles now.

At 86, he's still helping students
Publication Date: May 25, 2013

"Most people think work is a dirty four-letter word," Mel Snyder says.

Obviously he doesn't.

He's 86 and a special education assistant at Creekside High School, a continuation school in Murrieta.

For some, a continuation school might produce images of kids looking for second chances, or maybe not the easiest place to be an educator, especially when you could be kicking back in retirement.

Snyder, "Mr. Mel" to the kids, seems to see it differently: The proverbial foundation of youth we're all looking for.

He likes the kids, perhaps as much as they like him. He loves helping them and they sure appreciate it. Yes, they might have their "issues" from time to time, but around him not so much.

Asked how much longer he'll work, he says, "Until they put me in a box. I can't think of anything else I'd rather do."

Even if it involves fist bumping with the kids. While some seniors might wonder what the world's coming to when a sturdy handshake won't suffice, Snyder doesn't mind in the least.

This is why he's in the right place at the right time.

Take Brandon Sanchez, a junior.

"He's a good guy because he cares for the students," the 17-year-old says. "He always has something smart to say."

Eight decades and counting provides perspective. His work life was mostly sales and he once owned a successful diaper laundry service in L.A.

"Then some guy invented paper diapers and put me in the toilet," he says.

There's that sense of humor again. He's full of one-liners when we talk and with such a gift for gab, he must have been a heck of a salesman.

One of his three daughters and two of his son-in-laws were teachers and Connie, his wife of 66 years (There is that consistency again with Snyder), was a school office manager for 24 years. So it was natural for him to start subbing as an instructional aide six years ago. Four years ago, he accepted a regular position.

The best part of his job?

"I love when a student comes up to me and asks a question," he says. Such a simple thing, yet for Snyder, so powerful.

Another of his duties at Creekside is to lead students in the Pledge of Allegiance every morning. For him, pride in country means something — he served in the Navy for a couple years near the end of World War II — and no doubt the kids pick up on it.

Vince Rodriguez, 19, is interested in a career with the Border Patrol. He says Snyder keeps him motivated. If an 86-year-old dude can still work every day, why can't he?

"I find that amazing that he's still working," Rodriguez said.

Frank Castillon, the teacher who works with Snyder, says he's dependable and kids enjoy him.

"He brings a different perspective to the students, a walking U. S. history book."

Susanna Abarca, who does campus security, says former students who drop by for a visit always ask what's up with Mr. Mel. Like a favorite grandparent who always took the time to genuinely talk to them, they miss their old friend.

The good news for everyone at Creekside: He's not going anywhere.

Southwest crime, then and now
Publication Date: June 29, 2013

A recent front page had these jarring headlines — "Two former Marines draw death verdicts," "Wine country slaying," and "Sex offender takes plea deal."

Inside was more happy news: "16-year sentence for molestation" and "Found skeletal human remains identified."

Wow, that's a lot of gruesome stuff. What is this, some big city newspaper?

No, it's this one and the "big city" is Southwest Riverside County where all these stories originated.

There was a time in this area when people stormed city council meetings over such grisly matters. Today we seem to give a collective sigh and turn the page.

The past I'm referring to was 1992 and the place was Murrieta. Old Carriage Road — located in a development called Country Walk, the kind of name developers slapped on projects back then in the hopes of luring "big city" folks here — had the dubious distinction of having Murrieta's first crime wave.

Murrieta's first drive-by shooting happened on the block and residents feared they were in the midst of a war between white supremacists and Latino gang members. About 20 neighbors went to a City Council meeting to ask their leaders to do something.

At the time, Murrieta Mayor Jerry Allen said the city was trying. Councilmen Gary Smith and Joe Peery were out cleaning up graffiti. (Yes, our elected officials used to do that back then.) Extra police patrols were added to the area.

Allen, a former L.A. deputy, said the city's first drive-by shooting was unfortunately inevitable. "I honestly believe we're going to be dealing with it from now on."

Such crime here was unheard of at the time. Of the residents who went before the council, I wrote back then: "Their reaction speaks well of us as a community. Imagine neighbors parading before the Los Angeles City Council to complain about a shooting in which nobody was hurt. They'd be laughed out of town."

Today we have more serious crime and large groups of citizens aren't storming the council chambers. Clearly something's changed.

It's not like I feel we're under siege. Local cities such as Temecula and Murrieta like to brag about being rated among the safest anywhere. The statistics back them up.

What's changed is our perspective. Twenty years ago — when we were about 25 percent of the population we are today — there was a sense that we could create on this blank canvas of undeveloped space a land that was truly special, where crime was nonexistent, our schools were the best and traffic was something we left behind in the big cities we fled.

Clearly that didn't happen. So we've adjusted. Our land is way more developed now, our schools are solid but not the best, the traffic isn't great, but it's certainly not the 91 or the 405, and crime isn't nonexistent, but we feel safe enough.

And so when we stare at a front page full of local crime we stop and think, this isn't Mayberry. Once upon a time, we'd hoped it would be.

A community standing as one
Publication Date: July 12, 2013

When it comes to our response to the missing autistic Menifee boy, we walked our talk.

We walked by what was estimated to be a thousand through the rugged terrain of rural Menifee in our collective quest to find the boy.

We only called off our monumental search when a child's body was found in a shallow grave near the family's home and a 16-year-old relative of the boy was arrested on suspicion of murder. The remains are those of a boy matching the description of Terry Dewayne Smith Jr., but authorities did not confirm the body is his.

The dramatic story and our overwhelming response drew the attention of journalists far and wide. Here in Southwest Riverside County, we don't just talk about family values (the conservative lingo) and the notion that it takes a village to raise a child (a liberal's take); we walk as one when one of our children is missing.

It was a moment for the most ancient of fears — is there anything more frightening than the notion of a missing child? — driven by the newest of tools, social media. I first heard of the search via an e-mail from Facebook inviting me to join, noting five of my "friends" were helping the cause. I learned the story turned even sadder in another message from Facebook early Wednesday afternoon alerting me that "Praying for Terry" was canceled by Elicia Hopkins.

Scrolling through tons of other Facebook posts, this one from Cathy Neumann-Bearse struck me the most: "You know ... I learned something new about my community these past few days ... I learned that we are different cities ... but we ARE ONE COMMUNITY and we are STRONG! Sweet Terry is with Jesus and he is watching us and thankful we helped him be free."

It speaks both to the bond we displayed as the masses marched through those Menifee fields and to the community's powerful beliefs. There is a reason we've been called the Bible Belt of Southern California.

Francy Honda, of Murrieta, went to Menifee four times to do her part in the search. Of her role, she says: "Knowing there is a child out there wandering around and what am I doing here? I could be helping."

She went out the first night after dark and just drove around Menifee looking. Another time she was with her daughter Tara, 21, and they brought back fliers to pass around Murrieta. The last time she brought her son Nate, 18.

Like the Menifee boy, Nate, too, is autistic. He also once went missing, though in his case he was fortunately found by authorities. It happened 14 years ago when somebody accidentally left the front door unlocked and Nate, then 4, wandered out, unbeknownst to Honda, who was working on the computer.

He drifted over to busy Whitewood Road where a concerned motorist spotted him and notified authorities. Murrieta police arrived quickly and with the help of a neighbor, returned Nate home within a few minutes. There's that village thing again.

Those long-ago fears — what could have happened to Nate if a stranger hadn't been so alert? — weighed on Honda's mind as she joined what will forever be remembered as an epic search for Terry.

If only his story had ended so happily.

Recalling both of Arlean Garrison's Murrietas
Publication Date: July 20, 2013

Back when Murrieta started to boom in the 1980s, a well-travelled businessman dropped by the local chamber to get some information.

The guy said he liked the pleasant company. The location was great too, right off the main drag of Washington Avenue. No big city traffic to fight.

Arlean Garrison recalled the visitor.

"He said, 'this is the only chamber of commerce in the United States like this and I don't see anything wrong with it.'"

The story speaks to the Murrieta that once was and to the folksy Garrison who died earlier this month at age 97.

At the time the chamber was tucked in Garrison's Murrieta Machine Ship, amid the fix-it supplies. It was identified by a sign dangling from a big old eucalyptus tree out front. The actual office was no bigger than a walk-in closet. Heck, it even smelled like a musty old closet. The carpet looked like it should have been tossed out, which is where it was headed until the chamber rescued it.

"It's got character," said Bob Crane, who helped run the place then.

And so did Garrison. She was both Murrietas, both yesterday and today, a difficult feat that she pulled off with charm. She moved here from South Dakota in 1939, so she had the past well covered. Yet she never begrudged today's suburban lifestyle and the 100,000 who joined her here. Trust me, plenty of old-timers felt differently.

Now the Murrieta chamber brags on its website that it has a conference room that sits 70, or about 68 more than Garrison's version. Today it's in a suite on busy Madison Avenue in new Murrieta, far removed in time and place from its old home. Today, a passing businessman would say it's a chamber like most others, not the one-of-a-kind place Garrison's office represented.

Garrison always lived in old Murrieta when I knew her, next to her shop, in a place that looked like it was still 1939. During one of the times I visited, a sign called it "Garrison Acres," and with the rabbits, raccoons, opossums and chickens she had running around, it had the feel.

She wrote a history of her favorite place, "My Children's Home," in 1963. It was a little bit of everything of Murrieta, from stuff on historical folks such as Don Juan Murrieta — yes, the city is named after him — to local businesses of way back when. It was written in a folksy way that was all Garrison and all Murrieta.

She had a terrific sense of humor. She got an award for her service on some local history board, about the time Murrieta was going through a bitter City Council recall campaign.

"That's nice that they all sat down and agreed to something," she said with a chuckle that was all Arlean.

Asked if she would ever move, she said she had it made in Murrieta. "I got two bars just down the street." Once again, all Arlean.

In the same conversation she told me she never minded all the change. She just hoped to maintain what she fondly called "the friendly little atmosphere" Murrieta always was for her.

Here's hoping we can honor her memory by keeping it that way.

Murrieta's Triangle Could Be Cursed
Publication Date: September 20, 2012

It once was known as The Golden Triangle.

When it comes to development of this most epic slab of real estate in Southwest Riverside County, it's more like the Bermuda Triangle.

All projects seemingly go there to die for some mysterious reason, from the Murrieta mall to one of Zev Buffman's tantalizing schemes to so many others that it's hard to keep track of it all.

Once again the 64-acre site between Interstates 215 and 15 is in play as the Murrieta City Council considers a massive project including more of those dreaded fast-food restaurants. The last meeting on the monumental matter was a long-winded six hours -- anything but fast.

In the interest of trying to see whether The Triangle is more Golden or Bermuda, yours truly tried to walk the property recently.

Alas, the site is now fenced off on busy Murrieta Hot Springs, so there's no reasonable way to investigate the matter from the ground.

But wait, signs promoting The Triangle have had many areas whited out, as if somebody has something to hide. Could this be the work of a ghost of Buffman, the man who first haunted Old Town Temecula with one of his visions before shifting his plans to another Murrieta property, where they also died?

After all, don't ghosts travel in white? White out makes perfect sense. Or is it the handiwork of the lost souls of the mall? At the time of Murrieta's incorporation nearly a quarter century ago, the mall was envisioned as the city's financial soul, the project that would fills its coffers with sales taxes as far as the eye could see. Golden, indeed. Then Temecula aced out Murrieta for the mall. Instead of lucrative Penney's, Murrieta was left with mere pennies and an invaluable piece of real estate that remains empty.

It's amid this backdrop that the town is vexed once again. Landowner Andy Domenigoni proposes a massive 18-story office tower, hotels, entertainment venues and tons of restaurants. Yet Murrieta leaders are fixated on plans to also include fast food.

The Golden Arches isn't what we envisioned for The Golden Triangle, huff some of the Murrieta powers that be. In so many words, they're telling Domenigoni to go jump in that lake his name's associated with.

Yet there's another streak that runs through conservative Murrieta, the one that says private property owners should get to do what the heck they want with their land. Why, we can't have foolish government bureaucrats dictating to the sacred market place.

Why, why, next thing you know they'll make all those weeds on the property sign up for Obamacare!

Marketing signs with white out, the ghost of Buffman, the Bermuda Triangle, the Golden Triangle, the lost souls of the mall, the last thing Murrieta needs is another fast-food joint, this is the best property in the whole dang area so why can't it ever get developed? The place is cursed, I tell you; the place is cursed!

The randomness of life

Publication Date: November 3, 2013

The southbound side of Interstate 15 in Lake Elsinore is a stretch of road we've all been on.

Probably on the way home from something in the big city, be it a job or something fun.

Michael Smyth was travelling that way when somebody rear-ended him and sent his car spinning out of control into a freeway call box.

He died about seven hours later. He was 53, husband of Ronda, a Murrieta teacher for forever, father of Sean and Kevin, who attended a Murrieta elementary school where I teach.

Nicest guy in the world, a cancer survivor, and just like that he's gone. Could have been me, could have been you.

The randomness of what happened to Smyth has me spooked something fierce.

A BMW driven by a Montebello man was following Smyth's Hyndai in the fast lane and failed to slow down before the crash, a CHP officer said.

Smyth was remembered at a giant funeral service that my wife Joanne attended. The front of the program is a shot of the handsome, black-haired guy smiling in his bicycling gear. If you knew him, you know it's the perfect picture.

Our kids used to get together for play dates and birthday parties a long, long time ago. The Smyths lived a few blocks away in Murrieta, our wives met at the California Oaks Sports Park playground.

Over the years, our kids grew apart and we grew apart, we all know how it goes. I'd see Michael from time to time, maybe at a store, maybe at a sporting event, maybe at Vista Murrieta High School where our kids all went, maybe on Whitewood Road while he rode his bike and I walked my dogs.

We'd always chitchat for a few minutes. He was one of those people who always greeted you warmly, always asked about the family, always made you feel good.

I'd heard about the cancer a few years ago and I suppose a better person would have dropped a card or made a call. The program described him as "a strong-willed man, who courageously battled and beat cancer in recent years."

I knew about his competitive nature, how he once aspired to be a professional open wheel race car driver before settling down like most of us do. He turned his inner fire to bicycling and became a fixture in the local community, touring with friends for three decades.

He carried the Olympic torch locally as it made its way to Atlanta for the 1996 Olympics. They don't let just anybody do that.

Ever since I knew him, he'd been a financial planner. The program says he was a man of great integrity who carried it out in every aspect of his life. I agree.

I'm left with the haunting image my wife described as Ronda stood at his funeral service and spoke movingly about her wonderful guy. Sean and Kevin, basically the same ages as my kids, stood on each side of her, their presence speaking louder than any words.

Could have been me, could have been you.

Escaping From the sheltered life
Publication Date: August 9, 2013

My daughter Julia and I see about 15 folks wearing "Free Bradley Manning" T-shirts milling around.

Suddenly they break into a formation and a Michael Jackson song starts booming. The group does a choreographed dance to the thumping music.

They finish a couple minutes later, pass out fliers about their cause supporting the WikiLeaks leaker, and leap into vehicles, off to their next flash mob performance on the always-fascinating streets of San Francisco.

My daughter lives there, not here. And after spending a weekend recently visiting her, it got me thinking about what exactly happens to our kids after they grow up in Southwest Riverside County.

We all know the other mantra we've preached since parents began piling into this place about a quarter century ago. Our schools are solid, the streets are safe and the housing's affordable, so we're willing to make ungodly commutes to raise our kids here.

I did it, you did it, we all did it. And in the case of my wife Joanne and me, we were lucky enough to see our kids go off to great colleges. It's what many parents strive for.

There's just one problem to this happy ending. It's the ending actually. My kids aren't settling here. At least not yet.

Obviously part of it is employment. Despite decades of hard work and the best of intentions, we don't have enough good jobs here. We can debate why until the cows come home — we know our kids won't — whether it's because we don't have any four-year colleges headquartered here, we don't have much of an industrial base, we don't have the political clout, we don't have a transportation infrastructure, whatever reason you want to cite, they're all valid.

The end result is my daughter lives in San Francisco and my son David, who will graduate from college next year, plans to get a job in some big Western city, most likely L.A. It's the luxury of being an accounting student; he can pretty much go where he wants. Anywhere but here.

All but one of Julia's local friends who are college graduates live elsewhere. Almost all of my son's local college-bound friends will settle other places too. A brain drain is not good for our community.

So I ask Julia if she's glad she spent her childhood in sheltered Murrieta. Well, she says, not trying to hurt dad's feelings, the schools were good and she got what she needed to get into Duke University. (David got into his dream school too, UC Santa Barbara.)

But, she says, she wasn't around enough interesting people. In other words, we're boring, at least to her. We don't have flash mobs connected with political causes, to cite one instance.

There's a sad irony in this. We devote all this energy to raising our kids right, to keeping them protected and to making sure they go to good local schools. Yet apparently many of these kids feel too sheltered, and in the end, to paraphrase the famous book, they can't go home again.

ACKNOWLEDGEMENTS

There are so many people to acknowledge, it's hard to know where to start.

Actually, it's easy.

It's our local politicians. Silly, some of you say, all they care about is lapping up what they can from the public trough. Like they need my thanks.

But somebody has to take care of our business. And if you've seen the near- empty chambers at most of our public meetings, you know most constituents can't be bothered.

Plus, the few people who do pay attention – such as journalists like me looking for something to write about – subject them to a fair amount of ridicule.

And so I've made a living off them in many respects. So thanks to folks such as Jeff Stone, Ron Roberts, Chuck Washington, Jerry Allen, Austin Linsley, Margi Wray, Barbara Tooker, Kris and Gary Thomasian, Peg Moore, Gary Smith, Kevin Jeffries, Maryann Edwards, Bob Buster, Barbara Tooker, Stu Morris, Joan Sparkman, Doug McAllister, Brian Youens, Margi Wray, Jeanie Corral, Mike Naggar, Jeff Comerchero, Bridgette Moore, Wallace Edgerton, Gary Washburn, Doug McAllister, Maryann Edwards, Rick Gibbs, Rosie Vanderhaak, and countless, countless others.

They never wrote me off, even when what I wrote infuriated them. Two quick stories make my point. Once I wrote a piece comparing the then new Murrieta Police Department to Barney Fife of Mayberry TV fame. Jerry Allen, then on the Murrieta City Council, called me at home on a Saturday morning to berate me. By the end he'd cooled off and he's continued helping me ever since. For you newcomers, yes, he's the guy with the street named after him.

A few years back, I wrote something about the Temecula City Council that had incumbent Jeff Comerchero irate. He sent me an e mail detailing all that was wrong with my piece. I replied back, he replied back, and by the end he said we were still good, he understood why I wrote what I wrote, didn't mean he had to like it, but he'd still talk to me.

See what I mean about letting bygones be bygones, letting me savage them and still leaving me with a smile and a quote. So thanks guys because a columnist needs outspoken politicians like a kid needs good parents.

Then there are my journalism colleagues who have been the source of endless tips throughout these years. There were the folks in the first Press-Enterprise office on Jefferson Avenue in the Old Adobe Plaza in Temecula, Mark Petix, Paula Kriner, Oscar Guerra, Sandy Stokes, Pat Murkland and Sue Boyce. Then there were the people who came and went, Frank Bartholomew, Bob Scally, Sheryl Oring, Andy Silva, Jeff Crider, Terri Hardy, Steve Moore, Denice Hilts, Rocky Salmon, Lyle Spencer, Thomas Kelsey, Greg Vojtko and many others. Finally there were the others who still help me today, such as John Hunneman, Gordon Johnson and Peter Surowski.

Then there are – How exactly do I put this without losing my mojo as a writer? -- my editors at The Press-Enterprise. They've OK'd most of my ideas. They've reigned me in when I probably needed reigning, and generally let me write what I want, damning, maddening or just plain silly as it could be at times. So thanks Doug Beeman, Tony Borders, Mark Coast, John Francis, Jim Rothgeb, Mark Acosta, Liam Truchard and Nels Jensen, the guy who not only OK'd this book, but backed me 110 percent.

There are others who've passed on to wherever it is we go after you know what. My favorite person ever to write about, former Temecula councilman Karel Lindemans, died last year. He'd moved away from Temecula to the desert many years ago and so I hadn't written about him for a long time anyway. Still, it was a loss, mainly for Temecula (he did a lot for the city that most people today have no clue about) and secondarily for local journalists. He was as quotable as they come. Cheers, my friend.

There were others who've passed on. They weren't nearly as quotable, but still interesting to write about: Pat Birdsall, Kevin Walsh, Bob Taylor, Dave Haas, Arlean Garrison, Eve Craig, and George Alongi, to mention a few of many.

There are the folks who may as well have died for all that I write about them anymore. I'm talking about you, Sal Munoz, Jack Van Haaster, Warnie Enochs, Zev Buffman, and tons of others who've dropped out of the limelight. Thanks, wherever you are.

As to this book, I had wanted to make one out of these columns for many a year. Yes there is self-publishing, but how exactly do you do it? I'd like to thank Mark Fletcher of Sun City and Robbie Adkins of Temecula for showing me how. My old friend Mark Henry offered me invaluable advice. My dad was a source of constant encouragement, as was Alain Jourdier, the father of a former student of mine. Not only are Dan Bernstein and Gordon Johnson great writers, they came through when I needed it the most. And Carl Kravats and Cindy Quick take the best photos.

There is the source of much of my merriment, my family. My daughter Julia, now 24, was four months old when I started writing this column. My son David, now 21, whose birth I chronicled here. My wife Joanne, the butt of many a joke, the source of many of my ideas because she's a former journalist and definitely still knows a good story. And I certainly want to mention our three dogs: Smiley, Midnight and Happy. Together my family has been the soul of my column, the ones who have made me a part of the most prominent demographic of Southwest Riverside County: Parents raising kids and pets in what they hoped would be a safe place with good schools and places to play. It's been all that and more.

Finally, there is the biggest, and, most important group of all, you guys, the readers. I don't know how they measure the popularity of this column, but somehow, someway, it's been allowed to continue far beyond what I ever could have imagined in 1989. Presumably enough of you like what I write – or at least tolerate it – to let this column continue, for so, so long.

For that, I am forever grateful.

ABOUT THE AUTHOR

Carl Love was born in Eugene, Oregon, in 1958 and grew up all around the world as an Army brat. During his K-12 years, he attended 11 different schools, living in Germany for six years and India for one year, as well as California, Oklahoma, Kansas, Washington D.C., North Dakota, Iowa, Pennsylvania and New York. His journalism career began as a junior for a high school newspaper in Bettendorf, Iowa. He attended St. Ambrose University and the University of Iowa, before graduating from California State University, Northridge. He has worked as a dishwasher, food server, door to door salesman of aluminum siding, fast food boy, college cafeteria milk guy, golf course maintenance dude, furniture warehouse driver, grocery store bagger, real estate shill, playground aide and bartender. He wrote for newspapers in Los Angeles, Santa Monica, Thousand Oaks, Porterville and Palm Springs, before settling down with The Press-Enterprise in Riverside in 1985. He became a teacher in 1997. Today he writes a weekly column for The Press-Enterprise and teaches fifth grade at Rail Ranch Elementary School in Murrieta, where he has lived since the last day of 1988.

Carl can be contacted at:
Email: carllove4@yahoo.com
 Carl Love @carl_love_

Made in the USA
Charleston, SC
12 November 2013